MERCHANT SAILING SHIPS
1850~1875

MERCHANT SAILING SHIPS

1850~1875

HEYDAY OF SAIL

David R MacGregor
MA, FSA, FRHistS

NAVAL INSTITUTE PRESS

FRONTISPIECE

The small wooden barque Natal Queen *is actually under tow as she leaves Hobart and in the light breeze the sails are not really drawing. The man on the fore royal yard indicates her size. She was built at Grangemouth in 1866 and measured 230 tons.* (Arthur D Edwardes)

By the same author

The Tea Clippers (1952; reprinted 1972)
The Tea Clippers 1833-1875 (1983, enlarged and revised edition)
The China Bird (1961)
Fast Sailing Ships 1775-1875 (1973)
Square Rigged Sailing Ships (1977)
Clipper Ships (1979)
Merchant Sailing Ships 1775-1815 (1980)
Merchant Sailing Ships 1815-1850 (1984)
Schooners in Four Centuries (1982)

Plans drawn by the author
Additional drawings by Paul A Roberts, T W Ward, F A Claydon and R Bird

First published in 1984 by Conway Maritime Press Ltd
24 Bride Lane, Fleet Street, London EC4Y 8DR

© David R MacGregor 1984

Published and Distributed in the United States of America and Canada by the Naval Institute Press, Annapolis, Maryland 21402.

Library of Congress Catalog Card No. 84-61562

ISBN 0-87021-951-0

Manufactured in the United Kingdom

CONTENTS

Dedicated
To Frode Holm-Petersen
a friend for 35 years

PREFACE

This book is the culmination of a project begun twenty years ago when I contracted with the Gregg Press to write a book on sailing ships for the years 1815-1875, comparing clipper ships with cargo carriers. The provisional title was 'Heyday of Sail' and due to the fact that the American branch of the business issued a leaflet on it, I have been credited in bibliographies with having had this book published in 1964. But this was impossible as the work was not finished until 1969 when it had run to some 250,000 words. Eventually the sections on clippers and construction were extracted to form the work which came to be published in 1973 under the title of *Fast Sailing Ships, their Design and Construction*. The date had now been pushed back to 1775, thus making a century up to 1875.

This left over half the manuscript and as many drawings unpublished – really everything about 'Slow Sailing Ships', unglamorous as it might sound – and so the series now called *Merchant Sailing Ships* was evolved. At the same time, many new plans were drawn, the original chapters were re-written and expanded, and much research undertaken on the eighteenth century. The first volume covered forty years; the next work was somewhat bigger but covered five years less; the present volume is still larger, yet deals with only twenty-five years. It is my intention to complete the series with a fourth book which would cover the subject down to the present century.

I was fortunate enough to be able to study plans in the possession of two Clyde-side shipbuilders, Alexander Stephen & Sons and Barclay, Curle & Co, and I am grateful to the directors for the permission granted. I spent three months in Glasgow in 1961 and should like to acknowledge the assistance from my fellow clansman, Robert W McGregor, chief draughtsman at Stephen's, and R Campbell, chief draughtsman at Barclay, Curle's. The collections at these two yards really form the backbone of the drawings presented here.

Over a period of thirty years I have received much help and encouragement from numerous museums and libraries in Great Britain where I have been able to copy plans or measure models, but the curators and members of staff who rendered assistance may have left by now. In particular, I should like to thank Basil W Bathe when he was Curator of Shipping at the Science Museum, London; Daniel Hay, Borough Librarian at the Whitehaven Central Library and Museum; A S E Browning, Curator of Technology at Glasgow Museum & Art Galleries; Mr Crawley, Director of Sunderland Museum in 1954; Michael K Stammers, still Keeper of Maritime History at the Merseyside County Museums; and David Lyon in charge of the Draught Room at the National Maritime Museum, Greenwich.

Of private collectors whose primary interest is ship plans, I must thank first and foremost James Henderson for imparting some of his great store of knowledge about Aberdeen ships and for providing plans and other data; in similar vein I am grateful to William Salisbury for particulars about shipbuilding at Glasson as well as for data and plans of Blackwall frigates; also to Benjamin E Nicholson for allowing me to measure his half-models of Annan ships; and to Frode Holm-Petersen who provided plans and illustrations of Danish vessels. In America, Howard I Chapelle gave me many copies of his drawings as well

as discussing naval architecture in a highly stimulating way.

Also in America, the later William A Baker of the Francis Russell Hart Nautical Museum at the Massachusetts Institute of Technology provided copies of plans, as did John Lochhead, Librarian at the Mariner's Museum, Newport News. In Canada, Dr George MacBeath of the New Brunswick Museum sent me plans; so also did John R Stevens when curator of the Maritime Museum of Canada at Halifax. Dr Charles A Armour has also helped in like manner.

The age of photography commences with this volume and whilst conferring benefits does present problems due to the large number of illustrations to choose from, although many of the ships were photographed in old age when cut down in rig. Captain Poyser of the Nautical Photo Agency was a good friend and supplied many of the pictures used here. Latterly, David Clement has made his collection available and generously copied any photographs I have selected. Richard H C Gillis also let me choose photographs and I am grateful to Mrs Anne Gillis for permission to use some of them. Others who have kindly allowed me to use their pictures include Reece Winstone, Richard Cookson, Dan MacDonald and Peter Catling.

In the United States, Karl Kortum has helped me with photographs, both in his private capacity and as Director of the Maritime Museum at San Francisco; likewise also Robert A Weinstein of Los Angeles. On the East Coast, I am especially grateful to the Curator of Maritime History at the Peabody Museum, Salem, a post occupied by John S Carter when I last did research there; also for permission to reproduce photographs from their collection. Among several friends in New England I should like to thank Andrew Nesdall who has always been willing to offer advice and information. In Australia, Cyril L Hume and Roderick Glassford have sent fine selections of photographs, and I have greatly valued their friendship over the years.

Others nearer home to help with photographic illustrations include Hans Jeppesen, Director of the Maritime Museum at Kronborg, Denmark; Ronald van den Bos of Amsterdam; and Atle Midthassel of Stavangar. In Great Britain, I should like to acknowledge assistance received from Dennis Stoneham of the Photographic Department of the National Maritime Museum, Greenwich, and from Paul Elkin, Curator of Technology at the Bristol City Museum.

As a contrast to real photographs, I have used engravings and paintings where possible to vary the form of illustrations and I am most grateful to Bertram Newbury of the Parker Gallery, London, for permission to use pictures from their files; also, for the same reason, to Paul Mason of the Paul Mason Gallery, and to Colin Denny. James Fairweather of Salcombe has also allowed me to reproduce photographs of paintings made by his father which feature West Country vessels.

For information on shipbuilders I have received assistance in the past from James Steele (died c1955) and from the late W Stewart Rees; also from Dr Peter L Payne of Glasgow University, Peter Barton, and Robert S Craig. The Committee of Lloyd's Register of Shipping permitted me to examine their records. The National Maritime Museum, Greenwich, is a great storehouse for information and many of the former staff have aided me over the years among whom were George P B Naish, Arthur L Tucker and George Osbon, all now gone; also Arthur H Waite and Michael S Robinson.

Several friends helped me considerably by drawing plans at my request especially for this work; they are Paul A Roberts, Ralph Bird, Frederick A Claydon and Bill Ward, and I should like to extend to them my warmest thanks.

In the matter of copying plans for reproduction my thanks go to John Mayes of Kingprint Ltd for his efforts. The bulk of the manuscript was typed by Joanna Fairey with additions by myself, but I am also grateful to my wife and to Janet Bennett for additional typing and for help in checking the proofs.

David R MacGregor
Barnes, London, 1984

LARGER SCALE COPIES OF THE PLANS
REPRODUCED IN THIS BOOK CAN BE OBTAINED
ON APPLICATION TO THE AUTHOR
AT 99 LONSDALE ROAD, LONDON SW13,
ENGLAND

1 FREE TRADE 1850~1875

CHANGING PATTERNS IN SHIPBUILDING

The quarter century after 1850 coincided with a period of widespread development in mechanical engineering as it applied to shipbuilding: considerable progress was achieved in the manufacture and design of steam engines and propulsion units, and the methods of fitting them satisfactorily into a hull; the building of iron hulls advanced from experimental stages to technological

success; and countless improvements in windlasses, anchors, steering gear, rigging and sails improved the efficiency and safety of the ships. Books were full of these innovations and numerous periodicals carried regular features on them to the almost total exclusion of wooden sailing ships. Yet the latter improved in the quality of their construction, due to the survey regulations instituted by classification societies, on whose assignment of years the insurance and freight markets based their premiums and rates. Trade expansion and gold fever, following the repeal of the Navigation Acts in 1849, produced the clipper ship era in which large iron and wooden ships were designed and built with a sharpness of form that astounded their contemporaries and possibly horrified their masters. It is fortuitous that so many forces of change should have coincided at the exact half-century; historians are often regarded with suspicion in using such a date as the fulcrum point of their conclusions.

The Great Exhibition of 1851 in London focussed

Fig 1. This coloured print of J & R White's shipyard at Cowes shows three vessels in frame and two others planked, one of which is ready for launching. There is a steam chest in the centre foreground and two chimney stacks suggest sawmills and machine shops. Although the date is given as 1856, some timber in the left foreground has the wording 'C. Gregory 1838'. (Private Collection)

Launch of H. M. Steam Despatch Gun-Vessel
"LAPWING"
From Mess.rs John & Robert White's Establishment, Medina Docks, Cowes, Isle of Wight.
Jan. 26th 1856.

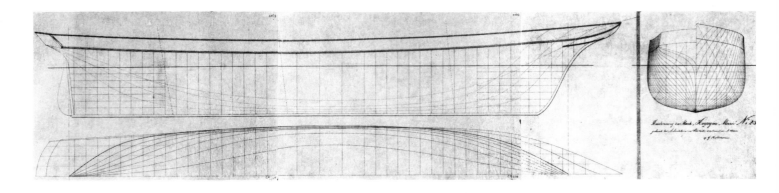

Fig 2. Lines plan of the German iron barque Herzogin Marie *as drawn by G Hillmann, probably c1860. The plan was in three pieces without overlap and so the joints are somewhat pronounced. Photographed from plan in Mariner's Museum, Newport News.*

attention on the engineering skills and inventions of the British nation, while the Prince Consort urged the expansion of such knowledge. New universities with engineering departments were eventually established in industrial towns and greater interest was shown generally in providing the necessary training for future engineers. The improved quality of machinery in factories and shipyards was enhanced by the new steel-making techniques, introduced by Henry Bessemer in 1856 and by Siemens in the sixties. These processes reduced the cost of production and soon made steel shipbuilding a viable industry.

During the unquestioned superiority of wooden shipbuilding, a great deal was left in the hands of a capable shipyard foreman and practically no drawings of a ship were required; but the wider use of iron changed this. Shipbuilders drew plans of mechanical parts, and drawings of the ship were necessary to explain the new construction methods. Within the short space of a few years considerable data becomes available for individual ships and restraint is needed to avoid overloading the twenty-five years after 1850 with more examples of ship design than the overall picture warrants. The migration of shipbuilding to Scotland and the north of England is reflected in the plans presented here which, from the early fifties, include few examples of ships or barques from the English yards south of the Mersey. Such selections must naturally be dependent on the circumstances surrounding the survival of plans of models and their suitability for study purposes.

Several important British collections of plans date from the early 1850s because the shipyards which produced these drawings began business during this boom period. Three such yards were situated on the River Clyde: Alexander Stephen & Sons, Barclay Curle & Co, and William Denny Brothers. Today these plans are all housed in the National Maritime Museum, Greenwich, and whereas Stephen and Barclay Curle built a mixture of sail and steam, Denny built steamers almost exclusively. Another collection comes from the yard of T & J Brocklebank of Whitehaven, while at Aberdeen the account books of Alexander Hall & Sons include spar

dimensions and some offset tables. For other shipbuilders, the records consist of shipbuilding lists and a selection of half-models and offset tables; both the latter require considerable work before lines plans can be drawn out, and so it takes longer to appraise the work of such shipbuilders.

In America and Canada, shipyard records comprise half-models rather than plans, apart from some celebrated clippers and isolated merchant ships, although the enterprising builder, William H Webb of New York, collected many of his plans and published them in 1895.[1] Some examples of his plans are given here. A modern example of how lines plans can be employed to build up a picture of merchant ship and fishing boat design is demonstrated by the late Howard I Chapelle who painstakingly took the lines off over thirty of the many half-models in the National Watercraft Collection at the Smithsonian Institution in Washington, and published them in book form in 1960.[2]

Although sailing vessels continued to be built almost exclusively of wood in North America, there was a slow move to experiment with iron for steamers and a few coastal craft. New York and Philadelphia led the way, but other yards were opened at Boston and Wilmington. The American Civil War gave iron shipbuilding an added impetus and although new work was limited after 1865, orders accelerated from 1870 when the cost of iron fell to $16.50 per ton. Nevertheless, compared with Great Britain, the output was tiny – in 1872 only twenty iron vessels were built totalling 12,766 tons, excluding any constructed for foreign orders or for the United States Government service. The cost of building in iron remained generally in excess of that for a wooden ship.[3]

The taxes levied in America on an important shipbuilding material such as iron had risen from 24 per cent in 1857 to 112 per cent in 1864 and it was proposed to further increase this to 168 per cent in 1868. This meant, it was claimed in 1870 by the treasurer of the Atlantic Iron Works of Boston, that only two iron sailing ships had been built in America, a barque of 600-700 tons, and the barque *Novelty* which was built by his yard. Iron shipbuilding seems to have been confined almost entirely to steamers until the 1870s.[4]

An important result of the growth of iron shipbuilding in Great Britain and an entirely new feature for the shipping industry, was the concentration on shipyards in Scotland and the north of England where most of the coalfields and iron deposits were located. Of course shipbuilding, principally in wood, continued in southern and south-western England for as long as orders were received, but after the mid-1850s orders for ships of over 500 tons were becoming less common for southern shipbuilders, with the exception of the larger building centres. Similarly, the prospects became increasingly hazardous for southern shipbuilders to sell large ships built on speculation. Contracts for constructing iron ships progressively tended to be awarded to northern shipyards, and such yards simultaneously collected orders for any large wooden ships that were required. Exceptionally, some shipyards on the Thames continued to build large iron ships until well after 1870. Although all raw materials had to be imported, these Thames-side yards benefitted from the fact that London was such a great entrepôt of trade and the consequential avoidance of special shipping charges. However, some smaller

Fig 3. The scene at San Francisco in 1853 from a daguerreotype taken by William Shew from Rincon Point looking across to Telegraph Hill with the semaphore station at the top. This is the centre section of a five-part panorama. Most of the ships here have been abandoned by their crews when they rushed off to the gold-fields. No name is visible on the ship in the foreground, but she is full-bodied with two deckhouses and a wheel house; her topgallant masts and yards have been sent down, as well as the topsail yards, and her jibboom has been rigged inboard. In line with her mainmast is a brigantine and amongst the ships between lies one whose deck has been roofed over to act as a warehouse. Such a scene was repeated in Australian harbours which became choked with abandoned craft. (Smithsonian Institution, Washington)

shipyards, such as Harvey & Co at Hayle and W H Nevill at Llanelly, adopted iron shipbuilding to satisfy local customers and prevent this drift of orders to the north, but by degrees many yards that had been accustomed to build wooden brigs, small barques and even an occasional full-rigged ship were finding that their orders were limited to wooden schooners and smacks, with an occasional barquentine. This is reflected in the falling fortunes of shipbuilding at Chepstow after 1847 where the annual production of barques and brigs were superseded by that of trows and sloops.[5]

In Germany, the first iron sailing ship was the brig *Hoffnung*, built in 1844 at Ruhrort on the Rhine and fitted with a centreboard, and in the following year the same yard built an iron barque. The next iron vessel was the *Orientale*, built in 1854 at Rostock, and thereafter came the *Herzogin Marie* (1857), *Deutschland* (1858 of 838 tons net), and *Prinz Albert* (1861 of 570 tons net). After a gap of three years, two iron vessels were built in 1865 and from then on there was a steady trickle of iron ships, but the industry did not really start to expand until 1875 when three more yards launched iron ships, in addition to the Reiherstieg Yard. The first steel vessel built in Germany was the barquentine *Hedwig* built in 1885.[6]

In Holland, iron shipbuilding was established by 1860 and a few square-rigged vessels were so built in the early 1860s, although composite construction appears to have superseded the use of an all-iron hull between 1865 and 1871. In 1867 the large auxiliary ship *Utrecht* of 2200 tons om was built at Bolnes. Composite construction lasted

Fig 4. *Ships discharging cargo at the Railway Pier, Sandridge, Victoria, in the 1860s. Stunsail booms are much in evidence: on the left, one is shown triced up; on the right, another is rigged under the lower yard. The second vessel on the right is a barque with double topsail yards.* (C L Hume)

until 1885 although by this date it had developed into wood planking laid over an iron-plated bottom.[7]

Composite construction, in spite of its greater cost over iron construction, was adopted for a number of vessels built in the British Isles, as the following totals show:[8]

Fig 5. *Emigrants embarking on the 478-ton* Ballengeich *at Southampton en route for Australia. This ship was built at Glasgow in 1849 and this engraving appeared in the* Illustrated London News *in 1852.*

ANNUAL TOTALS OF COMPOSITE CONSTRUCTION VESSELS 1862-67

Year	Number of vessels built	Total tonnage
1862	5	2779
1863	11	8114
1864	19	12,164
1865	41	27,749
1866	39	24,420
1867*	22	17,162

*(Jan-June only)

Prior to 1850 the shape of ordinary merchant ships had remained fairly constant throughout Europe as regards hull-form and construction, but soon after 1850 many shipbuilders were giving their vessels slightly finer lines to make them eligible for the new requirement of additional speed. It becomes a moot point whether or not a sharpened version of a general cargo ship enters the category of a medium clipper – indeed such niceties of

definition are impossible unless hundreds of plans are available for inspection and comparison. But the extreme clippers do belong to a section of their own and although there are bound to be borderline cases, there are many indisputably fine-lined ships of extreme form which can easily be set apart.

It is the policy here to include ordinary merchant vessels designed for cargo capacity rather than for speed, but after 1850 these cargo carriers are often becoming the equivalent of the fine-lined merchant ships of twenty or thirty years earlier, so one must reorientate one's thoughts to take account of the changing values. Some such metamorphosis of the cargo merchantman was occurring during the fifties and sixties; indeed the full-bodied ship was never so bluff again. These merchant ships did not lose capacity by being given a finer entrance and run as the hull length was increased and the floors made flatter. Iron construction, by reducing the thickness of the shell, saved considerable internal space which could be utilised to increase capacity by at least 15 per cent.[9] Alternatively this saving could be employed to design a finer-lined hull, whilst retaining the same capacity as a wooden ship. In other cases, an iron ship resulted in a longer and narrower hull which inevitably possessed a higher speed potential.

THE AUSTRALIAN GOLD-RUSH

In Great Britain there were few native-built ships above 900 tons available for the rapidly expanding Australian trade, with the exception of a few old East Indiamen and the aristocratic passenger frigates. Many Dutch ships were chartered for voyages to Australia, and French and German ships also made the passage out. However, Canadian shipbuilders had had their eyes on the British market for some years and had already been sending over so many softwood ships that by 1847 colonial-built ships, of which Canada was the principal supplier, actually comprised one-sixth of the tonnage owned in the United Kingdom.[10] By 1851 many of the Canadian-built ships were of over 1000 tons and as soon as the news of the Australian gold discoveries arrived and was confirmed, it became obvious in Canada that here was a rich market for their ships. For the shipowners too, these ships provided a quick way to make a profit because their low initial cost was quickly offset by the high freights available, so that the first cost was sometimes cleared in a single voyage. Great efforts were also being made by British yards to build larger ships and the new vessels so constructed were probably built on finer lines than would have been the case a year or two earlier, although only a limited number were built as extreme clippers. This new trade absorbed a vast amount of existing shipping that was never originally intended for this type of work, but given the necessary incentive the ships so employed could and did make fast passages. Although ships of over 800 tons were well-suited to this work, especially for the conveyance of passengers, the bulk of the Australian trade was for many years carried on in ships of between 200 and 500 tons. In January 1853, forty-seven vessels cleared for Australia and Tasmania from London and Liverpool, with a total tonnage of 21,629, making an average of 460 tons per vessel. The smallest ship was 100 tons and the largest 1324 tons.[11]

During 1852 the Canadian ships reaching Liverpool for sale were found to be improved in model, in materials, and in the quality of finish, so that the class received from Lloyd's Register was 6 or 7 A1, and ships of this class were fetching prices of £6–£8 10s per ton which was an advance of 17 per cent on the previous year. Tonge & Co's annual circulars which gave this information stated that the enormous emigration to Australia was mainly responsible for this advance. In 1852, 120 Canadian ships reached Liverpool and were sold. Such was the demand for these big softwood ships that prices advanced throughout 1853 until ships of 7 A1 were fetching £10–£11 5s per ton, and even spruce-built ships that only received a class of 4 A1 had advanced from £4 10s–£5 10s in 1852 to £7 10s–£9 in 1853. This sometimes resulted in the higher-classed Great Britain-built ships being preferred, even if they did cost £3 or £4 more per ton than the most expensive softwood Canadian ones. In any case, iron ships with a complete Baltic outfit could be had at a contract price of £14 10s–£16 per ton in 1853 which made them an excellent proposition.[12]

In 1854 the number of new colonial ships registered in Liverpool increased from 112 to 123 but the figures were particularly notable for the increase in tonnage of the ships which advanced to an average of 1048 tons. Prospects for the Canadian shipbuilding trade were not as rosy in the spring of 1855 as they had been twelve months before, because shipwrights' wages had risen and the market was becoming well stocked with cheaply-built ships.[13] The absorption of so much shipping into the Australian trade permitted many ships of poor model and defective build to be purchased.

There had been a boom of emigration to Australia between 1837 and 1844 but this had petered out during the later forties, and even by the close of 1851 the reports of the gold discoveries had had little effect on the labouring classes of Great Britain. Australia was sending urgent calls to the mother country for increased emigration to fill the vacuum caused by the desertion of the working population to the gold-fields, and it was feared that lack of labour would endanger the wool crop. Due to the great demand for ships, the Emigration Commissioners found themselves having to pay exorbitant rates to charter suitable vessels, and in 1852 they countered this to some extent by chartering a larger class of vessel than formerly.[14] Unfortunately, four of the large ships they chartered achieved the description of 'floating pest-houses' due to the high rate of mortality on board.[15] These were the *Borneuf*, *Wanata*, *Marco Polo* and *Ticonderoga*, the mortality rate on which was 88 out of 830 statute emigrants, 39 out of 821, 52 out of 749½, and 102 out of 795 respectively.[16] These totals did not represent the actual number of persons aboard, as the Passenger Acts allowed two children under fourteen to class as one statute adult, and infants under one year old did not count at all.

The shock occasioned by such a heavy death roll produced an enquiry, although it was shown that the ships were not legally overcrowded and that death occurred through a variety of reasons, such as bad water supplied by the dock authorities, the uncleanliness of Irish and north Scottish emigrants, and proneness of masters to sail far south on great circle tracks resulting in the inevitable cold. The standard laid down by law was very low and strict adherence to it brought great hardship to the emigrants. By contrast, the societies which sponsored emigration had a far higher standard, as did the passenger ships run by individual shipping companies. Captain C Patey RN, the Government Emigration Officer at Liverpool, was superseded by Charles F Schomberg, after whom James Baines undoubtedly named his monster Aberdeen clipper.

By the middle of 1855 the emigration mania to Australia was over and although many ships were still on the berth every month, they took out a wealthier class of passenger, many of whom wished to join their relatives. In addition there was also a large volume of manufactured goods to be exported. It is interesting to note that although just under 42,000 emigrants sailed from Liverpool to Australia in 1854, almost five times as many went to the United States of America.[17]

REPEAL OF THE NAVIGATION ACTS

The repeal of the Navigation Acts was passed in 1849 but did not become effective until 1 January 1850; the regulation on manning by Englishmen was retained until 1853 and a year later the coasting trade was thrown open to all. British shipbuilders and shipowners found that they were not ruined after all, as some had feared, because the repeal coincided with the gold discoveries which, coupled with free trade, brought a vast demand for ships of all kinds and kept British yards busy for some years at full stretch. In addition, the demand for shipping was accentuated by the urgent need for transports in the Crimean War, and as first-class ships were hired by the government a general redeployment became necessary. Steamers were so desperately required for war purposes that practically all those on the Australian run were chartered by the British or French governments with the result that postal communication suffered severely until the Post Office contracted with James Baines & Co (Black Ball Line) and Pilkington & Wilson (White Star Line), both of Liverpool, for a monthly sailing of each line to Melbourne. The Black Ball Line clippers rashly agreed to land their mails within 65 days of sailing and accepted penalties for delay. In any case, steamship companies found it hard to make their services pay and the long run from the Cape of Good Hope without any ports of call encouraged many steamers to be fully square-rigged sailing ships with only auxiliary engines. If not subsidised by a mail contract, steamers continued to obtain poor remuneration in the Australia trade until after the opening of the Suez Canal.

In the China tea trade, competition with America brought orders for faster and larger clippers and proved a great incentive to British shipbuilders. Indeed all forms of trade were interested in speedier deliveries although, as usual, orders were late in reaching the shipbuilders so that it was not until 1853 that the majority of the clippers began to be built.

Even during the boom, news of the failure in October 1854 of the Liverpool shipowner Edward Oliver had a dampening effect on the market when it was realised that his immense fleet of 98 ships would have to be sold. At a public auction an average of £6 2s 6d per ton was obtained.[18]

The termination of the Crimean War in April 1856 found Great Britain heavily overstocked with unwanted ships; consequently freight rates dropped and shipbuilding orders were cut back. Thus the 1850s are evenly divided between boom and slump. In the boom, cargo capacity was irrationally sacrificed to speed and the ordinary cargo carrier given finer lines. In the slump, few ships of high speed were ordered and the cargo carriers reverted to full-bodied hulls; here, the improved techniques of iron shipbuilding permitted the building of long, box-like structures which were ideally suited for the moving of bulk cargoes at low, but profitable freight rates. It was the profit motive which governed the shipping industry, as indeed any branch of business, a fact which is often overlooked in sailing ship histories.

The entrenched position of Lloyd's Register and the support given its classification system by insurance societies and the freight market continued to offer protection to the higher-classed British ships. Nevertheless, the construction of American ships increased rapidly, challenging Great Britain for supremacy in the international carrying trade until the fortuitous circumstances of the American Civil War removed this dangerous competitor. By the end of the war 750,000 tons of American shipping had been sold. The figures below indicate the rapid rise of American shipping and its decline; and totals for France and Holland are added for the sake of comparison.

SHIPPING REGISTERED IN FOUR COUNTRIES
(sail and steam included)

Year	Great Britain[19]	United States[20] of America	France[20]	Holland[20]
1830	2,202,000	1,167,000	-	-
1840	2,768,000	2,141,000	673,308	-
1850	3,565,000	3,486,000	688,153	396,124
1860	4,659,000	5,299,000	996,124	588,772
1870	5,691,000	4,195,000	1,072,396	528,578

In Europe there was also a general expansion in shipping and total tonnages rose during this period.

British shipping increased through the development of trade with India, Australia and Africa which the opening of the Suez Canal later benefitted; but an important factor in the rejuvenation of British shipping was the change in the methods of ship construction, enabling the shipbuilders to survive and progress without protection. This change was first to be seen in the gradual and later

Fig 6. Some of the transports engaged for the Crimean War lying in Cossack Bay, Balaclava, as photographed by Roger Fenton in March 1855. The ship on the right has been identified as the St Hilda which was built at Quebec in 1849 of 791 tons nm; in the centre are some steamers and beyond are further sailing ships. (Library of Congress)

Fig 7. George's Dock, Liverpool, bristling with masts and the spire of St Nicholas' Church on the right. The overhead railway was erected over this road in about 1875. Printed from a stereo negative loaned to me in 1954 by Samuel H Porter.

rapid adoption of iron as the chief building material, so that by 1863 the combined tonnage of iron sailing ships and steamers built that year in Great Britain greatly exceeded those built of wood, although it was not until 1868 that the tonnage of new iron sailing ships exceeded that of purely wooden ones.[21]

In his work on the Navigation Laws, Lawrence Harper shows how the British shipbuilder had to 'scour the world for masts and ship timber' and other maritime raw materials, and that he needed the protection afforded by the Navigation Acts to avoid being undercut by foreign shipyards. But once protection was removed he quickly began to make use of his own raw materials, namely of iron and coal and this soon gave him an advantage. 'The rapidity with which the English changed their methods', commented Harper, 'suggests how unpleasant former conditions must have been'.[22]

Until the advent of the great Merchant Shipping Act of 1854, government action consisted of a series of piecemeal Acts designed to correct certain abuses, but once the repeal of the Navigation Acts had been passed it became possible to consolidate the various shipping Acts into one. The Mercantile Marine Act of 1850, besides organising examinations for masters and mates and tightening up regulations concerning the crew, also clarified the Board of Trade's position which was to 'undertake the general superintendence of matters relating to the British Mercantile Marine'.[23] Other Bills flowed thick and fast, covering such items as steam navigation, carriage of passengers, seamen, pilotage, lighthouses and Trinity House. The Merchant Shipping Act of 1854, consisting of 548 clauses, repealed numerous outdated statutes but rationalised a vast range of shipping legislation covering every aspect of the industry. The Act defined anew the functions of the Board of Trade, in the first of its eleven sections, and also produced a new method of tonnage measurement which has since been universally adopted. The latter was detailed in *Fast Sailing Ships*.

Agitation about unseaworthy ships and overloading continued and it was in 1870 that Samuel Plimsoll first submitted his views on this subject to Parliament. There

was a Royal Commission on the subject in 1873 and 1874 but it was not until 1876 that the load line was established by statute.

SAIL VERSUS STEAM

The boom of the early fifties coupled with the heavy demands of the Crimean War for additional tonnage to serve as transports, resulted in a combined record total of 323,200 tons of sail and steam shipping being built in 1855. The resultant slump was in turn superseded by steadier conditions, and by the early sixties trade was reviving and shipyards were busy again, so much so that 1864 proved, by later figures, to have produced the largest tonnage of sailing ships ever constructed in a single year, namely 272,500 tons, against 159,400 tons of steamers.[24] The late sixties witnessed an extraordinary display of clipper-ship building for the China and Australia trades in an effort to curtail the advance of steam propulsion which was encountering difficulties on these long hauls around the Cape of Good Hope, where distances between bunkering depots were too great. True, the number of extreme clippers built at the end of the sixties was very small compared with those built in the boom of 1853-55, but many medium clippers were launched for passenger and general cargo work; later in life these same ships carried bulk cargoes of coal, grain, wool, rice, timber and nitrate.

The opening of the Suez Canal in 1869 abruptly terminated the construction of any more tea clippers, apart from an odd experiment, but it was found that the trade with Australia and the west coast of North and South America was uneconomical for steamships in terms of coal consumption and cargo capacity. This resulted in a flood of orders for fast sailing ships of maximum cargo capacity, which were more efficient to run by reason of their all-iron construction, wire rigging, and steam-assisted windlasses and cargo winches. Although 1870 had seen the tonnage of steamers built in Great Britain for British owners exceed that of sailing ships for the very first time, this new style of sailing ship was financially successful for many years. This book closes when the boom for iron sailing ships was at its height, but it is worth remembering that some ten years later, in the mid-1880s, the tonnage of newly-constructed sailing ships again

Fig 8. Lying off the Chincha Islands near the small seaport of that name in north Peru, a variety of ships wait to load guano. Possibly photographed c1865. (Nautical Photo Agency)

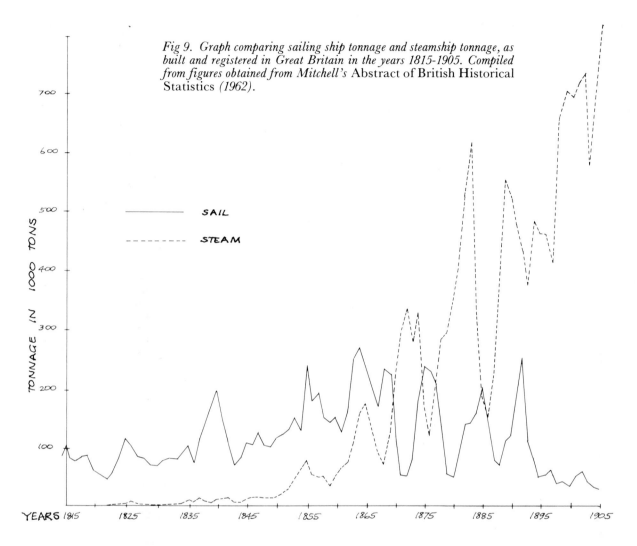

Fig 9. Graph comparing sailing ship tonnage and steamship tonnage, as built and registered in Great Britain in the years 1815-1905. Compiled from figures obtained from Mitchell's Abstract of British Historical Statistics *(1962).*

exceeded that of steamers, although this was to be the final year in which such an event occurred.

There is an informative table in *The Dismasting of Large Iron Sailing Ships* which indicates the rapid decline of orders for sailing ships due to the advent of the Suez Canal and the equally speedy resurgence of orders after the effects of the opening had been digested.

NUMBER OF SAILING SHIPS BUILT IN GREAT BRITAIN[25]

Year	Total
1868	138
1869	132
1870	51
1871	10
1872	14
1873	37
1874	109
1875	198
1876	119

The annual tonnage totals for the years 1814 to 1905, separating sail from steam, are plotted in figure 9. Prior to 1869 it will be noticed that the rise and fall in the building of sailing ships was complemented by the building of steamers; but after 1869 the position was reversed, and the tonnage of sail increased in years when that for steam

declined. In periods of depression, sailing ships could be laid up cheaply, wait inexpensively for cargo, and obtain depressed freight rates that were similar to those for steamers, with the result that owners hurriedly ordered sailing ships when a depression loomed. Hence orders for steamships declined in these periods. The slumps of 1873-79, 1882-86 and 1890-96 coincided with large orders for sailing ships and reduced orders for steamers. The low cost of steamer construction and the efficient triple expansion engine finally gave steam the supremacy after 1885, because shipowners naturally went for the cheapest form of vessel that would provide the most efficient and reliable service and yield the highest profits. Yet it must be strongly emphasised that the coming of steam was no walk-over and that sail was retained because it was economically successful. This subject of 'Steam Competition' was treated in more detail in *The China Bird*, particularly with regard to the China trade, and the subject warrants a detailed study of its own.[26] Professor Gerald S Graham is greatly to be thanked for his forthright article on 'The Ascendancy of the Sailing Ship 1850-1885', in which he demonstrated that steam propulsion required many years to oust sail from its supremacy in the carrying trade of the world.[27]

17

2
SQUARE RIGGED SHIPS OF OVER 300 TONS 1850~1860

Fig 10. This unidentified barque hauled out on the slip at Ramsgate shows the type of hull-form commonly found in many vessels. Copied from an old photograph in Ramsgate Central Library.

APPRAISAL OF CARGO CARRIER DESIGN

Although three-masted barques of less than 300 tons continued to be built as frequently as ever, full-rigged ships of such small tonnage were increasingly uncommon, and indeed the average size of ships was steadily growing larger. Many of these smaller barques were constructed at shipyards whose records have long since disappeared, but at yards specialising in iron construction, where more detailed records were kept, plans have been preserved in a number of cases. Up to this point, all classes of rig have been compared in the same chapter, but owing to the great disparity in sizes now appearing it has been decided that in this volume the larger square-rigged vessels shall be separated from their smaller brethren, and that the fore-and-aft rig be grouped with the latter.

During the 1850s there was a considerable degree of shipbuilding skill available in Great Britain for the

and depth but is some ten feet shorter. Deck arrangements of all three ships must have been very similar. The *Polmaise* carried tea regularly from China after 1859; her shortest passage was 103 days from Shanghai to Deal in 1865-66.

The following list of ships built at the Dundee yard in the fifties indicates the similarity in dimensions of several ships:

financial connection with the Glasgow yard after the launch of *Tyburnia* in July. Alexander jnr and his younger brother, James, had equal shares in the Kelvinhaugh yard from this date.[6] In April 1859 James gave up his interest and the yard was then the sole responsibility of Alexander jnr, until 1 January 1861, when his youngest brother, John, who was up to that time on a salary, joined as a partner with a quarter share.[7]

SHIPS BUILT BY ALEXANDER STEPHEN AND SONS AT DUNDEE 1850-1894[4]

All are sailing ships built of wood except No 24 which is auxiliary

Yard No	Year	Name	Dimensions	Tons nm	Tons om	Rig	Class
14*	1850	Amazon	144.0ft × 31.6ft × 21.6ft	791	667	S	14 A1
15	1851	Cossipore	148.7ft × 28.8ft × 21.0ft	707	838	S	9 A1
16	1851	Elizabeth Duncan	94.5ft × 23.2ft × 14.5ft	220	227	Bg	9 A1
17*	1852	Harkaway	168.0ft × 32.6ft × 21.3ft	899	830	S	15 A1
18	1853	Polmaise	178.9ft × 32.2ft × 21.2ft	887	878	S	14 A1
19*	1854	Whirlwind	187.0ft × 33.6ft × 21.1ft	978	1003	S	9 A1
20	1855	Beemah	188.0ft × 33.6ft × 21.2ft	887	1020	S	11 A1
21*	1856	Eastern Monarch	239.0ft × 40.3ft × 24.9ft	1631	1849	S	14 A1
22*	1859	Dartmouth	185.4ft × 34.3ft × 21.6ft	933	-	S	14 A1
23	1858	Ianthe	135.6ft × 26.0ft × 16.6ft	400	427	Bk	13 A1
24	1859	Narwhal	151.4ft × 30.1ft × 18.5ft	533 (gr)	-	S/aux	-

*signifies owned by Joseph Somes.
The *Narwhal* was Stephen's first auxiliary whaler.

At the Kelvinhaugh yard, a variety of vessels were launched in the years 1852-60, numbering twenty-seven in all, of which only the full-rigged ships *Cyclone* (1853) and *Tyburnia* (1857) were built of wood, the remainder being of iron.

SHIPS BUILT BY ALEXANDER STEPHEN & SONS AT GLASGOW 1850-1860[5]

CONSTRUCTED OF IRON

Full-rigged ships and barques	*Typhoon* (1852), *Hurricane** (1853), *John Bell** and *Storm Cloud** (1854), *White Eagle** (1855), *Charlemagne* (1857), *Sea Queen* and *Edmund Preston* (1858), *City of Lucknow*, *Carnatic* and *City of Madras* (1859), *Clyde* and *City of Calcutta* (1860).
Schooners	*Angelita* (1859)
Paddle steamers	Four in number
Screw steamers	Six in number of which *Euphrates** (1855) and *Dahome* (1857) were auxiliaries with full suits of sails.
Dredger	One

*signifies clipper hull-form

CONSTRUCTED OF WOOD

Full-rigged ships	*Cyclone* (1853), *Tyburnia* (1857)

Both the Dundee and the Glasgow yards of Alexander Stephen & Sons were building several large wooden ships for the London shipowner Joseph Somes, and these conformed to the contemporary style of passenger frigates. Amongst these was the *Eastern Monarch* which measured 1631 tons register and was the second largest wooden sailing ship to be built in Great Britain during the fifties.

The Dundee business was divided equally between William Stephen and his father as from November 1856; and in the following year, the father ceased to have any

The diaries of Alexander jnr show how he was sometimes away from the shipyard in order to obtain orders for new ships. His method, which most of the shipyards likewise employed, was to tour the principal shipowning centres, in Great Britain, especially London and Liverpool, visiting the owners, quoting prices and discussing ships with them and other shipyard representatives.

It was less easy to obtain orders at the end of the fifties, and Stephen's policy must have been to keep his men occupied on a new ship, when no repair work was on hand. Ship no 23 at Dundee was obviously laid down after no 22 – the *Dartmouth* – but being smaller and finding a buyer more quickly, was sold and launched a year earlier in 1858. A letter to a possible purchaser for no 23 is given below.

Letter to Simon Hardy & Sons, Cork, dated 18 November 1857:

The 13 A1 wood ship building at Dundee is 135 × 25¾ × 16½ and measures about 427 tons BM. The frame is principally of seasoned Sussex oak; upper and lower deck beams are of East Indian teak and also her planking inside and out, except the bottom which as usual is of elm. She has diagonal straps on the frames. At present she is planked up to the top of the wales. The beams are finished and are ready for putting in at spaces to suit your trade. She has a long midship section and a very full round bilge for stowage and she has only about nine inches rise of floor, all of which gives great carrying capacity and her great length at the same time gives her two excellent ends. She could be delivered in January, sheathed with yellow metal and with a Baltic outfit. The lowest price is £17 per ton BM.[8]

The vessel referred to above was finally sold in May 1858 to a Sunderland firm for £16 7s 6d per ton om including an East India outfit and received the name *Ianthe*.[9] An 'East India outfit' was more expensive and extensive than a 'Baltic outfit' and a ship intended for ocean trade would receive the former, the latter being reserved for coasting and short sea service.

Because many owners personally liked to superintend the fitting out of their ships, it was common for builders to quote for 'hull and spars' only. In a letter accompanying a quotation, Alexander Stephen & Sons listed in 1856 the items which comprised 'hull and spars', as follows:

> Blacksmith's work for the hull and spars, also blocks; boats according to Act of Parliament including oars, boat hooks and davits; joiner's work in cabins complete in pine and properly painted (but exclusive of upholstery and other furnishings); windlass with patent purchase; hatch and hold ladders; hen coops and meat safe; houses on deck on either side of wheel for carpenter etc; application of copper sheathing (the copper sheets and nails being supplied by the Owners), the Builder supplying sheathing paper and tacks; plumber's work, namely scuppers, bilge and head pumps, water closet in cabin; vessel to receive three coats of paint to outside.
>
> The Builder does not supply the following: sails; canvas; rigging; cordage; anchors; chains or chain cables; water tanks; any other outfit or furnishings.[10]

The price for a wooden ship strictly in accordance with the above list and the rules for building wooden ships laid down by Lloyd's Register of Shipping would, the letter concludes, be £15 17s 6d per ton BM classed 13 A1 (12 A1 for materials and one year extra for yellow metal fastenings). Alternatively, it would be only £13 15s 6d per ton BM for the lower class of 10 A1 (9 A1 for materials and one year extra for yellow metal fastenings).

The Glasgow yard appears to have always built to order, although this involved considerable travelling to the principal shipowning centres. This was necessary to make contacts, visit previous clients, and talk over business with other shipbuilders. Prices per ton were being quoted continuously in an endeavour to secure orders, and many quotations were sent by post. To obtain the contract for the auxiliary steamer *Sea King*, Alexander Stephen jnr of Glasgow visited London three times in 1862. At that time a four-day visit to London, including hotels and travelling expenses, cost about £10.

After obtaining the agreement to build, Alexander Stephen would make a half-model for the owner's approval before laying the lines down on the mould loft floor. A lines plan was probably prepared by the chief draughtsman, William Robertson, while the model was being made. Stephen made many of the models himself, often working late into the night, and it usually occupied him for three or four days. The sequence of events in preparing plans and building a ship up to the time of her launch are illustrated by no 14, the iron ship *Charlemagne*, constructed at Kelvinhaugh in 1856. The items are summarised from Alexander Stephen's diary.

CHRONOLOGICAL SEQUENCE OF EVENTS IN BUILDING THE *CHARLEMAGNE*

24 Jan 1856	Offered to build iron sailing ship for R Catto & Son, Aberdeen, 986 tons BM at £17 10s per ton BM.
4 Feb	Letter from Catto & Son agreeing price, but want tonnage and length increased; also want some accommodation as regards periods of payment.
5 Feb	James Stephen went to Aberdeen to arrange terms with Catto & Son.
15 Feb	Sent model of ship to owners at Aberdeen.
26 Feb	Model received back from Aberdeen with a few comments: Catto & Son ask for the hull to be a little finer forward and a little more flair to the bow 'aloft' but 'they think it a very good model'.
27 Feb	Began laying down lines in mould loft.
5 Mar	Began transferring after body lines from mould loft floor to platform preparatory to commencing setting the frames.
28 Mar	After body frames all set out; began on fore body.
1 Apr	Visited Catto & Sons at Aberdeen; some of the fittings discussed.
5 Apr	Contract fixed for supply of iron plates and angles.
11 Apr	Frames all set out.
14 Apr	Began on reverse angles and flooring plates.
16 Apr	Ordered keel from Parkland Forge Co.
30 Apr	Quoted Catto & Son for altering the stern to take a screw. Price £469 including £42 for 10 per cent interest over two years.
2 May	Catto & Son offer £200 for proposed alterations. Any sum less than previous quotation refused; alternative of charging for time and materials offered.
5 May	Catto & Son abandon idea of installing screw.
12 May	Keel laid and stem erected.
20 June	One third of contract price *ie* £6063 paid, vessel being in frame.
9 July	Deck plan and cabin plan agreed with Catto & Son yesterday. Plating proceeding.
8 Aug	Sent Catto & Son spar plan for approval.
29 Aug	Poop deck laid and caulked.
26 Sept	Work began on cabins.
2 Oct	Iron hull almost finished.
4 Oct	Caulking almost finished. Working on masts. Could be launched in a month's time.
21 Oct	Began putting in masts.
31 Oct	Lower masts in position.
10 Jan 1857	Launched.

[There is a gap in the diaries between 3 December 1856 and 8 November 1857.]

The weight of the materials used in the construction was: iron plates, 373 tons; iron angles, 182 tons; iron rivets, 32 tons; woodwork, 172 tons; sails, 5 tons: total 774 tons. On a draught of 19ft 6in, her displacement was calculated as 2130 tons.

Owing to the gap in the diary entries there is no description of *Charlemagne*'s launch but when the 873-ton iron ship *Sea Queen* was launched by Stephen in August 1858, she had all her masts in position up to royal masts, but without any yards crossed, and 85 tons of ballast was aboard.[11]

The *Charlemagne* measured 195.0ft × 33.0ft × 21.0ft and about 1014 tons om; she was not classed by Lloyd's Register. Her lines plan is dated 10 April 1856. Intended as a fast cargo carrier, she was a fairly long ship in proportion to her breadth, with moderately fine, convex ends; slight hollows were worked in where the plating met the stem and the sternpost; there was some deadrise, with wall sides and tumblehome, and a heavy round stern. She

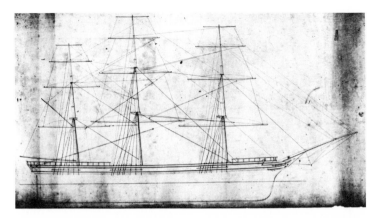

Fig 14. Charlemagne. Sail plan photographed from original when in possession of the builders, A Stephen & Sons. Built of iron at Glasgow in 1857, she measured 195.0ft × 33.0ft × 11.0ft and about 1014 tons om. Note the jibboom and flying jibboom which slid into each other and also into the bowsprit.

was under construction at the same time as the *Tyburnia* and similarities in the hull-form and midship section are unmistakable. Her sail plan was broad but not lofty and no skysails were carried.

With the production of *Tyburnia* and *Charlemagne*, ship design returned to normal at Kelvinhaugh after the excursion in designing the extreme clippers *Hurricane*, *John Bell*, *Storm Cloud*, and *White Eagle*, as well as the auxiliary clipper *Euphrates*.

The first of many ships built for George Smith & Sons was contracted for in April 1858. This was yard no 19 and the price was £13 per ton BM on 859 66/94 tons BM; she was to be built under cover to class 13 A1; payment was to be in four installments viz when framed, plated, launched and finished.[12] Framing was completed on 1 October and she was launched on 5 March 1859 as the *City of Lucknow*. The final payment was made by Smith's a month later on 8 April, and the final cost worked out at £11,320. The total weight of iron and rivets was 490 tons. She sailed on her maiden voyage from Glasgow on 11 April 1859, with 2004 tons deadweight, for Calcutta.[13]

The *City of Lucknow* did not have much deadrise but the

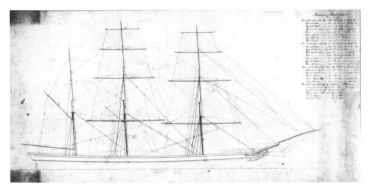

Fig 15. Carnatic. Sail plan photographed from original when in possession of the builders, A Stephen & Sons. Built of iron at Glasgow in 1859. Dimensions from register: 171.7ft × 27.1ft × 18.4ft and 604 tons. The fore and main lower masts seem rather short. A typical sail plan from Stephen's drawing office in the 1850s, being drawn in ink on heavy cartridge paper without any colouring. The spar dimensions are in the top right-hand corner. Lloyd's Register of 1863 has her rig as that of a full-rigged ship.

bilges were rounded; however the next two ships built for George Smith were almost flat bottomed with vertical sides and must have been good cargo carriers. These were the sister ships *City of Madras* and *City of Calcutta* launched in 1859 and 1860 as nos 23 and 27. The sail plans of all these ships show that no skysails were carried and in fact the sail plan of *Tyburnia* was a good model at this time. The *Carnatic* and the *Edmund Preston* were the only barques built in the fifties; the schooner *Angelita* is described in Chapter Four.

THE IRON BARQUE *EDMUND PRESTON*

Alexander Stephen jnr wrote in his diary in November 1857: 'Business at an exceedingly low ebb, very little doing. There is a monetary crisis all over the country and in no place is it so great as in Glasgow.'[14]

He noted that there was a great run on the Glasgow banks, that Dennistoun & Co had failed with liabilities of £2 million sterling, that the City of Glasgow Bank had suspended payment and that the shipbuilder Alexander Denny of Dumbarton had failed. Other shipbuilders were in difficulties. The Bank of England had raised the discount rate to 10 per cent. There were only apprentices left in his yard and no ships were under construction. With prices pared down, the firm must have been glad to sign a contract early in 1858 with Edmund Preston of Liverpool for an iron barque.[15]

The introduction was made by Frederick Preston who was inspector to Joseph Somes and who received a private commission of 1 per cent for this business. But in spite of having identical surnames, Alexander Stephen merely refers to Edmund and Frederick as being friends. Edmund Preston was probably a partner in the engineering firm of Fawcett, Preston & Co of Liverpool who may have built the engines of the auxiliary iron steamer *Antelope* which James Hodgson constructed in 1846. Edmund Preston and James Hodgson were probably involved in further business transactions so that it became quite natural for Preston to have the specification for his ship prepared by Hodgson, particularly if this was his first venture into shipowning. This lengthy document runs to about 13,000 words and specifies in detail the barque's construction and outfit, with lists of blocks and sails and an inventory. Alexander Stephen & Sons normally prepared their own specification after discussion with the owner, but this case was an exception. The gilt-tooled lettering on the front cover states: 'Specification for an iron barque for Mr Edmund Preston of Liverpool by James Hodgson'. The specification is not quoted here as it is proposed to publish it in full in a later work.

How the price was negotiated is not known, but a letter was received from Preston dated 13 January 1858 in which the above specification was mentioned. Alexander Stephen & Sons thereupon prepared a model and drawings, and calculated that the gross tonnage would be 428 $\frac{72}{100}$, and that on a draught of 15ft 6in the ship would carry 620 tons deadweight or about 1000 tons of measurement goods at 40 cubic feet per ton.[16] The first drawing was made on thin, flimsy tracing paper, now brittle with age and considerably foxed, and consisted of the sheer elevation with figurehead and carved work, on which was superimposed both the outline of the hull at deck level and the correct number of transverse sections for calculating the tonnage. In this case, seven sections are drawn and the length of each ordinate to the centre line is written in ink beside the section. The shape of the sections was presumably taken from the newly made half-model. Because the quotation was made on builder's measurement tonnage, which was normal practice, James Hodgson was smart enough to realise that the depth of hold was not measured and he must accordingly have specified a proportionally deeper vessel than usual, because Stephen protested that the vessel was 'very deep which you are aware is not favourable for the Builder when the price is rated by Builder's Measurement'.[17] This point is further emphasised in a quotation sent to Hodgson for quite another vessel, 'assuming ordinary dimensions'.[18]

The contract for the *Edmund Preston*, which was the name given at her launch, was agreed on 26 February 1858: she was to be a flush-decked iron barque classed 12 A1 and fitted with an East India outfit on dimensions of 144ft 0in × 25ft 3in × 17ft 4in, and with a tonnage of 436 $\frac{54}{94}$ BM; she was to be delivered by 31 October 1858. The price was based on a tonnage of 412 tons at £15 10s per ton BM or £6386 payable in five installments, viz: first – keel laid, and stem and sternpost erected; second – frames erected and beams across; third – plating completed; fourth – on launching; fifth – finished and builder's certificate delivered.[19] The specification was amended and signed on 31 March 1858. The price quoted included cabin stores such as cooking utensils, cutlery and crockery; but no 'napery', silverware or chronometer. The contract was signed some time after 20 April. 'Price is very bare in keeping with these times', observed Alexander Stephen.[20] Subsequently, it was decided to build the barque ten feet longer than the contract for an extra £625; also to build her under cover to obtain an additional year's classification with Lloyd's Register at an extra £150.[21]

James Hodgson supplied some drawings himself: constructional plans of each deck and a longitudinal section, dated 13 April; specification notes and sketches of main lowermast and bowsprit, both of iron; plan and section of after cabin, dated 14 April; plan of masts, spars and standing rigging with spar lengths tabulated, received by Stephen's on 16 April. Alexander Stephen & Sons' own sail plan, without any running rigging, was dated 29 June.

The keel, stem and sternpost were in position by 10 May 1858, the vessel being launched on 25 September of the same year, which indicates that her construction had been very rapid. Stephen's deck plan and longitudinal section was completed a month after launching and was dated 23 October. The *Edmund Preston* sailed on her maiden passage for Valparaiso at the end of November with a cargo of 1002 tons – 60 tons short of the estimated maximum – making a total freight of £1521, which were 'very good results in such times'.[22]

The plans presented here of the *Edmund Preston* are drawn from Alexander Stephen & Sons' own drawings, with additional material from James Hodgson's plans in a few cases. The plans show the vessel as built, with the additional ten feet incorporated. Lloyd's Register's survey report gives her dimensions of 163.0ft × 25.5ft × 17.25ft and a tonnage of 489 $\frac{54}{100}$; the surveyor reported that the 'workmanship throughout is well executed'.[23] The dimensions give a proportion of 6½ beams to length and the plans show that the depth as built was not excessive. The box-like shape of the midship section is largely influenced by the wooden ship *Tyburnia*, because the sudden tumblehome just below the sheer strake is totally unnecessary in an iron ship. The small amount of deadrise, hard bilges and wall sides must have produced good cargo capacity, but she has fine, evenly-balanced ends with slight hollows near the stem and sternpost. The stem is plumb vertical for some five feet which differs from the sheer elevation on the tonnage calculation and all Stephen's other ships; it is assumed to have been requested by James Hodgson, as his constructional drawing of 13 April has ten feet of vertical stem. The *Edmund Preston* could have possessed a good turn of speed and would rate as a medium clipper.

The following list is extracted from the specification, and provides in abbreviated form the most important points relating to the fittings and equipment; not all these fittings are drawn on the plans.

SPECIFICATION NOTES ON FITTINGS OF EDMUND PRESTON

Windlass To be fitted with patent purchase by Henry Wood & Co of Liverpool, with Gryll's patent whelps on the barrel.

Capstans Two of iron, raised on 12in high pedestals.

Main Deck 5in × 3in Quebec yellow pine; two 10in × 3in planks of teak, 8 feet apart, to run between foremast and mizzen, to take ring bolts for lashing down longboat, galley, spars, etc.

Hatchways Of African oak or greenheart, 4in thick and 12in high at lowest point rising to 15in high at centre, with iron cleats at side for battening down.

Gangway To have mahogany gangway in topgallant rail on each side, with teak ladders over each side.

Davits Pair of iron davits fitted on each quarter; also two fish tackle davits for anchor.

Winches Of iron; also two gipsy winches each side.

Pumps Three 6in diameter cast iron pumps; one 4in diameter brass pump by forward bulkhead, and another similar to pump out after compartment, with two brass buckets each etc, and when not in use, a brass screw cap is to close the pipe flush with deck.

Fire Engine Standard fitting with 70 feet of 2in leather hose.

Forecastle Companion of teak with doors, sliding

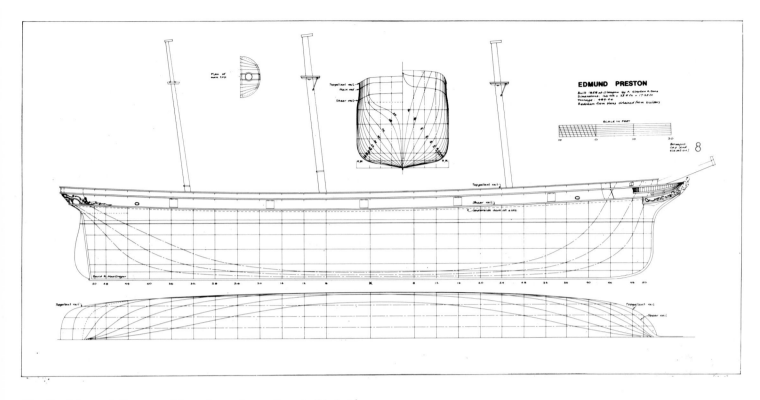

Fig 16. Edmund Preston. *Lines plan redrawn from builder's plan.*
Built of iron at Glasgow in 1858 by A Stephen & Sons; measurements
from Lloyd's Register Survey Report: 163.0ft × 25.5ft × 17.25ft and
489½ tons. Reconstruction: bowsprit and lower masts added.

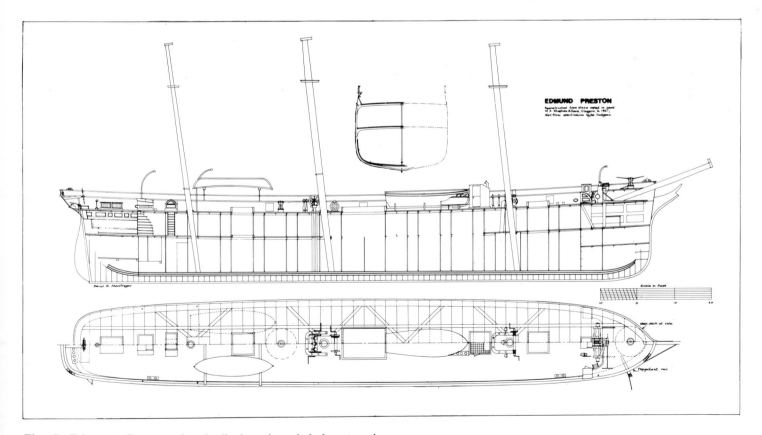

Fig 17. Edmund Preston. *Longitudinal section, deck layout and*
midship section. Redrawn from tracings made of builder's plans with
further particulars taken from the specification.

top and brass hinges; [Hodgson's plan shows accommodation for twelve seamen].

Fife Rails   Of mahogany with mahogany stanchions; any sheaves and facings to be of brass; belaying pins of iron.

Cabin   [Hodgson's plan shows accommodation for master, mate, two spare pairs of berths, steward's pantry, store room and saloon.]

Anchors   Three Trotman's patent (19, 19 and 16 cwt), one Rodger's (6 cwt), two Rodger's kedges (3 and 2 cwt).

Armoury   Two cast iron 6lb carronades on carriages complete with gun tackles, etc; also muskets, revolvers, cutlasses etc.

Masts and Spars   Fore and main lower masts and bowsprit to be of iron; also bibbs, trestletrees and tops. Mizzen lower mast of teak; topmasts, lower yards, topsail yards, jibboom, spanker boom of red pine or pitch pine; smaller spars of American black spruce.

Fig 18. Edmund Preston. Sail plan traced from builder's plan. Reconstruction: all running rigging; stunsails including booms and yards. Principal sources: oil painting by J Semple as in figure 19, and specification of vessel. Since the text was written, Mark Myers has drawn my attention to a note on the back of the painting referring to a scale of ⅛in which suggests that it may have been based on the sail plan, but the differences between the two pictures remain.

Rigging   All standing rigging of galvanised iron wire; running rigging of St Petersburg hemp, but braces and halliards can be of Manilla hemp if desired.

Sails   Of best, extra long, flax cloth; topsails to be fitted with Cunningham's patent reefing gear complete.

Cooper's Stores   Two oval harness casks with brass hoops; fourteen wash deck buckets (6 brass hooped, 8 galvanised iron hooped); [the 6 brass hooped are drawn by the longboat; the 8 others around the stern.]

Steering   Screw purchase gear to be agreed; mahogany wheel.

Cargo Derricks   One fitted to main hatch and one to fore hatch.

Boats   Longboat 23ft 0in × 7ft 6in × 3ft 4in deep, carvel built; 'fitted in chocks of height required projecting for boom rests on main deck and securely fastened with chain grips and housed over and fitted up for livestock inside'.

Pinnace
22ft 0in × 6ft 6in × 2ft 4in, carvel built.
Half-gig or life boat
22ft 0in × 5ft 6in × 2ft 3in, clench built.

Gratings   Teakwood grating on turned legs around steering gear; also platform for helmsman.

Galley   To be of iron, securely fastened, paved with fireclay tiles.

Bumkins   To be of iron, with strong joints and stays; to lie along bulwarks when in port.

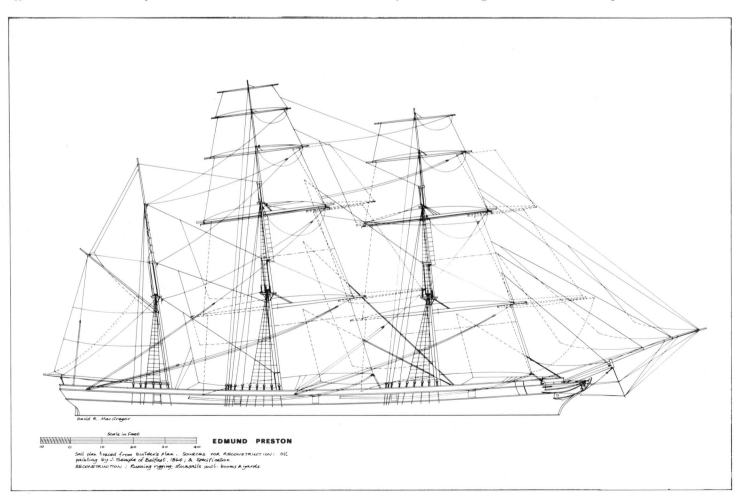

David R. MacGregor

Scale in Feet

EDMUND PRESTON

Sail plan traced from builder's plan. SOURCES FOR RECONSTRUCTION: oil painting by J. Semple of Belfast, 1864, & specification. RECONSTRUCTION: Running rigging, stunsails incl. booms & yards.

Fig 19. Edmund Preston. *Oil painting signed 'J. Semple, Belfast 1864'. I made a drawing of the picture when in the Bideford Public Library, and I am grateful to Mark Myers for providing this photograph of it.* (North Devon Museum Trust)

These deck fittings are used to reconstruct the deck plan and longitudinal section in figure 17. Points of interest are the short anchor deck forward; the iron galley; the companionway placed athwartships close abaft the mizzen which may have given access to the accommodation for petty officers and apprentices; the companionway abaft this was for the master, officers and steward; the arrangement of the steering wheel and grating for helmsman to stand on; and of course the presence of a flush deck which must have resulted in a wet ship if she was deeply laden. Flush decks were probably more common after 1850 for ocean going vessels of over 300 tons than one imagines; the big iron carrier *Aphrodita* (1858) has one, and so does Brocklebank's barque *Petchelee* (1850), and Barclay Curle's ship *City of Perth* (1857). The tea clippers *Ariel* (1865) and *Titania* (1866) are two other well-authenticated cases.

An oil painting, formerly in the Bideford Public Library, signed 'J.Semple, Belfast, 1864', provided sufficient detail to add running rigging to the sail plan in figure 18.[24] Stunsails have been reconstructed from this painting as some are shown set; the booms are under the yards and a description of the gear is taken from the specification. The Cunningham's patent reefing topsails confirm the specification, and a single row of reef points gave added security when close-reefing the topsails; a dotted line on the sail plan indicates their position. The rake to the masts and the presence of a main skysail gives the *Edmund Preston* a very pleasing appearance.

However, another oil painting was later discovered in the David Geider Gallery in London, just prior to its sale to an American buyer, and this gives conflicting data. The painting was signed 'S.Walters 1860', and one would assume that Samuel Walters would have produced an authentic work. The principal differences in Walter's painting are the replacement of roller-reefing gear in the topsails with three rows of reef points; stunsail booms on

top of the yards; no royal or skysail backstays; four (instead of five) freeing ports in bulwarks at a different spacing; bumkin for main braces placed further aft; no brails on spanker; no stay from mizzen cap; a long pole head to fore royal mast, but no skysail stay to flying jibboom; omission of davits; omission of fore capstan. It seems unlikely that Walters is correct in omitting the roller-reefing gear, and some of the other differences throw doubt on the accuracy of his painting. If the dates of the two paintings had been reversed, then one could have believed that alterations were made by 1864. As it is, the plans reproduced here probably show the vessel correctly after she was completed in 1858.

After examining the construction and outfit of the *Edmund Preston* in some detail, the conclusion is that iron construction provides the opportunity of gaining additional cargo capacity, partly by the thinness of the shell and partly by the ease with which a longer hull can be built; but in a timber ship of these proportions, the longitudinal members would have had to be unnecessarily large, and so valuable cargo space would have been wasted. For many years, ships in the 300-500 tons range remained popular with owners who did not wish to invest too much capital in a single bottom, and one has only to glance through the pages of any shipping register to realise how large was the percentage of full-rigged ships and barques below the 500 tons mark.

Fig 20. Edmund Preston. *Oil painting signed 'S. Walters 1859'. The differences between the two pictures are listed in the text.* (David Geider Gallery)

SHIPBUILDING ON THE CLYDE[25]

By 1850 the techniques of iron shipbuilding, coupled with the manufacture of marine engines, were well established on the Clyde, and many steamers in wood and iron were launched and engined on the river. The marine engineer, Robert Napier (1791-1876), began building hulls for his

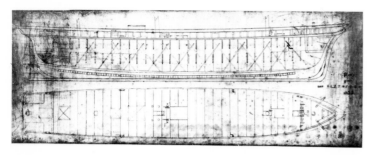

Fig 21. City of Perth. *Longitudinal section and deck plan photographed from original when in possession of the builders, Barclay, Curle & Co. Built at Glasgow in 1857 of wood; measurements from register: 155.4ft × 27.4ft × 18.3ft and 459 tons. The two stern houses can just be discerned on plan but less clearly on elevation.*

engines in the early forties, but apart from an occasional sailing ship all the vessels he built were steamers, although many had canvas as important auxiliary power. The brig *Haiti* (1852) and the ship *Twilight* (1855) were

Fig 22. *Photographed at Circular Quay, Sydney, in 1877, the* Wave of Life *was 21 years old and her rig had been cut down to that of a barque. Of 894 tons, she was built by Walter Hood at Aberdeen. It was considered to give a smart appearance if the upper topsail and upper topgallant yards were partially hoisted as seen here.* (James Henderson Collection)

two iron sailing vessels he built in these years. Many later shipbuilders and engineers served in his yard, such as William Denny, James and George Thomson, and Smith of Smith & Rodger.

An old established firm was Barclay & Curle of Glasgow; when Robert Barclay (born 1804) took over control of his father's shipyard he appointed Robert Curle as his manager, later taking him into partnership in 1845. The firm then became known as Robert Barclay & Curle. They built their first iron ship in 1847 and the following year had three berths for building wooden ships of up to 500 tons and another for iron ships of the same tonnage; in addition there were two slipways which could accommodate ships of up to 900 tons. During the fifties they built eight ships for George Smith & Co's 'City Line' to India, in which each name was prefixed with the words 'City of'. Several of these, such as the *City of Perth* (1857) were built of wood with diagonal iron trussing and had flush decks. According to plans of this ship there was a short anchor deck forward, which reached as far as the pawl post; abaft the mainmast was a small deckhouse; and right aft, there were two small houses on each quarter. This after layout can best be described by Captain John Smith in his book *Rise and Progress of the City Line* where he writes on page 33: 'Another feature about them all was an arched covering over the wheel to protect

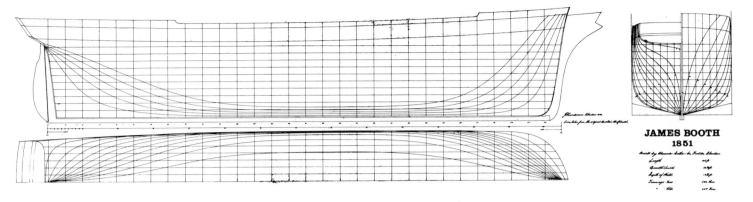

JAMES BOOTH
1851

Fig 23 James Booth. *Lines plan; drawn by James Henderson who took lines off the half-model. Built at Aberdeen in 1851 by Alexander Duthie & Co; measurements on this drawing: 145.0ft × 26.6ft (inside) × 19.9ft, 596 tons nm, 637 tons om.*

the man at the wheel from the sun, and the one side contained the second mate's room and bosun's locker; the other, paint and oil room and WC. This archway was painted blue, and the houses below stone colour, which looked very pretty. The masts and yards were all of a very pretty straw colour known as the City Line mast colour. The ships could be distinguished at a distance by the colour of their masts . . . while a City [ship] was painted grey colour with ports'.

From a study of the Barclay Curle plans it is evident that at least five of these 'City' ships had this deck layout; so did the wooden ship *Jacatra* which was launched sideways in 1852; the *Roseneath* of 1857 was also fitted thus although she had a topgallant forecastle. The latter's faintly-drawn sail plan shows the trucks close above the topgallant yards, and no sliding gunter royal poles are indicated. On the other hand the topgallant sails are very deep – almost as deep as the topsails – and perhaps it was intended to fit them with roller-reefing gear and so save the cost of one yard and its gear on each mast, a scheme which appears to have been adopted in the iron ship *Shandon*, launched two years earlier. Unfortunately no sail plan of the latter has survived, but Basil Lubbock says that she had 'patent reefing gear for topgallant sails, topsails and courses'.[26] This would have been most unusual, but doubtless other oddities have gone unrecorded. The unmistakable hallmark of a Barclay Curle medium iron clipper with rounded bilges, tumblehome and graceful stem, first made it appearance in the *Shandon*. The latter had dimensions of 183.7ft × 32.5ft × 19.0ft and 886 tons om.[27]

Many shipbuilders on the Clyde were building under cover as were other firms throughout the country. David Tod and John MacGregor, who commenced business about 1837, had two building berths covered in 1853 with a glass roof, similar in style to Paxton's Crystal Palace; the contract price was £12,000 and the ss *New York* was expected to be the first ship launched out of it.[28] Unfortunately it was blown down on 7 February 1856 during a very severe gale on the Clyde and fell on top of two small iron steamers which were in the course of construction. The total weight of the 'beautiful' structure was approximately 250 tons.[29]

Oher Clydeside building firms to produce numerous sailing ships during the fifties were William Simons & Co, with yards at Whiteinch and Greenock; John Scott & Sons and Robert Steele & Co at Greenock; and John Reid at Port Glasgow. All were building in both wood and iron.

Robert Steele's first iron ship was ss Beaver, launched in 1854; in the fifties they built twelve iron steamers, five iron full-rigged ships and four iron cargo flats. Simultaneously, they constructed nine wooden steamers and twenty-three wooden sailing vessels of all rigs. Of the wooden sailing ships there was one drogher, two schooners, nine brigs, four barques and seven full-rigged ships. The only one of the above ships for which both lines and sail plan are known to exist is the tea clipper *Falcon* (1859).[30]

In the museum at Glasgow there are half-models of some of John Reid's sailing ships: *Vanguard* (1852), *Trojan* (1853), *Helen Nicholson* (1862), *Marpesia* and *Antiope* (1866). The *Vanguard* of 687 tons was built of iron for the India and China trades and the model shows a vessel with a fair amount of deadrise, slack bilges and tumblehome; the *Trojan* of 425 tons is more full-bodied and has less rise of floor. Reid also built the extreme iron clipper *Cairnsmore*.

At Aberdeen, all the surviving half-models of ships built by Alexander Hall & Sons after 1850 are of clippers, and as such were fully described and illustrated in *Fast Sailing Ships*. The lines of the *James Booth*, built by Duthie in 1851, show the hull form of a fast cargo carrier, with her fairly full ends, but there is some deadrise with slack bilges. An engraving of her in the *Illustrated London News* indicates trysail gaffs on all masts and a skysail only on the mainmast. No plans or half-models have survived for Walter Hood's ships.

SHIPBUILDERS ON THE WEAR AND TYNE

The principal shipbuilding centre in north-east England was situated at Sunderland, on the banks of the River Wear. Many of the yards were laid out on the narrow foreshore beneath high banks and were dwarfed by the old iron Wearmouth Bridge, erected in 1796. Further upstream where the river was narrower, the land levelled out and there were yards as far up as Hylton. Shipbuilders on the Wear benefitted by the great boom of about 1840, and many firms sprang into being without any capital behind them. When trade and orders dropped suddenly in the early forties, between thirty and forty yards were forced to close down. However, after some lean years, trade began to revive and the early fifties saw another large building boom, with shipyards jostling each other on both the Wear and Tyne. The following table indicates the cyclical nature of it all.

SHIPBUILDING AT SUNDERLAND[31]

Year	Number of ships	Total tonnage	Average tons
1835	98	26,000	265
1840	251	64,446	257
1845	131	38,260	292
1850	158	50,374	325
1855	151	61,159	405
1860	112	40,201	359
1865	172	73,134	423
1870	103	70,084	686
1875	91	79,904	876

Of particular interest is the big increase of high class ships among these totals. In the past, Sunderland had been thought of as a ready place to purchase cheap ships but standards were undoubtedly improving even though

Fig 24. The full-bodied ship Bury St Edmunds *still crossed a single mizzen topsail when this photograph was taken. She was built at Sunderland in 1853 for Blythe & Greene of London, presumably for their sugar trade with Mauritius. Her class of 13 A1 indicated that she was built with good materials. She measured 153.0ft × 28.4ft × 21.0ft and 822 tons.* (Nautical Photo Agency)

many ships were still built on speculation there. In the early 1850s, the number of ships built to class 10 A1 or higher at Lloyd's Register is shown in the table:

SHIPS BUILT AT SUNDERLAND TO CLASS 10 A1 OR HIGHER[32]

Year	Number of ships	Total tonnage
1850	34 ships	17,737
1851	36 ships	20,637
1852	51 ships	27,565
1853	55 ships	30,702

No less than seventy builders were named in a contemporary report dated 1852 and many of the famous names fall from the tongue like an Arthurian legend – John Crown, James Laing, William Pile jnr, S P Austin & Sons, Bartram & Sons, George Haswell, William Pickersgill & Sons, William Doxford, Robert Thompson & Sons, Robert Thompson jnr, and many others.[33] One of James Laing's ships, the *Dunbar*, is illustrated in figure 62.

But few people think of Sunderland ships without remembering William Pile. This gifted designer was born in 1823, the son of William Pile who was also a shipbuilder. The father had three sons: John the eldest, William and Thomas. William served his apprenticeship partly in his father's yard at Stockton and partly with other Wear-side firms. In 1845 he rejoined his father who, together with the eldest son John, had a yard at Southwick, a mile or two above Wearmouth Bridge. The following year the three of them moved to a yard at North

Sands, below the bridge, where they built small barques, brigs and schooners under the name of W & J Pile. Then William jnr took over part of the yard in 1848, to build on his own account. One suspects that the father may have retired at the same time. When his brother John transferred his activities to West Hartlepool in 1854, William took over complete control of the North Sands yard, where he remained until his death in 1873.[34] In 1861 he took Richard Hay into partnership for six years during which time the firm was styled Pile & Hay. During the years 1845-54 considerable confusion is caused by the indiscriminate attribution of ships to either John or William, and accurate building lists for the combined or individual efforts of the brothers have yet to be completed. A list begun in 1857 indicates that from this year William built 76 wooden ships and 132 composite and iron ones; also nine others at the 'Low Yard'. During the sixties, many steamers were produced. The last wooden ship was launched in 1863 and the first iron one in 1861.[35]

Sunderland whose length was more than five times her breadth. Tonnages of 781 om and 893 nm indicate that she was much bigger than the vessels which Pile had previously been accustomed to build. Her ambitious figurehead of a Bengalese struggling with a tiger was carved by Messrs Lindsay of Sunderland.[36] Her half-model in the Sunderland Museum shows a kettle-bottomed hull with slack bilges and maximum beam well forward of amidships. A passage from London to Melbourne in 1852 occupied 121 days, 4 March to 3 July.

Commenting on the greater length of Sunderland ships in proportion to their beam, an article in 1852 remarked:

> The improvement not only adds greatly to beauty of model but to practical excellence in sailing. It gives a ship not only greater speed but greater 'sea kindliness' (as the phrase is), and does away in a great measure with the heavy pitching and rolling motion of those 'old familiar tubs' . . .[37]

On the Tyne, shipbuilding was in full swing in the fifties. Coutts & Parkinson, some of whose products were

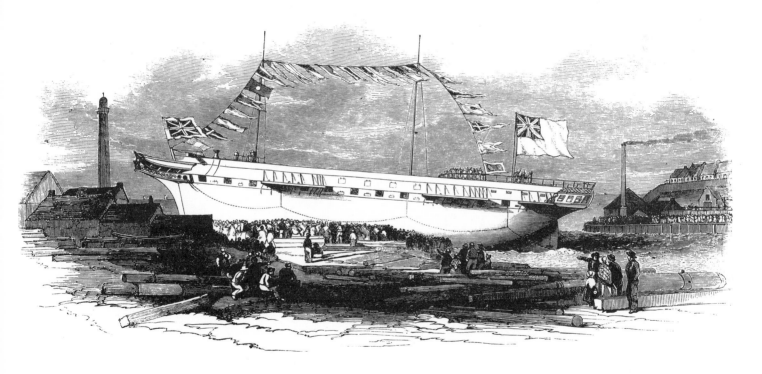

Fig 25 Launch of the Chowringhee *from an engraving in the* Illustrated London News. *Was she really painted white as the engraving suggests?* (MacGregor Collection)

Of the nine or ten ships launched by William Pile during 1852, at least four were built on speculation. Three of the reports completed by the surveyor representing Lloyd's Register gave no ship's name whatsoever. Other sources prove that the biggest of them was named *King Richard* which was later bought by Richard Green who renamed her *Roxburgh Castle* and her hull-form is described in Chapter Three. Pile is listed as the owner of some of the speculatively-built vessels.

When William Pile launched the *Chowringhee* in May 1851 it was reported that she was the first vessel built at

listed in Chapter Three of *Merchant Sailing Ships 1815-1850*, built some large iron ships in this decade, among which was the *W.S. Lindsay* built for the shipowner of that name. Of 900 tons register, the upper deck was flush and the longboat was sunk into it, and an open railing was substituted for solid bulwarks. Some 280 cabins were provided, of which sixty were for first class passengers. She was launched in 1852 with topmasts on end but no yards crossed.[38] Another ship built for W S Lindsay was the auxiliary iron ship *Tynemouth*, launched in 1854, which measured 238.0ft × 34.5ft × 18.6ft and 1364 tons gross, but the engines were only 80 horsepower. Another of Coutts & Parkinson's iron ships, the *Swarthmore* (1853), put into Tahiti in distress in 1854, homeward-bound from Melbourne. Her total depth of hold was no less than

26.2ft. On arrival home, her spar deck was completely removed, thereby reducing her tonnage from 1381 to 923.[39] Although iron-framed, the iron plates only extended up to the main deck above which there was wooden planking to the spar deck.

Many of the Tyneside yards only built in wood and then principally barques and brigs of less than 500 tons. John & Joseph Hair was one such firm and several of their plans, as listed in Chapter Four, are preserved at the Science Museum, London, although they are attributed to Robert Harrison who was perhaps the yard manager or draughtsman. The site of Robert Harrison's yard at Bill Quay is still in existence. A number of the ships must have been built on speculation as Hair's name appears as the owner for the first year. One of the plans depicts the barque *Parsee* which was built in 1851 and measured 112.3ft × 25.6ft × 18.1ft with tonnages of 412 om and 437

Fig 26. Parsee. *Lines plan and deck beams plan drawn by Paul A Roberts. Built at Newcastle in 1851 by J & J Hair with measurements of 112.3ft × 25.6ft × 18.1ft and tonnages of 412 om and 437 nm. I traced the original builder's plan in the Science Museum, London, through the courtesy of Basil W Bathe, at that time in charge of the Water Transport Collection. Reconstruction: waterlines added and projected; diagonals omitted; height of lower masts obtained from rake of chainplates; length of bowsprit.*

nm. She classed 12 A1 and her framework was of English and African oak. In the Science Muesum drawing, only the waterline at the light load line is projected on the half-breadth plan, the body plan being faired by the use of diagonals; but additional waterlines have been projected on the half-breadth plan, as reconstructed in figure 26. The bilges are rounded and very slack, and she is wall-sided above. Amidships there is about fourteen feet of almost parallel body; at either end she is moderately full, although finer in the run. Nevertheless, she is an attractive design and a good example of a merchant ship of her date. From the plan of the deck beams, a reconstructed deck layout can be made, and from the rake of the chain plates the height of the lower masts has been reconstructed.[40]

One point of particular interest is the great similarity both in hull-form and presentation between the plan of *Parsee* and plans of the *Emerald, New Express* and *Great Britain* built at Poole by Richard Pinney over the years 1836 to 1843. The shape of the midship section is very similar and also the stem, headwork and sheer elevation. The chief difference is that in Pinney's plans the waterlines are projected and the diagonals, when drawn, are in a solid line. These pronounced similarities suggest either that there was some connection between the yards

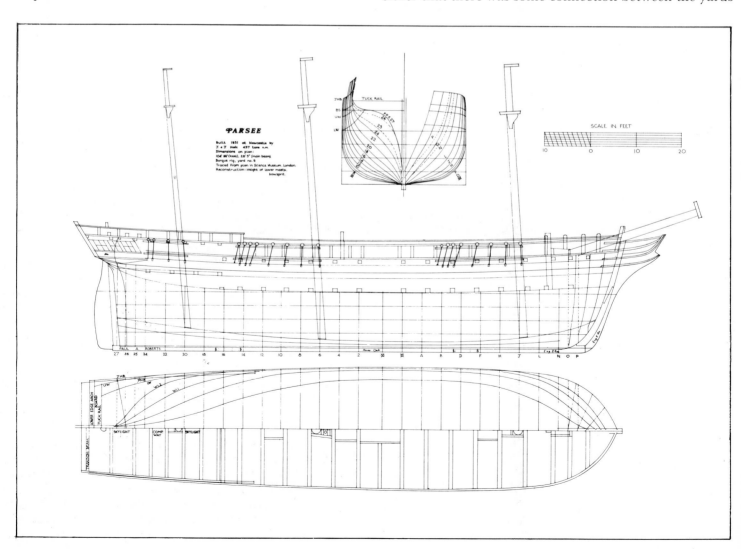

Fig 27. Ravensworth. *Whole-hull model in National Maritime Museum, Greenwich, drawn by William Ward. Built at Newcastle in 1856 by Gaddy & Lamb with measurements of 131.0ft × 29.0ft × 19.0ft and tonnages of 512 om and 508 nm. See text for description.*

Fig 28. Stern of Ravensworth *with unusual arrangement.*

Fig 29. Steering gear with cover broken to show lead of chains to drum.

Fig 30A. Binnacle and skylight, two views of companion and detail of davit.

Fig 30B. After end of forward deckhouse with 'V' slot to take bow of longboat; chock for this boat is between hatchway and house.

Fig 31A. Foot of mainmast with pumps inside fiferail, and cargo winch beside small hatch.

Fig 31B. The pumps in figure 31A with the adjacent fittings removed and also with two pump handles shipped in the lower slots provided. In the upper arms, ropes could be rove through the ends to provide additional purchase power in an emergency. The well-known painting by H S Tuke entitled 'All Hand to the Pumps' shows just such a pump as this in use aboard a brigantine.

Fig 32. Armstrong patent windlass with pump handles shipped and several turns of chain cable around the port side barrel, but there seems to be no arrangement for the use of normans. On the left, the foremast is broken off close to the deck to give a clear view of the windlass, but on each side of the mast is a short pinrail supported by balusters at each end.

of Richard Pinney and John & Joseph Hair or, what is more likely, that ship design in small and medium sized cargo-carrying vessels was strongly repetitive both chronologically and geographically. Indeed, this style of hull continued throughout the period during which small wooden square-rigged barques and ships were built, whenever speed was of secondary importance. Plans and half-models from shipyards scattered throughout the country and dating from the fifties and sixties, confirm this continuation in style.

DECK FITTINGS OF THE *RAVENSWORTH*

A contemporary unrigged model of the barque *Ravensworth* in the National Maritime Museum, Greenwich, provides a good opportunity to describe the deck

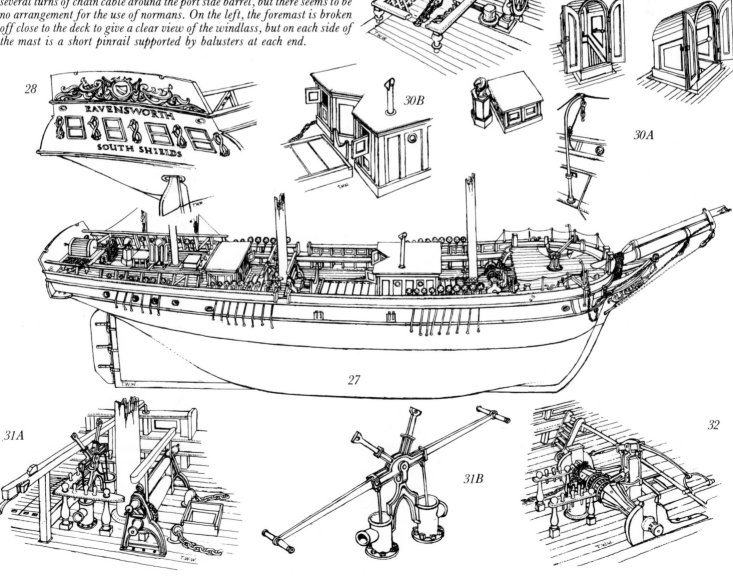

layout and fittings of a wooden vessel of the 1850s, and is made possible through the medium of William Ward's meticulous drawings of the model and of the individual fittings, as reproduced here. Corroborative evidence in paintings and models suggests that this deck layout was not uncommon in the fifties.

The *Ravensworth* was built in 1856 at Newcastle by Gaddy & Lamb for R W Hodgson of Newcastle; she measured 131.0ft × 29.0ft × 19.0ft, 508 tons nm and 512 tons om, and classed 11 A1. David Gaddy and Lewis M Lamb were in partnership from about 1843 until Gaddy's death in 1859, but the firm's name was continued during the 1860s with other Lambs in the business. The yard was at Tyne Main, Gateshead, where they installed a patent slip worked by a steam engine in 1844. Here ships of up to 700 tons were built in the fifties, the *Hotspur* of 1855 being the largest. In the sixties, barques in the 350-500 tons range were built and an occasional schooner. The *Lewis M. Lamb* of 1871 seems the last vessel to have been built. I am grateful to Adrian G Osler of the Tyne and Wear Museum Service for this information on the shipyard.

Because the *Ravensworth*'s fore hatch is placed abaft the foremast, the galley is sandwiched between the fore and main hatches, thus shortening the space available to stow the longboat. However, this difficulty has been overcome by making a V-shaped indentation in the afterside of the galley, to accommodate the bows of the longboat. In 1862, the Swedish naval architect, N C Kierkegaard, showed a semi-circular indentation in a deckhouse on one of his plans, doubtless to overcome a similar situation.[41] On the *Ravensworth*, chocks for the longboat are placed at each end of the main hatch; there is another tiny hatch between the pumps and the after deckhouse; the winch, pumps and forward boat skid are crowded tightly around the mainmast; the gallows frame above the winch is the vestigal rest for the spare spars, although the forward equivalent across the galley roof is missing. The Lloyd's Register survey report assigns the ship a longboat, a lifeboat and a gig. The latter two would be stowed on skids between the mainmast and the after deckhouse; their after ends would rest on a skid or on chocks (missing on the model) placed on the deckhouse roof, and the forward ends on the skid immediately abaft the mast. This arrangement was repeated in other vessels.

The aftermost deckhouse is squeezed into the space between the after hatch and the raised quarterdeck, and the after companionway has a delightful shape. A curious feature is the great inward rake given to the stanchions along the quarterdeck rail. T G Dutton's watercolour of the Tyne-built barque *Dennis Hill*, built in 1856 at Shields by Adamson & Son of 348 tons, is in the collection of the National Maritime Museum, Greenwich. It shows a similar position for the after deckhouse, but in this case the longboat is stowed between the galley and the foremast. The *Ravensworth* could well have looked like the *Dennis Hill* when at sea. It is interesting to note that the method of terminating the forward end of the topgallant rail in the *Dennis Hill* is similar to that employed in some of the Aberdeen clippers such as *Acasta* and *Phoenician*.

Leaving London on 27 December 1857, the *Dennis Hill* made a long passage of 167 days to Shanghai; she continued trading in Eastern waters until the early sixties. Her dimensions were only slightly larger than those of the *Parsee*.

SHIPBUILDERS OF NORTH-WEST ENGLAND

Wooden ships continued to be built by T & J Brocklebank at their Whitehaven yard, although during the depression in the 1840s, fewer were built than in former years. A small flush-decked barque was launched in 1850 named *Petchelee* of 357 tons nm and dimensions of 118.8ft × 22.7ft × 17.5ft. A plan showing her longitudinal section surmounted by a sail plan was reproduced as figure 110 in *Merchant Sailing Ships 1815-1850*. No lines plan is known but the lines of the larger *Harold*, built the previous year, appeared in the same volume as figure 109, and she was probably the last of the fleet to be designed on arcs of circles. Brocklebank's built the *Arachne* in 1851 as an 'improved' model to the *Harold* but with somewhat similar dimensions, and perhaps she was the first of the new style of ships as revealed in the plans of *Martaban* (1852) yard no 138 and *Aracan* (1854) yard no 139. These two ships had much finer lines comparable with ships from other yards, even though Brocklebank vessels were still only required to carry goods for their own merchant house and did not really have to compete for freights so strenuously as other ships.

Later in the fifties, with falling freights and profits harder to make, the ships were again designed on fuller lines. The full-rigged ship *Juanpore* was built in 1859 with dimensions of 144.4ft × 26.7ft × 18.6ft and a tonnage of 459; her lines were surprisingly like those of the *Harold* although her very convex entrance was not quite so short, her run was longer, and she only had about 16ft of deadflats amidships. She had less deadrise than the *Harold* with straight rather than curved floors. Of course, she had a longer and narrower hull with a L/B ratio of 5.41 compared with *Harold*'s 4.47. No deck fittings other than a small galley abaft the foremast are given on her plans and she was flush-decked.

The *Juanpore* was heavily sparred and carried skysails on all three masts. The mainyard measured 54ft within the cleats, ie excluding the yardarms or 61ft overall, and the main skysail yard measured 20ft 6in 'cleated'. As the distance from the centre of the foremast to the centre of the mizzen measured 84ft, it means that the mainyard occupied much of this space. The topsails were

Fig 33. Juanpore. *Lines plan redrawn in pencil from a tracing I made of the builder's plan. Built of wood at Whitehaven in 1859 by T & J Brocklebank with measurements of 144.4ft × 26.7ft × 18.6ft and 459 tons. Reconstruction: buttock line projected.*

Fig 34. Juanpore. *Sail plan reproduced from tracing I made of builder's plan. See text for description. No reconstruction. As the sheet of cartridge paper ended just outside the bowsprit cap, the length of the jibboom could be reconstructed from the angle of the stays leading from the foremast. Original drawn to ¼in scale which resulted in a large plan.*

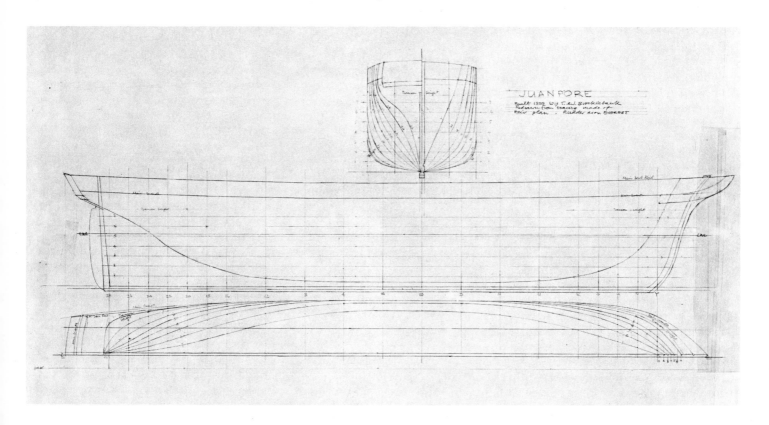

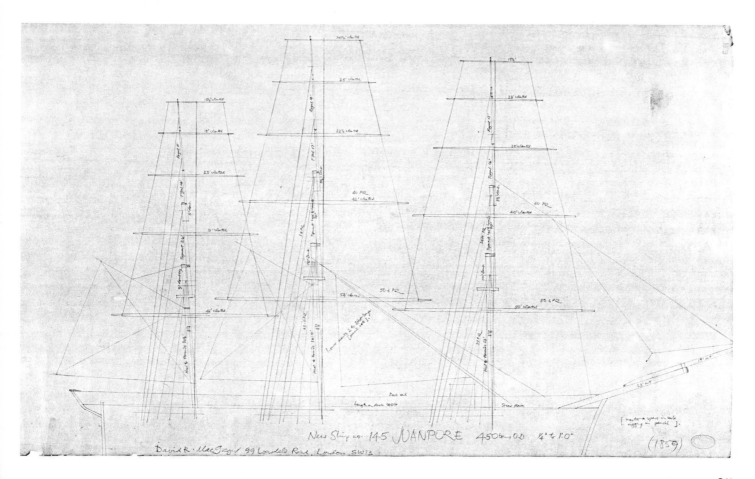

comparatively shallow and the main topsail had a drop of 26ft at the bunt, and as a result the cap of the lower mast was well over half way up the topsail. These shallow topsails and lengthy mainyard are reminiscent of the big Aberdeen clipper *Schomberg* (1855) whose sail plan appears as figure 207 in *Fast Sailing Ships 1775-1875*. No stunsail booms are drawn or listed on *Juanpore*'s sail plan and only two staysails are drawn, but the main trysail was exceptionally large with a boom extending almost to the mizzen.

This large sail plan made up for the fullness of her hull-form and produced some fast passages in the China trade as listed below:

JUANPORE'S FASTEST PASSAGES FROM CHINA
1860, dep Macao 19 Jan, arr London 7 May, 109 days
1863, dep Shanghai 8 Jan, arr Liverpool 24 April, 106 days
1864, dep Hong Kong 2 Jan, arr Liverpool 13 April, 102 days
1865-66, dep Foochow 7 Dec, arr London 25 March, 108 days

Of course, these passages were all made with the favourable monsoon. When sailing against the monsoon her average on five passages increases to 157 days. Brocklebank's sold her in 1877.

The days of wooden shipbuilding at the firm's Whitehaven yard were almost over, although in 1858 they built the large wooden ship *Rajmahal* of no less than 1302 tons, but the increasing use of iron forced the closure of the yard in 1865. By that date 157 vessels had been launched, from the commencement of business in 1788.[42] Thereafter the firm ordered ships from other builders.

The work of another Whitehaven builder, Lumley Kennedy & Co, is described in *Merchant Sailing Ships 1815-1850:* he was in business until the yard closed in 1864.

Shipbuilding was prolific at other Cumberland yards and especially at Workington in Peile, Scott & Co's works. This firm appears to have been in operation during the years 1834-57 and Lloyd's Register 'Visitation Committee' on their annual inspection of Great Britain shipyards in 1851 saw work in progress here and remarked that 'it seemed scarcely possible to produce a finer standard of naval architecture'. Four years later, the Committee visited the yard again and inspected a ship of 800 tons being built under a shed to class 14 A1 and the keel of another similar one laid. 'The materials and workmanship at this establishment', they reported, 'are unsurpassed in Cumberland or elsewhere. The whole management of the yard is under Mr Jonathan Fell, the patentee of the screw binding for beams'.[43] Between 1849 and 1857, fifteen vessels built by the firm were surveyed for Lloyd's Register and apart from the brig *Cronkbane* (1850) all were ships or barques. The classification achieved varied between 12 and 15 A1. The *Invincible* was a fast ship in the China trade; the *Maha Ranee* (1853), *Blackburn* (1854), *Mary Ann Wilson* (1856), *Banian* (1856) and *Kamehameha the Fourth* (1857) were built under a roof. Plans of their ship *Camertonian*, built in 1848, appeared as figures 130-135 in *Fast Sailing Ships*. In 1857, Fell left Peile, Scott & Co and became manager of the Workington & Harrington Shipbuilding Co, his first ship being the China trader *Jubilee*. Two years later his own name replaced that of the company in the Lloyd's Register survey reports.

MERSEY SHIPBUILDERS AND THE *APHRODITA*

Shipbuilding activities on the River Mersey continued at a high rate during the fifties as more and more builders in this area were turning to iron, and finally steel, as the sole shipbuilding material. A list of iron ships built in the 1850s of more than 900 tons, which appeared in *Fast Sailing Ships* (pages 146-47), listed a number of yards in this district. Amongst these were Jordan & Getty who experimented in the early fifties with composite construction, but although later shipbuilders had to pay royalties to John Jordan because of his patent rights, his firm switched over to building entirely in iron.

The correct attribution of ships to Jordan & Getty and their successors has not yet been fully clarified. Jordan appears to have separated from John Getty about 1854, and shortly afterwards a firm called Getty & Jones emerged. The big iron ships *Ellen Stuart* and *James Pilkington*, both built in 1854, are sometimes accredited to John Getty and at other times to Getty & Jones. This Jones was probably Josiah Jones jnr who was building under his own name from 1856 to 1859. In these few years he produced a great variety of iron vessels ranging from barges to paddle tugs, screw yachts, steamers, barques and full-rigged ships. The manager of his yard was William Quiggin (1821-1892) who had managed George Cram's yard at Chester and is credited with the design of the auxiliary iron ship *Royal Charter*, launched in 1855.[44] William Quiggin presumably lost his job when Cram became insolvent in 1856. In 1859 Quiggin became a partner with Jones, and the firm was restyled Jones, Quiggin & Co. In 1862 there were four partners, three of whom were Joneses. In 1868 the firm changed its name to the Liverpool Shipbuilding Co. Between 1856-59, sailing ships cost from £13 to £16 per ton in Jones' yard.[45]

William Quiggin's connection with Josiah Jones lends added interest to a set of plans in the National Maritime Museum, Greenwich, of one of the latter's ships, the large iron full-rigged ship *Aphrodita*, built in 1858 for Jones, Palmer & Co of Liverpool. The deck fittings are unusually well-detailed both on plan and elevation although the sail plan is not of the same quality.[46] The plans have been redrawn by Paul Roberts (figures 36 and 37).

The *Aphrodita* measured 227.0ft × 36.3ft × 25.6ft, 1427 tons om, and 1601 tons register. These dimensions give ratios of 6.25 L/B and 8.87 L/D. On the plan the beam scales 35.3ft. This long ship had an almost parallel body for some ninety feet. The floors are nearly flat with firm bilges and wall sides up to the load line; above, there is some tumblehome. There is no external keel. The entrance and run are full and convex; the sternpost is vertical, and there is a square transom stern – surely an anachronism in a ship of her kind; forward, there is hardly any rake to her stem, although a fair amount of sheer has been introduced. The new techniques developed in iron shipbuilding enabled lengthy box-like hulls, such as this, to be constructed which provided cheap transport for bulk cargoes on a far larger scale than in previous years. This

Fig 35. The Ellen Stuart *photographed off San Francisco during the later part of her life.* (National Maritime Museum, San Francisco)

was particularly valuable when freight rates were depressed, as was the case at the end of the fifties, and it meant that the *Aphrodita* was better suited to make a profit than fine-lined vessels. She was the forerunner of the big iron and steel ships which moved immense bulk cargoes in the last two decades of the nineteenth century.

About 1000 tons of iron was used in her construction. Her bow on the building slip faced east but after launching it was kept facing west as much as possible; this was done to reduce compass deviation which was causing much concern in iron vessels, as suitable correction was

still the subject of experiments.[47]

Apart from a short anchor deck forward, on which there is a form of patent warping capstan, the *Aphrodita* has a flush deck. She is provided with both an old style barrel windlass and one of a modern Brown & Harfield pattern. For the latter, a riding bitt and two cable stoppers are provided for each chain cable. There are three pairs of pumps, one pair being beside each mast. The galley is a square timber house sitting on the upper deck just forward of the main hatch. Both the main and after hatches are longer than normal; the longboat stows partly over the after hatch and appears to be fitted inside for poultry houses; forward of the mizzen, two boats are carried on skids, beneath which there are two capstans and a pair of riding bitts. Abaft the mizzen is a booby hatch, saloon skylight, after companionway and wheel. The companionway is placed athwartship as in *Ravensworth*, but there is an entry from each side, with dog-leg stairs meeting on a half-landing. The 'tween decks are 6ft 6in high, deck to deck. Crew accommodation is provided in the forward 'tween decks for eighteen men in six three-tiered bunks; further accommodation for another twelve men is given aft, entered through the booby hatch, but the mizzen mast and two pump shafts pass through the centre of the floor space. Right aft there are five staterooms, the saloon, and two store rooms or pantries.

The undated sail plan of the *Aphrodita* shows double topsails on the fore- and mainmasts, and the knowledge of

Fig 36. Aphrodita. *Lines, longitudinal section and deck plans redrawn by Paul A Roberts from a feint photostat of the builder's plan supplied by the National Maritime Museum, Greenwich. Built of iron at Liverpool in 1858 by Josiah Jones with measurements of 227.0ft × 36.3ft × 25.6ft and tonnages of 1427 om and 1601 register. Reconstruction: accommodation plans separated; companionway to saloon; reverse angles omitted on floors.*

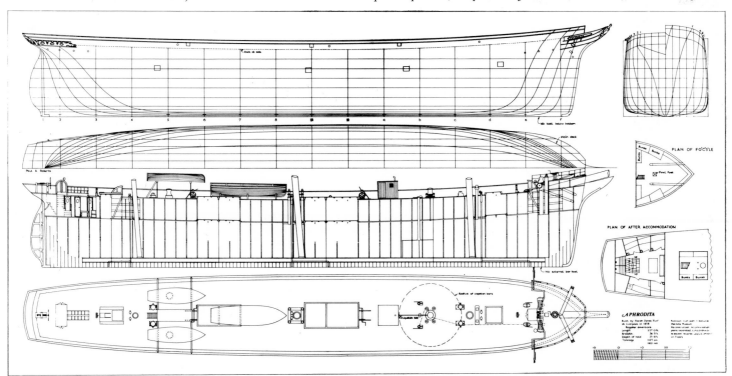

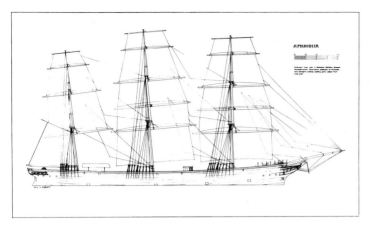

Fig 37. Aphrodita. *Sail plan. Redrawn from plan in National Maritime Museum, Greenwich by Paul A Roberts. Reconstruction: alternative positions of foremast and bowsprit omitted; loading ports added from lines plan.*

Fig 39. *Bow view of the* Oronsay *ex-Slieve Donard in drydock; the keel blocks look well-worn. This iron ship was built at Liverpool in 1859 by Thomas Vernon.* (Nautical Photo Agency)

William Quiggin's previous connection with the auxiliary steamer *Royal Charter*, which was also fitted with double topsails, strongly suggests that the *Aphrodita* was fitted with them from the first. As such she is one of the earliest known examples of a British ship so equipped, although it may be that some of Josiah Jones' earlier ships were also fitted with them, such as the *Khimjee Oodowjee* or *Lalla Rookh*, both built 1856, or the barque *Chiloe* of 1857. At this date, such a rig was called 'Howes' rig' even in England.

In the plan of the *Aphrodita*, the ship looks somewhat under-canvassed, although stunsails would be set each side when at sea; the yards on the fore- and mainmasts are similar in length, the lower yards measuring 78ft 0in long

overall. An alternative position for the foremast, 8ft 6in further forward, is indicated on the sail plan. A single topsail is still retained on the mizzen.

Aphrodita's first two voyages were to Calcutta and back and were on the slow side as befitted such a full-bodied ship. The return passage on her maiden voyage occupied 158 days after getting clear of the land from Calcutta on 18 February 1859, to off the Old Head of Kinsale in South Ireland on 26 July. She was still afloat in 1866 under her original owners.

In 1857, I K Brunel was enquiring about many types of ship fittings for the *Great Eastern* and he received a letter from Bradford Leslie concerning the work of Mr Brown who was a mast and blockmaker at Liverpool. Brown made iron rings that could be shrunk on to timber mastheads and yardarms, and Bradford Leslie had seen ships in Josiah Jones' yard thus fitted, and some mastheads were being exported to America. The *Aphrodita* was built a year after his inspection, but summing up the advantages of the iron rings Leslie commented that 'it also facilitates the application of double topsail yards by enabling the mast head to be made of the increased length required for that purpose'.[48]

Many of the large iron ships being built on the Mersey were placed in the India trade. In 1859 John Laird rebuilt at Birkenhead the large iron ship *Accrington* which had been built at Nantes by Guibert Fils some years earlier; when rebuilt she measured 243.4ft × 38.8ft × 30.2ft, with a gross tonnage of 1932. She had a spar deck.

At Preston on the River Ribble, Smith & Co opened a yard in 1859, their first vessel being the small iron full-rigged ship *Thomas Blythe* of 387 tons. Initially she traded to China. Smith's subsequent vessels were wooden schooners.[49]

Fig 38. *This painting is entitled* 'Accrington *signalling for a pilot', and a cutter may be seen under her lee as she clews up her topgallants and men lay out on her mainyard to furl the sail. This somewhat ugly-looking ship had been built at Nantes in 1855 with the name of* Francois Arago. *She was still afloat in 1873 under the ownership of W T Jacobs, Liverpool.* (Parker Gallery)

supervise the building of a large iron ship which he had designed for Edward Bates, the Liverpool shipowner, and which was launched the following year with the name of *Bates Family*. She measured no less than 2154 tons. In 1858 Hodgson described himself as 'Civil Engineer and Inspector for Building Iron Ships', and as he had recently surveyed Bates' iron ship *Flying Venus*, he may well have designed some of his other iron ships.[51] In March 1858 Bates had a fleet of seven iron ships of which four were of over 1000 tons each; this suggests that he was a very progressive shipowner.

SHIPBUILDERS OF SOUTHERN ENGLAND

Due to the absence of iron deposits and coalfields in the south of England, there was considerably less iron shipbuilding in progress because the additional transport costs would have advanced the price of the finished vessel. Yards on the Thames did, however, build ships of considerable size in iron because London was such a large importer that prices of goods were proportionally less than they would have been to a smaller port such as Littlehampton. Warships, steamers and sailing vessels

Fig 40. Ships drying their sails at Bristol in 1854. On the extreme left is the stern of what looks like an American vessel; beyond the full rigged ship, there are two others stern-on: a brig to the left and a barque to the right. The latter has an exceedingly wide stern, similar to the Dutch barque in figure 41. This photograph was copied from one in the collection of the late Harold Wyllie.

JAMES HODGSON OF LIVERPOOL

Another Liverpool specialist in iron ships was James Hodgson who practised as an engineer, shipbuilder and consultant for some thirty years from the late thirties. His busiest years as a shipbuilder were during the 1840s and he is known to have constructed at least seven iron ships. Although most of his products were steamers or auxiliaries, such as the *Sarah Sands*, he did build the iron clipper barque *Richard Cobden* in 1844 (see figure 129 in *Fast Sailing Ships*) from designs by Thomas R Guppy of Bristol. In 1855 he supervised the building of the ss *Carbon* in the yard of Rennie, Johnson & Rankine at Liverpool.[50]

At the end of 1857 he prepared a very detailed specification on behalf of a Liverpool engineer named Edmund Preston, who had contracted with Alexander Stephen & Sons to have an iron barque built at Glasgow. The specification for this barque, which was named *Edmund Preston*, was referred to earlier in this chapter. In August 1858 Hodgson was at Samuelson's yard at Hull to were built of iron on the Thames throughout the fifties, sixties and seventies, and the biggest yards must have imported immense quantities of iron plates and angles. Elsewhere in the south, there was a limited amount of iron shipbuilding especially in the Bristol Channel area where yards in south Wales, Cornwall, north Devon and Somerset received the benefit of Welsh industry. During the boom in the early fifties, shipbuilding of all kinds was actively pursued wherever a building slip could be laid down, and the majority of the vessels were probably built on speculation. In the south, this boom resulted in several yards building vessels of much bigger size than either before or since, such as the *Speedy* of 1031 tons nm built at Bridport or the *Sarah Neumann* of 1004 tons nm built at Bideford.

By 1850 only a handful of sailing ships were produced annually on the River Thames and the principal builders of such vessels were R & H Green and Money Wigram & Sons at Blackwall, Bilbe & Perry and William Walker at Rotherhithe, William & Henry Pitcher at Northfleet, Charles Lungley at Deptford, Maudslay, Sons & Field at East Greenwich, J & W Dudgeon at Poplar and some others.[52]

Some of the dry docks and slipways in the London area most frequently mentioned in the Lloyd's Register survey

reports in the early 1850s included Fletcher's Dry Dock, New Crane Dry Dock, West's Ways, Dowson's Dry Dock, Nelson Dry Dock (operated by Bilbe & Perry), Young & Co's Dock, Ratcliff Cross Dock, Wigram's Dry Dock, Tebbut & Co, Limekiln Dry Dock, Globe Dry Dock, Carter's Dry Dock, Somes' Dry Dock, Bull Head Dry Dock, Tindall's Dry Dock and Fountain Dry Dock.

During the fifties Bilbe & Perry built some well-known sailing ships such as the *Orient, Red Riding Hood,* and *Lauderdale*. At first they employed Thomas Bilbe's system of diagonal framing in wood with a single skin of outer planking in the conventional manner, but later they switched to iron frames and diagonal timber planking. A fuller description of their system and a list of some of the ships so built is given in *Fast Sailing Ships* together with remarks on other unusual ships and constructional systems.

Not many plans and models of London-built ships appear to have survived, but there seems little reason to suppose that the style of vessels built differed much from those constructed elsewhere in the country at this date, whether designed to carry cargo or to sail at maximum speed.

The surge in shipbuilding activity which took place in the north during the late forties and first half of the fifties was repeated in identical fashion in the south and in Wales. Very little tonnage was built in iron and that to order only. Many of the wooden ships were constructed on speculation and were launched with the suffix 'pro tem' after their name, indicating that no purchaser had yet been found. In boom conditions a speculatively-built

Fig 41. The small Dutch barque Calypso *from a watercolour signed 'J.Spin, 1855'. Her wide square stern is like the barque in figure 40. Although the masts have long pole heads to display flags without lowering the yards, she does not cross a royal yard on the fore. (Peabody Museum, Salem)*

vessel might be sold soon after the keel was laid; but if no purchaser was found or if times were bad, a ship might lie in the yard with the decaying timber of her hull being replaced when repair work was slack.

In August 1852, Hill's yard at Plymouth had a ship of 400 tons ready for launching which had been a long time in frame but for which no purchaser had yet been found.[53] Two years later the Visitation Committee of Lloyd's Register, on their annual tour of inspection, found in Kelly's yard at Dartmouth a large ship in frame of about 750 tons built to the order of Col Woolrich who had just failed in business. In 1857 the Committee found the vessel still in frame 'much discoloured by time and exposure to the weather', and recommended the removal of some planking, a careful examination and the dubbing over of the whole frame before any more work was executed. A similar case was to be found at Hocking's yard in Plymouth with a ship of 950 tons which had been on the stocks for a like period of four years, although she had been under a roof; nevertheless the sternpost was decayed and many butt ends of the planking were warped and started.[54] At Emsworth, a ship of 617 tons om had quite an adventurous career before she was even launched.

Fig 42. *This dramatic engraving from the* Illustrated London News *of 1859 is entitled 'Ship* Blervie Castle *in a Whirlwind' and presumably represents the ship of this name launched at Emsworth in 1857 as described in the text.* (MacGregor Collection)

'This vessel', reported E W Jobling, Lloyd's Register's surveyor, 'was set on the blocks in May 1851 but for some years very little progress was made with the frame. On the death of Mr Walker in 1855, by whom the ship was set on, the Trustees of this gentleman's estate sold the frame to Mr Henry Harvey of Littlehampton, who has since his purchase at my recommendation taken out the entire keel fore and aft; as also the stem and seven floors, four first futtocks, fifteen top timbers, seven third futtocks, and three second futtocks, all of which have been replaced . . .'. She was launched in January 1857 and was provisionally named *Adelaide*; later the name was changed to *Blervie Castle*. A class of 12 A1 was awarded.[55]

The activities at John Gray's yard at Newhaven are

given in Chapter Four. In the West Country, shipyards were working at full stretch throughout 1854, as this report indicates:

All the shipbuilding yards in Devonshire are now full, and there is a great demand for shipwrights. During the past week several vessels have been launched from ports in various part of the country. At Bideford a first-rate schooner has been launched; she is the *Alma*, and is intended for a shipping company at Hayle in Cornwall. Another vessel, registered A1 at Lloyd's for 13 years, has been sent afloat from Mr J Westacott's yard at Barnstaple. She was named *Robert Bright*, and was built for Mr Edwards and other merchants of Bristol, by whom she will be used for the West India trade. The interest attached to the launch was increased in consequence of its being performed by torchlight. At Teignmouth the *Avery*, of 500 tons burden, has been launched from the yard of Mr Follett. Several other vessels of large tonnage are also nearly completed.[56]

Fig 43. *This broadside view of the barque* Zodiac *might almost be the sail plan itself. Built and owned in Salcombe, she was launched in 1852 with tonnages of 320 om and 340 nm. The staysails all seem on the large size.* (Fairweather Collection)

At Cleave Houses, in the port of Bideford, George Cox (1809-1877) was taken into partnership by Thomas Evans in the early forties; by 1845 Cox was building on his own account and in 1858 took his son John into partnership. During the fifties he produced some large wooden vessels.

The last four ships on the table overleaf were all owned by John Leech of Liverpool, the *Sarah Neumann* being the largest ship ever built at Bideford. Her lines plan is reproduced as figure 209 in *Fast Sailing Ships*. The quotations are all taken from the appropriate Lloyd's Register survey report.

At Barnstaple, John Westacott was equally active in the fifties, although his square-rigged productions were not as large. Most of his vessels were built under a roof, which gave them an extra year's class and many received 14 A1. He built *Lady Ebrington* and *Parana* in 1852; *Sea Snake* and *Springbok* in 1853; *Mary Ann Bruford* and *Robert Bright* in 1854; *Star of Peace* in 1856. Leaving Liverpool on 4 October 1852 with 153 passengers, the *Lady Ebrington* took 108 days on a passage out to Melbourne.

At Padstow, F H Thomas launched the ship *Morning*

SHIPS AND BARQUES BUILT BY GEORGE COX IN THE 1850s[57]

Date	Name	Tons nm	Tons om	Rig	Remarks
1850	Rajah of Sarawak	525	458	S	
1851	Nepaulese Ambassador 'pro tem'	804	698	S	Renamed Joshua, 13 A1 (owned by Joshua Prowse)
1853	Vocalist	275	336	bk	
1854	Jane Leech	910	871	S	13 A1, 'Is a most handsome model; materials and workmanship of the best description'
1854	Shuttle	310	365	bk	12 A1
1855	Sarah Neumann	1004	1220	S	13 A1, 'Is a clipper style and handsome model, materials and workmanship of the best description'
1857	Bucton Castle	886	1014	S	'She is a handsome model . . .'

Star in August 1855; with a tonnage of 480 om she was described as one of the largest vessels ever built in Cornwall.[58]

Apart from the lines taken off the half-model of the *Sarah Neumann*, plans or models are rare of other Devon and Cornish square-rigged vessels of this date, although a sail plan of the small Appledore-built barque *Mary Lord* (1859) is reproduced in Chapter Four. In hull-form and deck layout, many of the smaller vessels probably resembled the barque *Parsee* (figure 26).

DONALD McKAY OF BOSTON AND WILLIAM WEBB OF NEW YORK

Although the building of large ships was passing from wood to iron in Great Britain, timber construction remained unaltered and undiminished in North America where the United States and Canada were producing larger and larger ships constructed entirely of wood. In a table on page 154 of *Fast Sailing Ships*, seventy-two clippers of over 1500 tons were shown to have been built in the United States alone in the years 1850-59, and thirteen of these were of over 2000 tons. Non-clipper ships, never having caught the public imagination to the same extent, are not at present so well documented, but all shipyards produced examples because the full-bodied ship or medium clipper probably formed the bread-and-butter work of the yard, whilst the clippers graced the ways for only a few years. Their heyday was in the first five years of the 1850s but by 1856 the rush to the Californian gold-fields was over and the trade was over-stocked with large ships; added to which the market was flooded with ships released from transport service by the ending of the Crimean War. The depression was world-wide and the big American clipper had difficulty carrying sufficient cargo to earn a living, and when these clippers were sold or lost they were not replaced. But the medium clipper proved a successful replacement. As Henry Hall commented in his report on the United States' shipbuilding industry, the medium clipper was a 'handsome [ship] with towering masts and spars, full on the floor, with a good bow and fair run, capable of carrying a great cargo at an excellent rate of speed'.[59] He added that they carried one-and-a-half times their register tonnage, although many were undoubtedly designed to carry a larger proportion of cargo.

The seaman journalist, Duncan McLean, writing in the *Boston Atlas* in 1856, further defines this emerging type of medium clipper when he commences his description of the new ship *Susan Howland* with these words:

The great clipper building enterprize [sic], consequent upon the discovery of gold in California, has been the means of introducing many improvements in naval architecture. Among these may be cited, beauty of outline in all other classes of vessels. The eye became accustomed to beauty in the clippers, and demanded its embodiment in full-modelled vessels also. This gave our designers more scope for the exercise of their talents, than they had before enjoyed, and the result has been highly satisfactory. Before clippers became general, shipowners were in the habit of furnishing their own models, and these were designed mostly for capacity, without reference to beauty or speed; but now, shipowners, though still desirous of great capacity, are not indifferent to beauty. The consequence is, that nearly all our full modelled vessels vie in beauty of outline with many of our most approved clippers. What they lose in airy lightness, is made up in harmony of outline. The *Susan Howland* is a full modelled vessel, designed to stow a very large cargo compared with her register, but is of a beautiful model. She is 180 feet long between perpendiculars on deck, has 38½ feet breadth of beam, 28½ feet depth of hold, including 7 feet 10 inches height of between decks, and registers 1137 tons. Though full modelled, having only 9 inches dead rise at half floor, yet she has easy waterlines, finely formed ends and a rounded stern. Her bow rakes and flares enough to give an air of lightness to her general outline, and is finished without head or trailboards. It is tastefully ornamented with a full figure of the lady whose name she bears, and the figure is painted white, relieved with gilding and carved flower-work.[60]

The report goes on to describe her cabins and deck fittings, to specify her construction and scantlings, and to list her spar dimensions. She had single topsails, carried nothing above royals, and her mainyard was 70 feet long and 19 inches in diameter. Her maiden passage was scheduled for Enoch Train & Co's line of packets sailing to Liverpool.

Writers in America have for long ascribed a ship's hull-form to either the Baltimore clipper or packet ship model, implying either a ship with steep deadrise or one with flat floors. (Some of the clippers certainly possessed flattish floors with extremely sharp ends, but this variation is outside the scope of the present work.) Packets, like Webb's *Havre* of 1845, had short full ends, but with a run longer than the entrance in the lower body, and the floors had little deadrise with firm bilges. The medium clippers tended to possess a similar midship section, but they were finer at the ends with convex waterlines, and the entrance and run were more evenly balanced. Above the waterline, the medium clippers had dispensed with most, if not all, of the heavy headwork and

Fig 44. Donald McKay's shipyard at East Boston, probably taken in the 1850s. All the midship frames have been erected for some vessel but the stem and sternpost have not yet been set up. In the foreground are stacks of timber some of which is 'grown'. (Peabody Museum, Salem)

Fig 45. The wooden ship Abbot Lawrence *hauled out for repairs to her coppering. Her deep hull and full ends indicate large cargo capacity; she has built wooden masts with iron bands, a wooden stock anchor, a lowering gaff and large houses on her poop. She was built by Donald McKay in 1856 and measured 1497 tons.* (Peabody Museum, Salem)

trailboards, and the square stern was replaced with a round or elliptic one, thus giving a far neater and more graceful appearance, which is how McLean describes the *Susan Howland*. He does not actually employ the term 'medium clipper' but uses other interesting descriptions. The *Caroline* of Charleston (built 1851 of 722 tons) is

described as 'a beautiful freighting ship';[61] the ship *Samuel Lawrence* of Boston (built 1851 of 1035 tons) was 'designed . . . to sail as fast as the general run of packet ships';[62] of the ship *Witch of the Wave* (built 1856 of 1198 tons) he writes: 'This ship is not a clipper. She is a noble freighting ship, of the most approved European packet model . . .' and built in the same yard as the famous clipper of the same name.[63] In the titles to his articles, sailing vessels were designated as 'clipper', 'packet' or just 'new', the last term indicating a full model.

One item of interest concerning the reporting of the dimensions of a new ship occurs in his report on the 'new packet ship *Commodore Perry*' in which he comments that 'we have not been able to procure her exact dimensions, but by pacing her deck and guessing, we give her length on deck as 212 feet, extreme breadth of beam 47½ feet and depth 29 feet'. This was a very honest statement, and one

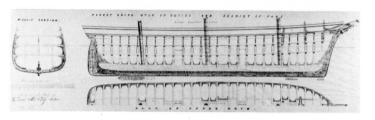

Fig 46. A tinted drawing of Donald McKay's ships Star of Empire *and* Chariot of Fame *which illustrates the huge amounts of timber consumed in their construction. In the midship section on the left, the many keelsons to give longitudinal support can be seen. The* Chariot of Fame *measured 220.0ft × 43.0ft × 27.6ft and 2050 tons. (Peabody Museum, Salem)*

built on speculation by Donald McKay as medium clippers, and both were sold to James Baines in 1854 whilst still on the stocks. Duncan McLean said that the former could stand upright without ballast, which was a useful quality for any ship. Although McKay's clipper ships usually varied in design from one to another, it may be that these two ships were somewhat of the same style to be seen in the *Donald McKay* whose lines appear in figure 47.

This latter plan is signed and dated: 'Cop[ied] G. Hillman, L'pool Sept 1862'. It is drawn to the unusual scale of ⅛in to 1ft. Hillman copied many plans in Europe and these are now in the Mariner's Museum at Newport News, Virginia. This large ship was the fourth of the celebrated quartet which James Baines had ordered from McKay for his Black Ball Line service to Australia, the others being the *Lightning* (launched January 1854), *Champion of the Seas* (launched April 1854), and *James Baines* (launched July 1854). The *Donald McKay* was launched in January 1855. The first three were clippers of which *James Baines*'s design was halfway between the extreme *Lightning* and the slightly fuller *Champion of the Seas*. By contrast, *Donald McKay* was much fuller in design but her large powerful hull, supported by a huge sail plan, enabled her to make fast passages in strong winds.

The *Donald McKay* has not much hollow in her entrance and run, but the ends are generally convex and evenly balanced, and the floors have little deadrise with hard bilges and the minimum of tumblehome. It was a hull designed to carry the maximum amount of cargo and yet to sail reasonably fast, and it would be fascinating to know how and why James Baines decided to switch from a

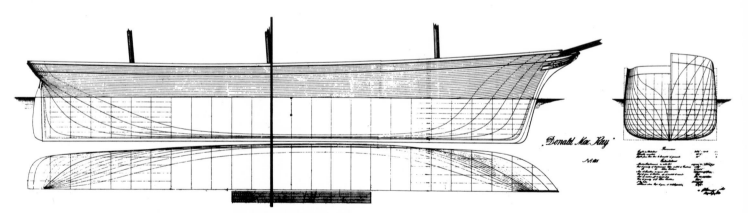

Fig 47. Donald McKay. Lines plan; this is a photostat of the original which was drawn by G Hillmann and dated 'L'pool Sept 1862'. Built 1855 at East Boston by Donald McKay; measurements listed on plan. Note: the vertical black stripe by the mainmast was a join in the paper.

wonders how many other contemporary reports of measurements were determined in a similar fasion. His estimate was very accurate because the official measurements are given by John Lyman as 212ft 0in × 44ft 11in × 29ft 0in and 1964 tons. The smaller breadth figure may be a moulded breadth. An interesting point about her sail plan is that she had sliding-gunter royal masts.[64]

The *Commodore Perry* and her sister ship *Japan* were both

full-blooded clipper to a cargo carrier, because when he must have ordered the ship at the end of 1853 or beginning of 1854, the Australia trade was at its peak and clippers were rolling off the stocks. The ordering of a medium clipper called for an extra degree of shrewdness and foresight of how the trade could turn out, and his decision was undoubtedly correct, as the new ship must have carried a large cargo which at even the depressed freight rates would have permitted her to earn a good living.

Donald McKay built thirteen medium clippers, if one is to accept the definitions in Richard McKay's book, although the latter labelled the ship *Donald McKay* as a clipper. The particulars of these ships are as follows:

LIST OF PROBABLE MEDIUM CLIPPERS BUILT BY DONALD McKAY[65]

Date	Name	Tons	Comments
1854	Santa Claus	1256	
1854*	Commodore Perry	1964	Bought by James Baines of Liverpool
1855*	Japan	1964	Bought by James Baines; renamed *Great Tasmania* when registerd in Liverpool
1855	Donald McKay	2594	Ordered by James Baines; hulked at Madeira 1886; burnt and broken-up 1888
1855	Zephyr	1413	
1855	Defender	1413	Wrecked 1859
1856	Mastiff	1030	Burned 1859
1856	Minnehaha	1695	
1856	Amos Lawrence	1396	Traded to California and the East
1856	Abbott Lawrence	1497	
1856	Baltic	1372	Atlantic packet
1856	Adriatic	1327	Atlantic packet
1858-59	Alhambra	1097	

*Date of delivery

Duncan McLean gave the *Donald McKay* a detailed report, and thanks to the careful public relations attitude adopted by the masters of such ships, the newspapers of the ports at which they called often reprinted McLean's report verbatim. In the case of the *Donald McKay*, the *Argus* of Melbourne reprinted it and the *Tasmanian Daily News*[66] quoted the *Argus* in full. This report assigns her

Fig 48. An engraving of the Donald McKay *hove-to in the Mersey off Liverpool. Her Howes double topsails have no braces to the lower topsail yards. The skysail yards are not crossed. (MacGregor Collection)*

dimensions of 266ft length 'between perpendiculars on deck', 46ft extreme breadth, 29ft depth of hold, and 2588 tons register. She was thus the biggest of the quartet ordered by James Baines and the largest ship McKay built with the exception of the *Great Republic* whose dimensions when first built were 325ft long, 53ft extreme beam and 39ft depth of hold, with four decks. As rebuilt after the disastrous fire which burned her to the water's edge prior to her maiden passage, she was cut to three decks and her masts and yards shortened considerably. Duncan McLean comments on the relation in size between these two huge ships in these words:

> Although not so long nor wide at the measuring points as the *Great Republic*, yet [the *Donald McKay*] has more spread of floor, is much fuller in the ends, has more cubic capacity, and therefore is the largest sailing merchant ship in the world, and spreads 27 per cent more canvas than the *Great Republic*.[67]

The *Donald McKay* had three decks, and was designed to carry passengers on two decks. Her scantlings were massive in size: the keel of rock maple was comprised of two logs 16in square, placed on top of each other; the floors were 20in × 14in; the keelson was made up of four logs, each 16in square, placed above each other and there were sister keelsons each side; there were 96 beams under each deck, the size on the lower two decks varying from 15 to 17in square; her external planking was 5in thick, increasing to 7in at the wales. The dimensions of her spars were prodigious: the foreyard measured 105ft in length and the mainyard 115ft. As first built, the *Great Republic*'s foreyard was 110ft long and the mainyard 120ft, but when

THE "DONALD M'KAY," MONSTER CLIPPER, OF THE BLACK BALL LINE OF PACKETS.

rebuilt after the fire, these were cut down to 90ft and 100ft respectively, which were identical to those carried by the *James Baines*. Of British ships, the longest mainyard belonged to the Aberdeen-built *Schomberg* with 111ft 6in; next came the *British Ambassador* (1873) with 108ft, followed by *Stuart Hahnemann* (1874) with 100ft.

Her rig of Howes' double topsails required the topmasts to be fidded abaft the lower masts. It should be noted that whereas the lower topsail was set by its sheets, the upper topsail had none, but its foot was laced to a jackstay on the lower topsail yard. In a squall, the upper topsail could be lowered and the sail would hang in front of the lower topsail, so that the ship could quickly be reduced to close-reefed topsails without a man leaving the deck. This was also the claim made for roller-reefing single topsails, but in Howes' gear there were no mechanical parts to get jammed or frozen.

On her maiden passage, she took 17 days to Liverpool from Boston which she left on 21 February 1855, but sighted the land at Cape Clear after only 12 days at sea; thereafter easterly winds slowed her down. On 27 February she ran 421 miles and logged 18 knots in strong west-north-west winds, under topsails and foresail. At Liverpool she loaded for Melbourne and made the passage out in 81 days, returning in 86 days. The average

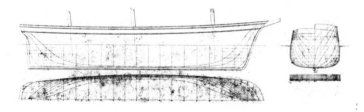

Fig 49. Amos Lawrence. *Lines plan drawn by F Schüler from Mariner's Museum, Newport News. Built at East Boston in 1856 by Donald McKay. Dimensions scaled off plan: 186.0ft length foreside stem under bowsprit to aftside sternpost, 39.75ft moulded breadth, 23.0ft approx depth of hold. Tonnage 1396.*

time for her first six outward passages between these ports was 83 days.[68]

The lines and sail plan of another medium clipper built by McKay have survived in the Mariner's Museum at Newport News. This represents the *Amos Lawrence* built in 1856 of 1396 tons for Boston owners. She has evenly balanced ends but is much fuller in the entrance and run than the *Donald McKay* so that her after buttocks are much steeper; she has equally flat floors but more deadrise. The lines were drawn by F Schüler and the Museum considers them to be contemporary. The sail plan of *Amos Lawrence* shows masts, yards, sails and standing rigging, although the deadeyes are omitted. She carries nothing above royals, and neither staysails between the masts nor stunsails are included. The three headsails are large sails; each has a long foot with the clew kept high as in later ships.

William H Webb, son of Isaac Webb, was another shipbuilder with a large output, and again it was in the fifties that the majority of his ships were launched. He was

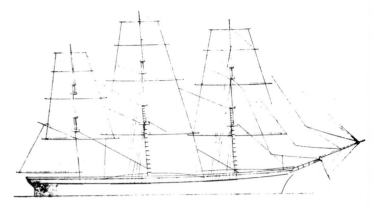

Fig 50. Amos Lawrence. *Sail plan from Mariner's Museum, Newport News. Source of the plan not identified.*

in business from 1840 to 1869 at New York during which period he built 138 vessels of all kinds and from the plans which he published in 1895 one can form an excellent picture of his designs. Although best known for his packet ships and clippers, there are plans of some medium clippers such as the barque *Snapdragon* (1853 of 619 tons) and the barque *James A. Borland* (1869 of 637 tons). His clippers had their maximum beam placed right forward which gave them a very long fine run, but the two vessels named above had balanced ends with less hollow in the run. The lines of the *James A. Borland* appear in figure 226, Chapter Five. Some of his clippers were given round or elliptic sterns, but all his other sailing vessels continued to be constructed with square ones. The old style head with heavy trail boards was retained on the packets, but other craft discarded it in favour of a lighter stem head with a bust figurehead.

His two largest sailing ships were the extreme clipper *Challenge* (1851 of 2006 tons) and the medium clipper *Ocean Monarch* (1856 of 2145 tons). The latter's combined lines and structural plan appears in figure 51 to illustrate that her hull-form was somewhat similar to the *Donald McKay* with convex entrance and run, and flat floors; but the interesting part of this plan is the structural timber work which is shown in immense detail. Dimensions given on the plan are 242ft 2in length between perpendiculars, 43ft 7in breadth for Custom House tonnage, 45ft 10in breadth extreme, and 30ft 2in depth of hold. She had three decks and could carry 882 steerage passengers. She should not be confused with Donald McKay's packet ship of the same name which in 1848 was burned off the coast near Liverpool with a great loss of life. Webb's ship carried cotton, corn and other commodities; on her maiden passage she had the deep draught of 23ft. In the early years of the 1850s, building costs at New York were about $55 per ton, fitted-out ready for sea.

Fig 51. Ocean Monarch. *Longitudinal section, deck beams plan, midship section and hull lines photographed from plan in William H Webb's* Plans of Wooden Vessels. *Built at New York in 1856 by William H Webb; measurements on plan 242ft 3in length between perpendiculars, 45ft 10in extreme breadth, 30ft 2in depth of hold and 2145 tons.*

Fig 52. Ocean Monarch. *Outline sail plan from same source as figure 51.*

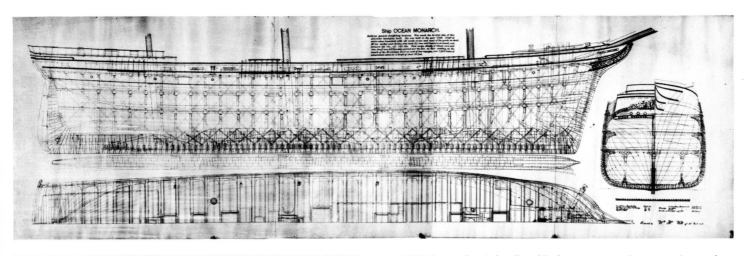

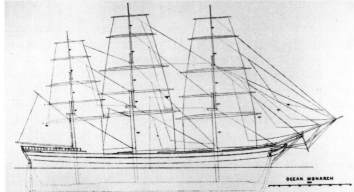

OCEAN MONARCH

SHIPBUILDERS OF SAINT JOHN, NEW BRUNSWICK

Although lists of ships built at individual yards have survived to show the vast extent of building in the Maritime Provinces of Canada, few plans are still in existence to show what these ships were really like. The lines of the celebrated *Marco Polo* are reproduced here in figure 53, in which can be seen her great depth of hold, flat floors and hard bilges, and full convex ends at the load waterline; while lower down, there are pronounced hollows in the waterlines. It cannot be said whether this is a typical form of hull or not, due to the lack of other plan data, but many builders operated a yard for only a short time and the records, if they kept any, were dispersed or destroyed when the yard closed. In a recent work on Canadian ships and shipbuilding, Stanley Spicer comments on the *Marco Polo*'s design by saying that she 'was not modelled after a true clipper ship but she was sharper under water than the usual Saint John vessel'. And in a later chapter he states that the 'Maritime square-riggers were first and foremost cargo carriers'.[69] He suggests that but few real clippers were built and that they were all intended for the Australian gold rush.

James Smith who had built the *Marco Polo* at Saint John

in 1850 launched the *Ben Nevis* two years later and sent her to Liverpool loaded with timber where she was purchased by Pilkington & Wilson and promptly dispatched to Melbourne as one of their 'White Star' packets. Frederick William Wallace calls her a 'deep-draughted timber-drogher of full model'.[70] She had dimensions of 181.0ft × 38.6ft × 28.0ft and 1420 tons (presumably om), which were very similar to those of *Marco Polo*, namely 184.1ft × 36.3ft × 29.4ft and 1625 tons nm, 1400 tons om — his description therefore is probably correct. It seems also likely that her design was a variation on the earlier ship, but her builder was unsuccessful in repeating the speed of the *Marco Polo*. On the other hand, the *Illustrated London News* published an engraving of *Ben Nevis* and produced a description as seen from the passenger's viewpoint by a writer who knew little about ships: 'Commanding as a frigate in appearance, the *Ben Nevis* is of very handsome model, and she sits upon the water with an ease and grace that afford the happiest augury as to her sailing qualities'.[71] Carrying 564 passengers, she took 96 days on her first passage to Melbourne under Captain Herron, 27 September 1852 to 3 January 1853. The engraving of her under sail illustrates a very lofty ship for the length of hull, the height of mainmast from deck to truck equalling the length on the load waterline. On the mainmast, there is another stay above the skysail stay which suggests that a moonsail was carried, and above this the pole is some ten feet long up to the truck. Like many of these ships, she had painted ports.

In 1853 James Smith built the *Prince of the Seas* of only seven tons larger, but she was of much shallower draught with dimensions of 193.0ft × 35.3ft × 22.3ft; this was a normal depth of hold for this length and breadth.

Another Saint John shipyard which adjoined Smith's premises belonged to William and Richard Wright who built thirty vessels between 1839 and 1855. Richard Rice has written an account of their yard from the business history viewpoint, listed their ships and reconstructed a balance sheet.[72] All of Wright's vessels were full-rigged ships with the exception of a steamer, a schooner, a brig and two barques. Size varied greatly from the schooner *Spitfire* of 83 tons built in 1841 up to the *Morning Light* of 2377 tons which was the last ship they built. The year 1848 was the only one in which no vessel was launched.

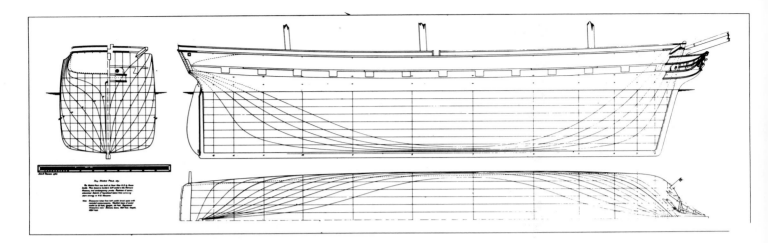

Fig 53. Marco Polo. *Lines plan drawn by John R Stevens from lines taken off builder's half-model in the Mariner's Museum, Newport News. Built at Saint John, New Brunswick, in 1851 by James Smith; measurements in England 184.1ft × 36.3ft × 29.4ft, 1625 tons nm and 1400 tons om. Reconstruction: position of masts; headrails and figurehead; cathead; painted ports.*

Fig 54. *Lithograph portraying the* Marco Polo's *arrival in the Mersey, flying the Black Ball Line swallowtail at the main truck, and firing a bow gun. This episode was recorded by the artist T Dove after the ship reached Liverpool in September 1853 at the end of her second round voyage to Melbourne and back.* (New Brunswick Museum)

Large ships could be built easily and cheaply with timber that was readily available, and as early as 1841 they had produced a ship of almost a thousand tons; this was the *Eglinton* of 949 tons. Their first vessel of over 1000 tons was the *Queen* of 1847 which measured 1098 tons. When Wright's first opened their yard the cost of building a ship, excluding the cost of timber, iron and sails, has been calculated by Richard Rice as £3 1s per ton. Newly-built Canadian ships in the 1840s fetched from between £7 to £12 per ton, and many of the builders, like the Wright Brothers, built on speculation, registered the ship in their own names, loaded her with timber and sent her across the Atlantic to Liverpool where both ship and cargo could be sold.

It was ideal for an owner to have a ship built at a

Fig 55. The box-like hull of the Importer *has prevented her from settling over further in the mud of the River Avon just off Bristol, but it gives a view of her flush deck, the wide square stern and how small the white deckhouse looks on her broad deck. She was built with the name of* Wasp *at Portland, New Brunswick, in 1853 by W Potts & Sons and was of 1447 tons. In 1878 she was registered at Liverpool and given the name of* Importer. *(Nautical Photo Agency)*

Fig 56. Another Canadian ship at Bristol. This photograph, taken on 4 June 1858, shows the Morning Star, *bow on, off Princess Wharf, but the two barques on the right have not been identified. She is described in the text. The photographer was Chas Wm Warren who made the exposure at 2.30pm on that June afternoon; the weather was sunny and exposure time was 3½ minutes using a dry plate. (Reece Winstone, Bristol)*

loading port, because the maiden passage did not have to commence with a profitless trip along the coast to a loading port nor incur the loading and discharge of ballast. This was just the point that Alexander Stephen of Glasgow was never tired of recommending to prospective clients after 1855, whenever they asked for a quotation. Shipbuilding prices in the early 1850s for Canadian ships were referred to in Chapter One. The Wright Brothers were registered as first owners in every ship they built from 1843 onwards with the exception of two vessels. Beginning in 1850, W & R Wright retained shares in several ships after they were sold in Liverpool, and in the case of the large *Morning Light*, they were unable to find a purchaser.[73]

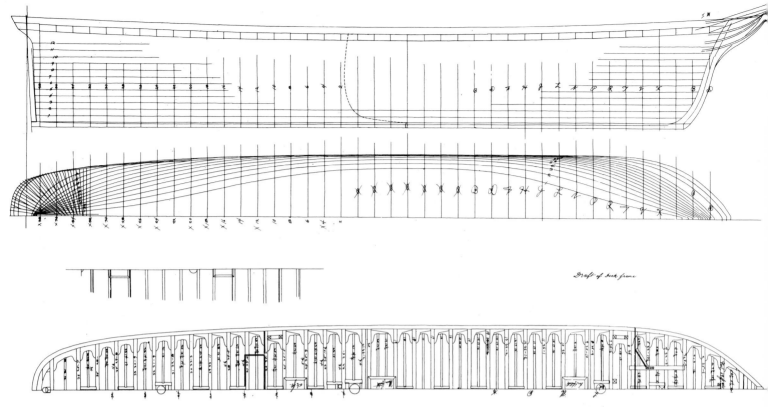

Fig 57. Inkermann. *Lines and deck beam plan traced by George MacBeath c1955 from original in New Brunswick Museum, Saint John. Built at Saint John in 1855 by Brown & Anderson with measurements of 214.6ft × 39.2ft × 22.9ft and 1545 tons. Reconstruction: I plotted the line of mid-section on the sheer elevation to indicate the amount of deadrise and tumblehome which the half-breadth plan contains.*

The ship *Bhurtpoor* which the Wright's built in 1851 received the following description in the Liverpool *Mercury* upon her arrival in that port:

> The new ship *Bhurtpoor.* This handsome ship which is now discharging the cargo brought by her in the Brunswick Dock, made a very rapid run from St John's, [*sic*] NB. She is consigned to Messrs Fernie Bros & Co of this town. The *Bhurtpoor* has just been built by Messrs W & R Wright, of St John's, and in the construction of this ship, those celebrated builders, have adopted every recent improvement. She is 169 feet long, keel and forerake, 36 feet beam, and 22 feet deep, registering 978 tons, but from her graceful proportions and appearance, looks much smaller. Her frame is of hardwood and hackmatac, beams of pitch pine, planking and ceiling of pitch pine and hackmatac; the whole materials and fastenings being extra strong and heavy, and the ship thoroughly copper-fastened. Her masts and spars are exquisitely proportioned and tapered, so much so that, on looking from the mainsail to the skysail-masthead, off the deck, the whole might be taken for one stick. The main deck is clear, except the topgallant forecastle and handsome round-house cabins, the waterways and other upper works, giving the appearance of great strength and solidity. The fore cabin has a handsome skylight, and the after cabin is also well aired and lighted by the stern windows. She is fitted with Robinson's patent steering apparatus, which is contained in a substantial wheelhouse, while a dipping needle compass is fixed on a very neat brass stand before the mizenmast, for the use of the officer of the watch. No expense appears to have been spared in the building and outfit of this splendid vessel, and it is hoped the spirited builders will find a profitable employment for her.[74]

In *Record of Candian Shipping*, F W Wallace gives the *Bhurtpoor*'s measurements as 162.8ft × 32.0ft × 22.4ft and 978 tons. Wilson & Chambers of Liverpool purchased her but she drove ashore near Wexford on the Irish coast on 18 September 1853 and became a total wreck. This was at the start of her second voyage between Liverpool and New Orleans. I can find no record of her having gone out to Australia in her short life.

Although paintings exist of W & R Wright's ships, no plans or models are known, but by all accounts, *Star of the East* (1853 of 1219 tons), *Guiding Star* (1853 of 1472 tons), *White Star* (1854 of 2339 tons), and *Morning Light* (1855 of 2377 tons) were all built on clipper lines. Some authorities, such as Wallace,[75] give the *White Star*'s tonnage as 2467 tons, but presumably this was the gross tonnage and the smaller one the net register.

An early photograph of a Canadian ship appears in figure 56 to show the *Morning Star* in the docks at Bristol in 1858. This is probably the ship built at Saint John in 1854 by F & J Ruddock of 1327 tons which was bought in Liverpool in the same year for £17,000 and placed on the Australian run. She is presumably fitted with Howes double topsails, as the upper topsail yard is lowered right on top of the lower yard. An interesting point is that the lower yards are supported by standing lifts taken to the topmast just below the futtock shrouds, and that they are secured to the yard some distance inside the upper topsail yard lifts.

The age of building large clippers had passed by 1855, but in that year Brown & Anderson at Saint John produced the full-rigged ship *Inkermann* of 1545 tons and dimensions of 214.6ft × 39.2ft × 22.9ft. A lines plan of this ship in the New Brunswick Museum at Saint John proves her to be a medium clipper with a short convex entrance but a longer convex run, and although no body plan was drawn it is possible to reconstruct one from the waterlines. This results in a slight rise of floor, slack bilges and sides that round up all the way to give noticeable tumblehome. She has a round stern, a raking stem with a built-up head and trail boards. Although seven stations amidships are marked with a midship station notation, covering a length of 30ft, there really is not this length of deadflats as the waterlines are curving all the way. A deck beams plan at the bottom of the sheet shows the extent of poop and forecastle, and the position of windlass, masts, hatchways and pumps. This is surely more typical of the type of ship built in Canada in the 1850s rather than the *Marco Polo* type.[76]

Howard Chapelle who saw this plan in 1957 said it was probably drawn from a half-model, by taking the lifts apart and tracing each one as well as the profile; the beam spacing could then be decided and the plan handed to the mould loft. The *Inkermann* was owned in Belfast by 1865. Wallace spells her name with only one 'n' in *Record of Canadian Shipping.*

No mention has been made of Quebec which was turning out many fine large ships, because no plans have been inspected for any ships from this centre. Many of the ships in the 1250-1750 tons range were ideal for transports in the Crimean War. The *Ocean Monarch*, built by Baldwin & Dinning in 1854 of 1887 tons, was sold for $53 per ton while only half-finished on the stocks, because the demand for new ships was so great.[77]

A mass of low-classed wooden ships were released on to the British market in the first half of the 1850s which could not hope to be re-classed at A1 when their original term expired. Even though they may have carried passengers during their first years at sea they rapidly deteriorated without constant and expensive maintenance. Such large numbers of huge wooden ships had rarely been seen before and some rivers and creeks must have been choked up with decayed and rotting hulks which could no longer find employment.

As iron construction improved and became more readily acceptable, so the days of the big wooden ship declined although when constructed of high class materials these ships continued to find profitable employment.

Fig 58. This photograph, taken at Bristol in 1854, could show one of the softwood ships produced in the Martime Provinces of Canada. Her sides look strained but the sails are neatly furled; she is rigged as a barque. (Copied from a photograph in the collection of the late Harold Wyllie)

BLACKWALL PASSENGER FRIGATES

SHIP DESIGN IN THE 1850s

Ships like the Canadian *Marco Polo* had no direct counterpart amongst British-built ships either in size or model. Other than East Indiamen of the largest class, there were probably only two wooden merchant sailing ships built in the United Kingdom of over 1500 tons – the *Eastern Monarch* and the *Schomberg* – the reason being that shipowners found it cheaper to buy or charter softwood American or Canadian ships for short-lived, speculative trades such as the gold-rush or the Crimean War. Then again, the deep-bodied hulls of the biggest three-deckers could only enter a few of the better dredged British rivers and harbours. The majority of the large British-built ships were employed in the passenger service out of London to India and Australia. Some of them were built on the Thames but an increasing number were the products of other yards such as those of Alexander Stephen & Sons at Dundee and Kelvinhaugh, James Laing, William Pile and numerous other builders at Sunderland, and T & W Smith at Newcastle. Such vessels were magnificent examples of the shipwright's art, in which the massive baulks of timber were converted into the sweet lines of a hull.

An examination of ship plans after 1850 reveals that the

Blackwall passenger ships were of a different form to their predecessors such as the *Blenheim* and conformed more closely to the general shape in vogue for a fast, cargo-carrying ship. They were certainly not intended to be clippers although they could carry their canvas and sometimes made passages which were quite as fast as ships built purely for speed. Safety and regularity was their aim. The large number of high class ships built for the passenger trade in the first half of the fifties reflects the rising activity in the shipping industry. Plans and models of many of these ships have survived, and lines of the *Dunbar* are reproduced here.

Several of the ships were built on semi-experimental lines such as the *Kent*, which Money Wigram built at Blackwall in 1852. From her plan in the National Maritime Museum at Greenwich it will be noticed that she has sharp ends but a long parallel middle-body – thirty-six feet of it – extending all the way from rabbet to bulwarks. She has hollow garboards but hard bilges and little deadrise. Another variant was the *Roxburgh Castle*, built at Sunderland by William Pile in 1852 and with

much the same profile as the *Seringapatam* of 1837. Her lines plan, also in the National Maritime Museum, was drawn by H J Croad to the usual $\frac{1}{4}$-inch scale, and shows little deadrise although the floors are almost concave between the hollow garboards and the firm bilges, and the maximum beam is placed only twelve feet above the rabbet line, thus resulting in a kettle-bottomed midship section. It is worth noting that a similar midship section occurs in half-models at the Sunderland Museum of Pile's wooden ship *Chowringhee* (1851) and his iron ship *Ganges* (1861) which suggests that this was his favourite form of design. The *Roxburgh Castle* was probably built on speculation because she was launched under the name of *King Richard*, but was renamed shortly afterwards when Richard Green bought her.

As to performance, the *Kent* was celebrated for her quick passages to and from Australia, her average to Port Phillip Heads from Plymouth or Start Point on her first five passages being $75\frac{1}{2}$ days, the shortest of which was 71 days. Her maximum speed is given as 12 knots, 13 knots being obtained for a few minutes in a squall. Her main truck was 130ft 0in above the deck which was identical to the *Tyburnia*, a ship of approximately the same size.[1] Gold-rush fever forced up the price for scarce cabins on well-found ships and on 7 January 1853 the passage money for a cabin aboard the *Kent*, measuring 8ft 6in square, was advertised in *The Times* to cost £120 for the trip to Melbourne.

Homeward-bound from Melbourne in 1853, the *Marco Polo* and *Kent* made a race of it. The latter left five days earlier but the two ships met in the Southern Pacific in 57° south, 161° west. Captain Coleman, master of the *Kent*, reported that the ships were so close 'you might have thrown a biscuit from the deck of one vessel on to the other'.[2] He claimed an advantage for the *Kent*'s sailing powers in going to windward when the two ships were in sight, but Charles MacDonnell, master of the *Marco Polo*,

Fig 59. Established in 1855, F C Gould of Harmer Street, Gravesend, was constantly photographing ships at anchor off the town or moored to buoys before sailing. He must have found the passengers good customers, and this Blackwaller Kent *could have been no exception. Of course, this photograph must have been taken in the early seventies when some of her flying kites had been docked. (Copied from old album)*

Fig 60. Roxburgh Castle. *Lines plan redrawn by F A Claydon from a tracing I made of the plan in the Croad Collection at the National Maritime Museum, Greenwich. Built of wood at Sunderland in 1852 by William Pile and launched under the name of* King Richard. *Dimensions on plan: 180ft 3in length between perpendiculars, 153ft 11in length of keel for tonnage, 35ft 9½in extreme breadth, 35ft 5½in breadth for tonnage, 34ft 9½in breadth moulded, 1029⁹⁰/₉₄ tons om; 1863 Lloyd's Register gives 22.1ft depth of hold and 1121 tons nm. Reconstruction: 7 stations omitted in body plan and sheer elevation for greater clarity.*

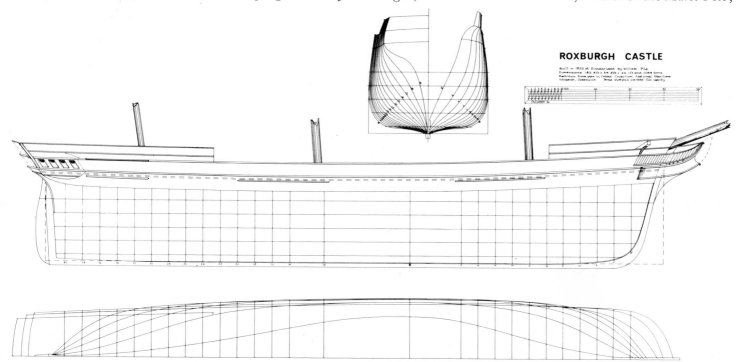

ROXBURGH CASTLE

Fig 61. Richard Green went to William Pile for other Blackwall Frigates after the Roxburgh Castle, and thus the Windsor Castle pictured here was built five years later in 1857. Although her stern is round, she may have looked somewhat similar to the earlier ship. This photograph is copied from one of F C Gould's at Gravesend; surprisingly the hull is without painted ports. (Nautical Photo Agency)

Fig 62. Dunbar. Lines plan drawn by the author from lines taken off half-model by himself and Basil Greenhill c1955; model then owned by Gellatly, Hankey & Co, London. Built of wood at Sunderland in 1853, by James Laing with measurements of 201ft 9in length of keel for tonnage, 35ft 0in extreme breadth, 22ft 7in depth of hold, 1171 tons om and 1321 tons nm. See text also for comments on these. Reconstruction: head rails, figurehead, forecastle and poop.

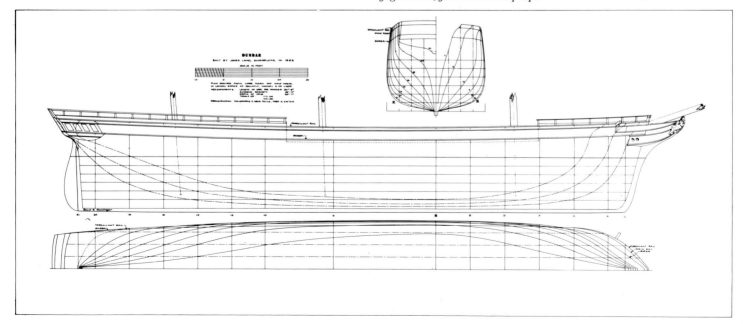

put this down to the *Kent* being more close-hauled.[3] The two ships reached Liverpool and London at about the same time.

In 1853 the *Roxburgh Castle*, with 198 passengers aboard, made a splendid run out to Melbourne in only 72 days from Plymouth having left on 10 May. She had taken her departure from London on 3 May and spent 2 days at Plymouth.[4]

The *Kent* and *Roxburgh Castle* are examples of original designs that resulted in fast ships. Ships with up-to-date but more conventional hull-forms include *Vimeira* and *Dunbar*, built by Laing at Sunderland; *Ballarat*, built by Duthie at Aberdeen (her lines are shown in figure 167 of *Fast Sailing Ships*); *Eastern Monarch* (figure 67) built by A Stephen at Dundee; *Tyburnia* (figure 69) and the *Clyde*, built by A Stephen jnr at Glasgow; *Highflyer* and *Superb*, built at Blackwall by Green. These conclusions are the result of having examined the builder's plans or lines taken off half-models. The *Dunbar* was a finer version of *Vimeira*; the *Clyde* and *Superb* were built of iron, the latter being a very lofty ship crossing three skysails; the *Tyburnia* and *Highflyer* were both in the Australian and China trades, and often brought home cargoes of tea. All these vessels were designed by the shipbuilders concerned.

JAMES LAING AND THE *DUNBAR*

Launched in 1853, the *Dunbar* affords a good example of the type of Blackwall passenger ship being built in the fifties and of the fine degree of workmanship that Sunderland could produce. The lines plan of the *Dunbar* (figure 62) is from a builder's half-model in the possession of Gellatly, Hankey & Co, London, who took over Duncan Dunbar's business on his death in 1862. Edward Gellatly had been Dunbar's general manager and was one of his executors; the firm originally bore the name of Gellatly, Hankey & Sewell.

Duncan Dunbar ordered the *Dunbar* from James Laing of Sunderland especially to participate in the booming Australian trade of gold-hungry passengers and high freight rates. She has appreciable deadrise, tumblehome and well-rounded bilges. The midship section is twenty-five feet forward of amidships, which is unusual for a ship so large and at this late date. The run is longer and finer than the short, hollow entrance and the design is for a powerful ship that could make fast, safe passages in the southern hemisphere. At station E in the body plan can be seen the shoulder worked into the hull below the load line and the fullness at the fore foot, both being intended to increase the bearing qualities forward and to deter the pitching motion. The *Dunbar* is very similar in design to the much larger *Eastern Monarch*, which was built three years later, except that her entrance is shorter and more concave.

The Illustrated London News, after referring to the building of large ships on the River Wear being 'a proof of the mastery which science, capital and perseverance have obtained over natural obstacles in these go-ahead days of

Free-trade and stimulating competition', gives a more concise description of the ship herself:

The dimensions of the *Dunbar* are: length of keel for [tonnage] measurement, 201ft 9in; extreme breadth 35ft 0in; depth of hold 22ft 7in; height between decks 7ft 3in.[a] She is of 1980 tons burthen,[b] her register tonnage being 1321 [new measurement]. Her timbers are of British oak, and she is planked and decked with East India teak. She is built for strength, stowage and durability, yet withal is a graceful model. She is extra copper-fastened throughout, and her iron knees and other fastenings are of enormous strength. The masts of the *Dunbar* are in keeping with the rest of the ponderous structure. They are built of teak. The mainmast weighs nine tons, the foremast eight tons, and the mizen in proportion. The poop is 82ft 0in in length and 7ft 0in in height; it is tastefully panelled in front and ornamented with a row of pillars of polished teak; and it will be fitted up with all the elegances of modern upholstery for the enjoyment of first-class passengers. Great attention has been paid to ventilation in all parts of the vessel. The between-decks has the appearance of a large hall, each berth being separately lighted.

The *Dunbar* has been carefully inspected by many of the first shipping authorities, who have unanimously declared her to be the finest merchant ship afloat.[5]

Fig 63. Two sketches by William Ward of Dunbar's *lion figurehead.*

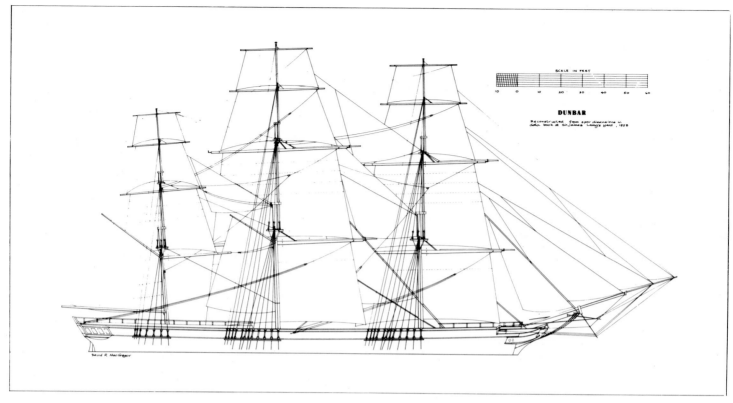

SCALE IN FEET

DUNBAR
Reconstructed from spar dimensions in data book at Sir James Laing's yard, 1858

Fig 64. Dunbar. *Sail plan reconstructed from spar dimensions in data book inspected at Sir James Laing's yard, Sunderland, c1858. See also text.*

[a] These measurements are confirmed by the builder's old data book, which breaks down the length measurement: 190ft 9in keel, 10ft 0in fore rake, 11in aft rake. The length as given by the magazine is therefore only 1in too long.

[b] This tonnage figure must represent estimated cargo capacity as the builder's old measurement tonnage is 1171.

Some additional details are supplied by the *Sydney Morning Herald* quoting a Sunderland paper. In the lower hold were six orlop beams and twenty-eight riders, the latter measuring 18ft 0in long, 5in wide and 3in thick. These must have been in iron as the scantling would be too small for timber and would have been a form of diagonal iron trussing, bolted to the frames. She also had eight large iron breasthooks. The patent windlass and other gear was made by a Monkwearmouth engineer named Duxfield. The figurehead was a British lion rampant, as was usual in Dunbar's ships, and was carved by James Brooker of Maryport, whose work was much in demand for figureheads. The stern carvings were designed and carved by James Lindsay, carver to the Queen.[6]

The figurehead of the *Vimeira*, built by Laing two years previously for Dunbar, was also carved by Brooker and the stern carving was executed by Mr Bridges of Sunderland.[7]

The *Dunbar* was laid down on 17 September 1852 and launched on 30 November 1853. Her cost is stated to have been 'upwards of £30,000'.[8] On a new measurement tonnage of 1321, a total of £30,000 results in £22 15s per ton. Alternatively, on a builder's tonnage of 1171, the cost is £25 12s 6d per ton. These high prices were the current costs of a first class wooden ship completely equipped with an East India outfit for sophisticated passenger routes; such an outfit cost about £3 per ton. For the *Tyburnia*, Joseph Somes paid Alexander Stephen £20 8s per ton om or £22 12s 1d per ton nm; for the *Eastern Monarch* he paid £23 13s 4d per ton nm.[9]

A data book which I inspected in Sir James Laing's shipyard in *c*1956 gave spar lengths and rigging sizes for *Dunbar*, and these were used to reconstruct the sail plan. A lithograph of the ship, drawn by Thomas G Dutton, indicates the run of the rigging and general proportions of the sails. This data book does not give the lengths of the topgallant yards, bowsprit, or main trysail gaff, but these were reconstructed from spar lengths of *Vimeira, La Hogue* and *Duncan Dunbar*, all of which were built by Laing. The *La Hogue* had trysail gaffs on all three masts. The absence of a crossjack is typical of these ships. The extra length of the arms to the crossjack yard are of interest: this was possibly intended to permit greater ease in bracing the yard round, if the brace pendants were secured to the outer end. The whisker gaffs on the bowsprit are similar to those on the *Blenheim*, and the arrangement of the flying jibboom, which is not listed in the data book, is based on Dutton's lithograph. The division of the huge standing jib into inner and outer jibs was being adopted by several builders; it provided a complement of four regular headsails instead of three.

THE *DUNBAR*'S RIGGING SIZES

Fore- and mainmasts		Mizzen mast	
Shrouds	9¼in	Shrouds	6¼in
Stays	9in	Stays	7½in
Backstays	8in	Topmast backstays	6¼in
Topmast stays	7½in	Topgallant backstays	4in
Topmast rigging	5in		
Topgallant backstays	5¼in		
Sheets	4¼in		
Tacks	4in		
Lifts	5¼in		

Lanyards range from 1½in to 4⅝in

Four years after her launch, this popular and successful ship was dashed to pieces at the foot of the cliffs by Sydney Heads, there being only one survivor out of a total complement of 122 persons.

The *La Hogue*, built for Duncan Dunbar by Laing in 1855 had the same beam and depth measurements as *Dunbar*, but was about twenty feet longer. She was diagonally trussed inside and out, the iron riders being laid on in opposing directions. Twenty tons of copper was used in the fastenings and the iron knees weighed sixty tons. An engraving in the *Illustrated London News* shows that *La Hogue* was launched bow first into the River Wear.[10]

Lloyd's Register's Visitation Committee reported on her as follows:

> Proceeded to the wet dock and inspected the ship *La Hogue* of about 1300 tons built under special survey for Mr Dunbar, member of the General Committee. The Visitation Committee, in common with all the surveyors and other persons who have seen this ship, have much pleasure in bearing their testimony to the excellence of the material and workmanship, and their admiration of this beautiful model of British naval architectural skill.[11]

The Committee also inspected in Laing's yard a ship of 700 tons being built under special survey for 13 years A1 grade. The frame was of British oak, well squared. 'The whole scantling was converted in Herefordshire, where the timber was grown, and brought round in a vessel of 200 tons. The advantages were stated to be good sound timber prepared where grown and the saving of expense in freight.'[12]

At about the same time, Alexander Stephen & Sons of Glasgow were obtaining the timber for their wooden

Fig 65. Lithograph by T G Dutton of the Dunbar *standing out to sea after dropping the pilot. The main topsail and topgallant are still shivering as the yards are being hauled round after the ship was hove-to for the pilot's lugger to come alongside. The royal yards have not yet been sent up.* (Parker Gallery)

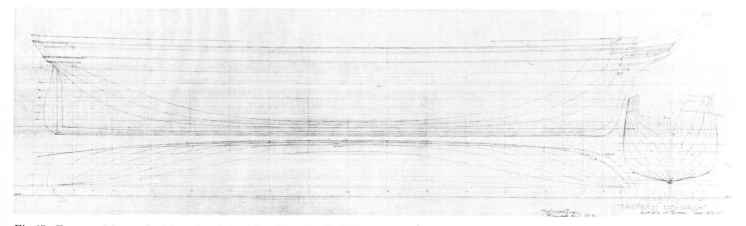

Fig 67. Eastern Monarch. *Lines plan derived from lines I took off the builder's half-model in 1961 in the offices of A Stephen & Sons. Built in 1856 at Dundee by A Stephen & Sons with measurements of 239.0ft × 40.3ft × 24.9ft, 1849 tons om and 1631 tons nm. Reconstruction: poop and forecastle rails; bowsprit. Note: this plan is reproduced from my pencil drawing and so is not as clear as from an ink drawing.*

Fig 66. *This bow view of a Blackwaller makes a welcome change from the everlasting broadside pictures. This is the* Holmsdale, *built at Sunderland in 1858 by J Reed with a tonnage of 1257.* (Nautical Photo Agency)

Tyburnia from the Chepstow district and were likewise having the timber converted on the spot.

The firm of Sir James Laing & Sons traces its origin back to 1793 and a yard at Monkwearmouth. The early partners were the brothers John and Philip, but this partnership was dissolved in 1818 and Philip carried on alone. His son James (afterwards Sir James, 1823-1901) took control of the business at the age of twenty and a year later built the firm's first ship for Duncan Dunbar. This association lasted eighteen years. Although the firm specialised in high class wooden ships they moved with the times and built their first iron vessel in 1853. They continued to build sailing ships and steamers in wood and iron, but only constructed four composite vessels: the sailing ships *Collingrove*, *Beltana*, and *Torrens*; and the steamer *C.J. Texbor* – all four were launched between 1869 and 1875.[13]

ALEXANDER STEPHEN'S FRIGATES

The operations at their yards in Dundee and Glasgow were described in the previous chapter, where names of ships built in each yard were listed. The London firm of J & F Somes specialised in passenger-carrying and bought seven vessels from Stephen. These were the *Harkaway, Whirlwind, Eastern Monarch, Dartmouth* and *Star of India* which were all built of wood at Dundee; and the *Tyburnia* and *Clyde* built at Kelvinhaugh, the last-named ship being of iron. Of these seven, the *Eastern Monarch* was

not only the largest but also the second largest wooden sailing ship to be built in Great Britain in the 1850s.

When I was doing research in Stephen's Glasgow office in the summer of 1961, I took the lines off the half-model of the *Eastern Monarch* which was hanging on the staircase with all the other half-models. A study of her lines plan shows her design to be somewhat like that of the *Dunbar*, but with greater deadrise, hollow garboards and a longer entrance; in addition, she has her midship section placed amidships.[14] Her headwork is also somewhat lighter. Built in 1856 for Joseph Somes of London at a cost of £38, 165, the *Eastern Monarch* was employed in the India trade, being capable of carrying 800 troops, and was lost by fire in 1859 at Spithead. Although no sail plan has been found, an oil painting by W A Knell (figure 68) shows that she could set three skysails and that she was not a lofty ship but had a good spread of sail with particularly large courses. The spanker was a large boom-less sail and the clew is sheeted to an outrigger projecting some feet beyond the taffrail. There was presumably one outrigger on each quarter, secured along the sides just below the rail cap. A sail plan of the *Harkaway*, built in the same yard four years earlier and for the same owner, shows a similar spar projecting about seventeen feet beyond the stern. In both these ships the large standing jib had been split into an inner and outer jib, and in *Harkaway* the flying jib hoisted to the fore topmast, thus making four headsails from the topmast.[15]

Like several of Stephen's ships, *Harkaway* was fitted with a telescopic jibboom which slid into the bowsprit, so that the bowsprit was a hollow iron spar. Other ships to have this arrangement were *Storm Cloud*, *White Eagle*,

John Bell, Charlemagne, Hurricane, Cyclone and *Typhoon*. The last three as well as *Harkaway* had four headsails from the fore crosstrees, like the *Hurricane*'s sail plan in figure 173 of *Fast Sailing Ships*.

A summary of the principal costings for the *Eastern Monarch* is as follows:[16]

Carpenter's time and materials	£21,498	19s	1d
Blacksmith's work including copper bolting	4,798	15s	4d
Glasgow account	2,188	1s	7d
Cash account, including many items of the outfit	6,216	5s	6d
	£34,702	1s	6d*
Contract price	£36,080	0s	0d
Additional tonnage	640	0s	0d
Teak decks, masts and iron plates	1,445	0s	0d
TOTAL received from Messrs Somes (including all the extras)	£38,165	0s	0d

*In Stephen's letter book this total appears as £34,712 16s 11d.

Fig 68. A spirited oil painting by W A Knell of the Eastern Monarch *close hauled on the port tack; the royals are furled and the yards are braced athwartships so that they are foreshortened and difficult to see; the skysail yards have not yet been crossed. There is a crossjack furled to its yard.* (Parker Gallery)

These figures suggest that a good profit was made by the builders.

Alexander Stephen's diary indicates that during her construction and prior to being named at her launch, the *Eastern Monarch* was referred to as the 'Belcarres', a name which harks back to the East Indiamen *Earl of Balcarras*. The *Eastern Monarch* was fitted with iron garboards, and in the previous year the *Beemah* was also fitted with them in the same yard. This was presumably an iron plate running between the planking and the floor timbers, possibly across the top of the keel as well. The *Beemah* measured 887 tons net.

The *Eastern Monarch*'s dimensions were 239.0ft × 40.3ft × 24.9ft. Knees, breasthooks and bowsprit were of iron and she was trussed with diagonal iron straps let in flush on the outside of her frames. This trussing was standard practice in large wooden ships. A vast amount of timber was consumed including much Moulmein teak, and Alexander Stephen snr bought a cargo of 550 loads of it in London in March 1856 at a cost of £13 15s per load. It was estimated by his son Alexander that wooden ships took about twenty-five loads of teak for every hundred tons of old measurement tonnage.[17]

Considering the difficulties in obtaining suitable timber for these large wooden ships, the remarks in Alexander Stephen's diary, regarding the construction of the *Tyburnia* for Joseph Somes, are full of interest.[18]

The total cost of *Tyburnia* was £21,774 or £22 12s 7d per ton on 962 tons net register, or £21 10s 5d per ton on 1012 tons om (as per contract). In addition, the twenty-year-old barque *Pestonjee Bomanjee*, valued at £5 per ton on 595 tons om, was taken in part payment. This was the only time Stephen accepted such a transaction, but many builders agreed to such terms in order to complete a contract. As shipbuilders were not usually shipowners, the acceptance of old vessels in part payment was often a liability; however, Stephen sent Somes' old ship out East to procure cargoes of teak for building his new ships.

The *Tyburnia* measured 185.2ft × 34.2ft × 22.0ft, 1027 tons om and 962 tons register. The timber for some of her frames was to be cut at Chepstow, the moulds being sent there from Glasgow. Walter Langton & Son of London had contracted to supply the timber, cut and bevelled to the moulds for 5s 9d per cubic foot, delivered in Glasgow. As mentioned earlier in this chapter, James Laing and Sons were using Herefordshire timber in 1855. Careful conversion of the timber was essential to avoid wastage and some of that received from Chepstow, two months after the moulds were sent down, was as much as 1½ ins in excess of that ordered. Alexander Stephen was evidently upset and Mr Langton offered a small compensation. The

larger scantling resulted in most timbers averaging eight cubic feet more than was ordered. Mr Langton knew only too well about wasteful conversion, as he confessed that he had lost £1400 over the supply of timber to frame the *Eastern Monarch*.

The timber for the *Tyburnia*'s midship frames had come from Perthshire and Forfarshire and cost only 3s 3d per cubic foot delivered in Glasgow, although it had to be sawn up in the yard. The beams were all of wood but the breasthooks, lodging and hanging knees, and diagonal trussing were in iron. The builders' drawings of the longitudinal section and midship section show this quite clearly (figure 69).

There is a preliminary design plan of *Tyburnia* dated 6 May 1856 which is drawn in the style of Stephen's chief draughtsman, William Robertson. This was for a smaller ship measuring 176ft between perpendiculars, 31ft 11in extreme breadth and 20ft 6in depth of hold, resulting in 850 tons nm. The final design was dated 17 July 1856. Launched in July 1857, she was only the second ship built of wood at Stephen's Glasgow yard and also the last, although many composite ships were later constructed there. Her design must have been strongly influenced by the wooden ships under construction in the Dundee yard, as the shape of the midship section was unlike anything previously built by Stephen on the Clyde and embodied pronounced tumblehome. Joseph Somes may also have had a hand in the design. To outward appearance, she was yet another typical passenger frigate above the load line. It is difficult to determine today if her design should be attributed to Alexander Stephen snr, or to his son Alexander, but the latter reported Somes Brothers as saying that 'they consider her the best model in their numerous fleets as a carrying and sailing ship'.[19]

Fig 69. Tyburnia. Frame elevation, deck beams plan and midship section drawn by Paul A Roberts from copies of the builder's plan, obtained when in possession of A Stephen & Sons. Built in 1857 at Glasgow by A Stephen & Sons with measurements of 185.2ft × 34.2ft × 22.0ft, 1027 tons om and 962 tons nm. Note: the dimensions on the plan should be in feet and decimals of a foot not in feet and inches.

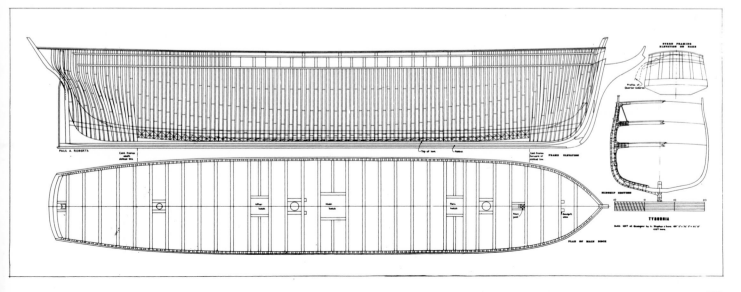

Fig 70. Clyde. *Elevations of bow and stern carvings photographed from original when in possession of the builders, A Stephen & Sons. The drawing is about 28in long. Pencil note at top reads: 'Clyde. The carver has drawn the ribbon in two ways — you can say which is right. Please send us the motto for the ribbon.' Colours are written on the mouldings. In the bottom right-hand corner, the ink note reads: 'Form of Drops for Stern & Galleries'; and below it is printed 'MOTTO VIVENDO DISCE MORI'.*

Evidently Stephen agreed with this verdict, for her design was copied and developed and left its imprint on the Kelvinhaugh ships for the next ten years.

The *Tyburnia*'s sail plan has a conventional bowsprit and jibboom, and she sets nothing above royals. The fore and main topsails have point reefing but the mizzen is Cunningham's roller-reefing pattern. No staysails between the masts are shown on the sail plan, and these could be reconstructed from paintings; paintings also indicate that the lower masts are built of timber.

Like other shipbuilders, Alexander Stephen snr of Dundee constructed a number of ships on speculation, and either he or his son William would visit London, Liverpool, Glasgow and other towns in an attempt to sell the hulls. After the *Eastern Monarch* (yard no 21) was launched in 1856, no 22 in the Dundee yard was laid down the same year; and two years later when Lloyd's Register's Visitation Committee visited the Dundee yard in August, they saw her still under construction and observed that she had been built under a roof for the 14 years A1 grade, and that the internal and external planking was almost complete.[20] This ship was sold to Joseph Somes in 1859 and named *Dartmouth*.

The last ship built at the Dundee yard for Somes Brothers was the *Star of India*, launched in 1861, with dimensions of 190.4ft × 34.2ft × 22.1ft and 1092 tons gross. She survived until 1892 when she was abandoned in the north Atlantic.

Two years before this ship was launched, Somes Brothers decided to order their first iron ship following a visit to London made by Alexander Stephen jnr in search of orders. Alexander returned to London and met Frederick Somes at Blackwall on 23 February 1859 and agreed a price of £18 per ton BM. Both then returned to the London office which Alexander named in his diary as that of Somes, Mullins & Co. Later he met the other partner, Samuel Somes, who was annoyed at not being consulted first. Three days later a contract was concluded whereby Alexander Stephen was to build a ship in iron to class 13 A1 with dimensions of 200ft 0in × 33ft 0in × 21ft 10in and tonnages of 1044 BM and 1150 register; decks to be of teak; to have a full East India outfit; all for a price of £18,792. Payments were to be in four equal installments: first when keel is laid, second when plated, third when

launched, and fourth when finished. This was Alexander's first order from a London shipowner.[21]

This ship, named *Clyde*, was yard no 22; her keel was laid on 26 October the same year and she was launched on 5 July 1860. Shortly before the time of the launch the shipyard were contacting the various sub-contractors and agreeing prices for work to be carried out. A Low & Co agreed to carry out plumber's work for the sum of £176 15s, but excluded the main pumps which had already been bought from Dundee at a cost of £25. Painting of the ship was to be carried out by McGrew of Partick for £105; wire rope and manilla cordage was to be supplied by John Black; chandlery was to be supplied by McSymon & Potter for a sum of £57; nautical instruments were to be supplied by Cameron & Blakeney at a cost of £31. The day before she was launched, Stephen's learned that the *Clyde* had been chartered by the Government to take troops out to Bombay from Cork and that Somes Bros wanted her to leave Glasgow on 16 July. Date for embarkation was extended to 24 July with a penalty of £20 per day for delay.

The master joined the *Clyde* two days after she was launched, on 7 July, at which date the stepping of the masts had not yet been begun. However, the mainmast was finished four days later and so were the others. The ship went down the Clyde on 26 July and the following day a photographer was dispatched to the Gareloch to take pictures, while the ship was having her compasses

Fig 71. The well-known marine painter, William Clark got £35 for this picture of the Clyde *hove-to at the start of her maiden passage. The sliding gunter masts, fidded abaft the royal masts for setting skysails, are not drawn on the builder's sail plan in figure 73. (Parker Gallery)*

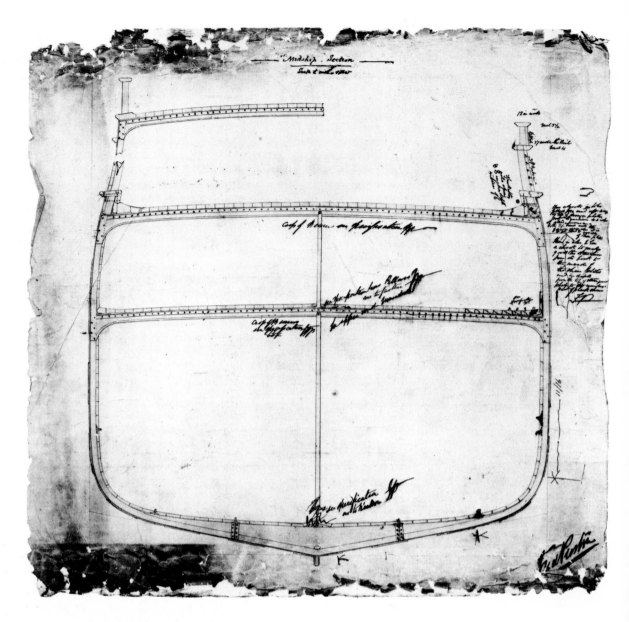

Fig 72. Clyde. *Midship section photographed from original when in possession of the builders, A Stephen & Sons. Drawn to ½in scale. Initials 'FP' after the various notes must refer to 'Fred Preston' who signed this plan in the bottom right-hand corner. Frederick Preston was inspector for Joseph Somes and he has already been referred to on page 23 as introducing to Alexander Stephen the enquiry to build the* Edmund Preston. *The thin flimsy and yellow tracing paper on which the plan was drawn had been mounted on cartridge.*

adjusted. The marine artist, William Clark, was making sketches of her at the same time in order to paint her portrait, the price for which was settled at £35.[22]

Alexander Stephen noted in his diary that there would be no profit on the contract. A week later he commented that Somes' ship, the old East, Indiaman *Earl Balcarres* [*sic*], had returned from India after a passage of 120 days bringing a freight of £22,000. This ship had been built back in 1815 at Bombay with a tonnage of 1417.[23]

The *Clyde* was of much the same hull-form as the *Tyburnia* but she had slightly less deadrise with vertical sides and not much tumblehome. She was some 15ft longer but breadth and depth were approximately the same. The sail plans of the two ships were generally alike. Although Clark's portrait of the ship has survived no photographs taken in the Gareloch have been discovered. The earliest photograph is that taken off Gravesend in which the high steeve of her bowsprit is plainly discernible.

The length of the *Clyde*'s outward passage to India on her maiden voyage has not been traced but on her return

Fig 73. Clyde. *Sail plan photographed from original when in possession of the builders, A Stephen & Sons. Built 1860 at Glasgow with measurements of 214.1ft × 33.1ft × 22.6ft and 1151 tons. Dimensions are written on the spars; the lengths of the lower masts are 'above deck'.*

she took 164 days to get home to Falmouth from Karachi, arriving back about 18 September 1861. Although there was talk of building another ship for Somes Bros, probably of iron, no order was placed, presumably because the price was not right, and in fact Stephen did not build any more ships for Somes.

END OF THE FRIGATES

The differences between a passenger frigate and any other sailing ship carrying passengers and cargo was growing markedly less as the fifties advanced. In particular it was the trade with Australia and New Zealand that attracted passenger ships, and there were many splendid such vessels afloat. Like the Blackwallers they combined speed with carrying capacity and, if possible, an easy motion and dry decks. Shipbuilders' plans show that many vessels had their 'tween decks lighted and ventilated for emigrants, and others so built were later used in the coolie run between India and the West Indies.

In *Reminiscences of a Blackwall Midshipman*, there is an account of a voyage in the *Orwell* which was built at Harwich in 1854 and which registered 1079 tons. She was owned by Green who also owned the *Trafalgar*; W I Downie who recounts his passage compares the two ships on several occasions.

I . . . was appointed to the *Orwell*, another ship of the same company, but engaged in the Australian trade, and bound this voyage for Sydney. She was, I fancy, an older vessel than the *Trafalgar*, and perhaps a trifle smaller; a fine, well-built craft, and a good sailer. Nothing particularly noticeable about her, except that her bulwarks, which were very high, tumbled home from the deck in such a pronounced fashion that in bad weather they made a most convenient shelter from wind and rain. She, like the *Trafalgar*, carried a few guns on her main deck. I missed, however, the swinging booms of my former ship; for the *Orwell* carried the triangular lower studding-sails generally found in merchant vessels of the day.

I think I have stated before that the discipline of the 'Blackwall liners' was much stricter than that usually prevailing in the merchant service. I now found that, even in ships of the same company, there was often a marked difference, that of the *Orwell* being very much inferior to the *Trafalgar*'s. Discipline, of course, there was, but much less formality. For instance, as long [as] you came on deck decently clothed, no one ever noticed if you sported a badge and band or not; and you might even stand your watch in one of those objectionable articles of head-wear called a 'Scotch cap'. The midshipmen were treated more like apprentices, and one of the first things said to me was, "Well, young fellow, you'll find it a bit different in the Australian service; you'll have to pull off your jacket and turn up your shirt-sleeves here; we don't want brassbound ornaments on this ship'. This, I found, was perfectly correct; but, I think, that while perhaps the *Trafalgar* carried man-of-war customs rather farther than was necessary, the *Orwell* erred in the opposite direction, considering the traditions of the service, and that, in those days, we ranked a bit above the ordinary merchantman; being, as we were, in a class by ourselves, and paying heavy premiums our first three voyages.[24]

Of course, Downie was wrong about the two ships he compares above as the *Trafalgar* was six years older, and their dimensions are as follows: *Trafalgar*, built 1848, 173.6ft × 36.5ft × 16.0ft, 1038 tons reg; *Orwell*, built 1854, 190.6ft × 29.6ft × 21.6ft, 1000 tons reg.

The depth of hold of 16ft must be to the underside of the lower deck so that she probably had three decks, which would not have been uncommon to find in a Blackwaller.

Of somewhat similar proportions to the *Trafalgar* was the *St Lawrence* which T & W Smith built on the Tyne in 1861 with dimensions of 180.0ft × 37.2ft × 22.5ft and 1094 tons. The builder's half-model which I saw about twenty years ago in Smith's offices in North Shields showed her to have very hollow garboards, a good rise of floor, rounded bilges and considerable tumblehome; otherwise she was of a short and rather full-bodied model. She was certainly an anachronism even when launched although she may have been a safe passenger vessel.

Gould's photograph which depicts her lying in the Thames off Gravesend in about 1870 is valuable as it shows what a Blackwall frigate looked like when crossing single topsail yards together with the original assortment of stunsail booms. Other points of interest are the boat carried on iron davits over her square stern; the lowered mizzen gaff which hoists on the lower mast; the lead of the foreyard and fore topsail yard braces which go to the mainmast and not to the deck; and the fore stay which sets up a long way beyond the knightheads at the position where the whisker booms are secured, which is halfway up the bowsprit. In the photograph these booms are seen end-on and so are barely visible.

Fig 74. St Lawrence. *Lines and general arrangement plans drawn by William Salisbury from lines taken off builder's model. Built 1861 on River Tyne by T & W Smith with measurements of 180.0ft × 37.2ft × 22.5ft and 1094 tons. Mr Salisbury has never been convinced that this model represents the Blackwall Frigate because the model's dimensions vary from the actual ship.*

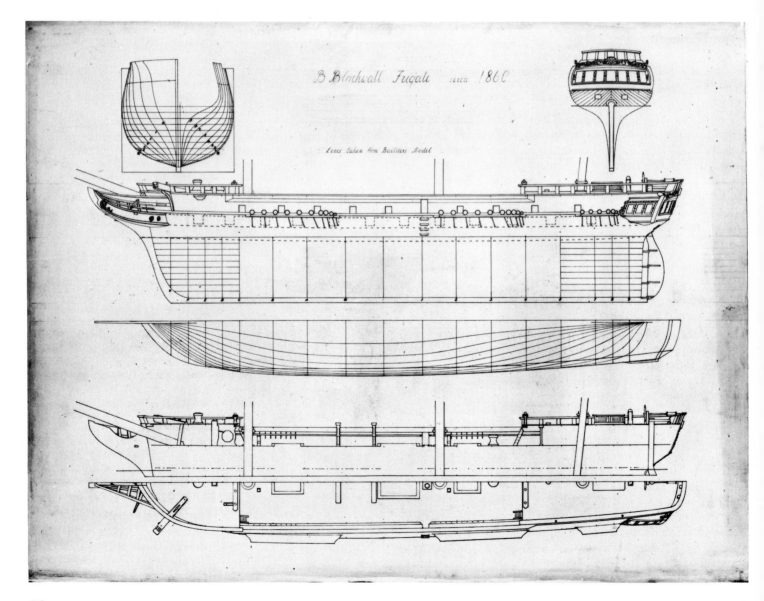

Fig 75. The St Lawrence *off Gravesend c1870, copied from a Gould photograph. She is described in the text. The collier brig hove-to in the distance, seen between the foremast and bowsprit, is the subject of an enlargement in figure 253.* (Private Collection)

During the 1860s the *St Lawrence* specialised in taking passengers and troops to and from India; she was afloat in the eighties in the Pacific trade between Puget Sound and Sydney carrying lumber.

Altogether not many of the frigates were built of iron but the Blackwall Yard launched two for R & H Green towards the end of the sixties. The *Superb* came first in 1866 followed two years later by the *Carlisle Castle*. Their dimensions show they were very similar in size: *Superb*, 230.3ft × 37.9ft × 23.1ft, 1451 tons; *Carlisle Castle*, 229.8ft × 37.8ft × 22.8ft, 1458 tons.

Both were lofty ships carrying double topsails – although the *Superb* set only a single mizzen topsail – and aloft each set skysails on every mast. The *Superb*'s foreyard was 81ft long and the mainyard was 85ft. Both ships were kept in the Australian trade and occasionally loaded wool.

Other examples of these passenger ships could be cited and in particular those owned or managed by Devitt & Moore, amongst which was the *Sobraon* which was noteworthy for two reasons: firstly, she was the largest composite-built ship ever constructed, measuring 2131 tons net; and secondly, she had accommodation when first built for 250 passengers who occupied almost the whole of the 'tween decks. After 1870 and with the exception of Green's *Melbourne* of 1875, few sailing ships were built specifically to carry passengers but those afloat continued in the business for another twenty years or so.

The era of the passenger frigates reached its zenith with the *Marlborough* and *Blenheim* in the late 1840s and then declined. Other modernising influences were being felt, and the hull-form changed from ship to ship as experimental forms were adopted. A few ships, like T & W Smith's *St. Lawrence* (1861), retained the old style, but by the end of the fifties the Blackwall passenger frigate had gone in all but name. True, above the waterline the hull and rigging remained unchanged for as long as single topsails were hoisted; the passengers expected it. The photograph of the *Parramatta* on the stocks, just prior to launching in 1866, shows the last vestiges of the Blackwall Frigate era.

1

2

3

1 *Fig 76. Also built in 1861, the* True Briton *was of a different hull-form to the* St Lawrence, *being longer and shallower for her breadth. This lithograph by T G Dutton shows an unusual arrangement of two staysails from the main topgallant mast; fore and main topsails have Cunningham's roller-reefing gear but the mizzen topsail has three rows of reef points. (Parker Gallery)*

2 *Fig 77. A good action picture of the* Macquarie *under topsails and foresail and quite a contrast to the following picture where the breeze is light but the viewpoint is much lower down. (Nautical Photo Agency)*

3 *Fig 78. A fine picture, probably by Captain Corner, of the* Macquarie ex-Melbourne *under full sail; ships were all too rarely photographed in such conditions with such dedication. There is some washing hanging up to dry under the bowsprit and more on the forecastle head. (Nautical Photo Agency)*

1 *Fig 79. This scene aboard* Macquarie *is well-known; nevertheless it portrays better than most the atmosphere aboard a passenger ship in fine weather on the poop. A three-sheave halliard block is in the foreground.* (Nautical Photo Agency)

2 *Fig 80. The* Parramatta *on the stocks in May 1866, just prior to being launched in James Laing's yard, Sunderland. She was the last wooden ship he built. The proportions of the hull are clearly shown; she measured 231.0ft × 38.2ft × 22.0ft and 1521 tons net.* (MacGregor Collection)

3 *Fig 81. Photographed later in her life when under Norwegian ownership, the* Parramatta *is seen loading lumber through a timber port cut in her bow. The Laing lion figurehead is unmistakable but the white paint band level with the underside of the topgallant rail cap is new. The scene is at Timber Coves at Sillery near Quebec.* (Public Archives of Canada)

3

4
SMALL SQUARE RIGGERS AND FORE-AND-AFT 1850-1865

INTRODUCTION

Fig 82. I apologise for including this well-known picture of the Ebenezer but it is one of the rare cases in which a Colling & Pinkney roller-reefing topsail has been photographed with the sail set. Here, as an added bonus the fore course is set on a bentinck boom. This brig was built at Shoreham by May in 1860 with a tonnage of 177 and a length of 108½ft. (Nautical Photo Agency)

Vessels of all kinds remained very small. In 1854 a Governmental return showed the average size of vessels in the home trade as 81.3 tons, each manned by 4.04 men; and of those partly in the home trade and partly in the foreign trade as 181.9 tons, each manned by an average of 6.94 men. 'Home trade' was defined as the coasts of the

Fig 83. The Tromso *built in 1862 under easy sail in ballast. When photographed late in their life, many brigs no longer set royals.* (Nautical Photo Agency)

British Isles and within the limits of the River Elbe and of Brest.[1]

Contemporary comments on size are interesting. The schooner *Mary* measured 24 tons nm and when surveyed at Bideford in 1860 the Lloyd's Register surveyor described her as 'this little vessel'. She had been built at Hayle in 1853 by Harvey and Co with dimensions of 48ft 2in × 12ft 9in × 6ft 8in.

Small size was no deterrent to trade because cutters, schooners and brigs regularly voyaged across the oceans; some doubled the Cape of Good Hope and others sailed out to Australia at the time of the gold-rush. Of the vessels clearing from London and Liverpool for Australia between March and December 1853, sixteen measured from 76 to 100 tons; ten from 51 to 75 tons; and one was below 50 tons.[2]

BRIGS AND BRIGANTINES

The brig remained very popular in Europe because of the great manoeuverability afforded by square sails on two masts; and by hauling the yards backwards and forwards, the wind could be brought against either side of the sails, thus making the craft sail in either direction or lie at rest. The hulls were strongly-built, and their almost flat bottoms allowed them to deliver cargo on the beach or lie aground in tidal rivers. They could get up and down estuaries unaided whereas other types of craft often needed the assistance of tugs. In the Baltic trade they were much in demand as they were also in the coal and heavy ore trades where they had to withstand constant punishment.

In Kierkegaard's folio of plans, published at Gothenburg in 1864, plans are given of four brigs, one brigantine, two schooners, two cutters and a sloop, as well as barques and ships. Of these four brigs, one is a clipper with a raking stem rabbet; two are square-sterned with trysail masts; and the fourth has a round stern. All four have single topsails, which also applies to the brigantine.[3]

The naval architect, G Hillmann, was drawing a number of plans of brigs at Copenhagen, several of which were built at Rostock, such as the *Wolgart* whose plan was copied by him in 1857. As can be seen in figure 84 there are no concave lines in her half-breadth plan, and although she has fairly full ends and a broad beam, she has appreciable deadrise and slack bilges. She carried two trysails, as did many of the European brigs. Her sail plan is reproduced in figure 85 to show one method of

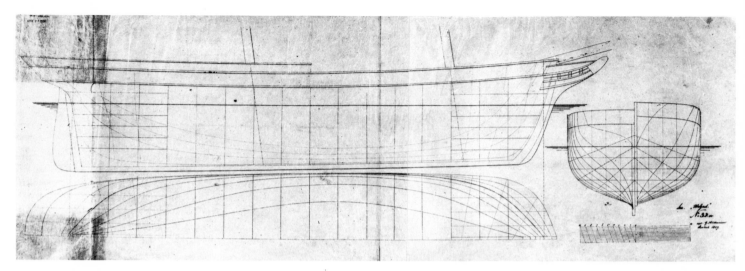

Fig 84. Wolgart. *Lines plan drawn by G Hillmann dated 'Rostock 1857'. Photograph from negative supplied by Mariner's Museum, Newport News. No dimensions on plan nor particulars of brig.*

draughtsmanship: the advantage is that there was no distortion to the shape of the square sails caused by the rake of the masts, and although this could be overcome by drawing the yards at right angles, a peculiar look could result with steeply raking masts.

The *Wolgart*'s sail plan is of a stylised variety which makes no allowance for the fact that the head of each square sail is shorter than the foot of the sail above. A more accurate representation of the shapes taken by sails can be seen in the plan of the snow *Peter* of Karrebeksminde (figure 86), which was probably drawn by the sailmaker. Points to notice are the hollow leeches of the topsails, and as only one row of reef points is dotted on halfway down the sail, it may be that these were roller-reefing sails; the headsails are drawn to show the generous cut of the canvas; and the distance of the head earing from the cleat by the yardarm is clearly indicated.

Fig 85. Wolgart. *Sail plan drawn by G Hillmann dated 'Rostock 1857'. Photograph from negative supplied by Mariner's Musum, Newport News.*

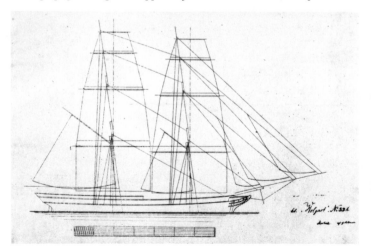

Two stunsails are shown on the foremast, and as the foot of the lower one is quite short it may be that a swinging boom was not fitted.

In Great Britain, the construction of brigs in southern and south-western ports was gradually being replaced by schooners, but in the north-east, the brig continued in popularity. At Whitby, for instance, only a single schooner was built between 1850 and 1871 amongst forty-five brigs, although after 1862 the barque rig was displacing the brig.

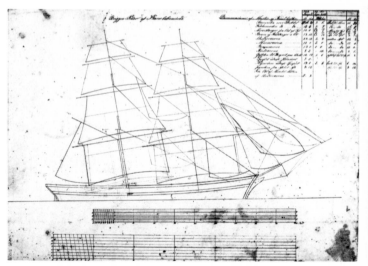

Fig 86. Peter. *Sail plan undated; no dimensions of snow on the plan. Photographed from original plan loaned by Frode Holm-Petersen.*

1 *Fig 87* Neptunus. *Lines and general arrangement drawn by Christian Nielsen from plan made by E P Bonnesen and dated 'Christianshavn 25 March 1847'. Built 1843-44 at Christianshavn; measurements on plan: 73ft 0in × 20ft 0in × 11ft 9in and 56½ Commerce Laster = 113 tons. I am grateful to Hans Jeppesen, Director of Kronborg Maritime Museum, for making the two plans of* Neptunus *available to me.*

2 *Fig 88*. Neptunus. *Sail plan drawn by Christian Nielsen from same source as figure 87. Port side of foremast shows square sails and stunsails set; starboard side shows them furled. Although built before 1850, brigantines of this rig were regularly seen in Denmark in the years 1850-75.*

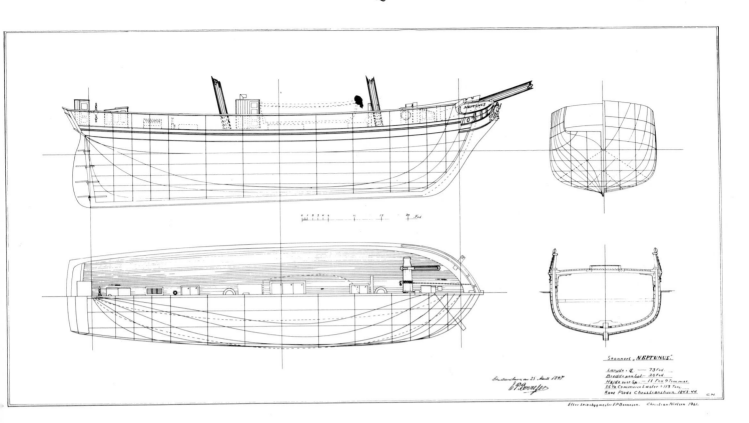

Skonnert „NEPTUNUS.“

Længde i H. — 73 Fod.
Bredde paa Spt. — 20 Fod.
Højde over Sp. — 11 Fod 9 Tommer.
56½ Commerce Læster = 113 Tons.
Kaas Plads Christianshavn 1843-44.

Efter Skibsbygmester E.P.Bonnesen. Christian Nielsen 1961.

Skonnertbrig

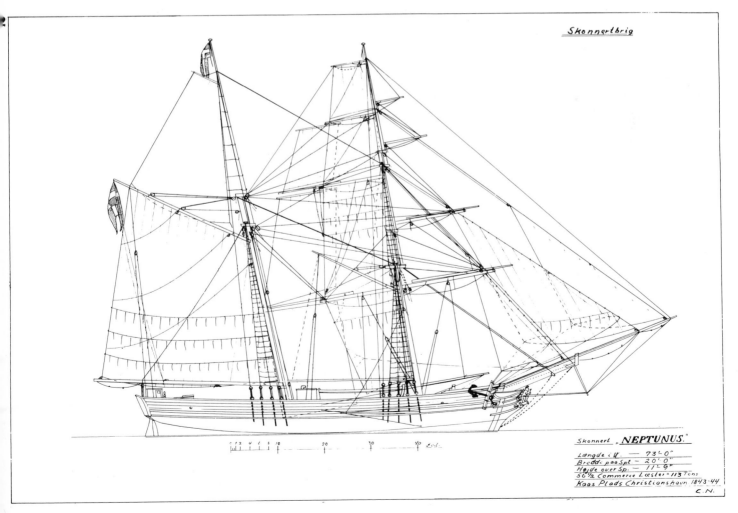

Skonnert „NEPTUNUS.“

Længde i H. — 73'-0"
Bredde paa Spt. — 20'-0"
Højde over Sp. — 11'-9"
56½ Commerce Læster = 113 Tons.
Kaas Plads Christianshavn 1843-44.

C.N.

Fig 89. Brigs in the River Wear at Sunderland just above Wearmouth Bridge, looking downstream. The scene is about 1855 and shipyards crowd the narrow strip between the water and the high banks. Copied from an old photograph. (MacGregor Collection)

An Aberdeen brig was the *Earl of Carlisle* of which James Henderson had drawn the sail plan, reproduced in figure 90. An Italian artist painted the brig off Naples in 1854 and he must have copied the sail plan exactly; now the reverse has occurred today and his watercolour in the Aberdeen Museum serves to provide measurements for the reconstruction. Brands & Scorgie built the *Earl of Carlisle* in their yard at The Inches, Aberdeen, in 1854. She measured 92.8ft × 21.6ft × 13.3ft and 192 tons. Although launched in November 1853, she was completed early in 1854 and so the later year appears as the year of build. The Lloyd's Register surveyor reported that she 'is formed with the flared bow and stem to a moderate extent; is flush-decked with square stern . . . '.[4] She classed 6 A1 and was equipped with a longboat 18.5ft long, a stern boat 16.5ft long, a windlass, a winch, but no capstan. The lower masts were of yellow pine.

The stem does not follow Hall's pattern of a raking stem rabbet but rather the style to be seen in Walter Hood's ships, and the mounting of the figurehead in the manner shown was rarely seen in the British Isles outside Aberdeen. In the matter of sparring, separate trysail masts are fitted on both fore and main, and the trysails are hooped to them. The main trysail boom is of similar length to the mainyard. In brigs of over 200 tons, the trysail or spanker boom becomes an unwieldy spar which accounts for the fact that the true snow set a spanker without a boom. Brands & Scorgie built another brig in 1854, the *Cynthia*, which was fitted with wire standing rigging.

In the same year, James Geddie launched the brig *Brothers* at Kingston, near Garmouth, of 159 tons nm and 190 ton om, and of the same beam as the *Earl of Carlisle*, but eight feet shorter in length. A lines plan of her in the Science Museum, London, shows a vessel with slight deadrise, and rounded, slack bilges; the ends are short and sharp; she is flush-decked with a square stern and little sheer. The plan is drawn very large to $\frac{1}{2}$-inch scale. The length of her bentinck boom is listed as 30ft, her foreyard 42ft and her fore topsail yard 34ft, according to dimensions on her plan.[5]

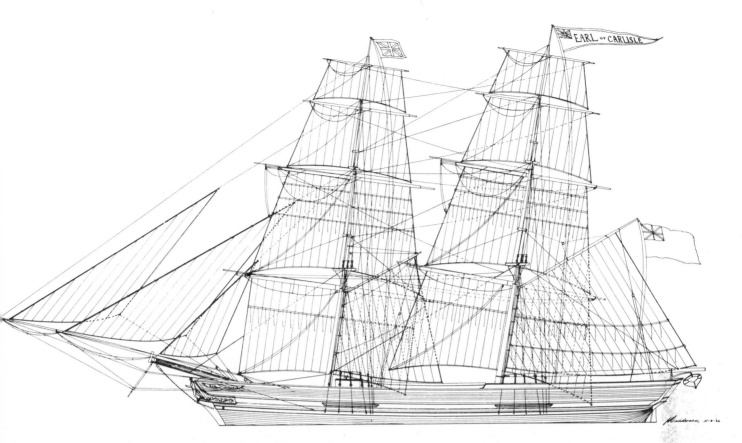

Fig 90. Earl of Carlisle. *Sail plan drawn and reconstructed by James Henderson from painting of brig in Aberdeen Museum. Built 1854 at Aberdeen by Brands & Scorgie with measurements of 92.8ft × 21.6ft × 13.3ft and a tonnage of 192. See text for further description.*

DEPARTURE OF "THE LIZZIE WEBBER," THE FIRST EMIGRANT SHIP FROM SUNDERLAND TO AUSTRALIA.—(SEE NEXT PAGE.)

Fig 91. *One of the smaller vessels taking emigrants to Australia was the Lizzie Webber of 213 tons nm, here seen leaving Sunderland on 1 August 1852 at the start of a passage to Melbourne. There were 64 passengers aboard and a stop was made at the Cape of Good Hope from which the brig sailed on 2 November, reaching Melbourne on 15 December, 136 days out. She had been built at Sunderland the same year to class 8 A1. Engraving from the* Illustrated London News *of August 1852.*

Fig 92. A busy scene in a shipyard with the Tweedside *of Cley hauled out to be re-coppered, as described in the text. I am grateful to the late Peter Catling for providing this photograph.* (Catling Collection)

Very few brigs were being built of iron – probably not more than two or three each year. In 1855 Hyde & Co of Bristol completed the *Locomotive*, a flat-bottomed, shallow draught, iron brig of 197 tons nm and measuring 110ft 0in × 22ft 6in × 11ft 10in. A rough sketch on her survey report indicates that the breadth of floor must have been about 16ft across and that the bilges were very hard, but without any chine. The floors were twelve inches deep; the keel was a U-shaped section, 2½in × ⁹⁄₁₆in, with a flange each side; the keelson was a repetition of the keel, but the other way up. Two bilge keels, each 22ft long, were placed seven feet out from the keel, and immediately above them were bilge keelsons, each 40ft long. The latter were all of the same section as the keel. Her first voyage was scheduled for Montreal.[6]

Brigs and brigantines were being built in New England and the Maritime Provinces of Canada for the Atlantic and West Indies trades, but brigs appeared in decreasing numbers. An example of a brigantine was the *Anita Owen* built in 1856 at Millbridge, Maine, at a cost of $20,000, with dimensions of 117ft 0in (moulded length at rail), 27ft 5in (moulded beam) and 13ft 6in (moulded depth).[7]

A brig built in Nova Scotia was the *Tweedside*, constructed by T Wallis in 1854 with dimensions of 112.2ft × 27.8ft × 13.2ft and a tonnage of 254 net and gross. It has not yet been ascertained when she was first owned in England, but she was registered in London in 1864 and the following year her registry was transferred to Wells, Norfolk. Here her owner was James W Porritt of Cley, but although she bore the name of Cley on her stern, she was much too big to get into Blakeney Harbour, let alone reach Cley Mill. *Lloyd's Register* did not class her when they listed her in 1874 and 1875.

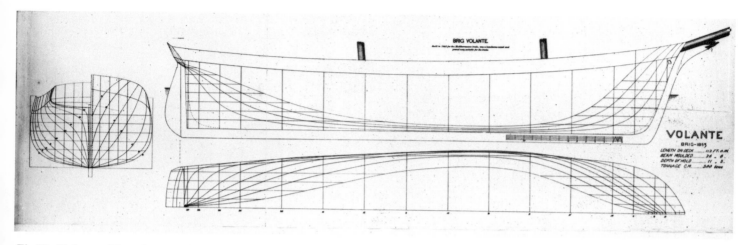

Fig 93. Volante. *Lines plan reproduced from plan in William H Webb's Plans of Wooden Vessels. Built 1853 at New York by William H Webb; measurements listed on plan: 112ft 0in (on deck) × 26ft 6in (moulded) × 11ft 3in and 300 tons CM. Inscription in centre under title reads: 'Built in 1853 for the Mediterranean trade, was a handsome vessel and proved very suitable for the trade'.*

The photograph of the *Tweedside* in figure 92, from the collection of the late Peter Catling, is an excellent study of a shipyard. She appears to have had new copper plating as well as new bulwarks, and the stern carving is newly painted or gilded. The hull looks to have a fine entrance and run with a fair amount of deadrise. Although the gaff is lowered, there is no trysail mast, but there is a standing gaff on the foremast. Unusually, for a Canadian ship, there are no outside channels. There is a steam chest on the left of the picture, and on the right, there is a small brigantine with standing fore gaff, bentinck boom and three-piece foremast.

American and Canadian ships were much quicker to adopt Forbes' or Howes' double topsails than British vessels, and the brigantine *Herbert Huntington*, built at Yarmouth, Nova Scotia, in 1856, was the first Nova Scotian vessel to carry double topsails.[8]

Probably the most famous, or rather, notorious, Canadian brigantine was the *Mary Celeste* which was built in 1861 on Spencer's Island, Nova Scotia. Originally christened *Amazon*, she measured 198 tons with a length of 99.3ft. She was transferred to American ownership in 1868 when she was renamed *Mary Celeste*. It was four years later that she was discovered abandoned on a passage from New York to Gibraltar. A sufficient number of articles and books on the mystery have been written to preclude the need of attempting anything further.

J & J HAIR OF NEWCASTLE

On James Geddie's plan of the *Brothers*, the waterlines are drawn dotted both on the sheer elevation and where projected, whereas the diagonals are drawn with a solid line. The same sort of technique is adopted in a plan of the snow *Julia*, built on the Tyne in 1853 by John & Joseph Hair, only here the diagonals are dotted on the half-breadth plan and the waterlines are not even projected, save for two or three of the upper ones at bow and stern. The use of diagonal lines and almost total omission of waterlines infers that the body plan was faired by means of the diagonals. Perhaps a half-model had already been made from which the body plan was drawn.

The Science Museum, London, possesses six plans of

Fig 94. Volante. *Outline sail plan from same source as figure 93.*

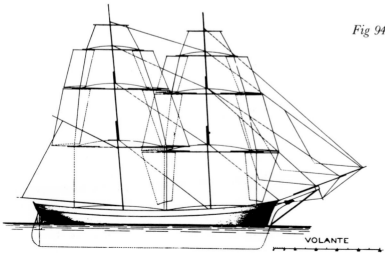

vessels built around 1850 which are ascribed to Robert Harrison, although the Lloyd's Register survey reports assign the ships to the builders John & Joseph Hair of Newcastle. The plan of the brigantine *Oberon* bears, on the back, the legend: 'Brigantine *Oberon*; launched Jany 3rd 1850; Robert Harrison'.[9] Perhaps Harrison was the yard manager or draughtsman; in any case it was rare for working shipyard drawings to be signed by the draughtsman. There are no surviving spar dimensions or sail plans.

In the plan of *Julia*, the general proportions and shape of hull-form are what one would expect for a brig, schooner or small square-rigger built anywhere in the country between 1840 and 1875, and she resembles their barque *Parsee* (see fig 26). In the *Julia*, the outline of the cutwater is not given, nor is that of the rudder. The lower deck beams have a laid deck only at bow and stern where required for crew accommodation. The dimensions given on the plan are: length of keel 83ft 6in, main breadth 23ft 10in, depth of hold 15ft 3in, length of floor 12ft 10in, 226 tons nm, 231 tons om. Six of their vessels are listed below:

PARTICULARS OF SIX VESSELS BUILT BY J & J HAIR 1847-1854[10]

Date	Name	Rig	Tons nm	Tons om	Remarks
1847	*Margaret Potter*	sch	81	107	Plan at Science Museum, London
1850	*Oberon*	bgn	173	-	Plan at Science Museum, London
1851	*Parsee**	bk	437	412	Plan at Science Museum, London
1853	*Julia*	bg	226	231	Plan at Science Museum, London
1853	*Abbey*	sch	98	-	
1854	*Choice*	bk	358	363	

*Further particulars are given in Chapter Two on p32.

There is also a plan at the Science Museum entitled 'Eagle Packet of N'Castle'. The vessel has two masts and is probably a schooner named *Eagle*. However no suitable vessel has been located in *Lloyd's Register*. Her bowsprit is fitted to the pawl post as in a cutter. An unnamed barque completes the set of six Science Museum plans, all of which have similar hull-forms and sheer elevations.

JOHN GRAY OF NEWHAVEN

A typical builder on the south coast of England was John Gray, whose yard at Newhaven lay on the west bank of the river, above the swing-bridge. He built brigs and barques of Sussex oak to a high class at Lloyd's; sometimes he built a schooner or even a full-rigged ship, and many vessels were taken into his yard for repairs. A plan of his barque, the *Watkins*, is reproduced in *Fast Sailing Ships* (figure 126) and it appears that at the close of the forties John Gray was influenced by the Aberdeen bow. The existence of this plan and the references made to Gray by Michael Bouquet[11] suggested the need of further research, and the surveyor's reports made on behalf of Lloyd's Register of Shipping have yielded informative comments on ships built in this yard.

SHIPS BUILT BY JOHN GRAY AT NEWHAVEN 1845-53[12]

Date built	Name	Rig	New tons	Old tons	Class	First owner and port of registry
1845	*Requiter*	sch	187	?	12 A1	Campion, London
1846	*Richard Dart*	bg	269	247	13 A1	R Dart, London (R)
1847	*Comet*	bg	225	260	12 A1	Reid, London (R)
1847	*Tiger*	bg	171	198	12 A1	Farrant, London (R)
1848	*Watkins*	bk	288	330	14 A1	Watkins, London (R)
1848	*Alice Maud*	bg	208	252	13 A1	Clark, London
	(lengthened 1851)	bk	253	297	13 A1	Clark, London
1849	*Emily Smith*	bg	141	162	13 A1	Smith, Pt Elizabeth
1849	*Fruiterer* ('pro tem')	sch	57	97	12 A1	Gray, Newhaven
1850	*Corsair's Bride*	bk	323	348	13 A1	Clark, London
1850	*John Gray*	bk	179	206	7 A1	Gray, Newhaven
1851	*Don Ricardo*	S	298	335	15 A1	C Ironsides, Liverpool (R)
1851	ss *Paou Shun*	3m sch	386	461	14 A1	Dent & Co, London & Canton
1852	*Electric Telegraph*	bk	215	285	13 A1	Gray, Newhaven
1852	*John Hillman*	bg	224	237	12 A1	Hillman, Newhaven (R)
1853	*Monsoon* ('pro tem')	bk	296	308	13 A1	Gray, Newhaven

(R) signifies that the vessel was built under a roof

Later vessels included the *Lewes*, launched as a barque in 1855 but later converted into a brig; and the well-known brig *Sussex Maid*, launched in 1856, and later made into a brigantine.

The first of Gray's vessels to be built under a roof was the *Richard Dart*, launched in 1846, and Lloyd's Register allowed one extra year to be added to the class, in accordance with the rules, providing the vessel had remained underneath the roof for twelve months. John Gray had built this roof at a cost of £600 in about 1845. Two of Gray's ships at this time were completed elsewhere: first there was the *Corsair's Bride* which was towed to London by a steam tug, with her lower masts stepped and the other spars aboard; then it was reported by Lloyd's surveyor that the three-masted schooner *Paou Shun* was to be 'fitted with a screw accelerating power to be worked by steam and is to proceed from hence to Newcastle, to be fitted with the same'. She appears to have been intended for a steamer at the time of her launch, according to the local newspaper, although the description offered by Lloyd's surveyor suggests auxiliary machinery. Her equipment included Thomas Brown's patent capstan, a double suit of stunsails, and the following sails: two foresails, two fore topsails, two fore topmast staysails and two jibs, two mainsails, one gaff topsail, two square sails and four topgallant sails. The mention of the last named suggests she carried square sails on both fore- and mainmasts. The *Watkins* and *Electric Telegraph* are described fully in *Fast Sailing Ships*.

That three barques and a schooner were first registered in Gray's name suggests that they were built on speculation and that he failed to find a purchaser before completing them, a view that is further strenghened by reading the words '*pro tem*' after the names of *Fruiterer* and *Monsoon*. The *Electric Telegraph* found a purchaser within twelve months but it took between two and three years in the case of the *Monsoon*.

Shipbuilders rarely combined the business of shipown-

Fig 95. Ashore on the beach at Durban lies the barque Bridgetown *which was built in 1857 at Newhaven by John Gray; her tonnage was 358 and she had a length of 131.8ft. The ship is described as 'wrecked' and perhaps the process of dismantling her has already been begun. The date is 28 July 1882.* (Local History Museum, Durban)

ing and building, although they sometimes took shares in vessels they had built. Builders intending to work on speculation would study the market to determine what types of ships were most in demand and make their plans accordingly, trusting to find a buyer before the vessel was too far advanced. It is probable that the majority of shipyards produced considerable tonnage built on speculation, although the ratio between this and that of contract work has not yet been determined; nevertheless, repair work was the great stand-by for the smaller yards although there was much fresh work available for all during the prosperous days in the middle of the century.

ALEXANDER STEPHEN'S IRON AND COMPOSITE BRIGS AND SCHOONERS

Unlike many shipyards specialising in iron construction, Alexander Stephen & Sons of Glasgow produced vessels of all sizes and rigs, and not merely large full-rigged ships and barques. Surviving plans illustrate some interesting vessels of smaller size which were built in the years 1859-68, as listed below.

SMALLER SAILING VESSELS OF UNDER 350 TONS BUILT BY ALEXANDER STEPHEN & SONS AT KELVINHAUGH[13]

Date	Name	Rig	Tons	Dimensions	Material
1859	Angelita*	2m sch	129	100.0ft × 16.5ft × 11.5ft	iron
1861	Mexico	bgn	156	105.4ft × 20.2ft × 11.7ft	iron
1862	Belle of the Mersey	brig	176	111.6ft × 21.6ft × 11.5ft	iron
1862	Arriero	bgn	167	105.0ft × 21.0ft × 11.7ft	comp
1863	Zircon	bgn	187	105.0ft × 21.0ft × 12.5ft	iron
1865	Belle of the Clyde*	brig	199	115.0ft × 22.0ft × 11.4ft	iron
1866	Metero*	3m sch	191	120.0ft × 26.0ft × 9.0ft	comp
1867	Janette	2m sch	91	87.7ft × 19.0ft × 8.9ft	iron
1868	Belle of Lagos*	3m bk	228	130.7ft × 24.0ft × 11.3ft	iron
1872	Belle of the Niger	3m bk	283	141.2ft × 25.0ft × 11.6ft	iron
1875	Osburgha*	3m bkn	346	146.7ft × 26.1ft × 13.0ft	iron

*plans reproduced here

The *Angelita*, *Mexico* and *Arriero* were all owned by Nelson, Ismay & Co, Liverpool while all the 'Belles' were owned by George Eastee also of Liverpool. Unfortunately no plans have survived of the *Mexico* and the *Zircon*.

All the 'Belles' except the *Belle of the Niger* and the *Arriero* are all of the same basic hull-form and demonstrate how a successful design could be enlarged or contracted as demand arose, and also receive a variety of rigs. It is probable that the *Mexico* and *Zircon* conformed to the same hull-form. The *Angelita*, although of similar depth, is much narrower and so correspondingly deeper in relation to length and breadth. The other schooner, the *Metero*, is a very shallow draught design with large beam, and altogether a surprising type of hull to send around Cape Horn to the West Coast of South America. As she stranded off Valparaiso on her maiden passage it may be that her shallow draught denied her sufficient weatherly qualities. A proposed sail plan of her as a three-masted schooner with topsails on two masts is described in Chapter Six. *Janette* was smaller, sharper-lined and of quite a different hull-form.

When Alexander Stephen & Sons came to design the *Angelita* they would have had no previous designs of small craft to consult, because none had been built in the Kelvinhaugh yard and the last built at the parent yard in Dundee was the wooden brig *Elizabeth Duncan* in 1851. So perhaps it was natural to turn their eyes towards their most recent design, the iron barque *Edmund Preston*, for inspiration. The result seen in the *Angelita* (figure 114) is a deep, narrow hull with a proportion of six beams to length, the same as in *Edmund Preston*; the *Angelita*'s ratio of depth to breadth is 1:1.43, and in *Edmund Preston* it is

1:1.45. Other points of similarity are seen in the midship section, and the entrance and run. For a brig, the deep hull might be considered traditionally acceptable but hardly for a schooner. On her voyage to South America, the *Angelita* would have made considerable use of her square canvas – topgallant, topsail, square sail and stunsails – and there is an indication on her sail plan that a conversion to a brigantine was considered. The contract price was £14 4s per ton BM on 130 tons, but no profit was made by Stephen's on the contract. The deck layout adopted in her was repeated in the other two-masted vessels and can be studied in the plans of *Belle of the Clyde*.

The *Belle of the Mersey* had single topsails and carried nothing above her royals; she had no main trysail mast, but a brig's spanker boom and gaff. The brigantine *Arriero*'s foremast was similar to the *Belle of Mersey*'s; she was one of Stephen's earliest composite vessels and the contract price was £17 10s per ton BM on 216 80/94 tons.

The *Belle of the Clyde* has the same depth as the *Angelita* but is 15ft 0in longer and 5ft 6in broader; it is the extra breadth that really is the most noticeable difference and provides a more conventional hull for her date. The plans reproduced here in figures 96 and 98 are traced from originals when in the builder's possession, and there has been a small amount of reconstruction. The originals were drawn at ⅜-inch scale. Stephen's plans in the sixties did not employ a sheer elevation on which the buttock lines were developed, but in its place there was a longitudinal section showing construction and deck fittings; below it was the half-breadth plan and to one side, the body plan. Neither buttock lines nor diagonals were drawn. On the *Belle of the Clyde*'s plan given here, I have plotted the buttock lines which have been dotted across the longitudinal section, but Stephen's technique of drawing the sheer strake and the main and topgallant rails from stem to stern has been retained. The deck plan was originally on a separate sheet, but here it is combined with the half-breadth plan for the sake of compactness. The love of a particular curve for the stem became so engrained with the draughtsmen that Stephen's barque *Mabel Young* was thirteen years later repeating that seen in *Belle of the Clyde*.

The brig's lines show a sharp, concave entrance and run, but without any parallel middle body; the floors are straight with little deadrise, the bilges are firm, and there is appreciable tumblehome; the buttock lines are concave where they cross the load line aft. She would rate as a medium clipper. The builder's plan gives a draught of 10ft 6in on an even keel, at which the loaded displacement is 430 tons. It is interesting to compare comments made by the late Howard I Chapelle in describing the American wooden brigantine *J.W. Parker*, built at Belfast, Maine, in 1874, which had an approximately similar hull-form:

> Her model represents the final development of the American trading brigantine, combining swift sailing, weatherliness, and good handling qualities with excellent cargo capacity.[14]

In *Belle of the Clyde*, the harness cask on deck, the pair of water butts, the davits amidships, as well as the style and layout of the deck fittings are all typical of the small sailing ships built by Stephen's. Also of interest are the

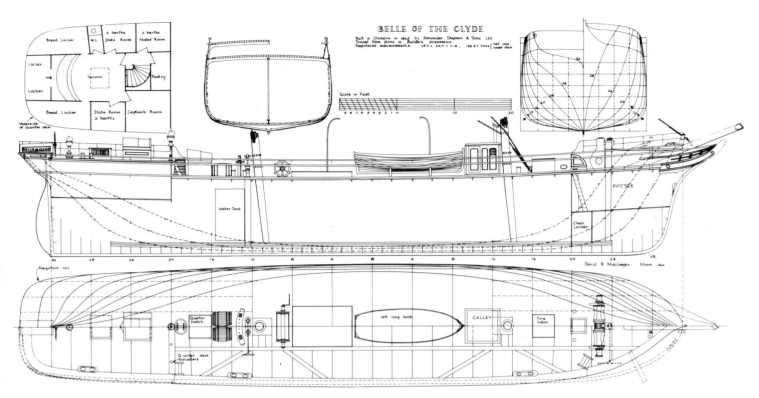

Fig 96. Belle of the Clyde. *Lines, longitudinal and midship sections, cabin and deck plans traced and redrawn from builder's plans when in possession of A Stephen & Sons. Built 1865 at Glasgow by A Stephen & Sons with measurements of 115.0ft × 22.0ft × 11.4ft and 198 tons. Reconstruction: buttock lines plotted; several plans now combined on a single drawing.*

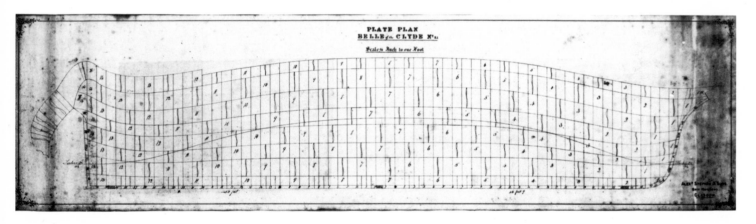

Fig 97. Belle of the Clyde. *Shell expansion drawing photographed from original when in possession of the builder's, A Stephen & Sons. Here the iron plates of the hull are drawn out as though each was flat which results in this shape for the profile.*

high iron hatch coamings to the fore and after hatches; the windlass is of greenheart; two boats are carried, a 19ft longboat and an 18ft gig; anchors consist of two bower, one stream and one kedge. As to construction, the frames are arranged at twenty-one inch centres; the keel is an iron plate 6in × 1½in; the garboard strake is ⁹⁄₁₆in thick and the sheer strake ½in.[15]

The four *'Belles'* built for George Eastee of Liverpool were engaged in the palm oil trade to ports on the Gulf of Guinea, the principal of which was Lagos. Light winds, malaria and a hostile coast gave the trade a bad name, and required fast vessels which could also defend themselves. 'The ships themselves were all light weather flyers,' wrote Basil Lubbock, 'beautifully modelled, heavily sparred

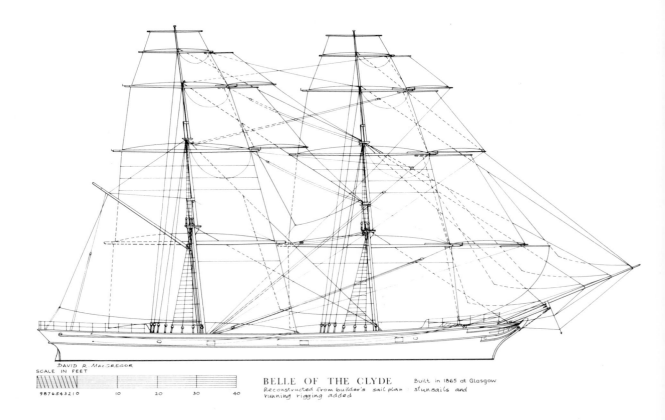

BELLE OF THE CLYDE   Built in 1865 at Glasgow
Reconstructed from builder's sail plan stunsails and
running rigging added

DAVID R. MacGREGOR
SCALE IN FEET
9 8 7 6 5 4 3 2 1 0   10   20   30   40

Fig 98. Belle of the Clyde. *Sail plan redrawn from builder's plan. Reconstruction: running rigging and stunsails. No boom drawn by builder for spanker or trysail thus making her a true snow. See text for type of topsails fitted.*

barquentines, brigs and schooners, which were the equals in speed to anything afloat of their date'.[16]

The *Belle of the Clyde* is no exception to this with her lofty sail plan and skysails on both masts (figure 98). The builder's plan does not show running rigging or studdingsails, but these have been reconstructed, partly with the help of the *Belle of Lagos*'s sail plan. Like most brigs of her time, *Belle of the Clyde*'s yards and masts on the fore are identical in length to those on the main, with the exception of the lower masts in which the fore lower mast is 2ft 6in shorter. The lower yards are 46ft long and the skysail yards 14ft. No braces are fitted to the skysail yards, a common practice when the sails were so small. When contracted for, the topsails were specified to be of Colling & Pinkney's roller-reefing pattern, and it is quite likely that this was adopted. The rig is actually that of a true snow in that there is a trysail mast on the main and the trysail has no boom, but this is contrary to the custom adopted by the middle of the century, in which a boom was almost invariably carried.

SMALL BARQUES

A fine example of a tiny barque is afforded by the *Mary Lord* of 196 tons register, which was built in 1859 at Appledore by William Clibbett, and for which a sail plan has survived. This plan (figure 99) may have been drawn by William Clibbett or perhaps by Henry Walter Lisslie in whose possession the drawing eventually resided; or it may have been drawn by William Bear of Northam who taught both Lisslie and Robert Cock's son, James, the mysteries of how to draught a ship's plan.[17] Plans depicting spars, rigging and sails were normally provided for the sailmaker, but if the latter made the drawing himself, the sails and spars were usually more accurately drawn than the hull. In the present case the sails are incomplete, but the spars and standing rigging are carefully drawn and so is the hull. The relative thickness of the rigging is clearly indicated by single or double lines. The plan was drawn to $\frac{1}{4}$-inch scale. A study of the handwriting, compared with other plans in the Lisslie Collection, would possibly provide the name of the draughtsman.

Points of interest on the plan are the lofty royal poles measuring 5ft 0in on the foremast and 5ft 6in on the mainmast, and this height is increased by the royal yards not being hoisted close up to the rigging. This may have been the practice at Clibbett's yard or it may have been a cumulative draughting error, because once the drop of the lower yard at the slings is established, the hoist of the other sails is governed by rules such as those recommended by Robert Kipping.

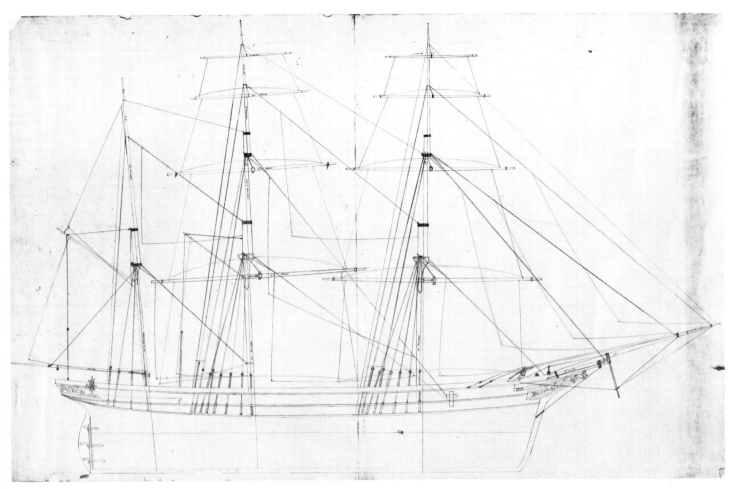

Fig 99. Mary Lord. *Sail plan reproduced from original at National Maritime Museum, Greenwich. Built 1859 at Appledore by William Clibbett with dimensions of 195ft 1½in × 22ft 4¾in × 13ft 0in and 196 tons. See text for provenance of drawing.*

Kipping was sailmaker and foreman to T & W Smith of Newcastle, builders of passenger frigates such as the *Blenheim*, and the first edition of his *Elements of Sailmaking* appeared in 1847; a second edition followed in 1851, both these having a page size of 8¾in × 5½in. Later editions appeared in a smaller size, as from 1858, and the work was so much in demand that it was in its twelfth edition by 1887. Although no foot is shown for any square sails on this plan of the *Mary Lord*, the head earing is correctly set in from the cleat. The main topmast staysail is unusually shaped and appears to have been hoisted upside down.

The *Mary Lord* had dimensions of 105ft 1½in × 22 ft 4¾in × 13ft 0in, according to the Lloyd's Register survey report, and classed 12 A1; the surveyor remarked that she 'has a raised quarterdeck 26 feet long and fifteen inches high and the frame is of English oak well square . . . '.[18] She was launched on 28 September 1859 and was owned in Liverpool by Bromham, being engaged in the South American trade. Later in life she was converted to a brigantine.

William Clibbett had begun building in about 1812 and his son in 1835; their last craft was launched in 1869 and together they produced thirty-three vessels. The following list indicates the variety in size and type which they built at this date:

LIST OF VESSELS BUILT AT APPLEDORE BY WILLIAM CLIBBETT 1850-65[19]

Date	Name	Rig	Tonnage
1853	*Devonport*	sch	160
1857	*Thomas*	sch	45
1858	*Hawk*	sch	45
1859	*Mary Lord*	bk	196
1860	*Susanna*	smack	40
1861	*Lubentia*	sch	96
1863	*Mary* (or *Mary Ann*)	bk	257
1864	*Wave*	polacca sch	65
1865	*Charles*	sch	87

Of course, barques were regularly being built of 250 tons or less at many yards in the country, and occasionally even full-rigged ships, although this was more common in the earlier part of the century. Conversely, brigs, sometimes grossed over 250 tons.

The lines plan of the barque *James Davidson* (figure 102) suggests the probable type of hull which might have been given to the *Mary Lord*, or for that matter to many small cargo ships of brig, barque, barquentine, and ship rig that were built throughout the country during the fifties and sixties. The *James Davidson* was built at Whitehaven in 1865 by Shepherd & Leech, and measured 107.1ft × 23.2ft × 14.0ft and 217 tons. The hull is deeper in proportion to length than the *Belle of Lagos* but has the moderately full, convex entrance, flattish floors and

Fig 100. The barque Woodville *of 302 tons, which was built at Arbroath in 1856, seen at Port Chalmers, New Zealand. Barques of this size commonly traded around the world in the nineteenth century. This may be an historic photograph because it is almost certainly the* Edwin Fox *against which the barque is lying, and her mainmast has just been pulled out and at the moment is hanging suspended from the crane of a third vessel lying alongside. The* Woodville *has a single topsail on the foremast but double topsails on the main.* (David Clement Collection)

partially concave run to be found in most ships of this type, and the *James Davidson* retains a square stern which was becoming less common. These lines were taken off a half-model in Whitehaven Public Library and Museum, through the courtesy of Daniel Hay, the curator.

Shepherd & Leech took over Lumley Kennedy's yard when he closed down in 1864, and the *James Davidson* was the first of seventeen vessels built in the years 1865-79. She was the only barque and was followed by brigs, brigantines, barquentines, trawlers and yachts; the sail plan of their barquentine *Chrysolite* is in figure 296 and she may well have had a similar hull-form. Joseph Shepherd had been foreman in Brocklebank's yard in the same town, and his designs probably continued some of the forms to which he had previously grown accustomed. For instance, the *James Davidson* has some similarities with Brocklebank's ship *Harold*, launched in 1849, such as the

midsection, rake of sternpost and form of after body. It is quite likely that the design for the *James Davidson* was repeated in all Shepherd & Leech's later ships with necessary modifications for changed dimensions. It was normal for shipbuilders to repeat a favoured hull-form in numerous vessels over a period of years, enlarging or contracting the hull as need arose and equipping it with a multitude of rigs. At Garmouth, James Geddie used a similar hull-form in the sixties for all his schooners, as well as for the barquentine *Union* and the barque *Florence Barclay*.

1

Fig 102. James Davidson. *Lines plan drawn from lines taken off builder's half-model in Whitehaven Public Library and Museum. Built in 1865 by Shepherd & Leech at Whitehaven with measurements of 107.1ft × 23.2ft × 14.0ft and 217 tons. Reconstruction: head, forefoot, keel below rabbet.*

2

Fig 101. A French barque of under 300 tons was the Alphonse Elisa, *built in 1864 at Nantes by Boju & Bertrand of 296 tons. She has a yard laced across the centre of each topsail known as a* baleston *and to which no braces are led; apparently it was common at Nantes.* (Nautical Photo Agency)

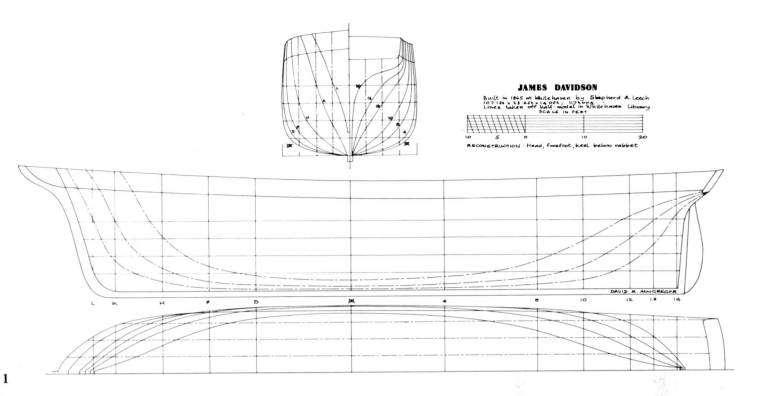

JAMES DAVIDSON
Built in 1865 at Whitehaven by Shepherd & Leech
107·16 x 22·2ft x 14·0ft; 117 tons
Lines taken off half-model in Whitehaven Library
SCALE IN FEET

RECONSTRUCTION: Head, forefoot, keel below rabbet

DAVID R. MACGREGOR

1

2

DESIGN OF SCHOONERS

It is important to realise that the rig of schooner did not imply any size of hull nor that it was an intermediate sized vessel between brigantine and ketch. There have been sufficient examples given here of conversions from one rig to another on the same hull to prove that hull size did not commence with a barquentine and reduce gradually through brigs, brigantines, schooners and ketches until it got right down to sloops. The photograph of a brigantine and a schooner lying at Saltash in 1859 (figure 105) shows two vessels similar in hull size and mast height. Or in the view looking down into Boscastle harbour (figure 310) one of the smacks is considerably bigger than the schooner; in the course of time this large smack might well have been re-rigged as a ketch or schooner.

In 1855 the term 'schooner' had not fully adopted the stricter meaning as used twenty years later, but still embraced barquentines and occasionally brigantines. In 1855 the *Illustrated London News* printed an engraving of the brigantine *Waterloo* being struck by a whale and called her a 'schooner'. Alexander Hall & Sons' account book defines the jackass barquentine *Kelpie*, the jackass barque *Ziba*, and the barquentine *John Wesley* all by the name of 'schooner'.[20] By about 1880, however, a schooner only referred to a vessel of two, three or more masts that was fore-and-aft rigged on each mast with some additional square canvas on the foremast. Whereas on the Atlantic coasts of America and Canada it was rare to find yards carried on a schooner's foremast after the sixties, the reverse was the case in Europe, so that here a schooner was automatically assumed to have a square topsail, and if not she was termed a 'fore-and-aft schooner'. Important

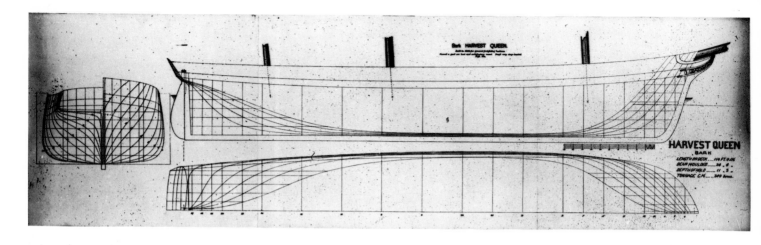

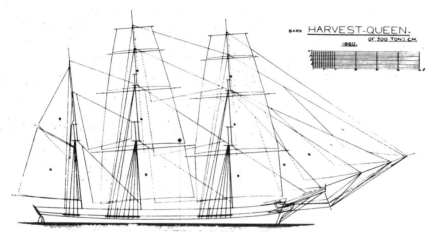

Fig 103. Harvest Queen. *Lines plan from drawing in William H Webb's* Plans of Wooden Vessels. *Built in 1860 at New York by William H Webb with measurements of 114ft 0in (on deck) × 26ft 6in (moulded) × 11ft 3in and 300 tons. Built for 'general freighting business' and 'proved a good sea boat'. She was a fairly broad vessel in relation to her length by British standards for this date.*

Fig 104. Harvest Queen. *Outline sail plan from same source as figure 103.*

exceptions to the rule of square canvas in European schooners were pilot boats and yachts.

Two basic forms of schooner hull had emerged by 1855 for British vessels of under approximately 200 tons: one was generally put into fast-sailing craft and consisted of a long convex entrance with almost vertical bow sections, and a very concave run; the other, normally intended for vessels where cargo capacity was the prime consideration, had more balanced ends, perhaps even with hollows in the entrance. Examples of the first type are the Brixham schooner *Fling* and the Cornish schooner *Rhoda Mary*; of the second type, there is the Glasson-built *Express*. Of course there are exceptions to each category. Perhaps the convex entrance and very concave run owes its origin partly to the British fast-sailing cutters of the eighteenth and early nineteenth centuries, while the hull with the more balanced ends is a scaled-down version of a brig. The cutters were principally constructed in ports along the southern coastline of England, from Land's End to

Dover, and it is not without significance that it was in the south-west area that more vessels had the hull attributable to the cutter than elsewhere in the country. The conversion of large trading smacks and barges to ketch and schooner rig inevitably assisted in perpetuating the influence of the cutter and sloop.

An examination of the plans at the Science Museum, London, shows that at Kingston-on-Spey, James Geddie was building two and three-masted vessels with sharp, well-balanced ends, and with straight floors which had a fair amount of deadrise. The sterns remained square and there was little rake to the stem; the hulls probably floated on an even keel, and the good beam and average draught made them satisfactory cargo carriers in addition to being good, weatherly ships. The *New Rambler, Lady Ann Duff, Isabella Anderson* and *Alma* were all two-masted schooners of this style built in the years 1857-61 and the barquentine *Union* of 1867 was really an enlarged and lengthened version. Geddie built his first barquentine, the *Eident*, in 1861. Two years later came the three-masted topgallant yard schooner *Chieftain* of 192 tons; neither gaff nor boom are listed for the foremast which suggests that she set staysails between the main- and foremasts, like a barquentine. Figure 107 probably represents her and shows a cross between a schooner and a barquentine. Her lines are very similar to the barquentine *Union*, but more concave in the run; the builder's plan of *Chieftain* shows the stem moved forward about 12in and finer waterlines

Fig 105. Brigantine and schooner lying at Saltash in 1858 while behind them Brunel's tubular suspension bridge has had one of the spans erected. (Museum of British Transport)

Fig 106. I was surprised to find this engraving in the Illustrated London News *of 20 August 1853 (page 155); after all, five-masted schooners usually come from the other side of the Atlantic. But the* Transit *of 1800 was a five-masted barquentine, and this drawing formed part of a submission to the Admiralty on coast defence. Briefly the idea was to be able to make use of fishermen in manning these vessels which would be of shallow draught but fitted with engines to give a speed of 10 knots and to be suitably armed. 'Each vessel to have three or five masts, according to her length, and rigged as a cutter.' The word 'schooner' is not mentioned. It was thought that this form of rig would keep the vessels more upright in strong winds and thus provide better gun-platforms. Unfortunately I trimmed the bottom off as the engraving on the reverse of ships of the line under sail was at one time considered of greater importance, so I cannot say who submitted this scheme to the Admiralty, nor what was the contemporary opinion; the right-hand margin also got trimmed!*

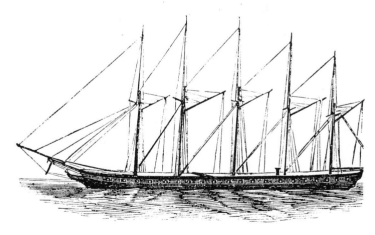

NEW COAST DEFENCE GUN-BOAT.

dotted in pencil. The plans of all these named vessels are drawn in ink at ⅜-inch and ½-inch scales; no buttock lines are projected, but waterlines and diagonals only are employed for the design and fairing. All have square sterns except the *Union* which was the first of Geddie's ships to be drawn with a round one.[21]

No models or plans appear to have survived of Alexander Hall & Sons' schooners of this period, and the spar dimensions in the cost accounts contribute no information about the hull-form. A reconstructed sail plan and a photograph of the schooner *Salamander* appear in *Fast Sailing Ships*. Between 1856 and 1875, Hall specialised in full-rigged ships and barques, and the following are his only small craft; schooners *Kitta Wake* and *Salamander* (yachts built in 1856), *Martinet* (1856), *The Oak* (1857), *Recruit* (1857), and *Elizabeth* (1872); four smacks; three brigs; one brigantine; two barquentines; and one jackass barque.

One of the characteristics of certain schooners and ketches built on the north-west coast of England was that of having what amounted to a double-ended hull with the sternpost and rudder 'outside', although the bulwarks sometimes raked aft to enclose the rudderhead. This is called an 'Irish Sea' stern and is a vestigial form of a pink stern. The billy-boys on the north-east coast had a similar arrangement. On the north-west coast it may have developed from the Mersey flats, which were sloop-rigged barges with double-ended hulls. There may also have been a derivation from the galliot as described in *Merchant Sailing Ships 1815-1850*, page 65. Appledore men disparagingly called these schooners 'Barrow flats' but

Fig 107. Early British barquentine, probably Chieftain *of 1863, as described in the text. I am grateful to George Smith of Herd & Mackenzie at Buckie for providing this picture.*

they had many advantages: they were of shallow draught, sailed on an almost even keel unlike the drag of some of the Cornish and south Devon craft, were good sea boats, could sail without ballast, and were comparatively cheap to build.[22] Plans of such a schooner, the *Millom Castle*, are given in figures 274 and 275.

The Lisslie Collection of plans at the National Maritime Museum, Greenwich, already referred to in this chapter, was formed by an Appledore shipwright and draughtsman, Henry Walter Lisslie (1859-1948), and contains hull lines of many schooners and ketches. Although names appear on many of the plans it has been possible to identify only two of them with actual vessels and several explanations offer themselves: some may represent proposed designs not carried out; others are perhaps of vessels built on speculation and christened at the launch with the builder's favourite name – *Hero, Pearl, Teazer* appear on several plans – only to be renamed later by the purchaser; again, others are given a number which suggests an actual vessel. All builders are very jealous of their designs, and Lisslie may have been obliged to give false names when copying them to avoid offence. The plans include designs from both types of hull-form outlined above, and many of them represent fine-lined vessels with little sheer and raking sternposts. As Lisslie would have been sixteen years old in 1875, it is probable that many of the plans are of ships built after this date. The lines plan of a fruit schooner appears as figure 278 in *Fast Sailing Ships*.

An example of a North Devon two-masted schooner is the *John Farley*, built in 1864 by John Johnson at East-the-Water, Bideford, and figure 109 is a photograph taken in 1951 of her half-model when in the possession of Mr Beard of Falmouth. Lines taken off this model show a

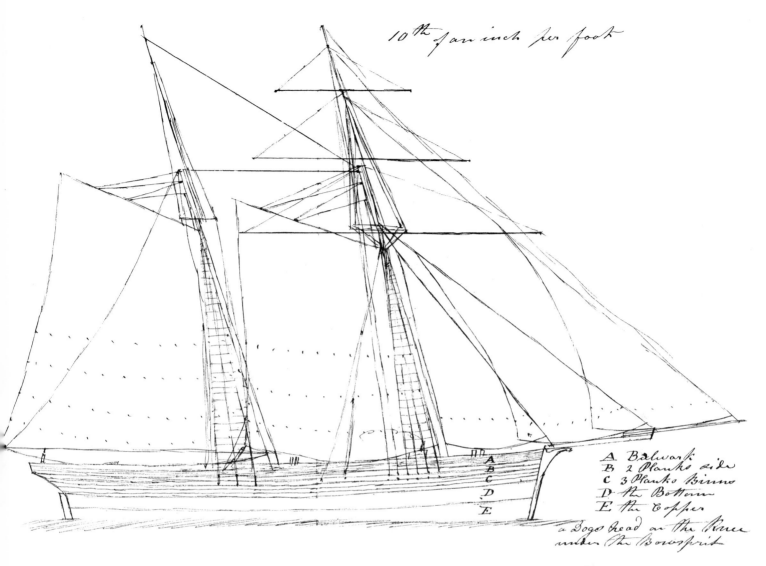

10th of an inch per foot

A *Bulwark*
B *2 Planks side*
C *3 Planks Birns*
D *the Bottom*
E *the Copper*

a Dogs head on the Knee under the Bowsprit

Fig 108. Although drawn c1840, perhaps by John Ward of Hull, the characteristics of this schooner were still much in evidence in the 1850s, and the notation of the side planking is of interest. (MacGregor Collection)

Fig 109. Half-model of the schooner John Farley *which I photographed in 1951. She was built at Bideford in 1864. (Author)*

vertical stem and fiddlehead, a convex entrance with vertical sections, considerable beam with some deadrise and slack bilges, a run formed with appreciable hollows in the waterlines, and a slightly rounded stern. Her measurements indicate her broad beam: 82.0ft × 20.2ft × 10.7ft and 108 tons, classed 12 A1

Until the end of the sixties, shipyards on the rivers Taw and Torridge were busy lengthening many of the shorter vessels of earlier years, and in this manner many smacks became converted into schooners. For instance, the *Pride*

Fig 110. The Pride of the Torridge *after being converted to a schooner in 1865 but still retaining a cutter's stem and running bowsprit. This photograph of a painting was made c1965 from a negative in the possession of Bideford Library.*

of the Torridge, which George Cox launched at Bideford in 1858 as a smack of 47 tons, was lengthened in 1865 and converted into a schooner of 78 tons; this explains why a painting of her as a schooner illustrates her with a smack's vertical stem and almost horizontal running bowsprit.[23]

It may be fairly said that the trend to build longer vessels after 1850 obtained everywhere. A report on shipbuilding in Wales in 1855 remarked that 'increased length is being given to the ordinary coasting vessels, 100 feet over all being now the length of a schooner or brig that formerly did not range more than 80 feet'.[24]

Although the tradition was for billy-boys to be clinker built, it was unusual for other trading craft; but reporting on the *Woodside* built in 1854 on the Tyne by Gaddy & Lamb, the Lloyd's Register surveyor wrote that 'this little schooner is clinker built and intended for coasting

purposes'. With a tonnage of 56 she was not all that small.[25]

Some qualifying references to the word schooner, encountered during the early fifties, are 'billy-boy schooner', 'flat-botommed schooner-rigged', and 'polacca schooner'.

Schooners built in northern European countries such as Denmark, were generally of shallower draught than British vessels if built for the Baltic and home trades, but naturally deeper if intended for Altantic or West Indies voyages. They continued to set square topsails and topgallants on the foremast, together with a flying square sail below the lower yard, and topmast and lower studdingsails were also provided. The lower studdingsail was usually four-sided with the foot shorter than the head. Although they frequently had a clipper bow, it was generally less ornate than British models, and did not have such elaborate head rails. The arrangement of headsails was often to have two from the fore crosstrees, one from a topmast stay to a point on the jibboom, and a fourth on a topgallant stay to the end of the jibboom. Main topsails were often jib-headed.

Fig 111. The Danish schooner Caroline *which was built in 1850 at Nykobing Mors. Of about 85 tons register, the photograph shows a long bowsprit but quite a short dolphin striker and a standing gaff on the foremast with the head of the foresail hooped to the gaff. (F Holm-Petersen)*

Fig 112. A Dutch schooner-rigged kof from the middle of the nineteenth century. Vessels like this were in use as coasters and traded around Europe. They had better lines for sailing than formerly and although full-ended no longer required leeboards. This one is illustrated as plate 58 in G C E Crone's Nederlandsche Jachten, Binnenschepen Visschersvaar-tuigen *(1926) (Nederlandsch Historisch Scheepvaart Museum, Amsterdam)*

Fig 113. The American two-masted schooner Henrietta Simmons *under sail in 1917. She was built in 1865 at Leesburg, New Jersey, with a tonnage of 228, and was assigned a 'full model' hull by the* American Lloyd's Register. (Peabody Museum, Salem)

In the United States, some two-masted schooners achieved enormous size and the three biggest were probably the *Robert Caldwell* of 446 old and 466 new tons, the *Walter Raleigh* of 487 old tons, and the *Langdon Gilmore* of 497 old tons. They were all built in 1856 by C C Jerolomon at Belleville, New Jersey, for carrying cotton from southern ports to New York.[26]

MATTHEW SIMPSON'S SCHOONERS AND THE *EXPRESS*

Glasson lies on the River Lune, below Lancaster, and there is an old dock here at the seaward end of the canal which up to the mid-1860s carried vessels to Preston and enabled them to by-pass the difficult navigation of the River Ribble. Matthew Simpson built fourteen schooners, some barges and pilot cutters here between 1849 and 1879, but it is not known if he launched his hulls into the dock or the river. Particulars about the ships he built are available through the kindness of William Salisbury, who in 1945 transcribed the account books, which were then in possession of Simpson's successor, Nicholson (Glasson Dock) Ltd. In 1961, the whereabouts of these books was no longer known.

William Salisbury took the lines off several of the builder's half-models, one of which has a register length of 84ft 0in and a maximum beam of 21ft 0in. This identifies the model as representing one of four very similar schooners built by Simpson, whose particulars are summarised below:

Name	Date launched	Tons net	Tons om	Dimensions	Cost per ton om	Total cost
Margaret Porter	22 Apr 1856	122.02	164	85.1ft×21.5ft ×11.5ft	£12 13 8	£2080 6 7
Gauntlet	1857	122.57	164	86.5ft×21.1ft ×11.3ft	£12 1 10	1983 7 0
Express	7 Mar 1860	119.10	164	86.5ft×21.0ft ×11.1ft	£11 8 10	1877 0 0
Kate	1861	119.22	164	86.0ft×21.3ft ×11.0ft ×11.0ft	£11 0 2	1805 19 0

The net tonnage and dimensions are taken from the builder's certificate, a copy of which is given in the cost accounts.

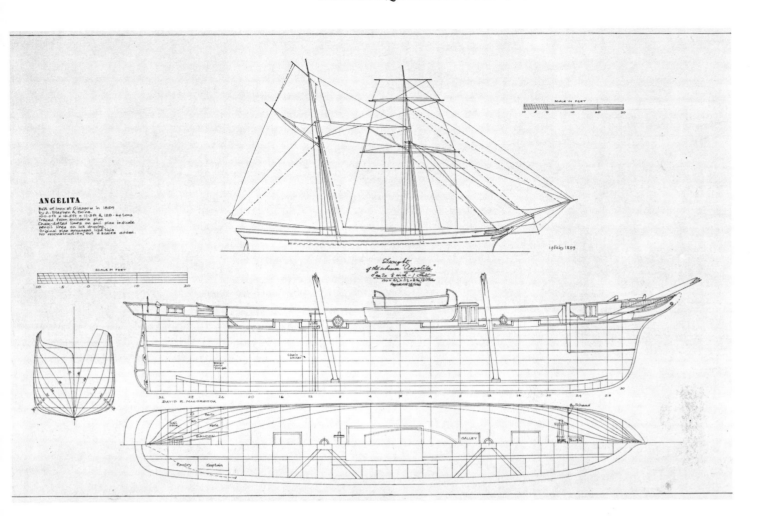

Fig 115. The Englishman *was built in 1864 with only two masts, but was given a third sometime this century. Here she is seen leaving Holyhead in 1932. (David Clement Collection)*

Fig 114. Angelita. Lines, general arrangement and sail plan redrawn from tracing made of plan when in builder's possession. Built of iron at Glasgow in 1859 by A Stephen & Sons with dimensions of 100.0ft × 16.5ft × 11.5ft and 129 tons. Reconstruction: rail and sheer omitted behind deck fittings. Some deck fittings on plan slightly out of line with corresponding ones on longitudinal section. Chain-dotted lines on sail plan represent pencil lines drawn on original and may indicate the conversion to brigantine rig which occurred later.

All were two-masted with topsail and topgallant yards, square sterns, classed 7 A1, and built for owners at Fleetwood, Barrow and Whitehaven.

The only schooner built by Matthew Simpson prior to these four was the *Valentine* of 125 tons, built in 1849. The schooners that succeeded the *Kate*, beginning with the *Englishman*, were larger vessels which were all built on speculation. By the system of book-keeping employed, all realised a loss compared with the cost price. Obviously this was not as serious as it sounds because Simpson continued building until 1879. The smallest loss was £6 in the case of *William Shepherd* (1870) and the second biggest was £291 for the *Dairy Maid* (1867); an exceptionally large loss was incurred in the last schooner built, the three-masted *Red Rose* (1879), with a loss of £1765, the sale price being £2000. Presumably Simpson made sufficient profit on his repair work to cover the losses which, with the exception of the *Red Rose*, amounted to £1,070 on seven vessels. The *Lancashire Lad* (1870) is excluded from these calculations as her account is incomplete and no costs are entered. The later group consisted of the two-masted schooners *Englishman, Result, Lancashire Lad, William Shepherd, Saxon Maid, Lord Howe,* and the three-masted schooners *Dairy Maid, Livingstone* and *Red Rose.* Some of the later group had round sterns.

Reverting to the first group of four similar schooners, the costs of two of them are summarised below:

	Margaret Porter			**Express**		
Wages	£ 416 19 0½			£ 455 15 2		
Timber	841 17 9½			689 12 0		
Masts and spars	67 12 10½			57 9 0		
Sundries	119 3 0			78 9 9		
Blacksmith's work	150 13 0			169 17 0		
Castings	12 10 0			9 6 9		
Outfit	-			129 2 0		
Surveyor's fees, insurance, carving, painting, steering wheel, launch dinner, &c.	60 0 5			53 6 3		
Blocks &c.	15 19 4			16 0 0		
			Sails	97 16 6		
Sails and rigging	222 5 2					
			Rigging	116 0 7		
Tools, augers	2 1 0			4 5 0		
	£2080 6 7			£1877 0 0		

The total given here for *Margaret Porter* is £171 4 11½ in excess of the summation of the figures listed for the various trades, but that of the *Express* is correct. In each case, the figures are copied direct from William Salisbury's transcript.

The blacksmith's work comprised all the iron work on board: hanging and lodging knees, pointers, breast hooks and staple knees – all in the hold; main sheet horse, whisker booms, knees to fife rail, 5in diameter pumps, fittings to catheads and wheel, iron straps for galley, windlass and winch handles – all on deck; binding to blocks, sheaves, sheerpoles, mast spider bands, hoops and slings to yards and masts – all aloft.

The four similar schooners whose measurements are tabulated above (the *Margaret Porter, Gauntlet, Express* and *Kate*) must have been built from the same set of moulds and it is probable that the half-model referred to would apply equally to any of these four. As there is a sail plan of the *Express* after her conversion into a three-masted schooner, it seems logical to concentrate on this particular schooner and to employ the lines from this half-model into building up a set of plans for her, and adding a typical deck layout. The result is shown in figure 117.

Fig 116. Bow of the schooner Carrie Bell *which was built by Matthew Simpson at Glasson Dock in 1862 with measurements of 95.3ft × 21.4ft × 11.3ft and 136 tons net. She must have been similar to the* Express. *Photograph by W A Sharman at Bridgwater. (MacGregor Collection)*

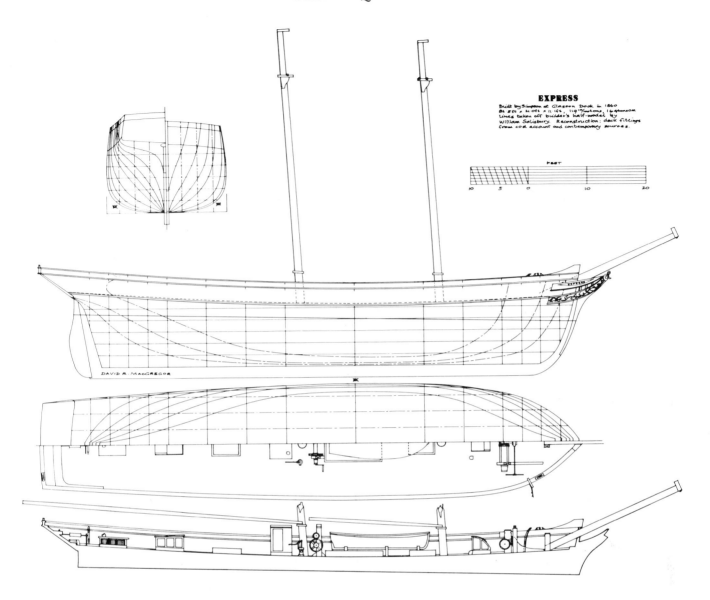

EXPRESS
Built by Simpson at Glasson Dock in 1860
86.5ft × 21.0ft × 11.1in, 119 7/100 tons, 16 guns on
Lines taken off builder's half-model by
William Salisbury. Reconstruction: deck fittings
from cost account and contemporary sources.

DAVID R. MACGREGOR

Fig 117. Express. *Lines plan and general arrangement redrawn from material supplied by William Salisbury. Built in 1860 at Glasson Dock near Lancaster by Matthew Simpson with measurements of 86.5ft × 21.0ft × 11.1ft and 119 tons net. Reconstruction: described in detail in text.*

The *Express* has a registered length which is 2ft 6in in excess of the half-model, but the 'room and space' occupied by the addition of an extra frame would account for this difference. In redrawing William Salisbury's take-off from the half-model, 2ft 6in has been added amidships to make the register length correct; the resulting length from knightheads to taffrail was confirmed by dimensions of the mast spacing which are written on the sailmaker's plan of her as a three-masted schooner. The curve of the stem and head, the deep keel, the proportion of depth to length and the drag of 1ft 9in aft are strangely reminiscent of non-English origins, such as some of the Baltimore clipper types taken into the Royal Navy. The shape of the body plan, on the other hand, does not remind one of a fast vessel but rather of a collier brig or small square-rigged ship accustomed to take the ground. The degree of drag was based on

waterlines drawn on the sailmaker's plan; also on her freeboard amidships, which in the early nineties *Lloyd's Register* stated to be 1ft 11½in. The sheer given to the hull is a compromise between the lesser sheer of the half-model and the greater one of the sail plan.

The lines of the *Express* show a hull with balanced ends which is unlike the West Country hull-forms found in schooners such as the *Fling* or *Rhoda Mary*, or the trading smack *Mary*. The *Express* has some concavity in the entrance and run up to a height of about six feet above the rabbet, but above that the waterlines are convex; the ends are fairly sharp, but the quarter-beam buttock is rather concave above the load line in the after body although fairly straight at the point of crossing and below it; the flat floors round up into very slack bilges, and the curve continues to give pronounced tumblehome. The unusually deep keel, two feet below the rabbet, is a prominent feature as is the position of the rudder, the trunking of which abuts the lower margin of the long raking counter. Although Matthew Simpson employed both square and round sterns on his vessels, the majority of British

97

schooners and ketches throughout the nineteenth century were constructed with square sterns.

The deck layout had become fairly standard by 1860 and the reconstructed arrangement is based on deck beams sided nine inches and spaced four feet apart, both of which were fairly common dimensions. Some particulars of the deck fittings are obtainable from the cost account, and the mast positions come from the sail plan. From the former we learn that she was steered with a wheel; that she had a female figurehead 3ft 6in high and carved at a cost of £3 10s by J J Venn, who carved many of Simpson's figureheads; that the stern ornament cost £1 10s, the carving of two trail boards cost 18s, and of the two name boards 21s; that the windlass had a patent purchase, as one would expect; and that she was equipped with a 17ft carvel-built and copper-fastened boat. Other deck fittings comprised a brass binnacle; a cargo winch with an unspecified amount of iron castings; 5in diameter ornamental pumps, the flanges for which are described as 'too large – guard against this in future'; iron stock anchors; iron catheads and whisker booms; and an iron main sheet horse with a solid eye.

Naturally there were variations to all deck fittings and also to the layout, and the chief stumbling block in the reconstruction of the *Express* has been the great length of the longboat – no less than 17ft. Her three sister ships had longboats measuring 16-16½ft, so her's was not a freak, but it was considered far too tight a fit to place the galley, longboat and cargo winch between the two masts; the galley has been accordingly positioned abaft the mainmast. There are sound precedents for this as a number of other two-masted schooners had the galley abaft the mainmast such as the *Amanda* and the *Katie* (built at Padstow in 1867 and 1881 respectively), the *Catherine* (built at Portmadoc in 1856), and the *Walter Ulrich* (built at Nevin, Caernarvonshire in 1875); and many of the Aberdovey schooners illustrated in D W Morgan's book, *Brief Glory*, have a similar arrangement.[27] It is a fortunate circumstance that the examples emanate from the west and north-west coasts which is where the *Express* was built and owned.

Apart from the position of the galley, the siting of the other fittings is fairly standard and their individual shape makes the only real variation. The longboat has to be between the masts to be hoisted in and out; there are the usual three hatchways; the chain locker is situated under the forecastle, and the spurling pipe leads down on the foreside of the hold bulkhead; iron catheads were beginning to make their appearance fairly widely and sometimes iron standards were fitted to the cargo winch, but this method removed the convenient rest for the fore boom on the gallows top. The great steeve of the bowsprit in *Express* has necessitated that it be housed between bitts as was once the practice, whereas a more horizontal bowsprit was tenoned into the fore side of the pawl post.

The *Express* was first owned by Kelly & Co of Whitehaven which explains why sail plans were drawn for her there. The spar dimensions in the builder's accounts are unreliable for reconstructing a spar plan, because they do not give the finished size of the spars but only the

length and diameter of the logs out of which the spars were shaped. Admittedly this can be construed as offering a maximum dimension, but sometimes two spars are listed as having been made from a single log, such as the fore boom and studdingsail yard which came from a log measuring 38ft × 7½in. The reconstructed sail plan of *Express* is partly based on the cost account for the number and types of sails and spars carried, and a thorough check and comparison of log sizes was made with the three sister ships to determine maximum dimensions. But the chief source has been the sail plan drawn after her conversion to a three-masted schooner: this has been employed to give the profile of the stem and knightheads, and also for the mast positions and lengths of all spars except the main boom and gaff, studdingsail and yard, and square sail boom. The resulting plan provides a good example of a two-masted schooner for the period 1855-75.

It has been assumed that when converted to a three-masted schooner the fore- and mainmasts were left *in situ*, and a mizzen added between the mainmast and the stern, and it is on this basis that the mast positions were determined for the two-masted rig. The close spacing of the fore- and mainmasts, and the much greater length of the main boom, are typical of schooners for this date, but the great steeve to the bowsprit is less common. After her conversion from a barquentine to a three-masted schooner, the Whitehaven-built *Chrysolite* still retained such a highly-steeved bowsprit, as the photograph in figure 297 illustrates. Perhaps it was a custom amongst certain builders of the north-west coast. The square sails were receiving less hoist but the yards were longer, as can be readily observed when comparing the *Express* with the *Victoria* of 1838 (*Merchant Sailing Ships 1815-1850*, figure 124). The spar to boom out the tack of the square sail may also be seen in the sail plan of Denny's schooner *Caledonia* (*Fast Sailing Ships*, figure 125), and greatly improved the efficiency of the square sail when running before the wind. Beginning with the *Englishman*, Matthew Simpson equipped his remaining schooners with a lower studdingsail in addition to the topmast one. All the running rigging has been reconstructed, and the cost account indicates a fair amount of chain rigging which was fitted to the following: sheets to the three square sails, topsail and topgallant tyes, topping lift, span on gaff, boom jib outhaul, peak and throat tyes, bobstay, martingale stays, and bowsprit shrouds. Some of the chain rigging is indicated on the plan. The list of sails in the cost account names the headsails, working outwards as 'stay foresail', 'standing jib', 'boom jib', and 'flying jib'. The concave foot to the stay foresail is drawn thus on the sailmaker's plan of her as a three-masted schooner.

Fig 118. Express. *Sail plan as built. Entirely reconstructed as described in text.*

Fig 119. Express. *Sail plan as converted to a three-masted schooner. Reconstructed from sailmaker's plan; see text for fuller description.*

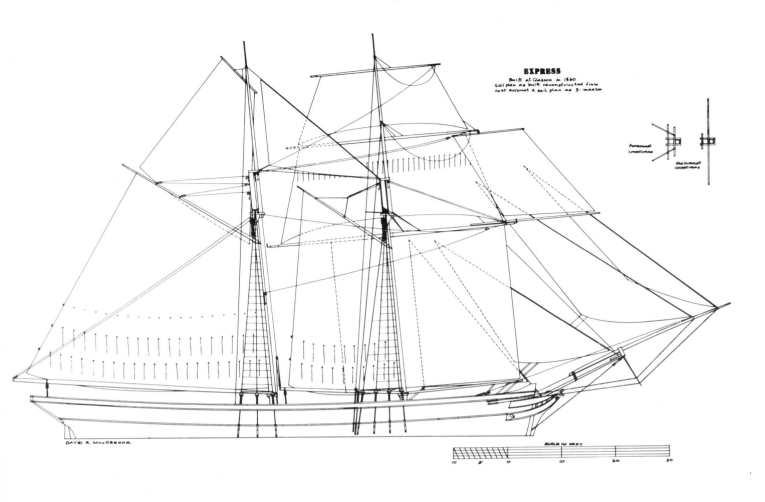

EXPRESS

Built at Glasgow in 1860
Sail plan as built reconstructed from
cost account & sail plan as 3-master

Foremast crosstrees

Mainmast crosstrees

DAVID R. MacGREGOR

SCALE IN FEET
10 5 0 10 20 30

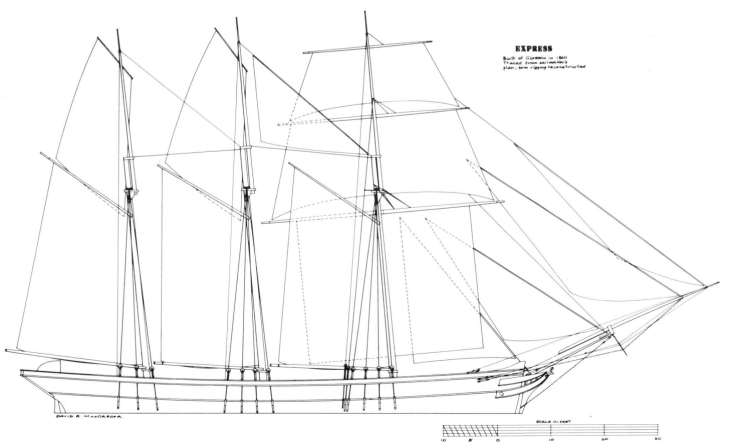

EXPRESS

Built at Glasgow in 1860
Traced from sailmaker's
plan; some rigging reconstructed

DAVID R. MacGREGOR

SCALE IN FEET
10 5 0 10 20 30

It is not known when the *Express* was given a mizzen but it was probably in the eighties. This second sail plan, figure 119, provides a valuable comparison with the two-masted rig, and the tall, narrow gaff sails completely alter the proportions of the sail plan. A chain span to each gaff is drawn on the original, but the running rigging is omitted here as it is broadly similar to the two-masted rig. The lead of the mizzen stays added to the difficulties of handling the main topsail, but if the latter had been a jib-headed sail the mizzen triatic and topmast stays could have been taken to the main topmast head and so cleared the main topsail. But the arrangement shown here in the *Express* is found in a number of other vessels, some of which are illustrated here. Another arrangement on the mizzen of a three-masted schooner or barquentine, was to fit a pair of stays from the mizzen crosstrees to the deck, one stay passing each side of the mainsail. The leeward stay could then be slacked off to prevent chafing the sail. This practice was adopted frequently prior to 1870, but later vessels abandoned it because of the work entailed in slacking off and setting up the stays.

The Whitehaven sailmaker's plan of the *Express* as a three-masted schooner has amendments to the rig superimposed, whereby she would have become a two-master again. This involved the removal of the mizzen mast completely, the shortening of the foremast's head by 1ft 3in and the fore topmast by 18ft 6in, the removal of the topgallant sail and the division of the single topsail into upper and lower sails. The old topsail yard was altered into the new upper topsail yard, and a new lower topsail yard was made. Unchanged were the square sail yard, fore boom and gaff, mainmast and main topmast, and bowsprit. The boom jib was now taken to the fore crosstrees and no flying jib was shown; the jibboom would probably have been shortened by about 6ft to comply with the altered headsails. On the mainmast, a jib-headed topsail is shown set, and the mainsail's gaff and boom are about 3ft shorter than those fitted when she was new. Unfortunately the above changes are not dated on the plan, but must have occurred late in the century, perhaps in the nineties when she was registered in Dublin.

The exact method of setting the topgallant on the *Express* is not known, but the yard was probably fitted with standing lifts and braces as it was a large sail. In some schooners there were neither lifts nor braces to the topgallant and the sail was set flying. This rig is presumably what Basil Lubbock called a 'butter-rigged schooner', and 'when the sail had to be taken in the yard was lowered down on to the topsail yard, and the sail furled in with the topsail'.[28] Lubbock added that according to Clark Russell the term 'butter-rigged' came from schooners of this type which used to trade to Holland for butter. On the other hand a 'butterman' usually referred to a clipper schooner designed to race fresh milk, butter and cheese from the Channel Islands to the London market. The photograph taken in 1859 of the Saltash Bridge under construction, figure 105, includes a brigantine and a schooner; the latter is rigged as described above; the brigantine, with bentinck boom, fore trysail

mast and gaff, has the royal yard lying close on top of the topgallant yard in the same manner as the schooner's topgallant.

THREE-MASTED SCHOONERS

Reports of schooners with three masts were becoming much more numerous in the fifties, and the Lloyd's Register surveyors were reporting on them, as the following selected instances show: at Newcastle in 1851, the Portugese *Emma* of 192 tons nm was described as 'quite a yacht'; lying at Bideford in 1854 was the first three-masted schooner ever built on Prince Edward Island, namely the *Choice* of 137 tons nm; also reported in 1854 was the narrow iron-hulled *Alma* of 190 tons nm built that year by Gourlay Bros, Dundee, for a voyage to Melbourne, with dimensions of 121.6ft × 20.0ft × 9.4ft. The three-masted *Phantom* of 210 tons, which George Steers had built at New York in 1853, was surveyed in the River Torridge in 1857, after her centreboard had been removed at Appledore. Some schooners were lengthened into three-masters as happened to the *Aurora* in 1852:

> The three-masted (formerly two-masted) schooner *Aurora* was launched on Monday evening from the building yard of Mr James Sebire [of Guernsey], where she had been hauled up to be lengthened. Her present gauge is 152 tons old measurement, 119 tons new measurement. Lengthened 24½ feet amidships, 3½ feet at the bows and at the stern, and her breadth of beam increased 3 feet. The *Aurora* came off the stocks fully rigged and was towed into the harbour of St Peter Port by the *Bolton*, Alderney steam-tug. Her appearance is very yacht-like.[29]

The *Aurora* had been built in 1838 by De Putro & Vandin in Guernsey for the fruit trade, and originally measured 58 tons. She was lengthened a second time in 1862. When first altered in 1853 she set a fore royal above a topgallant, topsail and a square foresail; jackyard topsails were carried on the main and mizzen masts.

But it was in America that the construction of three-masted schooners really got into its stride, because no less than forty-four of them measuring 300 tons and upwards were built in the decade of 1850-60.[30] They were built to compete with steamships on coasting voyages, although some of them went deepwater. They were of two kinds: either shallow draught with a big centreboard; or a deep hull. In rig they concentrated on fore-and-aft sails and abandoned square sails on the foremast, although a few carried a single yard. The masts were usually of the same height, but the mizzen gaff sail was larger than the fore or main. They set jib-headed topsails in addition to staysails from each topmast head. There were usually four headsails and the big sheer tended to give the bowsprit a high steeve. These three-masted schooners became known as 'tern schooners' or simply 'terns'.

Although three-masters had been built in America for many years, the first true tern was built in 1849 and the first similar schooner in Canada was the *Zebra* of 142 tons, built in 1859 at La Have, Nova Scotia. However, the Canadians only built two more in the sixties and it was not

Fig 120. Eckford Webb. *Sail plan photographed from original when in possession of A Stephen & Sons. Built 1855 at New York by Eckford Webb with measurements of 130ft 0in (between perpendiculars) × 29ft 8in (moulded) × 12ft 5in and 495 tons. Original drawn on thin flimsy yellow tracing paper.*

Fig 121. An English three-masted schooner had to have square sails on the fore topmast, and the Huntress *pictured here crossed topsail, topgallant and royal yards, and there are booms to set topmast and topgallant stunsails, and a square sail could have been set below the foreyard. The* Huntress *was built in 1862 at Salcombe by Vivian with measurements of 109.0ft × 23.5ft × 12.7ft and 176 tons. Here she is entering Malta.* (Fairweather Collection)

until the seventies that they really started adopting this rig.[31]

Probably the first tern to cross the Atlantic was the *Eckford Webb*, which sailed from Charleston to Queenstown in 21 days in 1855, her master reporting a maximum speed of 16 knots. She was named after her builder and was launched from his New York shipyard in April 1855 with dimensions of 137ft 0in register length, 130ft 0in between perpendiculars, 29ft 8in moulded breadth, 12ft 6in depth of hold and 495 tons. Howard I Chapelle reconstructed her lines which are reproduced in his book *Search for Speed under Sail* as plate XVI. She was a medium clipper with a shallow draught hull and a short, sharp entrance but longer run; there was little deadrise, but the floors rounded up into slack bilges with marked tumblehome. The foremast was stepped right up in the bows and the fore staysail reached to the bowsprit cap. There was no square canvas whatsoever.[32]

The *Illustrated London News* published an engraving of her, describing her as 'tern-rigged' and commenting that she only had a crew of six men, but 'each mast is supplied with a splendid winch, by the aid of which two men hoist the sails in five minutes'. She took her cargo of cotton to the Baltic. On 24 March 1856, Alexander Stephen & Sons took her on their slip at Kelvinhaugh, Glasgow, and she came off on 5 April. No comments were made on her by Alexander Stephen in his diary, other than giving the above dates, but from the fact that in 1961 I discovered her sail plan, rolled up with other drawings in their plan store, it is obvious her rig attracted considerable attention.

An attempt at copying a tern was made by the Shoreham shipbuilder James B Balley (1788-1863) who was a notable builder in the port over many years. The schooner in question was the *Wild Dayrell* which was launched on 16 August 1856 and was named after the horse which had won the Derby the previous year. In his *Ships and Mariners of Shoreham*, Henry Cheal writes that she was built on hollow water lines and 'was described as being "of Yankee three mast schooner rig", being built on a new principle, the sails in nautical phraseology being all "fore and aft"'. However, on her maiden voyage with her builder aboard, 'she rolled away all her gaffs and booms and had to put into Plymouth to refit. Mr Balley returned to Shoreham by rail!'. After being altered on Harvey's slip at Littlehampton in 1873, *Lloyd's Register* gave her rig as barque with dimensions of 121.9ft × 27.0ft × 14.3ft and 300 tons net. Prior to this year they did not list her.[33]

Another big three-masted schooner built by Balley was the *Osprey* of 1856 measuring 220 tons net; unlike the *Wild Dayrell* she carried four yards on the foremast and was considered a smart sailer. Henry Cheal writes that she cost £3164 to build and was owned by R H Penney.[34]

Contrary to what was happening in America, the size of schooners did not increase year by year because trade requirements were radically different and the regular use of square sails on the foremast remained.

Fig 122. Danish three-masted two-topsail schooner. *Sail plan traced by the author from plan loaned by F Holm-Petersen and redrawn by Paul A Roberts in ink for reproduction. Unidentified. Written across the flying jib, at right angles to the sail plan, are the words 'The Edinburg Roperie and Sail Cloath Leith'.*

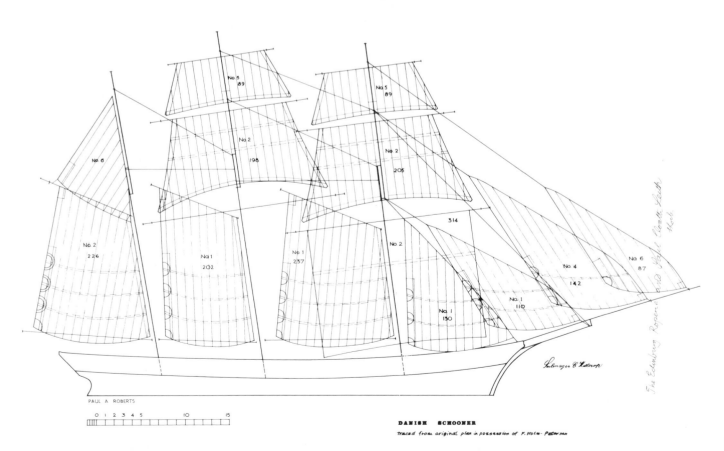

Fig 124. Kelpie. *Sail plan reconstructed from builder's spar dimensions. Built in 1855 at Aberdeen by A Hall & Sons with measurements of 94.8ft × 18.5ft × 9.2ft and 117 tons gross. Sails reconstructed from contemporary examples; plan first drawn 1965 but amended 1968 and 1984.*

Fig 123. *A photograph taken at Wisbech on 24 September 1861 by Samuel Smith includes in the foreground the three-masted schooner* Fredique *with topsail and topgallant yards on both fore- and mainmasts. The two lower yards are cockbilled and the foresail and mainsail are brailed into their respective masts, without lowering gaffs. I have so far not been able to trace this schooner and wondered if the spelling written by the photographer was correct. On the extreme right is the* Hannah & Eleanor *which was built at Sunderland in 1849; further to the left, the* Carolina *has heeled over, and ahead of the* Fredique *are the* Queen Alexandra *and the* Carey of Blyth — *both brigs.* (Wisbech Museum)

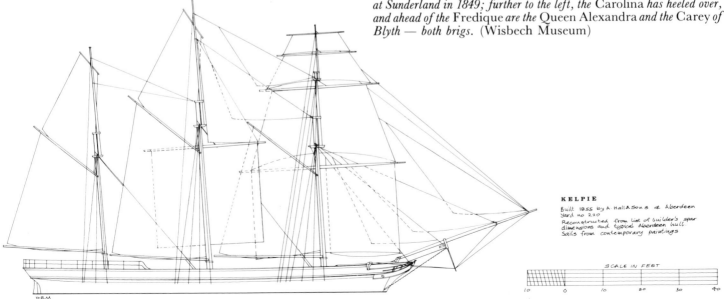

KELPIE
Built 1855 by A Hall & Sons at Aberdeen
Yard no 220
Reconstructed from list of builder's spar
dimensions and typical Aberdeen hull
Sails from contemporary paintings

SCALE IN FEET

10   0   10   20   30   40

1

2

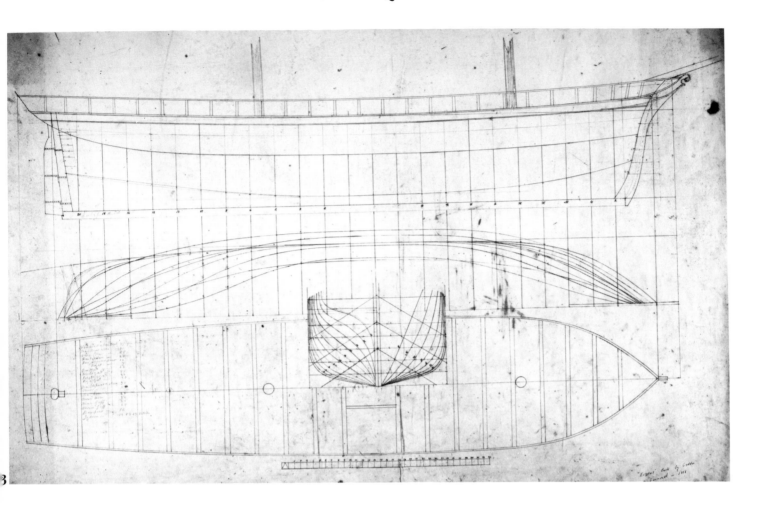

THREE-MASTED TWO-TOPSAIL SCHOONERS

North European countries occasionally employed this rig in which the main topmast was rigged with a square topsail and topgallant just as on the fore topmast. Jib-headed topsails would not have been carried, nor were any square sails set on the mizzen. A British example, the *Metero*, is described and illustrated in Chapter Six. There is a painting of the Danish schooner *Familia* (1855) of Troense in the collection of Frode Holm-Petersen who also has an undated sailmaker's plan which may be of the same schooner. In 1864 the Swedish naval architect, N C Kierkegaard, published a sail plan of a similar schooner,[35] and Hans Szymanski reproduced one of the *Anna und Meta* which was built in 1863 at Rostock.[36] A photograph taken at Wisbech in September 1861 (figure 123) obviously shows one such Scandinavian or north German schooner named *Fredique*; her two lower yards are cockbilled and she has standing gaffs on the fore- and mainmasts. She makes an interesting contrast to the British brigs. The rig was also to be seen on auxiliary steamers and warships; a few even carried a yard on the mizzen.

BARQUENTINES

Since T & J Brocklebank's *Bonanza* was launched in 1830, no evidence has been found as to the existence of the barquentine rig in the British Isles in purely sailing vessels until the appearance of the *Kelpie* in 1855. Admittedly, steamers employed this form of rig occasionally such as the paddle steamer *Forth*, which went missing in 1849. Others were rigged like the *Kelpie*, except that their foremasts were only two-piece masts. Although no hull lines of *Kelpie* have been found, the builder's spar dimensions have been employed to reconstruct the sail plan in figure 124. It may be objected that the fore gaff sail

Fig 125. A portrait of the Margaretha *which was built at Blankenese in 1851. (Dr Jurgen Meyer Collection)*

Fig 126. This picture of the Kelpie *is signed 'R.B. Spencer 1869' and so it is possible that the yard on the mainmast could have been removed. The name* Kelpie *is painted on the hull on the quarter and the hull has a round stern, raised quarterdeck and shield figurehead, all of which the barquentine of 1855 had also. But the five signal flags from the mizzen are a puzzle. There is a row of reef points on the fore staysail and fore topmast staysail; also on the main staysail. (Parker Gallery)*

Fig 127. Eident. Lines and deck beam plan photographed from plan in Science Museum, London. Built in 1861 at Kingston-on-Spey by James Geddie with measurements of 100.0ft × 23.3ft × 12.5ft and 174 tons.

is too big and the fore lower mast too long for a true barquentine, while the yard on the main makes her a cross between a barquentine and jackass barque. She could even have been rigged like the jackass barque drawn in Tyrrel E Biddle's book, in which a deep roller-reefing topsail is sheeted down to the mainyard; but Hall never specified a main topsail yard among the spar dimensions.[37] The proportions of the rig certainly owe more to a heavily-rigged three-masted schooner than to any square-rigged vessel, but the *Kelpie* nevertheless has the makings of a barquentine, with her three-piece square-rigged foremast. During the sixties the rig developed into the very attractive balance between square and fore-and-aft canvas that can be seen in the sail plans of the *Chrysolite* and the *Union*.

There can be no doubt that changes in rig were often the result of much discussion between masters and owners. For instance, Captain John Smith, a master in George Smith & Sons 'City Line' of Glasgow, recalls the dinners held during the fifties and sixties at the homes of the partners, and attended by business friends and shipmasters:

Sometimes it was very interesting to hear the different opinions how to make the best passages &c. I remember on one of these brilliant occasions Mr George [Smith] saying: 'If I was sailing a ship I would have her all fore and aft sails!' . . . I said he was right if the ship had square sails on the foremast.[38]

Unfortunately no year is allotted for this conversation but it obviously refers to the barquentine rig, yet the City Line ships continued to be masted as full-rigged ships.

On the Continent, a painting of the *Fanny* of Bremen, built in 1850, indicates a normal barquentine rig with four square sails on the foremast, which is a three-piece mast.[39] The following year at Blankenese, down river from Hamburg, the *Margaretha* was built of 152 tons. A painting of her in figure 125 does not conclusively determine whether she was a barquentine, or a schooner with four square sails, although the small drop to the topsail suggests the latter. The mizzen, which was stepped in the same position as in the *Bonanza*, was removed in 1860. In America, the barquentine *Mary Stockton* was launched in 1853 at Manitowoc on Lake Michigan and her plan was published the same year by John W Griffiths.

Fig 128. Ziba. Sail plan reconstructed from builder's spar dimensions with the assistance of James Henderson. Built 1858 at Aberdeen by A Hall & Sons; measurements in their certificate of 167.4ft × 28.4ft × 17.2ft and 465 tons net. Reconstruction: stunsail booms and yards, all sail outlines and running rigging from contemporary practice.

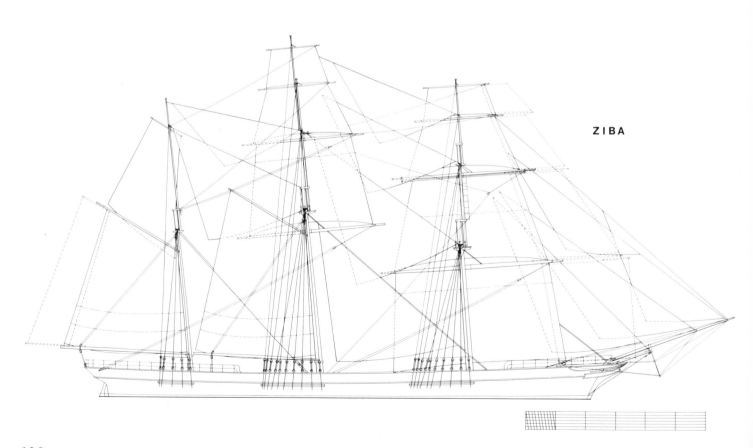

ZIBA

Barquentines continued to be built in America, and the term 'barkentine' was almost certainly first coined there at the end of the fifties, although Griffiths did not employ it in 1857 when publishing the lines and spar dimensions of such a vessel.[40] An early use of 'barkentine' appears in the log-book of the American ship *Cremorne*, covering the years 1861-63, in which an entry at Shanghai describes the *Fairy* as a 'barkentine'.[41] In Great Britain, an early use of this term occurs in Alexander Stephen's diary for 1866 where he refers on 17 January to a quotation for a 'composite 3 masted Barkentine at £15 per ton'. *Lloyd's Register* first included 'barquentine' in the 1874 register book among the list of abbreviations, but the *Mercantile Navy List* of 1876 spelled it 'barkantine'. For much of the sixties and seventies, the barquentine rig was described either as 'three-masted brigantine' – as late as 1880 the *Slyboots*, built 1868, was so described when put up for sale – or just plain 'schooner', and it is probable that the rig of many early barquentines is disguised under the latter term.

The *Kelpie* was built in 1855 by Alexander Hall & Sons for Charles Horsfall & Sons of Liverpool, who ran her in their West African trade to Gambia. She was presumably an experiment in rig aimed at beating the notoriously fickle and treacherous weather on this coast, and the single yard on the mainmast suggests that additional square canvas was provided when running with a fair wind. Studdingsails and other flying kites would have been standard equipment. As the builder only lists the spar lengths, the shapes of the sails are entirely hypothetical, particularly the square canvas on the mainmast.

The *Kelpie* measured 94.8ft × 18.5ft × 9.2ft, 108.51 tons under deck and 117.64 tons gross, and had a round stern, shield figurehead and raised quarterdeck; her builders called her a 'schooner'; perhaps we should call her a 'jackass barque'. Her total cost was £3000.

Although Inkerman Rogers has listed several early barquentines as built in the port of Bideford, later research has shown that this is incorrect: the *Mary Lord* (1859) is shown by her sail plan (figure 99) to have been a barque and Grahame Farr's examination of the Custom House registers has proved that it was the *Cazique* of 1863 which was the first Bideford-built barquentine.[42]

The next barquentine so far established as being built in the British Isles after the *Kelpie* was the *Eident*, launched at Kingston-on-Spey in 1861 by James Geddie and differing little in hull-form from his larger barquentine *Union* (1867). *Lloyd's Register* of 1863 lists the *Eident* as a 'schooner' with dimensions of 100.0ft × 23.3ft × 12.5ft and 174 tons. The builder's plan has only two masts marked on the sheer profile in the positions for a brig or brigantine, but the deck plan has two new mast positions in place of the mainmast and the spar dimensions confirm the barquentine rig. Geddie later built many fine barquentines.[43]

JACKASS BARQUES OR BARQUETTAS

A combination of the barquentine and the two-topsail schooner produces a rig which is crudely described as a 'jackass barque' but which in the Channel Islands was called a 'barquetta'. Without the mizzen it would be a 'true brigantine'. A well-known example is the China clipper *Ziba*, built in 1858, whose sail plan has been reconstructed in figure 128 from the builder's spar dimensions, and the sails added from a contemporary painting.[44] The hull is hypothetical but is representative of Alexander Hall's designs at the end of the fifties; the mast spacings are given with the spar dimensions so that the sail plan at least is accurate. The result is a very pleasing balance between square and fore-and-aft canvas, with a tall narrow area of square sails on the mainmast, and generously cut staysails between the masts; the fore topsail is of Cunningham's roller-reefing pattern but the main topsail is point reefing; the sliding gunter pole above the main truck forms a regular feature in many of Hall's ships. Her builders described her as 'schooner rigged', and gave her measurements in their certificate as 167.4ft × 28.4ft × 17.2ft, 497 tons gross and 465 under deck and net. Her total cost, equipped ready for sea, was £8909 10s 8d. No lines plan has been found for *Ziba*, so her clipper status cannot be verified, although it is probable that she was a fine-lined ship because she has a coefficient of under deck tonnage of .57.

A few examples have been found of other jackass barques of the period, such as the *Matchless* of Guernsey, built in 1859 and the *Erme*, built at Salcombe in 1863. A lithograph of the former appeared in *Fast Sailing Ships* as figure 221. Another Guernsey barquetta was said to be the *Lavinia*, but *Lloyd's Register* only lists an earlier vessel which was built in 1840 of 146 tons; of course, the 'schooner' rig attributed to her would cover a 'barquetta' in the eyes of the surveyor. Two examples of the actual use of the word 'jackass barque' have been seen in *Mitchell's Maritime Register* in the early sixties, when describing the launch of a new ship.[45]

Earlier examples of this rig were cited in *Merchant Sailing Ships 1775-1815*, page 47, and the rig appeared spasmodically throughout the century in many European countries. A provisional list of such vessels built after 1855 is given in Chapter Six.

Fig 129. A typical Danish galeeas of the mid-nineteenth century; the rigging of the square sail below the hounds was a practice sometimes adopted in Scandinavia, and here there are stunsail booms on the yard. (Maritime Museum, Kronborg)

KETCHES, SLOOPS AND BARGES

There were numerous types of local cargo-carrying craft, each with its own special features and individual design, several of which have already been described. By the fifties, the larger single-masted craft were being re-rigged as schooners or ketches, but the smaller sloops retained an unaltered rig until the end of commercial sail in the present century.

A single-masted billy-boy, the *Rival*, was described and illustrated in *Merchant Sailing Ships 1815-1850*, figure 60; a development of this rig was to shorten the main boom and step a pole mizzen with gaff sail and topsail, while still retaining the square canvas on the main. This form of ketch rig was employed in the billy-boy *Bluejacket*, as illustrated in figure 130. The material to produce this plan was generously provided by Peter Catling who measured the hulk beside Morston Creek, near Blakeney, Norfolk, in 1932 and conducted considerable research to establish

her rigging and deck layout. A plan he drew formed the basis of an article in *The Norfolk Sailor*, the journal of the Norfolk Nautical Research Society.[46]

The *Bluejacket* was built in 1860 in a yard at Walsoken, which lies downstream of Wisbech, and was carvel, not clinker, built and did not use leeboards. *Lloyd's Register* for 1863 gives measurements of 61.5ft × 16.5ft × 7.8ft and 57 tons with a class of 8 A1; the fastenings were iron bolts, and the builder's name was Henson. In later years *Lloyd's Register* gives the builder's name as Meadows. She was first owned at Boston but later at Wells and Blakeney; she usually loaded corn and farm products in Norfolk and returned with coal and general cargo, and her comparatively small draught and large beam enabled her to negotiate the shallow creeks of the north Norfolk coast.

The dimensions scaled from the plan give 63.0ft × 19.0ft × 7.0ft which show a considerable difference with the register figures; the discrepancies are partially accounted for by severe damage caused to the hull in 1887 when a truck dropped on her when she was under the coal staithes at Hartlepool, breaking her main beams and straining her keelson and bottom. In the subsequent rebuilding she might easily have opened out somewhat with a consequent decrease in depth. Her lines plan has been developed from two sections at each end, measured 3ft 3in and 6ft 6in in along the keel from heel of sternpost and forefoot, and also from a midship section. Five unevenly spaced stations render a fully accurate set of lines impossible but it is maintained that the resultant

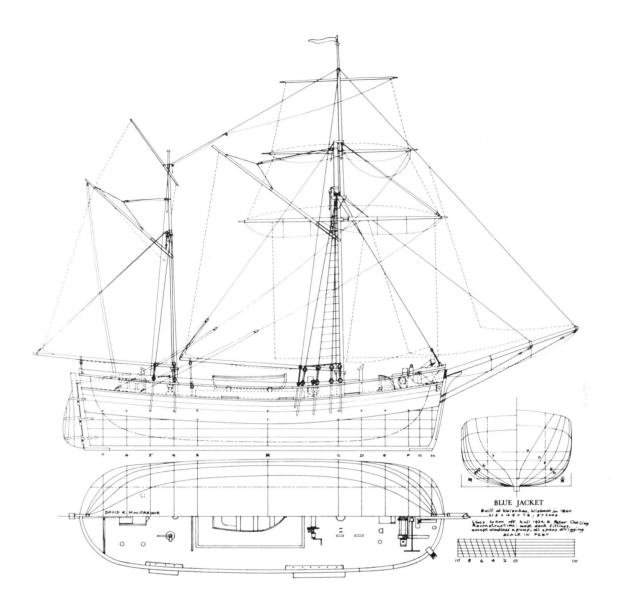

Fig 130. Bluejacket. *Lines, general arrangement and sail plan redrawn from plan provided by Peter Catling. Built in 1860 at Walsoken, Wisbech, by Meadows with measurements of 61.5ft × 16.5ft × 7.8ft and 57 tons. Reconstruction: see text.*

Fig 131. *The windlass of the billy-boy* Bluejacket *in 1935. It is a regular Armstrong patent type of the kind fitted to all coasters.* (Peter Catling Collection)

plan, developed in accordance with the hull-form of such craft as indicated in models and a few published plans, is fully typical of the billy-boy hull. The principal points of this hull-form are its full ends, flat floors and rounded bilges, almost parallel sides, round stern with an outside rudder, and big sheer. In addition, the lack of data on billy-boys makes this plan one of the most complete so far attempted.

The principal feature of the deck layout is the immense cargo hatch, reminiscent of the many barge hulls employed principally on estuary and short coastal services. Forward, the bowsprit is housed between bitts with a short pinrail above; the windlass has the usual lever arm purchase with a 7ft 6in octagonal barrel, of which the central portion has the wide teeth for the pawls to grip and

109

Fig 132. The billy-boy Bluejacket *at Blakeney Quay prior to 1885. The position of the two yards on the doubling when the sails were furled was a feature of her rig. The other vessels at the quay, from left to right, are the ketch* Mary Anne, *the lighters* Clam *and* Only Son, *the ketch* Lion, *and the stern of the* Tigris. (Peter Catling Collection)

the narrow teeth for the purchase levers; the forecastle scuttle is close abaft the windlass, and next comes a small caboose or galley which is too low for a man to enter, but which contains a small cooking range accessible through a pair of doors to a man kneeling on the deck. According to a photograph and a painting, the cargo winch is situated abaft the mainmast, and has wooden barrels like an enlarged washing mangle; but men who served aboard *Bluejacket* say that the winch was placed abaft the main hatch, between the iron horse and the mizzen, and it is conceivable that its position was altered. The main sheet block hooks on to a traveller on an iron horse, close abaft the hatch coaming; the pumps are situated just abaft the mizzen, as also is the after companionway with its sliding top; the long wooden tiller, with a dog's head carved at the

Fig 133. Here is the ketch-rigged Fanny Jane *in the River Parrett near Dunball below Bridgwater. She had been built there in 1858 and had a tonnage of 65 and was still steered with a tiller when W A Sharman took this photograph. The foresail set on a boom.* (MacGregor Collection)

end, reached sufficiently far forward for the steersman to sit on the companionway. In keels and billy-boys the tiller usually passed through the lower part of the bulwarks, but the *Bluejacket* may at one time have had the tiller mounted at a higher level so that it entered the hull above the main rail, through a gap in the wash strake. Relieving tackles were fitted to the tiller on each side.

Fig 135. *In this severe frost in January 1881 when blocks of ice were piled high on the banks of the Thames, the spritsail barge* Collingwood *was photographed on the western side of the Isle of Dogs. There were two barges of this name and the likliest was the one built at Grays in 1863 of 38 tons and owned there. The photograph shows tiller steering, a round stern, wooden stay fall blocks, a short mizzen and the topmast housed. I am grateful to Jocelyn Lukins for giving me this picture.*

Fig 134. *On board the* Fanny Jane *with the massive windlass in the foreground; on the right is the starboard anchor. Photograph by W A Sharman.*

The rigging plan has been reconstructed from excellent photographs taken in the early eighties, and before the damage of 1887 which resulted in the removal of her three yards. Like the *Rival* (figure 60 of *Merchant Sailing Ships 1815-1850*) the topsail yard hoists on the doubling with the halliards taken through a block lashed to the cap. There is a wire standing lift to the topsail yard, but the topgallant yard has no lift or footrope, and lowers close down on to the topsail yard where it is furled by the crew standing on the topsail yard's footrope. There is a traveller on the topmast through an eye of which the topgallant halliards

pass; when the yard is hoisted, the halliard holds it close to the traveller and so to the mast, but when the yard is lowered the traveller rests on the cap, and the halliards continue on down with the yard. A square sail is set from the lower yard and a topmast studdingsail was probably fitted in her early days. When the square sails were removed, she must have been somewhat under-canvassed and less weatherly on the inhospitable Norfolk coast. The photograph taken at Blakeney Quay, figure 132, gives a valuable contrast between the *Bluejacket* and a fore-and-aft ketch with a slimmer hull.

It was observed in Chapter Three of *Merchant Sailing Ships 1775-1815* that the earliest reference to a ketch which Grahame Farr had found in the Bideford and Barnstaple Custom House records was dated 1859 at Barnstaple. An examination of the Lloyd's Register survey reports for Bideford from 1851 gives the *Havelock*, built in 1858, as an earlier ketch-rigged craft. She was constructed in George Cox's yard at Bideford of 93 tons and was given a very

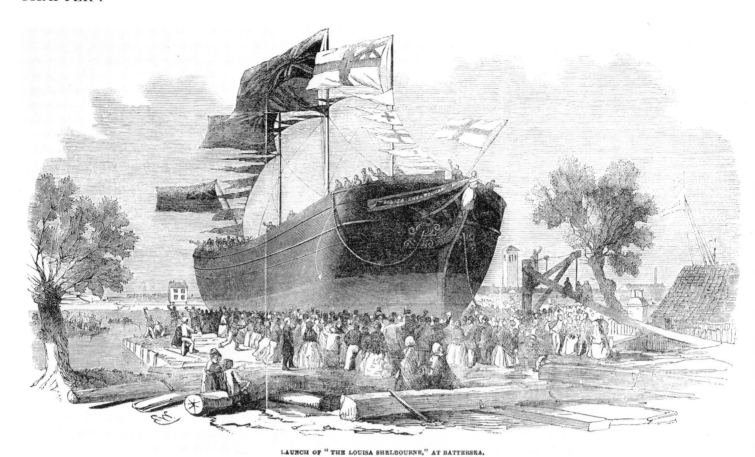

LAUNCH OF " THE LOUISA SHELBOURNE," AT BATTERSEA.

Fig 136. The Illustrated London News *in 1854 recorded the launch of the* Louisa Shelbourne *at Battersea, London. She was of 275 tons nm. (MacGregor Collection)*

large hatchway measuring 24ft long and 7ft wide, which suggests that the vessel was not intended for ocean trading but for close inshore work. In the West Country such a vessel generally went under the term of 'barge' and also that of 'smack'.

On the Severn, the trows were adopting an increasingly large area of fore-and-aft canvas by the middle of the century, and many were stepping a mizzen to give a ketch rig. Plans of a trow, the *Wave*, are given in Chapter Six.

In East Anglia, the spritsail barge was getting the swim-headed bow replaced by an upright stem, while at the stern, the transom was not so deep, thus producing a finer run. To the first barge race in 1863 and the subsequent events have always been ascribed the improved hull-form and sailing qualities of barges. Many of the participants were 'stumpies', that is to say, they carried no topmast and hence no topsail, but soon every barge was to carry them.

The construction at London of some larger barge hulls was reported by Lloyd's Register surveyors and the three following examples may be considered typical. The *Hannah and Sarah* was a 'ketch-rigged barge' built in 1853 by Buckeridge & Co at Blackfriars; she measured 78 tons nm with external dimensions of 80ft 0in × 19ft 6in × 7ft 2in and hatchways of 33ft × 9ft and 10ft × 8ft. Another was the *Advance*, built in London in 1854 by Fox & Son,

and described as a 'flat-bottomed schooner' of 107 tons with dimensions of 84ft 0in × 21ft 0in × 8ft 0in and a big hatchway measuring 30ft × 8ft; 'the sides and flat of this vessel are as a sailing barge, the ends are curved as other sailing vessels'. An accompanying sketch shows that she had a chine.[47] A much larger version was the *Louisa Shelbourne* of 275 tons nm, rigged as a barque; she was built 'on a principle similar to "Barges" with a chine amidships but ends like to a round-bottomed ship'; H Carne jnr of Lambeth built her in 1854, and her masts must have been placed on end below London Bridge.[48]

Another schooner barge was the *Stour*, built by Vaux at Harwich in 1857, and she was followed by other schooners and ketches which are often referred to as 'boomies' because the mainsail was set on a boom.[49]

5
SQUARE RIGGED SHIPS OF OVER 300 TONS 1860-1875

INTRODUCTION

The majority of square-rigged ships of over 500 tons built in Great Britain after 1865 had abandoned wood in favour of iron, although a small minority were framed in iron with external timber planking, a method already referred to and known as 'composite construction'. The history and progress of these modes of construction were recounted in some detail in *Fast Sailing Ships* Chapter Five in which I explained how steel shipbuilding was in favour for a short period in the late fifties and early sixties, but was not employed to any great extent until after 1878 when the Siemens-Martin process drastically reduced the cost of manufacture. Shipbuilders then gradually turned to the use of steel and eventually it replaced iron. But the forests of Canada and America, and those of Scandinavia, still provided timber in sufficient quantities and large enough sizes to permit the unchecked building of wooden ships in untold numbers, although in Europe, at least, iron was replacing timber for hanging and staple knees, and it was employed as diagonal trussing between the frames and the external planking. Ships constructed entirely of wood that were larger than 750 tons were rarely built in Great Britain after 1870, and an attempt will later be made to name some of them.

From the sixties onwards there is a growing mass of drawings and relevant data on square-rigged ships of all types, partly owing to the precision needed for iron and steel shipbuilding in which accurate drawings were essential, and partly owing to the rise of sophisticated shipyards in which more modern office techniques demanded the filing and cataloguing of documents. The complete sets of plans for ships built at the yards of William Denny Brothers, Alexander Stephen & Sons, and Barclay, Curle & Co, together with many partial collections from other yards bear witness to this fact, and their preservation at the National Maritime Museum, Greenwich, is a source for some satisfaction. This in turn presents the problem of evaluating the mass of documentary evidence and establishing lines of development.

JONES, QUIGGIN & CO OF LIVERPOOL AND THE *FORMBY*

This shipyard was referred to in Chapter Two; plans of the full-bodied ship *Aphrodita* which was built by Josiah Jones in 1858 appear in figure 36. William Quiggin became a partner with Jones in 1859 in the newly styled firm of Jones, Quiggin & Co. They produced a wide variety of vessels, including many paddle steamers, tugs and yachts. The sailing vessels which they built are listed below:

SAILING VESSELS BUILT BY JONES, QUIGGIN & CO 1859-1864[1]

Yard no	Date	Name	Tons om	Tons reg	Material	Rig	Total cost
69	1859	*Aconcagua*	501	498	iron	bk	£7462
110	1861	*Donietta*	134		steel	sch	£2050
111	1861	for Stewart Douglas & Co	134		iron	sch	£1769
112	1861	*San Lorenzo*	501	486	iron	bk	£8067
114	1861	*Jane Blythe*	465	486	iron	bk	£7128
115	1861	*Aminta*	1160	1132	iron	ship	£17,379
116	1861	*Oasis*	1160	1117	iron	ship	£16,533
122	1862	*Staffordshire*	1092	1173	iron	ship	£20,098
124	1862	*Seaforth*	1205	1189	iron	ship	£20,879
144	1863	*Derbyshire*	1092	1164	iron	ship	£20,763
145	1863	*Waterloo*	1205	1253	iron	ship	£21,332
147	1863	*Helen Scot*	1095	1118	iron	ship	£20,191
148	1863	*Evelyn*	1095	1179	iron	ship	£21,042
149	1863	*Victoria Cross*	630	669	iron	ship	£4587*
150	1863	*Ulcoats*	630	671	iron	ship	£12,951
151	1863	*Domitilla*	249	206	steel	sch	
152	1863	*Formby*	1271	1271	steel	ship	£24,003
153	1864	*Hecuba*	1265	1247	iron	ship	£22,693
154	1864	*Clytemnestra*	1367	1251	steel	ship	–
155	1864	*Andromeda*	1899	1876	comp	ship	–
156	1864	*Altcar*	1271	1283	steel	ship	£23,305

*This low price appears in the list

Note that the following pairs of vessels were built with similar dimensions: *Donietta* and yard no 111; *Aminta* and *Oasis*; *Staffordshire* and *Derbyshire*; *Seaforth* and *Waterloo*; *Helen Scott* and *Evelyn*; *Victoria Cross* and *Ulcoats*; *Formby* and *Altcar*. The *Andromeda* was the only vessel of composite construction and was actually the second largest such ship built in Great Britain, Alexander Hall's *Sobraon* (1866) being the largest at 2131 tons.

This list indicates the surge of shipbuilding orders at the commencement of the sixties, although after 1864 Jones, Quiggin & Co were fully occupied building steamers. In 1868 the firm's name was altered to the Liverpool Shipbuilding Co.

The *Formby*, built in 1863, is of interest not only because she was probably the first full-rigged ship to be built of steel but also because her plans were reproduced in considerable detail in Professor W J M Rankine's book on shipbuilding which was published in 1866.[2] It was unusual for a sailing ship to feature among the plans of such a work when the drawings mostly concentrated on screw and paddle steamers or on iron-clads. It is probable that many of Jones, Quiggin & Co's ships built in the years 1861-64 were similar to the *Formby* not only as regards hull-form but also in deck layout and sail plan. Many of the yard's ships had a depth of hold of 23ft 6in, and eight of them had a breadth of between 34ft and 35ft. The ships closest to *Formby* in point of dimensions are:

		Shipyard dimensions[3]	Register dimensions
1862	*Seaforth*	206.0ft × 35.0ft × 23.5ft	218.0ft × 34.8ft × 23.5ft
1863	*Waterloo*	206.0ft × 35.0ft × 23.5ft	215.0ft × 34.8ft × 23.6ft
1863	*Formby*	206.0ft × 36.0ft × 23.5ft	209.1ft × 36.0ft × 23.4ft
1864	*Altcar*	206.0ft × 36.0ft × 23.6ft	209.5ft × 36.0ft × 23.7ft

Unfortunately, shipyard dimensions often vary from the register dimensions, but they do indicate the intentions of the yard to produce a run of similar hulls from the same set of plans. Compared with the *Aphrodita* of 1858, the *Formby* had a similar breadth but is 18ft shorter and 2ft shallower. At a draught of water of 20ft 9in, the *Formby* has a loaded displacement of 2750 tons according to a table on one of her plans. Although she has the same hard bilges, wall sides and absence of deadrise to be found in *Aphrodita*, she has finer ends, a round stern and altogether a more attractive appearance.

Two of the five highly detailed plates of the *Formby* appearing Professor Rankine's book are reproduced here in figures 138 and 140. All of the plates would have been reproduced but for the fact that, in spite of examining two copies, they were creased and stained along the folds, and the plates would have had to be disbound to get them photographed. But the cross-sections do show the form to a limited extent. According to her lines plan the *Formby* would pass as a medium clipper but her flat floors and approximately 45ft of dead-flats would result in a large cargo capacity. The longitudinal section and deck plan

Fig 137. *The* Formby *might well have looked like the* Seaforth *as illustrated in this engraving from the* Illustrated London News. *Here the main skysail yard has not been crossed, and the fore and main topsails are given double rows of reef points.*

THE EAST INDIAN CLIPPER SEAFORTH. 1200 TONS. WITH STEEL MASTS AND YARDS.

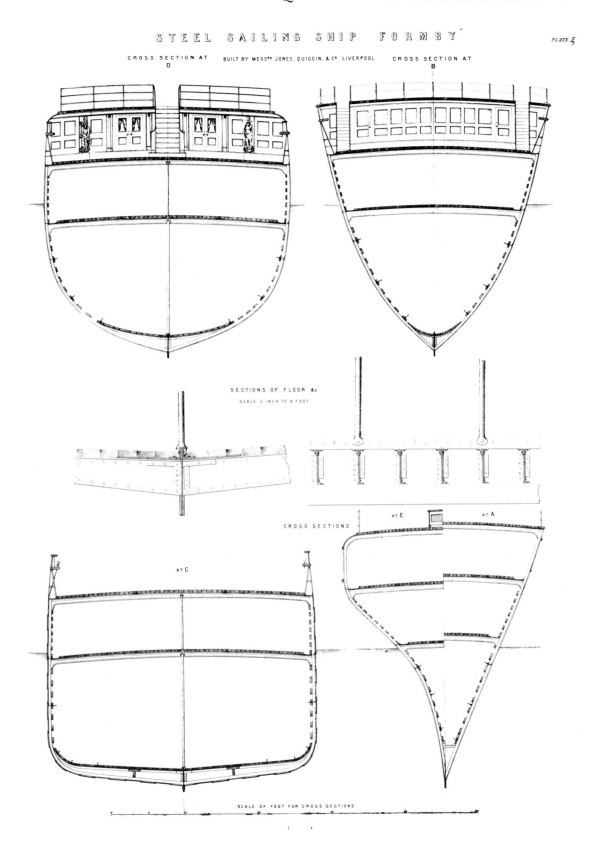

STEEL SAILING SHIP FORMBY

PLATE E/3

CROSS SECTION AT
D

BUILT BY MESSRS JONES, QUIGGIN, & CO LIVERPOOL

CROSS SECTION AT
B

SECTIONS OF FLOOR &c
SCALE ½ INCH TO A FOOT

CROSS SECTIONS

AT E   AT A

AT C

SCALE OF FEET FOR CROSS SECTIONS

Fig 138. Formby. *Cross sections and details of keel reproduced from W J M Rankine's* Shipbuilding, Theoretical and Practical *(1866) plate E/3. Built in 1863 at Liverpool by Jones, Quiggin & Co with register dimensions of 209.1ft × 36.0ft × 23.4ft and 1271 tons.*

EMERSON'S PATENT SHIP WINDLASS.

[FIG. 1.]

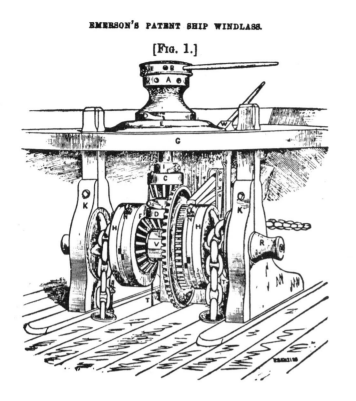

Fig 139. Drawings of the Emerson & Walker windlass of the pattern possibly fitted to the Formby *from the catalogue issued by the Emerson Ship's Windlass Co of Boston, Mass. I am grateful to Karl Kortum, Director of the San Francisco Maritime Museum for these particulars. The following description and key to the letters is best described in the words of the original catalogue. Incidentally, the letter on the deck beams below the capstan looks like a 'C' but perhaps is really a 'G'.*
DESCRIPTION OF THE WINDLASS: Figure 1, represents the windlass, as standing under the topgallant forecastle and a common capstan above. Figure 2, is a sectional side view of windlass and stopper. The same letters have reference to the same parts as in the other views. This view shows plainly how the windlass should stand when in place. A, is a common capstan working on the shaft J, of the windlass, but having no connections otherwise. B, is the lever head keyed to the shaft J. Turn the head round with the sun and the upper pawls O, catch into the pinion C, which turns the large gear on the starboard end of the windlass and gives great power. Turn the head against the sun the lower pawls O, catch into pinion D, which works small gear F, on the port end of the windlass and gives speed. The lower end of the shaft J, steps into a hole in the top of the centre piece V, the forward part of which extends sufficiently to reach the pawl bitt when the windlass is in place. The wheels which hold the chains we call wild cats; these are connected to the gears when heaving in chain by the keys N N. When paying out chain they are controlled by the friction bands H H. E, is the base of the capstan. W, is the cam which works the friction bands being connected by the rods M. P, is pawl plate firmly secured to the pawl bitt. T, is a hook which is hooked into the friction band at the top and fast to the deck at the bottom. S, is the clearing guard which prevents the chain from fouling. K, K, are the following pieces made as shown by the line on the side of the bitt; they open abaft the box, up to the top of the box; above that they open at the centre of the box.

[FIG. 2.]

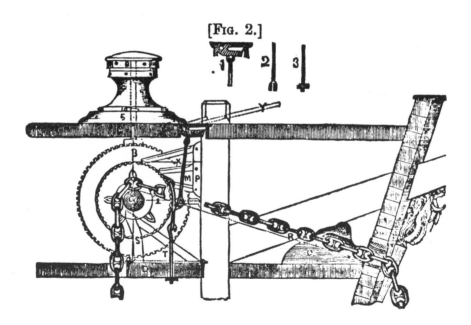

give good detail of the fittings and construction. The windlass is Emerson & Walker's patent in which the capstan spindle is fitted with a bevel pinion geared to a bevel wheel on the windlass, so that when the capstan is turned the windlass is made to revolve. But as a steam engine and donkey boiler are placed in the deckhouse, coupled to a driving shaft which projects each side with a dolly wheel at each outer end, it is likely that a driving belt could be taken to the windlass to provide an alternative source of power; also to the cargo winch and pumps if

required. The fitting of auxiliary steam power harnessed to mechanical handling gear was a new feature and permitted larger ships to be operated without increasing the crew, while simultaneously easing the labour on board. The cargo winch is placed at the forward end of the main hatch so as to be closer to the boiler. Most of Barclay, Curle & Co's plans show a similar type of auxiliary power – the first of their ships on which a steam winch has been observed is the steamer *Admiral Moorsom*, built in 1860, in which a piston and cylinder are fitted on each side of the winch. Frequently it is the steam cargo winch which provides the motive power, and this in turn is used to drive the pumps and windlass.

Other points of interest in the plans of the *Formby* are the placing of the longboat on top of the deckhouse; the wooden bitts in an all-steel hull; the booby hatch mounted on the after hatchway to give access to the 'tween decks when at sea; and the capstan beneath the three boats for such work as hoisting the upper topsail yards. Two carved figures grace the front of the poop, that to starboard being Neptune with his trident, and to port is his wife.

The sail plan shows double topsails on each mast with the foot of the upper topsail close to the lower yard; there is also a gunter pole fidded abaft the main royal mast to take a skysail yard in fine weather. No studdingsails are drawn, probably because they would have obscured other details on the plan, but the halliard blocks at the yardarms indicate that lower and topmast studdingsails were part of the quipment for the fore- and mainmasts; in addition, topgallant studdingsails would almost certainly have been carried. It may be that, as no swinging boom is shown the fore lower studdingsail was a triangular sail. The bowsprit is steeved rather steeply for a ship of this date but otherwise the sail plan forms a splendid example for a ship of the sixties. It should be noted that in the engraving the leeches of the inner jib, main royal staysail, and mizzen topgallant staysail are omitted in the gap

Fig 140. Formby. *Sail plan; reproduced from a loose plate cut from some encyclopaedia, but an examination shows it to be a faithful re-engraving of the sail plan in Rankine's work. (See figure 138.) This is a detailed sail plan of the kind rarely found in British books. The main skysail mast is a gunter pole, fidded abaft the royal mast. (MacGregor Collection)*

between the foot of one sail and the yard below. The letters and figures refer to tables carried on page 228 in the main body of Rankine's text.

The *Formby* thus forms an excellent example of the new type of iron or steel merchant ship that first appeared in the sixties in the 1000 or 1500 tons range, and which was well suited to shift large cargoes economically with a fair turn of speed. After 1864, the yard only built four more sailing vessels and all were of iron: no 241 was a barque of 490 tons; no 243 was the *British Navy* of 1198 tons built in 1869; no 246 was a ship of 1257 tons; and no 247 was the barque *Maypocho* of 751 tons built in 1869.

The late W Stewart Rees compiled a list of shipbuilders at Liverpool with the number of ships built by each and the length of time they were in business, which is tabulated below for some of the better known yards. The totals listed include sailing vessels, steamers, tugs, barges, dredgers and so forth.

LIVERPOOL SHIPBUILDERS

Years in operation	Shipyard at Liverpool	Number of ships 'as far as can be traced'
1847-1864	Cato, Miller & Co	32
1841-1865	Thomas Vernon & Son	118
1866-1975	Thomas Vernon (at Seacombe)	12
1847-1894	W H Potter & Co	177
1856-1871	Jones, Quiggin & Co (became Liverpool Shipbuilding Co in 1868)	258
1857-1894	R & J Evans	132
1864-1877	Bowdler, Chaffer & Co (at Seacombe)	118
1823-1893	T Royden & Sons	262

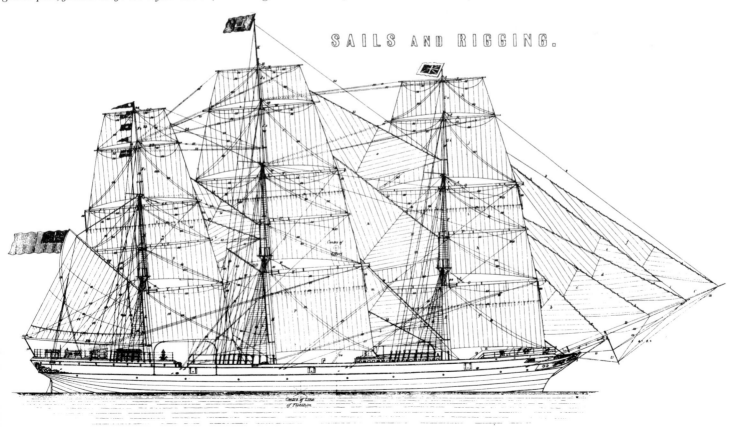

SAILS AND RIGGING.

At Birkenhead, John Laird started in business in 1829 and by 1947 had constructed over 1100 vessels. A number of iron sailing vessels were built such as the *Ellen Bates* (built 1853 of 1058 tons), *Eblana* (built 1864 of 1267 tons) and *British India*, ex-*Sorabjee Jamsetjee Jeejeebhoy* (built 1864 of 1156 tons). Many steamers at this date were fully equipped with masts and sails and so the design and construction of a pure sailing vessel was no problem. Another prominent shipbuilder at Birkenhead was G R Clover & Co who was operating during the 1860s and 1870s. Ships built in north-west England are dealt with later in this chapter.

SHIPBUILDING IN NORTHERN EUROPE

The beginnings of iron shipbuilding in Holland and Germany were outlines in Chapter One although wood shipbuilding continued for many years. Apart from sailing ship plans in museums and private collections, there are several fine examples of plans published in book form in the second half of the nineteenth century. Industrialists in Great Britain presumably considered such illustrations of historical interest only, but the insistence of publishers on the Continent to continue to issue these works stemmed from the practical use of such illustrations and the demand which must have arisen from a shipping community in which square-rigged sailing ships continued to play an active and important role. In fact, this was really the case in Great Britain although a perusal of published works would incline a casual observed to think the opposite. Furthermore, timber construction featured prominently in books on shipbuilding published on the Continent and the plans illustrated wooden hulls for many years.

A useful portfolio of sailing ship plans drawn by N C Kierkegaard was published in 1862 at Gothenburg.[4] All rigs were represented but the plans were confined to a lines plan, with the body plan and a cross-section often on a second sheet; another sheet comprised an outline sail and standing rigging plan. Apart from the deck beams, practically no deck details were ever given except in the case of a barque of 180 lasts (a last was approximately 2 tons), for which there was a detailed longitudinal section and deck layout, as reproduced here. The full-rigged ship of 500 lasts reproduced here as figures 143, 144 and 145, is a typical example of draughtmanship and presentation. She is the largest vessel appearing in the portfolio. The lines show a fine entrance and run with no hollow except in the lower body; and in the body plan there is appreciable deadrise with firm bilges and almost vertical sides. This would have resulted in a fast hull-form with good cargo capacity. The sail plan gives the ship double topsails with fairly deep topgallant and royals; staysails between the masts are included, but there are no studdingsails although they would undoubtedly have been carried. The sail plan of a smaller full-rigged ship of 345 lasts does have studdingsails on the foremast; she also has double topsails although the year 1862 is an early one

Fig 141 An example of an iron ship built by Clover of Birkenhead is the Bacchus, *here seen partially dismasted which was a common sight in the days of sail. She was built in 1867 with a length of 216ft and a tonnage of 1250 net.* (MacGregor Collection)

to have double topsails actually drawn on a published plan.

By contrast, both the three-masted barques in this portfolio have single topsails only; the barque of 230 lasts (about 460 tons) is more full-bodied with a short sharp entrance, maximum beam kept well forward, and a longer run. The other barque is of only 180 lasts but has a finer hull-form that more closely resembles the two full-rigged ships.

A fairly common practice on the Continent, rarely found in the British Isles, was to give vessels a flush deck from stem to stern and to erect a big deckhouse aft on the main deck. The mizzen mast passed through this house but the deck between the sides of the house and the bulwarks was not raised. In Great Britain, a deckhouse was certainly built on the main deck aft, but it was nearly always placed astern of the mizzen; in addition, the deck at its sides was usually raised one or two feet above main deck level. Barclay, Curle's small iron barque *Orange Grove* was, however, an exception to this as her plan in figure 170 proves.

At the bows, Kierkegaard's ship in figure 143 has a stem that follows the line of the cutwater in much the same way as in the Aberdeen clippers and there is no head knee nor trail boards, but the figurehead is stepped on the head of the stem. This was becoming standard practice in American ships and provided a very clear-cut profile, if a trifle bare by British standards. By contrast, Kierkegaard's barque of 230 lasts does have a head knee and trail boards, which gives her a different appearance.

Similar in hull-form to the ships of 500 and 345 lasts is a lines plan in the Mariners' Museum at Newport News of the ship *Caroline*, built at Apenrade, which G Hillmann drew. There is no date on his plan, but most of his drawings were made in Copenhagen or Liverpool in 1861 or 1862. A length on the waterline between perpendiculars is given as '141'-7" [sic] and breadth '30'-"'[sic].[5]

In France, free trade was introduced in 1866 when the protective laws which restricted the carriage of cargoes by non-French ships were removed. But whereas a great international upsurge in trade assisted Great Britain

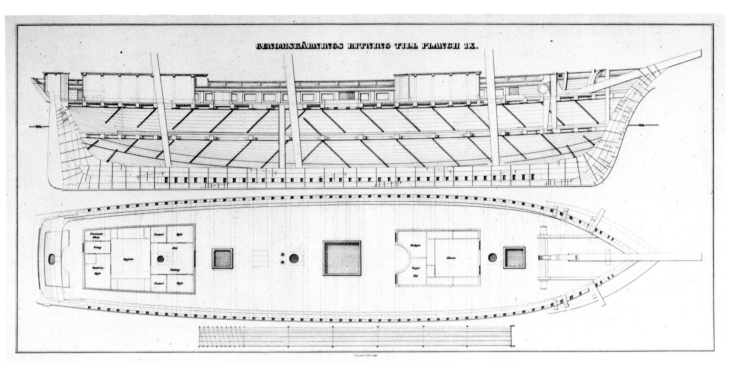

Fig 142. Barque of 180 Lasts (approx 360 tons). *Longitudinal section and deck plan reproduced from* Plancher till Praktisk Skeppsbyggnaskonst *by N C Kierkegaard (Gothenburg 1864).*

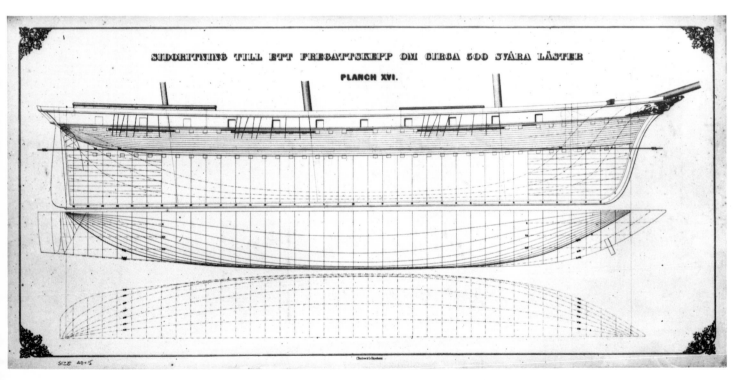

Fig 143. Full Rigged Ship of 500 Lasts (approx 1000 tons). *Lines plan including sheer elevation reproduced from book of plates by Kierkegaard as named in figure 142. To judge by the ports, she was flush-decked with a small deck abaft the house.*

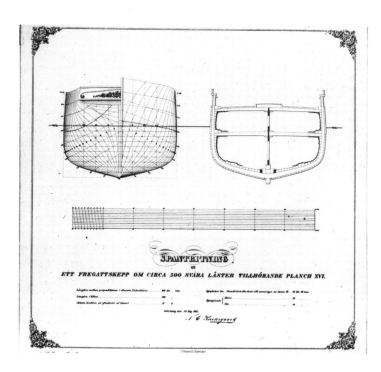

Fig 144. Ship of 500 Lasts. *Body plan and midship section of ship in figure 143 drawn on a separate plate.*

Fig 145. Ship of 500 Lasts. *Sail and standing rigging plan of ship in figure 143. Although the thickness of the yards is drawn, there is only a centre line for the masts, bowsprit, boom and gaff.*

Fig 146. *The after deck and deckhouse of the Argo of Fredrikstad which W A Sharman photographed at Bristol in 1911. She was built at Bergen in 1868 with a tonnage of 584. The arrangement aft may have been similar to the ship in figure 143.* (David Clement Collection)

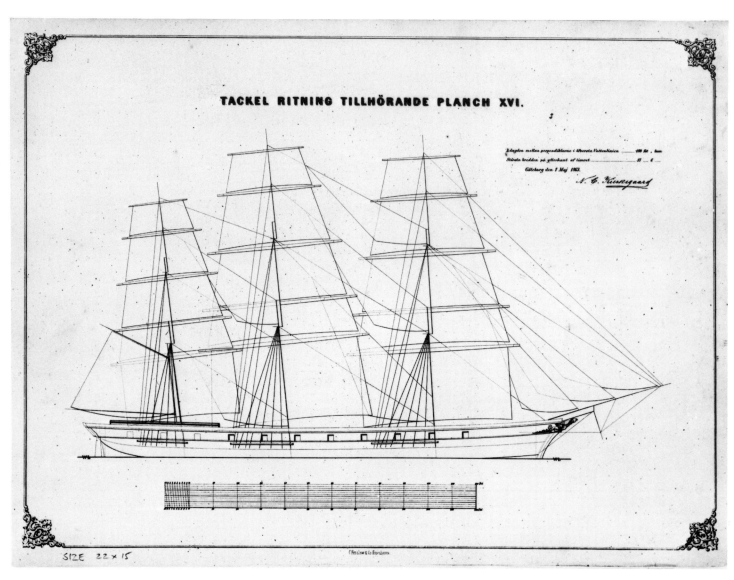

Fig 147. The bow view of the Impi illustrates a wooden hull with doubling, and upper and lower timber ports; also the trail boards and brackets. This barque was built at Brahestad, Gulf of Bothnia, Finland, by E Klubb in 1868; Bureau Veritas (1884) gives her measurements as 43.6m × 10.4m × 6.24m and 637 tons. Photograph by George Gjersoe. (David Clement Collection)

Fig 148. A scene off the harbour mouth at Granville: on the left is the Charles *of Granville with her 'baleston' topsails. She was built at this port in 1871 with a tonnage of 596.* (MacGregor Collection)

when she repealed her Navigation Laws in 1849, the same was not true in the France of 1866; her shipping industry therefore languished until a law of 1881 brought about the first of the 'bounty' subsidies which rejuvenated the industry. A cursory glance through the pages of the *Liverpool Underwriters [Red] Register* of 1873 lists the names of some French shipyards that were building iron and composite vessels. Nantes had such yards as E Gouin & Co who built the iron barques *Misti* (1869 of 432 tons) and *Uranie* (1865 of 409 tons); also that of T Dubigeon and P Jollet & Babin. At Bordeaux, L Armin had built composite vessels in the 1850s such as the *Panama* of 527 tons and the *Reine du Monde* of 941 tons. Iron construction was therefore still in its infancy.

At Bremerhaven, the shipyard of R C Rickmers was continuing to build in wood for itself and for others and in 1852 had employed 300 men in the yard. The first ship of over 1000 tons was the *Matilda Wattenbach* of 1575 tons gross, launched in 1855 for London owners. With orders constantly being received, it was found that accommodation was too limited and new premises were obtained in 1857 at Geestemünde. Here the first full-rigged ship built for the firm's own account was launched in 1859, named *Willy* of 855 tons. During the 1850s, eighteen vessels had been constructed for various owners, of which eleven were full-rigged ships, and a further seven sailing vessels were built up to the end of 1865. Thereafter a change of policy decreed that all construction was to be for the firm's own

fleet and 1869 was the only year at this period in which a new vessel was not launched. Six full-rigged ships were built in the ten years after 1865, but the other vessels were barques, with the exception of the barquentine *Laurita* of 1868. Excluding her, all the ships had the word 'Rickmers' in their name. The yard did not launch its first iron ship until 1890 and the first steamer came about the same time.[6]

Dreyer's yard at Altona on the Elbe, below Hamburg, built a number of fine-lined ships in the fifties and early sixties, but all in wood.

The first big iron ship built in Germany was the *Deutschland*, built by the Hamburg yard of Reiherstieg which specialised in iron shipbuilding. This barque was launched in 1858 with a tonnage of 838 net and dimensions of 176.9ft × 32.3ft × 20.4ft. Between and including the years 1858-75 this yard built 22 iron sailing ships, as well as many other classes of vessels. The only rigs employed were barques or ships, and the net tonnage never exceeded 1000 until the *Melpomene* of 1876. Three other shipyards launched their first iron ships in 1875: the Flensburg shipyards produced the *Doris Brodersen* of 647 tons; the Weser Shipbuilding Co of Bremen built the *Wilhelmine* of 842 tons; and H F Ulrichs of Bremen-Vegesack built the *Capella* of 915 tons. Smaller sized iron vessels had been constructed during this time at other yards.[7]

In Holland, iron and composite construction was

carried on throughout the sixties and many other ships were built on clipper lines. The ships constructed at the end of the 1860s and in the next decade are shown by their plans to have flat floors but a long entrance and run. Of these, the *Industrie* of 1846 tons, built in 1872, was probably the largest. Her dimensions of 228.9ft × 42.9ft × 24.1ft show her to have been exceptionally broad for her length.

In *Ships and Shipyards*, Olof Hasslöf quoted Lieut Toll's remarks on returning to Sweden in 1853 after studying shipbuilding in America, France and England:

> At the private shipyards in America, and occasionally in England as well, ships are not built from plans but from models . . . It is therefore not without difficulty that drawings can be obtained, as these . . . have to be made from measurements of the models; and the difficulties are increased by the desire to keep all such matters a closely guarded secret.[8]

Fig 149. The reason for the lack of upper yards is not known — perhaps in her old age the Astronom *had been cut down; in any case she is heeling over with this quartering wind. Her poop stretches to the mainmast which suggests she was intended to carry passengers. Owned at Bremen in 1881, she had been built at Burg on the island of Fehmarn, north of Lubeck, by Bosse in 1863 with dimensions of 153.0ft × 33.0ft × 21.5ft and a tonnage of 879.* (Nautical Photo Agency)

The use of models produces great difficulty for the researcher today as the names were usually not inscribed clearly on them and many were burned as firewood or else given away. General arrangement plans of Scandinavian wooden ships are also rare, as Kierkegaard demonstrated, although sail plans are more common as the sailmaker required diagrams for his work. Such comments apply to all yards specialising in wooden shipbuilding.

ALEXANDER STEPHEN & SONS OF GLASGOW AND DUNDEE

During the fifties there had been changes in the management of this yard: Alexander senior (1795-1875) handed over his entire interest in the yard at Kelvinhaugh to his sons Alexander (1832-1899) and James who became partners with equal shares as from 1 September 1857; but James left the business some eighteen months later, and Alexander assumed complete control as from 27 April 1859. His younger brother John (1835-1917) then joined the Glasgow yard, being paid a salary until the end of December 1860, when he became a partner with a quarter interest, three-quarters being retained by Alexander.[9] At

This Photograph of the Bremen Ship 'Nordstern', upwards of 1000 Tons Register, under repair in the New Camber Dry Dock at Portsmouth, in February, 1864, being the largest Foreign Ship Docked, is presented to His Worship The Mayor by L A Van Den Bergh & Son, Consuls, Merchants, and Ship Brokers, Portsmouth and Southampton.

Length of Deck from Cutwater to Head, 340 ft. 3 in. ; on blocks, 327 ft. 9 in. ; depth, 29 feet ; width 50 feet ; depth of water over blocks, ordinary spring tides, 17 to 18 ft.

Fig 150. The Bremen ship Nordstern *in drydock at the Camber, Portsmouth, in February 1864. The rubber stamp in the centre reads: 'Poaté & Co, Photographic Institute, Porstmouth'. There are stunsail boom irons under the fore upper topsail and main topgallant yards. It is interesting to see the double topsail yards as early as 1864. (MacGregor Collection)*

Fig 151. Helios I. *Outline sail and standing rigging plan reproduced from* Die Grossen Segelschiffe *by W Laas (Berlin 1908) figure 22. This work gives date of build as 1866, but* Bureau Veritas *for 1871 supplies the following data: Helios [I omitted] built 1865 at Hamburg by J C Godeffroy & Son; 735 tons; built of iron with one deck and orlop beams. Dimensions according to Laas: 50.29m × 9.94m × 6.49m.*

Dundee, Alexander senior and his eldest son William (1826-1894) had shared the business equally as from November 1856. William played an increasingly important managerial role and assumed complete control two years before his father's death which, in 1875, really marked the end of a shipbuilding era. In Glasgow, as the lease of the Kelvinhaugh yard was due to expire in 1871, the Linthouse estate was purchased in 1868 and the first vessel launched from the new yard was the steamer *Glendarroch* which took to the water in 1870.

The two exemplary histories of the firm describe many of the ships in some detail in the text and then proceed to list all the ships constructed by them over a period of more than one hundred years, giving name, yard number, dimensions, tonnage, owner and date built. It is a great pity that most histories of other shipbuilders do not include such useful material.[10]

The plans produced by Alexander Stephen & Sons of Glasgow are now deposited in the National Maritime Museum, Greenwich, but comments are based on examinations made of them when still in the possession of the builders. A century ago, only a few drawings were needed to delineate a ship, and Stephen's frequent practice for a sailing vessel was to have a large sheet of cartridge paper on which were placed the longitudinal section, deck plan and half-breadth plan, one under the other, and to the left were the body plan, midship section and displacement scale. The midship section was usually drawn at a scale of $\frac{1}{2}$-inch to 1 foot, and all the other plans at $\frac{1}{4}$-inch scale. In the case of *Mofussilite*, the longitudinal section had all the timber ceiling lined in and tinted different colours to indicate the type of wood used, but this was exceptional. Sometimes the deck planking was drawn, but often it was omitted to allow the framing to show more clearly. There were few sizes or notes to spoil the appearance of the tinted plans but additional drawings, traced in ink on to yellow tracing paper, now

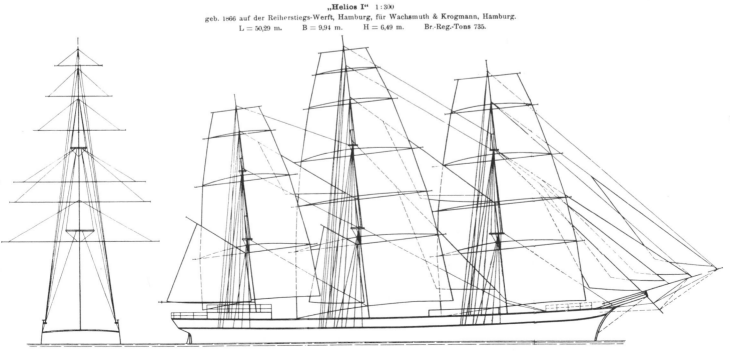

„Helios I" 1:300
geb. 1866 auf der Reiherstiegs-Werft, Hamburg, für Wachsmuth & Krogmann, Hamburg.
L = 50,29 m.   B = 9,94 m.   H = 6,49 m.   Br.-Reg.-Tons 735.

Fig 152. The German barque Maria *of Papenburg follows a two-masted schooner into Boston Harbour past Castle Island. The* Maria *was built in 1875 at La-Grana or La Grane and was of 319 tons; the after house is surrounded by a raised quarterdeck, and there is another deckhouse abaft the foremast. (Peabody Museum, Salem)*

Fig 153. This was copied from a postcard and has been identified as the Norwegian barque Ocean *of 490 tons which was built in 1861. The Nautical Photo Agency also issued this picture. (MacGregor Collection)*

Fig 154. The white-hulled Condor *was built at Apenrade in 1861 by J Paulsen and had a tonnage of 370. She was owned in Hamburg in the early 1870s. (Maritime Museum, Kronborg)*

Fig 155. In the breakers near St Michael's Mount, Penzance, Cornwall, the Norwegian barque Saluto is being driven ashore in 1911. This was all too common a sight in the days of sail when wrecks were counted by the score. The Saluto was built in 1867 at Nantes by T Dubigeon and was at first named Minna-Cords; tonnage was 733 net. (MacGregor Collection)

Fig 156. Starboard quarter of the Corona showing the stern windows, carving, and the booms for the spanker sheet. The latter was an old style arrangement and surprising to find on a full-rigged ship constructed in 1866. A Stephen & Sons of Dundee were the builders and she was of composite construction and registered 1202 tons gross. (David Clement Collection)

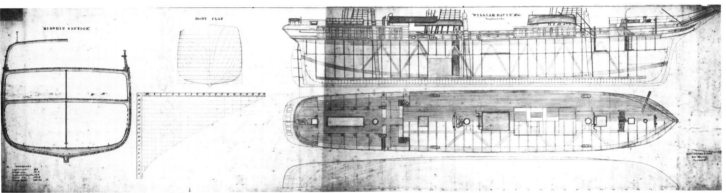

Fig 157. Kappa. *Sail plan photographed from original when in possession of the builders, A Stephen & Sons. Built of composite construction in 1865 at Glasgow with measurements of 156.3ft × 27.2ft × 17.3ft and 516 tons net.*

Fig 158. William Davie. *Lines, general arrangement and construction plans photographed from original when in possession of the builders, A Stephen & Sons. Built of composite construction at Glasgow in 1866 with measurements of 187.0ft × 31.6ft × 19.3ft and 841 tons net.*

Fig 159. *Parts of a 'Common Wooden Windlass' or an 'Armstrong patent' as it was usually termed. At the top left is the chain stopper; below it the two hand levers; and then a complete sketch of the windlass; on the right is a cross-section. (8) is the cross-head; (7) is the strong-back connecting the carrick bitts (2) on each side. The pawls (10) engage the teeth of the 'pawl rim' (11) and the shoes (not shown) at the bottom of each purchase rod (9) engage the teeth of the 'purchase rims' (12). From plate 70 in* Illustrated Marine Encyclopedia *by Capt H Paasch (1890).*

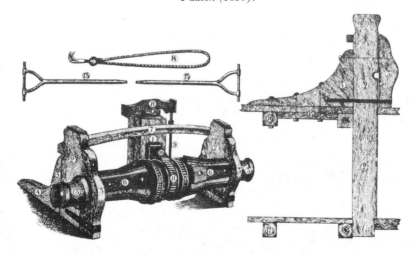

fragile with age, must have assisted with alterations or formed the means of passing drawings down to the machine shops. Occasionally, drawings on tracing linen are to be found amongst the plans, with the ship drawn in ink and copious notes added in pencil.

The sail plans were often very plain, consisting only of spars, sail outlines and standing rigging. For the 1860s, that of *William Davie* (1866) was by far the most elaborate (figure 160) and the usual practice was a compromise of the two extremes. A shell expansion plan was sometimes produced but this was apparently the extent of the range, apart from occasional drawings of deck fittings. After 1870, more detail begins to appear on the plans; perhaps this can be attributed partly to the move to new premises and partly to the ever increasing need for greater detailing of steamship plans.

During the years 1860-75, Stephen's were concerned with building thoroughly reputable ships of both iron and composite construction, and although they produced a variety of rigs, which adds greatly to the interest in this yard, none of their designs were ever again of the extreme clipper form to be found in the *Storm Cloud*. Indeed it is probably safe to state that none of their designs during the period now described were anything sharper than medium clippers. Admittedly, *Eliza Shaw* (1863) and *Mofussilite* (1864) did have greater deadrise than the

majority of their vessels, and as the former was built for the tea trade she was given a sharper entrance and run. *Gossamer* (1864) was also built for the tea trade as a medium clipper, but with flatter floors and fuller ends than *Eliza Shaw*; her maiden passage home from Shanghai against the monsoon occupied 145 days in 1865. The iron and composite ships and barques of over 400 tons mostly followed the midship section profile to be seen in the iron barque *Edmund Preston* (figure 16).

Killick, Martin & Co supervised the construction of *Eliza Shaw* for her owner, Charles Shaw, and she was composite built of 696 tons net with dimensions of 184.5ft × 30.7ft × 18.4ft. She had a remarkably consistent record, her first nine homeward passages being between Hankow or Shanghai and London, and the average works out as $124\frac{1}{2}$ days. All were made against the monsoon, the departure being taken between the middle of June and the middle of July, four days being deducted from the date of leaving Hankow if no time of passing Woosung is given. Freights from Hankow were £7 7s per ton in 1868 and £5 15s from Shanghai in 1865, so good profits must have been made, provided towage rates up and down the Yangtze-kiang were not excessive and no collisions or groundings occurred. In fact, none of the latter are recorded for her. Such a record was a good advertisement for her builder, which is probably why Stephen constructed about ten ships and barques for the China trade, none of which were sharper than medium clippers. The contract price for *Eliza Shaw* was £15,400 and Stephen's made a clear profit of £3300 on her construction. Her unusual after deckhouse was described

Fig 160. William Davie. *Sail plan photographed from original when in possesion of the builders, A Stephen & Sons. The plan provides more detail than do many of Stephen's sail plans and is described in the text.*

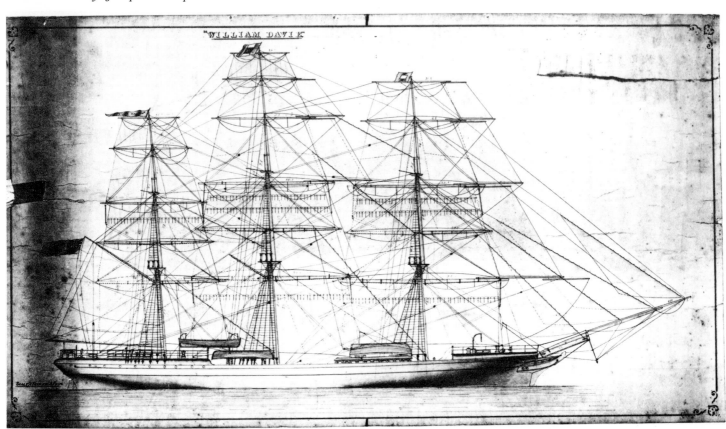

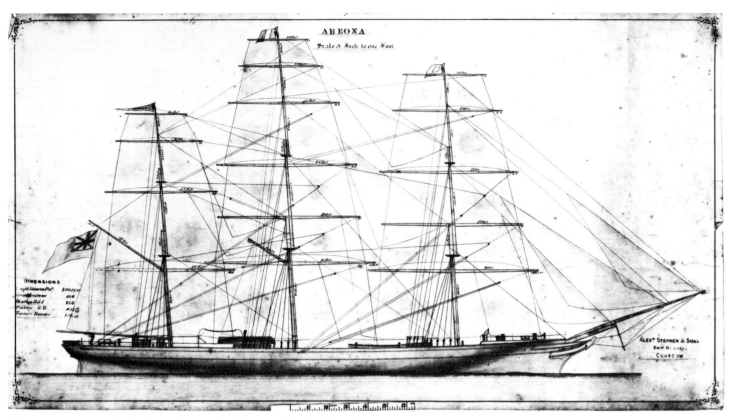

Fig 161. Abeona. Sail plan photographed from original when in possession of the builders, A Stephen & Sons. Built of iron at Glasgow in 1867 with measurements inscribed on the plan as follows: length between perpendiculars 200ft 0in; breadth extreme 33ft 0in; depth in hold 21ft 6in; tonnage BM 1853 15/94; tonnage register 979.48. This is more the standard sort of sail plan produced by the drawing office in the 1860s; the single mizzen topsail and large jib are the main differences to William Davie. The specification and inventory of Abeona are in Appendix IV.

on page 244 of *Fast Sailing Ships*; this particular arrangement was proposed by Killick, Martin & Co.[11]

Two large auxiliaries were built in the 1860s: the first was the *Sea King* which was a full-rigged ship and whose plans appeared in *Fast Sailing Ships*; the second was the *Zeta*, built in 1865 and rigged as a barque with a hoisting screw. The latter was of 734 tons gross and was built for the copper ore trade; with her engines she could go through the Straits of Magellan. She cost £13,500 excluding the copper ore trunk, condenser etc, but was converted to a sailing ship in 1874-75.

Plans of a small barque and an iron brig, both built by Stephen's, are given in Chapter Six, but an example of a typical larger full-rigged ship appears here and illustrates the composite-built ship *William Davie* which was launched in June 1866 for the New Zealand emigrant trade. Her dimensions were 187.0ft × 31.6ft × 19.3ft and 841 tons net and gross, and she was owned by the Albion Shipping Co of Glasgow. She was a medium clipper with short, sharp ends, a small amount of deadrise, rounded bilges and noticeable tumblehome. All information about the hull was contained on a single sheet 7ft 6in long and 2ft wide (figure 158). In the full-height poop are at least

ten staterooms for first class passengers, and approximately 150 emigrants were carried in the 'tween decks. The topgallant forecastle had about sixteen bunks and there was also a large deckhouse. There was no donkey boiler so that the pumps and winches were hand-operated in the conventional manner as was the Armstrong patent windlass. There is no separate plan of the poop deck, but the topgallant forecastle deck is curiously superimposed on the plan of the main deck. At this period, no buttock lines or diagonals were drawn on Stephen's plans.

The sail plan in figure 160 illustrates a typical full-rigged ship with a main skysail and double topsails. Points of interest are the double row of reef points in two of the upper topsails; a triangular lower studdingsail which was easier to handle than a square one; the small roach to the foot of the lower topsails and topgallants; and the separately fidded flying jibboom. Topgallant and royal staysails with a nock or straight luff were fairly common in ships at this date. Her fastest outward passage was one of 82 days to Dunedin in 1870 or 77 days land to land.

Stephen's sail plans usually avoided undue overlap to the square sails, although there was never a shortage of studdingsails; skysails were not a regular feature and then on the mainmast only. None of the flying kites claimed by Basil Lubbock to have been set on the *City of Hankow* are drawn on the sail plan, so they must have been the master's fancy.[12]

Most sailing ships at this date which began their name with the words 'City of' belonged to George Smith & Sons' 'City Line' out of Glasgow. In the thirties they were in the soft goods business and the sons, Robert and George, joined their father in the firm. They bought their

Fig 162 Bows of Stephen's ship City of Lahore *which was constructed of iron in 1864 for Smith's 'City Line'. The heavy whisker boom has been hauled inboard above the port cathead and the railing around the forecastle is plain and solid. Probably photographed in a New Zealand port.* (Alexander Turnbull Library, Wellington)

first ship, the *Constellation*, in 1840 and laid her on the berth for Calcutta. They soon began to order their own ships, their fifth being the first of the 'Cities' named *City of Glasgow*. This ship was ordered from Barclay, Curle in 1847, and they built many other ships for the City Line, as also did Robert Steele & Co. Alexander Stephen & Sons built their first ship for Smith in 1859: she was the *City of Lucknow* and was Smith's nineteenth vessel. She was followed from Stephen's yard by the iron full-rigged ships *City of Madras* (1859), *City of Calcutta* (1860), *City of Bombay* (1862), *City of Cashmere* (1863), *City of Lahore* (1864); then came *City of Hankow* (1869) the first built for them by Stephen's of over 1000 tons and the only one he supplied for them of composite construction; she was followed the next year by the iron *City of Sparta*, the last vessel he built for them.

Shipbuilding enquiries were dull in 1865 at Kelvinhaugh which perhaps explains why the yard built twelve schooner-rigged iron 150-ton barges for a London firm that year, to be shipped out to Bombay. In the following year, 1866, there was a monetary panic as the large discount house of Overend, Gurney & Co collapsed in May and the bank rate rose to 12 per cent. Alexander Stephen noted this in his diary and on 24 May listed other firms to fail, such as Fernie Bros and James Baines & Co of Liverpool, Gellatly, Hankey & Sewall of London. On the Clyde that November, Todd & MacGregor and A & J Inglis were working at 75 per cent capacity; but the bank rate was down to $3\frac{1}{2}$ per cent just before Christmas.

Alexander Stephen & Sons' development of composite construction was fully related in Chapter Five of *Fast Sailing Ships* as was also how the firm became the first builders to obtain a high classification for it from Lloyd's Register. Their first ship on this principle was the *John Lidgett*, launched on 29 August 1862. Their total number of composite vessels in the years 1862-76, comprised twenty-six ships and barques, one brigantine, one schooner, two steamers, and three auxiliary steamers. During the sixties the price of their iron ships gradually declined from £16 16s to £14 per ton, but composite ships were always more expensive and the prices ranged from £17 to £20 per ton. Although tonnage by builders measurements remained constantly in use when giving a verbal quotation, the tonnage used in the contract had generally, by the mid-sixties, changed to net, gross or under deck tons.[13]

Commenting on the new site for their shipyard, Captain John Smith wrote in 1908, in his book on the history of the City Line:

The Messrs Stephen bought Linthouse mansion and grounds, a mile below Govan, on the south side. The house in the centre of the ground still remains, and is little changed from the days when the wealthy occupants held their levees and dinner parties. The rooms remain as they were, and serve for counting-house, model rooms, draughtsmen's room &c, and plenty of windows look out in all directions, so that the works can be seen from the house on all sides. This yard was the only one on the Clyde in which was erected a travelling overhead railway, on which was a steam winch

that could lift engines and boilers into thirteen different ships building at the same time in the yard. When the Suez Canal was opened in 1870 [sic], and many steamers were required, the whole row of berths was filled.[14]

Fewer sailing ships were built by the firm after 1870 and none at all in 1873 although there was a big revival in 1875. In this year, five splendid sister ships were launched for David Bruce's 'Dundee Clipper Line' which brought jute direct to Dundee from Calcutta. The forerunner of this service was the *Lochee* which the Dundee yard of Alexander Stephen & Sons had built of iron in 1874, with dimensions of 264.2ft × 39.0ft × 23.4ft and 1728 tons net. The next year the Dundee yard built two iron sister ships for Bruce, the *Maulsden* and *Duntrune*, and the Glasgow yard built three sisters of similar measurements to these last, the *Airlie*, *Camperdown* and *Panmure*. The *Airlie* measured 246.3ft × 38.3ft × 22.9ft, 1578 gross and 1500 tons net. The contract price was £16 12s 6d per gross ton. The other four varied a few inches either way. Due to the great similarity in measurements it is almost certain that the two Dundee-built ships were built to the same plans as the three Glasgow vessels. The three Glasgow-built ships are shown by their plans to have been no more than medium clippers with slight deadrise and rounded bilges and not too sharp an entrance; there was a full height poop with a half-round, a topgallant forecastle and

Fig 163. Another view of City of Lahore *from the artist's viewpoint. No flying jib is painted and it would have needed a flying jibboom to set one properly. There is a deckhouse abaft the mainmast as well as the fore and there is a raised quarterdeck aft.* (Alexander Turnbull Library, Wellington)

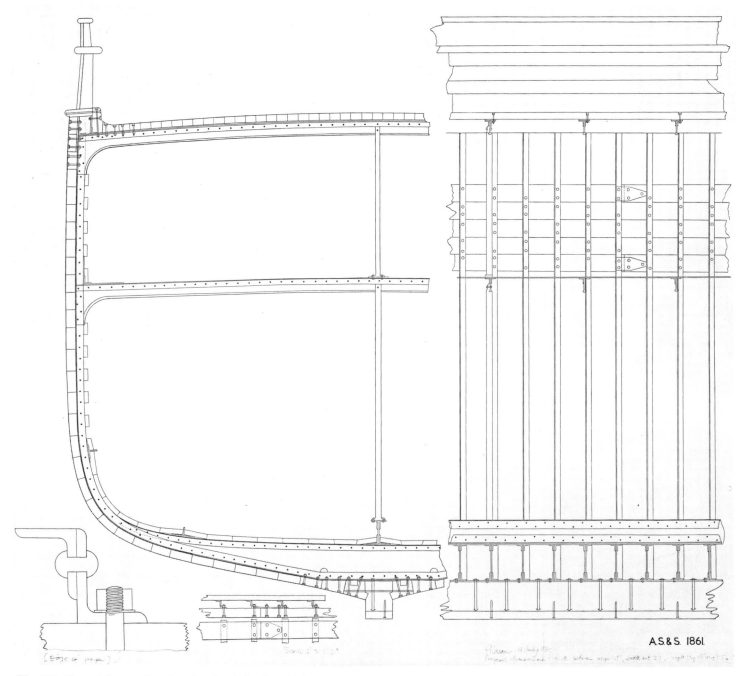

Fig 164. Traced from a drawing done by A Stephen & Sons in 1861 when experimenting with various methods of composite construction. On the left is a part cross-section and to the right is an elevation of the frames, keelson and keel with the bolts through the latter; in the bottom left is a frame and reverse frame bolted to a wooden plank, and drawn full-size on the original; to its right is a section through plank and ceiling, with an elevation below. The latter two are obviously drawn to the same scale as the plans above.

further accommodation in a large deckhouse abaft the foremast, in the after end of which was placed a steam engine to work cargo winch, pumps and windlass. No studdingsails are drawn on the sail plan and there is a skysail on the mainmast only, but this set on a gunter pole, and the legend written on it reads: 'This sail on no 180 only'; and *Airlie* was no 180. Basil Lubbock described these ships as 'good carriers and very powerful yet with a nice turn of speed, especially in strong winds'.[15]

The *Maulsden* was probably the fastest of them all, and after going out to Otago in 72 days in 1876, and to Melbourne in 79 days from Liverpool on the following voyage, she proceeded to make a record run from Greenock to Maryborough just north of Brisbane, of 70 days in 1883, 28 March to 12 May, the longest day's run being 335 miles.[16]

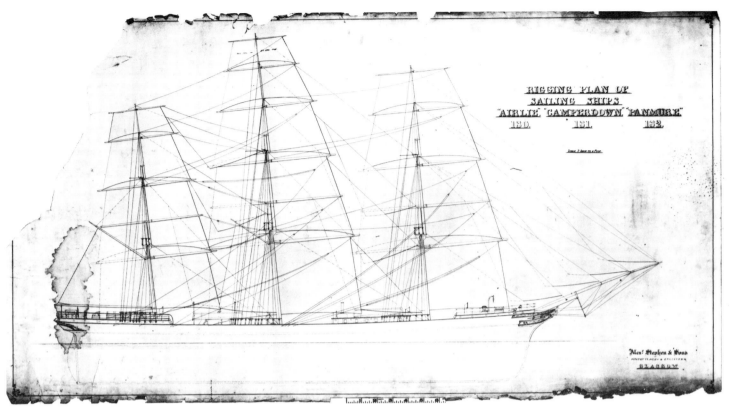

Fig 165. Airlie, Camperdown, Panmure. *Sail plan photographed from original when in possession of the builders, A Stephen & Sons. Built of iron at Glasgow in 1875; Airlie measured 246.3ft × 38.3ft × 22.9ft and 1500 tons net. As described in the text, a note on the main skysail indicates that it was only to be fitted on the Airlie.*

Fig 166. Germania, Britannia. *Longitudinal section, accommodation plan and deck layout photographed from original. Built of iron at Glasgow in 1874 by A Stephen & Sons with dimensions as listed in the text.*

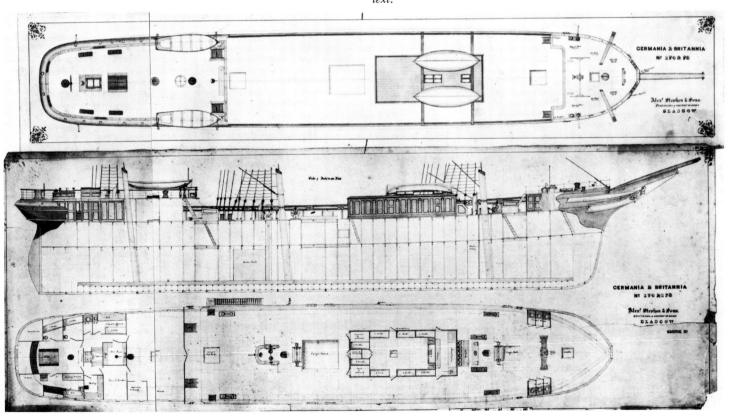

The Glasgow yard had built for a number of German owners such as R M Sloman & Co of Hamburg and D H Watjen & Co of Bremen, and in 1874 they built for the latter the barques *Germania* and *Britannia*. The shipyard plans were common to the two, although the dimensions varied slightly;

			Contract Price
Germania	175.0ft × 32.0ft × 19.6ft	870 tons iron	£16,300
Britannia	175.8ft × 31.3ft × 19.7ft	880 tons iron	£16,000

The sail plan, reproduced here in figure 167, is much more detailed than was usual with Stephen's plans and has a lot of running rigging drawn as well as the cloths of the sails. Two years later, in 1876, Stephen's yard built another barque for Watjen which was in fact their last to be built of composite construction; this was the *India*.

The opening of the Suez Canal and the impetus it gave to build steamers really stopped orders for extreme clipper ships and from then on any ship sharper than a medium clipper was a rare commodity. In some cases, sail areas were increased to make up for the fuller hulls as in the iron ships *Amana* and *Shenir* which Stephen's launched in 1875 and 1876 respectively, where a full suit of studdingsails was given to the fore- and mainmasts up to the royals, including a big square fore lower studdingsail.

Fig 167. Germania, Britannia. Sail plan photographed from original. Not many sail plans were showing stunsails by the mid-seventies but Stephen's continued them.

Fig 168: Amana. Sail and rigging plan photographed from original in 1961. Built of iron at Glasgow in 1875 by A Stephen & Sons; measurements given in text. This plan was drawn on cartridge paper which has yellowed with age, making the ink lines somewhat difficult to see clearly. The dark patches in the corners are the accumulated dust of years. Royal stunsails cannot have been too common in 1875.

Shenir was also unique in having a ringtail actually drawn on the sail plan – surely most unusual for this late date. These ships were in the 1150 to 1300 tons range with long hulls that had a small amount of deadrise and short sharp ends. Their dimensions are as follows: 1875, *Amana*, 239.2ft × 36.1ft × 21.5ft, 1299t net, 1229t under deck; 1876, *Shenir* 225.5ft × 34.8ft × 21.2ft, 1173t net, 1108t under deck.

It is worth comparing *Amana* and *Airlie* as both ships were built in the same year by the Glasgow yard. Comparing breadth and depth with length, the ratios are: *Amana* B/L 6.62 D/L 11.13; *Airlie* B/L 6.43 D/L 10.75.

The lines are somewhat similar but *Amana* is slightly finer and also narrower. I have no relevant sail areas to compare, but it appears that *Amana* has a slightly taller mainmast in relation to her length. Whether *Airlie* was fitted with studdingsails is not known. *Amana* cost £17 per ton gross to build and Stephen made a clear profit of £4600 on the contract. She was also built very quickly in only four months. From this year on, Stephen's ships became increasingly more conscious of cargo carrying requirements.

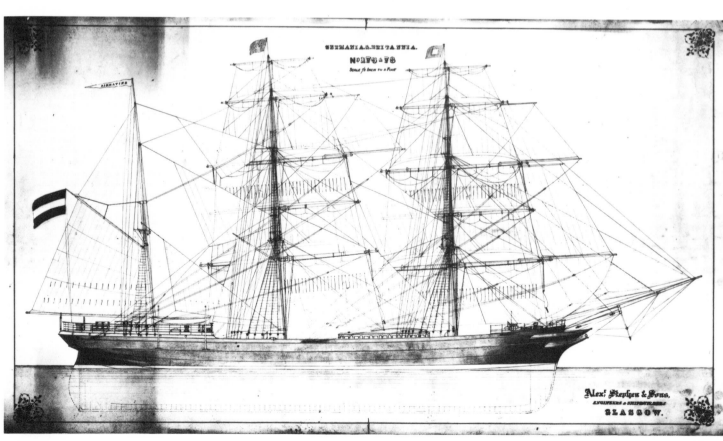

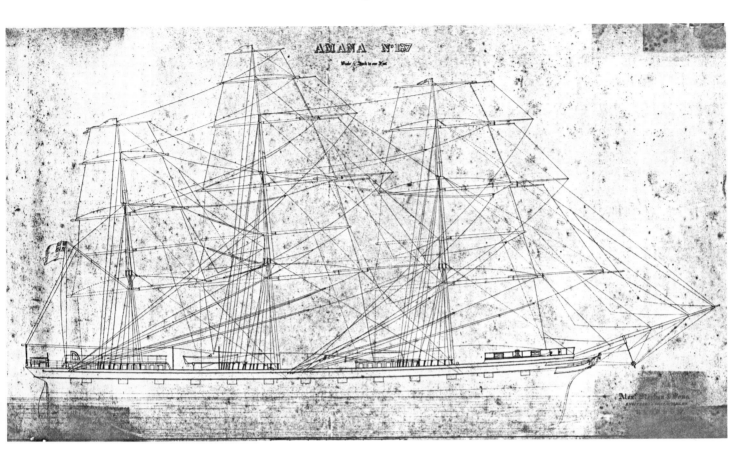

Fig 169. Amana. *Details of davits, bulwarks and deck at stern photographed from original in 1961.*

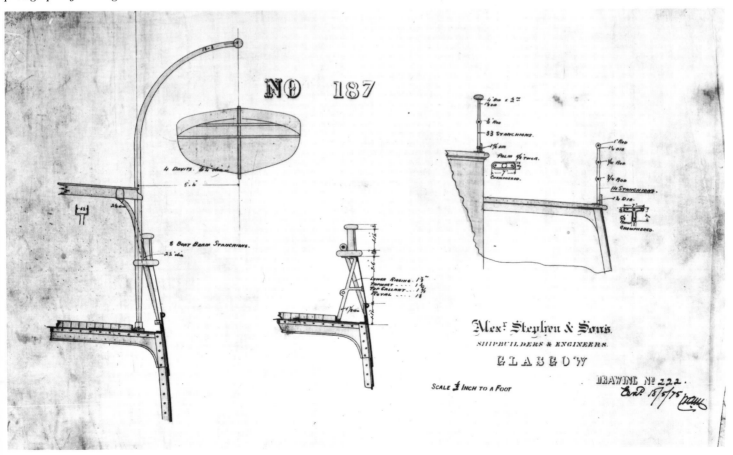

BARCLAY, CURLE & CO AND OTHER SHIPBUILDERS ON THE CLYDE

Another Clydeside yard where the majority of the plans have survived is Barclay, Curle & Co, but here the ships are more regimented in type and size, there being only one schooner before 1875 and no brigs, brigantines or barquentines. When I examined these plans in the summer of 1961, I found them to be in a bad state of repair and extremely dirty to handle. On page 179 of my book *The Tea Clippers* there is an example of one of their iron clippers (the barque *Derwent*) built to a house-style that originated in 1855 with the design of the *Shandon*. They constructed many ships for George Smith's 'City Line' and in the early fifties they were mostly of wood; their last wooden ship for Smith was the *City of York* (1859), but by that date several iron ships had already been launched.

An unusually small vessel for this yard was the *Orange Grove*, built of iron in 1861 with measurements of 146.6ft × 25.6ft × 15.9ft, 380 tons under deck and 398 tons net. She was owned by Campbell jnr of Glasgow and placed in the West Indies trade. Her lines plan depicts a hull-form

with sharp lines and a fairly long run but with not much deadrise; above the load line the stem rakes forward a long way with a full-length figurehead, and the bowsprit comes down on the sheer as in an Aberdeen clipper; there is a square stern, and she is flush-decked as can be seen by the deck plan and longitudinal section in figure 170. She was rigged as a barque, but unfortunately the sail plan has not survived. A painting of her appears as figure 171; the artist had painted the vessel with a green hull.

During the sixties, Barclay, Curle & Co built many iron ships in the 900 to 1200 tons range, and their design was fairly consistent, being a fuller version of the *Derwent*, the rig being normally that of full-rigged ship; many of these vessels appear to have been built in groups, so that a group of steamers is followed by a group of sailing ships. From 1860-66 three times as many steamers were built as sailing ships, but in 1867-69 ten steamers and lighters were built compared with about thirty-eight sailing ships. These latter are all very similar in design and of about 1000 tons each. The only two composite ships built in the yard were *Annie Duthie* (1863 of 471 tons) and *Loudoun Castle* (1868 of 895 tons); the wooden *Tamana* (1861) had part iron beams; so did ss *Toro* (1858), together with long iron hanging knees and an iron keelson. A paddle steamer for the Ottawa River Co, assembled in 1871, was of iron but planked with wood to the turn of the bilge and with iron plates above. Most of the full-rigged ships had a main skysail. The *Loch Tay* (1869) has a skysail on each mast hoisted on gunter poles, which are fidded abaft the royal masts and terminate at the topgallant rigging. The

Fig 170. Orange Grove. *Lines, sections and general arrangement reconstructed from two builder's plans by Ralph Bird. Built of iron at Glasgow in 1861 by Barclay, Curle & Co with dimensions of 146.6ft × 25.6ft × 15.9ft and 398 tons. Reconstruction: cargo winches on plan; boat; deckhouse panelling; buttock lines.*

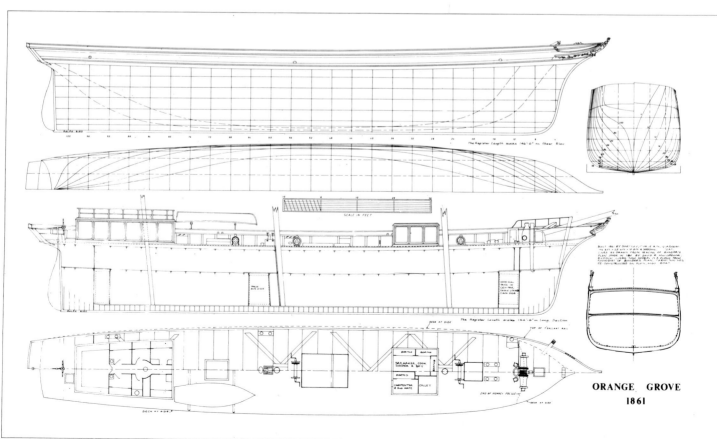

ORANGE GROVE
1861

Fig 171. Painting by an unknown artist of the Orange Grove *hove-to with a pilot lugger in attendance. The hull was painted green, and the flag at the fore truck had a white 'C' on a blue ground. (Parker Gallery)*

full-rigged ship *City of Corinth* (1870) has engines drawn in pencil on her sheer elevation together with a screw aperture and the base of a funnel.[17]

The full-rigged ship *Ben Nevis* which Barclay, Curle & Co built in 1868 has a steam-powered cargo winch which also drives the pumps and the Emerson & Walker windlass. In addition, a shaft is seen extending to the bulwarks, and by an ingenious worm gear is made to revolve an auxiliary screw temporarily fitted to the side of the hull, presumably for use in a calm (see figure 175). Perhaps there was one each side, as in the following description of Alexander Hall & Sons' tea clipper *The Caliph*:

In the after end of the house stands the steam engine of 8-horse power, which works cargo, lifts the anchor, pumps the ship, and hoists sails, yards, or warps ship. This engine is made in such a way that it can be attached to a shaft for driving two small screws, one on each side of the vessel, worked by a bevelled wheel on end of shaft across the deck, and a similar wheel on the end of the shaft which is along the ship's side, at an angle, and can be lifted out of the water at pleasure; this machinery is expected to drive the ship about 2½ knots per hour in a calm.[18]

Fig 172 Berkshire. *Sail plan photographed from original when in possession of the builders, Barclay, Curle & Co. Built of iron at Glasgow in 1867 with measurements of 237.2ft × 37.4ft × 23.1ft and 1472 tons net. The plan is badly torn along the bottom but the hull and jibboom could easily be restored. She was built for George Marshall's service to India and forms a good example of a heavily-rigged lofty ship with skysails on each mast.*

From time to time, ships made use of auxiliary propellers fitted on each side amidships, but usually they were abandoned as being not worth the trouble and as barely able to propel the ship to advantage, even in a flat calm. In 1869 Hall, Russell & Co of Aberdeen were reported as fitting 'patent slide propellers' to existing ships, and one vessel so fitted was the wooden barque *Zohrab* of 411 tons, which Parson jnr launched at Sunderland in that year. The following year she took about 168 days to sail out to Yokohama from London, so it would not appear that the auxiliary propellers were of much use on this trip. They were of 18hp and were claimed to move her at 3 knots in a calm.

Barclay, Curle & Co built some magnificent iron clippers in the 1870s whose good looks and fine performance have always earned praise from seafaring men. Their measurements are set out below.

IRON CLIPPERS BUILT BY BARCLAY, CURLE & CO 1870-1874[19]

Yard no	Name	Date	Dimensions	Under deck tonnage	Net tonnage
198	*Jason*	1870	253.0ft × 38.6ft × 23.2ft	1438	1512
219	*Strathearn*	1871	255.3ft × 40.4ft × 24.0ft	1625	1705
224	*Mermerus*	1872	264.2ft × 39.8ft × 23.7ft	1588	1671
237	*Ben Cruachan*	1873	255.5ft × 37.0ft × 21.7ft	1313	1468
238	*Ben Voirlich*	1873	255.6ft × 37.1ft × 21.8ft	1312	1474
239	*Loch Maree*	1873	255.8ft × 38.6ft × 22.9ft	1438	1580
244	*Brenhilda*	1874	240.4ft × 36.8ft × 22.3ft	1251	1321
245	*Thessalus*	1874	269.0ft × 41.1ft × 26.3ft	1709	1781

Fig 173. A deck scene aboard the Loch Tay, *looking aft with the mainsail in the foreground; one of the crew is attending to the fore braces; a boat is sitting in chocks on the skids and there are two harness casks below it. She was built by Barclay, Curle & Co in 1869 and was a sister to the* Loch Ness. *(Nautical Photo Agency)*

Fig 174. Another view of Loch Tay's *main deck, looking aft on the port side. One of the crew is sitting on the main hatch, perhaps wire splicing. (Nautical Photo Agency)*

The plans of *Mermerus* are typical of all these ships although it is impossible to say with absolute certainty as many of the plans are missing, but the hull lines and general arrangement plans in particular are typical. The hull-form is that of a ship with an easy entrance and run that was intended to sail fast, but the full midship section gave good cargo-carrying capacity and power to carry sail. Double topgallant on each mast and skysails above give a lofty sail plan but she was not alone in this respect, although *Brenhilda* only had single topgallants and a skysail on the mainmast. *Mairi Bahn* was a sister to *Brenhilda* and shared the same set of plans. Many of these ships were in the Australian and New Zealand trades. *Mermerus* made a fast run out to Melbourne of 66 days from London in 1876, but her life was a succession of fast passages and free from accident.

Surviving plans and models for the two Glasgow firms so far discussed in this chapter place them in an enviable position which allows their products to be appraised in some detail; for other firms the surviving information is much less definitive and so comparison of hull-form and deck layouts is not so easy. There were, of course, a large number of shipyards on both banks of the Clyde but to name more than a few selected firms would be to produce a mere catalogue of shipbuilders.

'Charles Connell was foreman [of Stephen's] – a clever man' writes Captain John Smith.[20] 'Like all other foremen, Mr Connell got Saturday afternoon off, and usually came down to the yard dressed with his coat on, and to see if all was right. He knew how to build a ship, and was not going to be content to be a servant all his days. There was a strip of land outside of Messrs Stephen's yard close to the Clyde. All of a sudden . . . a wooden partition was put up' to enclose his yard. This was in 1861. He was soon building ship after ship, all iron or composite. From 1862-69, he built 32 full-rigged ships, 2 barques and 1 schooner, as well as steamers.[21]

In the Glasgow Art Gallery and Museum are half-models of some iron ships built by John Reid & Co at Port Glasgow; one model is of the *Helen Nicholson* (1862 of 717 tons), and another is of the ships *Marpesia* and *Antiope*. The latter two must have been sisters, although there is a curious discrepancy in the length measurement as given by both *Lloyd's Register* and the *Liverpool Underwriters'*

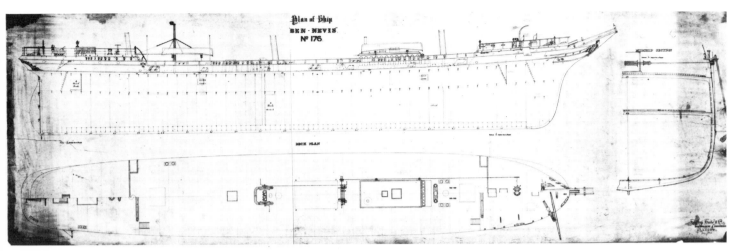

Fig 175. Ben Nevis. *Longitudinal section, midship section and deck plan photographed from original when in the possession of the builders, Barclay, Curle & Co. Built of iron at Glasgow in 1868 with measurements of 218.0ft × 34.6ft × 21.0ft and 1055 tons net. The auxiliary screw is described in the text.*

Fig 176 Barclay, Curle produced some magnificent iron clippers in the early seventies, but today it is difficult to imagine just how splendid they must have looked when newly completed. This photograph of Thessalus *does give some idea of the appearance and the great spread of sail they carried on their long yards. The only thing to mar this picture is the shortened jibboom and missing dolphin striker. This photograph was taken by F Wear at Port Adelaide in December 1898 when she was sailing under the Swedish flag. (Anders Ericsson)*

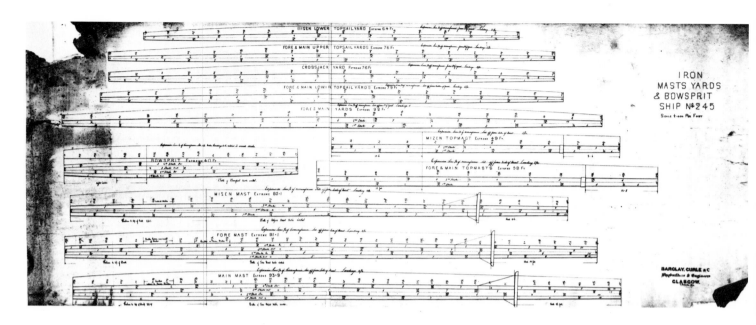

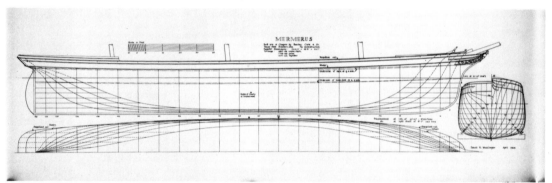

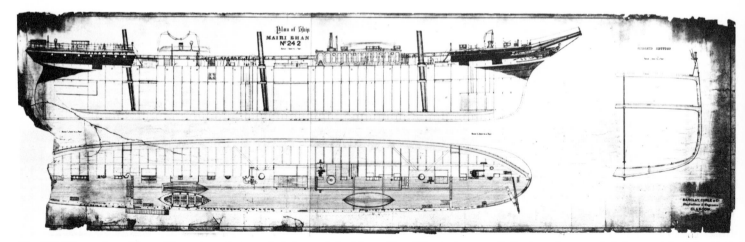

Fig 177 Thessalus. *Plans of iron spars photographed from original in 1961. This was a standard type of plan in Barclay, Curle's yard at this date.*

Fig 178. Mermerus. *Lines plan which I traced from the builder's plan in 1961. Built of iron at Glasgow in 1872 by Barclay, Curle & Co with measurements of 264.2ft × 39.8ft × 23.7ft and 1671 tons net.*

Fig 179. Mairi Bhan. *Longitudinal section and general arrangement photographed from original when in the possession of the builders, Barclay, Curle & Co. Built of iron at Glasgow in 1874 with measurements of 239.6ft × 37.0ft × 22.3ft and 1315 tons net. There is a steam boiler in the after end of the deckhouse and the chain or belt drive can just be made out running aft to the pumps and forward to the windlass.*

Fig 180. Ardmore. *Sail plan photographed from original in 1961. Built of iron at Glasgow in 1875 by Barclay, Curle & Co with measurements of 219.6ft × 35.1ft × 21.2ft and 1062 tons. This is a typical example of a sail plan from their drawing office in the 1870s, the belts of iron plating forming a pleasing feature in the way they are drawn and coloured. The creases and dirt spoil what must have originally looked a very smart piece of draughtsman's work.*

Fig 181. Builder's half-model of Marpesia *and* Antiope *in Glasgow Transport Museum, viewed from starboard quarter. Measurements of the two ships are compared in the text. Built at Port Glasgow by John Reid.*

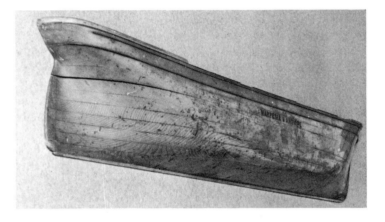

Register, yet the tonnage remains strangely unaffected. The '3' and '4' have probably been transposed in the length. The dimensions are for register: 1866 *Antiope* 242.3ft × 38.4ft × 23.7ft; 1443 net and gross; 1359 UD. 1866 *Marpesia* 234.2ft × 38.4ft × 23.9ft; 1443 net and gross; 1359 UD. The *Benmore*, according to Basil Lubbock, was also a sister:[22] 1870 *Benmore* 242.0ft × 39.2ft × 23.6ft; 1460 net; 1530 gross; 1368 UD.

Writing of the first two, Basil Lubbock says that 'it would be hard to say too much in praise, whether of their seaworthiness, speed or strength of build'.[23]

Marpesia's half-model shows a vessel with sharp ends, quite a fine run, a fair amount of deadrise and slack bilges. There was a topgallant forecastle almost to the foremast, and a poop stretching beyond the mizzen. Together with *Antiope* she was rigged from the start with both double topsail and double topgallant yards, which made them the earliest ships to be fitted with the latter. The photograph of *Antiope* in figure 182 shows the great length of the upper yards. *Benmore* was given the same sail plan but was drastically cut down in the seventies in such a way that the lower yards were removed and each of the three yards above moved one place down. By this means, the lower topsail yard became the lower yard, the upper topsail yard became the lower topsail yard, and the lower topgallant yard became the upper topsail yard. In this way, the double topgallants were eliminated.[24] Photographs indicate that *Marpesia* and *Antiope* also lost their double topgallants. It is not clear whether these reductions were made as a result of the dismasting of many over-hatted iron ships or to effect economies as freights fell.

All three ships were owned by Joseph Heap and they usually sailed out to Australia and then loaded a homeward cargo in India. *Antiope*'s fastest outward passage was one of 68 days to Melbourne in 1868.

In 1873, John Reid launched the heavily-sparred ship *John Kerr* of 1782 tons net. Her fore and main lower yards were each 95ft long and the crossjack yard was 79ft, and there were very few ships with lower yards longer than these. She was dismasted on her maiden passage, and was one of the eleven ships suffering this disaster which prompted the Lloyd's Register surveyors, B Martell, H J Cornish and W John, to compile their report on the *Dismasting of Large Iron Sailing Ships* which was first issued in December 1874, as described in the last section of this chapter.[25]

Two other lofty ships built by Reid were the *Lammermoor* of 1626 tons which was built in 1874 and her sister, *Cedric the Saxon* of 1619 tons, built the following year. Their midship sections have the same amount of deadrise as *Marpesia* which was large for anything other than a clipper and suggests that Reid designed his ships with a view to them being fast and weatherly. The *Lammermoor* had dimensions of 260.2ft × 40.7ft × 23.5ft and crossed skysails on each mast above double topgallants. Lloyd's Report on 'Dismasting' assigns her fore and main lower yards of 91 feet long, and she is no 59 in Appendix Table I of this report. *Cedric the Saxon*'s measurements were almost identical, but in her sail plan the skysails on the fore and mizzen were omitted, although the mainyard was no less than 112ft long. There is a half-model of the two ships in the Science Museum and this confirms how beautiful they were as does a painting by Jack Spurling.

Another example of the splendid iron ships being built on the Clyde during the seventies comes from the yard of

2

McMillan & Son of Dumbarton who produced the lofty ships *Thomasina MacLellan* and *Stuart Hahnemann*. The former, which the builders regarded as their 'masterpiece'[26] was built in 1873 of 1788 tons net; the latter appeared the following year and measured 273.7ft × 43.1ft × 23.6ft and 1997 tons net. She was given skysails on all three masts and the Lloyd's Register Report on 'Dismasting' lists her yards as the longest of the 82 ships given, and she is no 81 in Appendix Table I. For instance her fore- and mainyards are 100ft long; and the crossjack yard, and the fore and main upper topsail yards are each 80ft. Homeward-bound from India in 1875 she went over on her beam ends in a heavy squall, and because her sails and rigging had been specially strengthened against such an eventuality, nothing gave way; the result was that waves, washing over her, filled the courses and she capsized.[27]

Fig 182. The Antiope *at anchor with her double topgallant yards.* (Alexander Turnbull Library, Wellington)

Fig 183. The nearest ship is the lovely Lammermoor *lying at Hastings Moorings, Calcutta, and beyond her is the* Pendragon Castle. *The Lammermoor was built in 1874 by John Reid and was a heavily-sparred ship. Here awnings have been spread above the decks and the black dots on the stays are carrion crows.* (Richard M Cookson)

Fig 184. An example of MacMillan & Sons' work was the Thomasina MacLellan, *seen here at anchor. It would appear that the stunsail halliard blocks had not been removed from below the yardarms on the lower and topsail yards on the fore-and mainmasts, and also on the main upper topgallant yards. A flying jibboom is still rigged. Her dimensions were 262.6ft × 40.7ft × 23.8ft.* (Nautical Photo Agency)

A good example of the last word in building and equipping a large iron medium clipper may be found in the description of the *Baron Colonsay*, whose launch on 4 August 1875 was reported as follows:

Yesterday there was launched from the shipbuilding yard of Mr James F Scott, Main Street, Greenock, a magnificently designed iron sailing ship, of about 2187 tons, built to the order of James MacCunn Esq, for the East India trade, and is the latest addition to the Baronial Line. This really handsome ship has been built to the highest class at Lloyd's, under special survey, and the close surveillance of an efficient inspector, and is the largest iron sailing vessel afloat. Her dimensions are – length 270ft; breadth of beam 40ft 3in; depth 24ft. She has been fitted with every modern convenience and appliance for economising labour in loading and discharging cargo etc; was specially designed for quick sailing, and to shift without ballast. Judging from her very fine lines, great rise of floor, breadth of beam, and smart appearance, she will doubtless realize the most sanguine expectations of her designer; has a roomy and well ventilated forecastle, large deck-house and poop, fitted up in the most elaborate and chaste manner for convenience and comfort. Her lower masts are made of iron, 3ft 2in diameter, with four plates in the round, strongly bound with four heavy angle irons running the whole length; iron bowsprit has four angle irons, and a plate bulkhead inside, from end to end, and there is a thwartship bulkhead ten feet long at knightheads; has double bobstays, and double bowsprit shrouds and hoops, acting independently of each other, so that in the event of either being carried away, the head gear would still be as secure as in ordinary vessels. The masts are also doubled for 10 feet at the hounds in way of the rigging, and at the wedging; the fore and main stay plates are securely fastened to heavy iron plates 2 inches thick, and 4½ feet long, rivetted to deck plates and fore and afters. Besides this, the fore stays are fastened direct to bulkhead with large iron

Fig 185. Another lofty ship was the Baron Colonsay, *built in 1875 by J E Scott at Greenock. She was purchased from MacCunn by James Nourse in 1892 and renamed* Lena, *and it is with this name that she was photographed here at Calcutta. It is interesting that she had still retained skysail yards on each mast, but then Nourse did require his 'coolie ships' to be swift sailers. Her launch is described in the text at length.* (Arthur D Edwardes)

Fig 186. James E Scott (died 1915) built about 20 ships at Greenock until his yard closed down in 1878 after a strike. His wife was a daughter of Findlay who owned tea clippers. Later he lived in London. Photograph copied in 1955 from original owned by his daughter, Peggy Scott.

knees. Lower yards, and lower and upper topsail yards, are all of iron, with two angles inside, with doubling plates on each about 10 feet long, and strongly hooped every 30 inches. Has double sheerstake from poop to forecastle, and Stock's patent jackstay on mizzenmast. Calling and Pinkney's patent reefing gear on fore and main topgallant yards, thus dispensing with the immense top weight of double topgallant yards. Is fitted with Harfield's patent windlass, which can be worked either by steam or hand as required. Has four large capstans, two powerful steam winches, and donkey boiler for driving them; donkey engine and condensing apparatus, capable of condensing 600 gallons per day. At 2.15pm orders were given to let the daggers down. Immediately thereafter the ship glided majestically into her future element, the ceremony of naming her *Baron Colonsay* being gracefully performed by Miss Neil, daughter of John Neil Esq, Elderslie House, Largs, one of the owners.[28]

One of the patentees of the patent reefing gear is usually spelt 'Colling'. The reasons for choosing some of the equipment are of interest and indicate the close scrutiny being given by builders and owners to the ships under construction. J E Scott, her builder, was in business in the early seventies and produced about twenty ships but the yard was closed down in 1878 following a strike. Scott moved to London in 1882 where he was first a shipowner and later a shipbroker. He died in 1915.

Although lines plans and half-models have survived for a number of tea clippers built by Robert Steele & Co, Greenock, no such plans have been found for any of his other ships, and the only half-model found is of the sister ships *Knight of Snowdoun* and *Lord of the Isles* which were medium clippers built in 1864 of 633 tons under deck. The lines of this half-model were taken off when it was in possession of James Steele, but on his death in 1955 it passed to a relative and its whereabouts are today unknown. Some sail plans have survived, and these are all drawn to show masts, yards and standing rigging only, without any sail outlines; indeed the hoisting yards are drawn in the lowered position at the full extent of the standing lifts.

The last wooden vessel built by Robert Steele was the brigantine *Douro*, yard no 170, launched in October 1867 for Walter Grieve and measuring 195 tons. The last composite vessels were the auxiliary steamer *Hampshire*, no 176 launched in March 1870, and the barque *Lavinia*,

Fig 188. *Another of Robert Steele's ships, the* Lady Palmerstone, *under Norwegian colours and here loading timber from a lighter whilst anchored in mid-stream. Bow ports have been cut through her iron hull. She was owned in Kristiansand from 1898 to 1908 when sold to become a hulk at Adelaide. She measured 1247 tons net and had a beam of 35.4ft. I am grateful to Atle Midthassel for the picture and the data.*

no 175 launched May 1870. However, the following year, a composite cutter yacht was built of 63 tons. The first iron vessel was SS *Beaver* of 255 tons, built in 1854; and the first iron sailing ship was the *City of Madras* which was built the following year for George Smith & Sons. Thereafter, iron ships were produced regularly and included a number of schooner and cutter yachts. During the first half of the seventies, the fine sister ships *Hesperus* and *Aurora* were built in 1873 and 1874 respectively. The latter measured 250.0ft × 39.75ft × 23.6ft, 1577 tons UD and 1768 tons net; dimensions of *Hesperus* were identical in the builder's list although the underdeck tonnage was less at 1574.

Fig 187. *It is instructive to consider that the same year that the ship pictured here was built, namely 1868, that a tea clipper by the same builder was also launched, so we might almost be viewing the latter under sail. The builder was Robert Steele & Co, the tea clipper was the* Kaisow, *and the ship illustrated here was launched under the name of* Lake Superior, *but by this time had been sold to Norwegian owners and renamed* Superior. *Dimensions in 1870 were 231.9ft × 35.9ft × 22.3ft and 1274 tons net. The deep topgallant sails have been retained which was a mark of many ships of her date, but although a long bowsprit is still in place, the jibboom is very short; in fact, the total length of jibboom outside the knightheads might originally have been its length outside the bowsprit cap. There is a list of iron ships built by Steele in Appendix II.* (MacGregor Collection)

Fig 189. *This photograph illustrates the work of another Glasgow shipbuilder, John Elder & Co, who is not mentioned in the text. This ship is the* Rhone *ex-Gilroy which was built in 1875 with a tonnage of 1678. James Nourse bought her in 1890. Here she is seen stranded at Hotwells, Bristol, on 29 January 1896. She was repaired.* (York Collection, Bristol Museum)

SHIPBUILDERS AT ABERDEEN

All the shipyards at Aberdeen concentrated on wooden construction throughout the sixties, with many vessels in the 1000 tons range. At Duthie's yard, Alexander died in 1863 and the firm was restyled as John Duthie, Sons & Co, but their first iron ship, the *Cairnbulg*, was not produced until 1874. Many of their wooden ships were in the 950-1150 tons range, such as *William Duthie* (1862), *John Duthie* (1864), *Peter Denny* (1865), *Australian* and *Sir William Wallace* (1866), *Agnes Rose* and *Alexander Duthie* (1867), *Ann Duthie* (1868), *Abergeldie* and *Windsor Castle* (1869). These were lofty ships, setting skysails on each mast above single topgallants and double topsails. An examination of the *Ann Duthie*'s half-model proves that she had short, sharp ends, with well-rounded bilges, wall sides, slight tumblehome and about 15ft of parallel middle body. Most of Duthie's ships had this deadflat amidships, but they were powerful ships in strong winds and well-suited to the Australian trade.

John Duthie's fourth son, Robert (1831-1913), was an expert naval architect and responsible for many of the firm's clippers; he also built on his own account, producing *Robert Henderson* in 1857 and the smaller *Prince Alfred* in 1862. A photograph of the latter on the stocks displays her attractive hull and it is only the man on the quarterdeck which establishes her relatively small size.

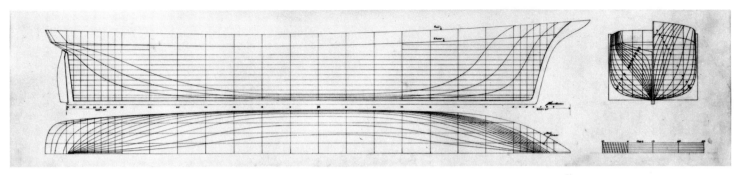

Fig 191. Ann Duthie. *Lines plan drawn by James Henderson from lines he took off builder's half-model in Aberdeen Museum & Art Gallery. Built of wood at Aberdeen in 1868 by Duthie, Sons & Co with measurements of 200.0ft × 35.2ft × 20.1ft and 993 tons net. No reconstruction.*

Fig 190. The John Duthie *lying at Circular Quay, Sydney, set the style for many of the ships built by John Duthie, Sons & Co. She was built in 1864 with a tonnage of 1031 and a length of 196.0ft. Hoisting the upper topsails halfway-up the mast was considered to give a smarter appearance.* (Cyril L Hume)

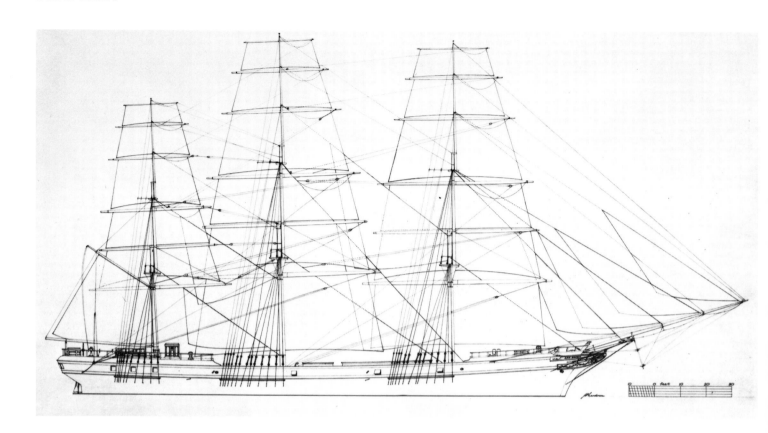

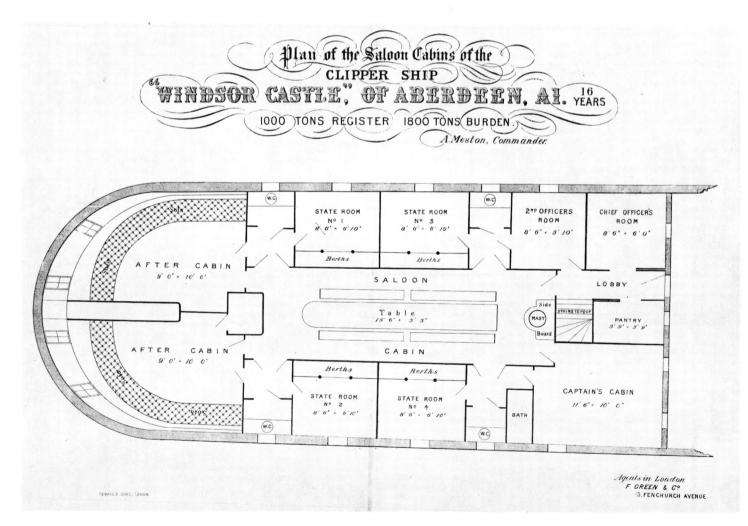

Plan of the Saloon Cabins of the
CLIPPER SHIP
"WINDSOR CASTLE," OF ABERDEEN, A1. 16 YEARS
1000 TONS REGISTER   1800 TONS BURDEN.
A. Meston, Commander.

Agents in London
F. GREEN & Cº
13, FENCHURCH AVENUE.

Fig 192. Ann Duthie. Sail and rigging plan reconstructed by James Henderson. Principal sources: lower masts of Agnes Rose, built by Duthie; a photograph of ship when new: contemporary text books on masting and rigging; photographs of other Duthie ships.

Fig 193. Windsor Castle. Saloon cabin plan reproduced from original in my possession. Built of wood at Aberdeen in 1869 by John Duthie, Sons & Co of similar form to Ann Duthie. These plans were used by agents when taking passengers' bookings.

Fig 194. The Prince Alfred ready for launching from the Aberdeen yard of Robert Duthie in 1862. This yard was at The Inches and the barque had dimensions of 131.0ft × 23.9ft × 13.0ft and only 258 tons which should really have placed her in Chapter 6. She is already coppered. (Nautical Photo Agency)

Another less well-known Aberdeen builder who had a yard at the Inches, was Smith who had originally been a German with the name of Schmidt, but was nicknamed 'Yankee' Smith. His chief draughtsman, John Humphrey, took over the yard and the business on Smith's death in about 1866, and changed the name to John Humphrey & Co. One of their ships was the *Invercauld* of 1311 tons, built of wood in 1874, which was a late date for such a large wooden vessel.

Like John Duthie, Walter Hood & Co clung to timber construction throughout the sixties and much of their production was for George Thompson's 'Aberdeen White Star Line'. Between the *Kosciusko* (1862) and *Ethiopian* (1864), the bow was remodelled. Hood's first iron ship was probably the *Glenavon* of 1868 and their only three composite vessels were the full-rigged ships *Thermopylae* (1868) and *Centurion* (1869) and the brig *Charles Chalmers* (1874). Throughout the 1870s there was one, sometimes two, iron ships built each year for Thompson: *Miltiades* and *Leucadia* in 1871; *Collingwood* in 1872; *Samuel Plimsoll* in 1873; *Romanoff* with fidded royal masts in 1874; *Salamis* in 1875. The large wooden ship *Aviemore* of 1091 tons was launched as late as 1870. Apart from the extreme clipper *Thermopylae*, no plans, other than midship sections, have been located for ships built by this yard in the period prior to 1875. The iron ship *Patriarch* (1869) is of interest because the masts were iron poles without doublings: the lower masts and topmasts were in one piece and the telescopic topgallant masts slid into the topmasts. This is reminiscent of what was proposed in 1853 for Stephen's clipper *Hurricane*. Walter Hood was drowned in Aberdeen harbour in 1862 at the age of sixty, but the firm continued under his name.

On the maiden voyage of the *Centurion*, which Hood built in 1869, her master, Thomas Mitchell, wrote a letter to the firm addressed to Mr Greig, in which he described the behaviour and performance of his ship, and from the tone of the letter it appears that Mr Greig was the yard manager or the chief designer.[29]

1 *Fig 195. Another Aberdeen yard at The Inches was Smith's which produced the* Umgeni *of 366 tons in 1864. Here she is seen drying her sails in Durban harbour. The photograph must have been taken in the 1860s as she still carries single topsails, and it is valuable in showing the sizes of staysails between the masts.* (Local History Museum, Durban)

2 *Fig 196. The composite-built ship* Centurion *came from Walter Hood's yard at Aberdeen in 1869 for the Australian trade. She was of 965 tons and had a length of 208.1ft. The artist has painted in every possible sail including a main sky staysail and a ringtail, but the fore lower stunsail is triangular.* Centurion *may have been too much of a clipper to justify inclusion in this work, but there is much useful data in this painting.* (Dr and Mrs Donald)

3 *Fig 197. Alexander Hall's shipyard in 1867, inscribed with the names of three sailing ships, and omitting the name of the tug in the foreground. On the left the* Illovo *is under construction; in the centre is the schooner-brigantine* Tom Duff *(built 1839) with a schooner's foremast but a fidded fore topgallant mast; on the right above the building shed are the masts and topsail yards of the clipper barque* Pilot Fish *built in 1848.* (MacGregor Collection)

4 *Fig 198. The crew standing at the bows of the* Calypso, *built by Alexander Hall in 1874 of iron, seen here in drydock in New Zealand. The elaborate carving and lovely figurehead are in stark contrast to the rough dress of the crew.* (Alexander Turnbull Library, Wellington)

Alexander Hall & Sons' first composite ship was the *Reindeer* – the second ship they built of this name – launched in 1863. She had a gross tonnage of 964 and cost £17,660. The fore and main lower yards each measured 72ft and she was very square aloft, the mainmast measuring 143ft from deck to truck. Upper and lower topsails were provided on each mast, but the lower topsail yards had no yardarms and were in fact 2ft shorter than the upper topsail yards. There was a skysail on the mainmast only, and also a sliding gunter pole for a moonsail. This pole measured 10ft 6in above the cranse iron and 42ft 0in overall length; the moonsail yard was 25ft 0in long with a maximum diameter of 5in. A full suit of studdingsails up to the royals was carried on the fore- and mainmasts. This is a rare case of a moonsail yard actually being specified by the builder.

Alexander Stephen jnr was fond of commenting in his diary about ships produced by other builders. Of the *Reindeer* he wrote that 'she is out in China and very bad accounts of her have come home; she had very [little?] longitudinal fastening, no sheer strake or diagonals and beams badly fastened'.[30] When in London in November 1863, Stephen went with Captain Killick to inspect Hall's new ship *Yang-tsze*, built for Killick, Martin & Co, and noted: 'She is much inferior to the *Eliza Shaw*. She is iron frame and wood planked – no sheer strake'.[31]

The first of Hall's ships to have iron spars was the *Pegasus* (1861), whose iron lower masts and bowsprit cost £314 18s to make and supply. A feature of Hall's sail plans was the long length of the skysail yard which made the sail very rectangular in shape, and the leeches did not follow the slope of the royals. This can be seen in the sail plan of *John Williams III* (figure 266 in *Fast Sailing Ships*).

Between 1863 and 1873, Hall's output of composite vessels comprised twelve ships and barques, one barquentine and two steamers – a considerably smaller output than Alexander Stephen & Sons. Iron shipbuilding at Hall's yard was only spasmodic in the later sixties and did not get into full swing until 1873; their first iron ship was the steamer *Douglas* completed in 1866. An all-wood ship, the *Commissary* of 941 tons, was built as late as 1868 and the following year saw the completion of a wooden steamer for the Japanese Navy, the *Jho-sho-maru* of 1459 tons. Many of the ships and barques were still built with speed in mind and some of these designs are discussed in *Fast Sailing Ships* and *The Tea Clippers* (1983). James Hall, brother to William, died of a heart attack in 1869 after a fire in the yard.

Another of their ships with gunter poles was the composite ship *Brucklay Castle*, built by Hall in 1867 of 1014 tons. An oil painting of this ship showed that the topgallant masts were short and only carried the topgallant yards, but that gunter poles were fidded abaft them to carry royals and skysails on each mast. These gunter poles were stepped on the cap of the topmast.[32]

Hall's last composite ship was the *Lufra*, built in 1870, although he did produce a small 30-ton composite steamer in 1873. In the seventies the square-rigged vessels produced by the yard consisted of the following:

SAILING SHIPS BUILT BY ALEXANDER HALL & SONS, ABERDEEN, 1870-1875[33]

(excluding 3 smacks of 77-81 tons)

Yard no	Date built	Name	Tons gross	Material	Rig	Contract price
265	1870	*Lufra*	704	comp	S	£10,000
268	1871	*Hokitika*	292	iron	bk	£3950
269	1871	*Juan de la Vega*	172	wood	bgn	£2780
273	1872	*Elizabeth*	99	wood	sch	£1846
283	1874	*Calypso*	1061	iron	S	completed £18 12s 6d for 1013 tons
284	1875	*Alive*	313	iron	bk	£4950
285	1874	*Avalanche*	1210	iron	S	£19,973
286	1875	*Bay of Naples*	1676	iron	S	completed £27,458
287	1875	*Ullock*	815	iron	bk	completed £17 7s 6d for 776 tons

A complete list of all their ships up to the end of 1875, together with rigs, tonnages and contract prices is given in Appendix 2 of *Fast Sailing Ships 1775-1875*.

These full-rigged ships were fine medium clippers and splendidly finished. The *Avalanche* and the wooden ship *Forest* collided in the English Channel in September 1877 and both ships sank; they were both close-hauled on opposite tacks in a south-westerly gale, force 8. The *Forest* was a Nova-Scotian ship of 1422 tons and was on the starboard tack, so having right of way; 104 lives were lost. At the official enquiry, it was reported that the *Avalanche* was under inner and outer jibs, fore topmast staysail, foresail, fore topsails, single reefed mainsail and spanker. There was no square canvas set on the mizzen and on the main, nothing above the mainsail. This was considered an extraordinary set of sails and doubts were expressed as to the accuracy of the evidence submitted by the survivors.[34]

Fig 199. A collision in the Channel in 1874 by two ships on opposite tacks which was re-enacted three years later by the Avalanche *and the* Forest, *as recounted in the text. In this engraving from the* Pictorial World *(24 Oct 1874), the* Candahar *on the port tack has just rammed and stove in the side of the* Kingsbridge *on the starboard tack. The latter sank in 3 minutes and 10 men were drowned.* Candahar *got in to Falmouth leaking badly, but was repaired. She had been built of iron in 1866 by Harland & Wolff with a beam to length ratio of 6.65 and a tonnage of 1418; the* Kingsbridge *was built at Sunderland by Oswald in 1869 and was about 80 tons larger.*

Fig 200. A contrast to the last picture is the motionless sleek hull of the Eastern Monarch *which Mounsey & Foster built at Sunderland in 1874. This engraving in the* Illustrated London News *is signed 'I R Wells'.*

WILLIAM AND JOHN PILE IN NORTH-EAST ENGLAND

The north-east coast of England from Hull to Newcastle remained one of the principal shipbuilding areas in the country, Sunderland being the chief centre. Here were concentrated a vast number of yards, but surprisingly little evidence in the form of plans and models has survived today in relation to the large numbers of ships produced. In the Sunderland Museum are to be found about twenty half-models of ships built by Robert Thompson & Sons, but only two from William Pile's yard.

Thompson's models cover the years 1857-92, but the majority are of barques built in the sixties in the 350-550

Fig 202. Model of England's Glory *in the Sunderland Museum. She was built by William Pile in 1869. The placing of three boats with davits between the main- and foremasts is unusual, but the rest of the model portrays a large iron ship of this date very well.* (Author)

Fig 201. Ready for launching into the River Wear at Sunderland from Robert Thompson's yard is the Vencedora *in April 1860. She had dimensions of 130ft 0in × 28ft 1in × 18ft 0in and 466 tons. She was the last wooden ship built in Thompson's yard at North Sands. Copied from an old photograph.*

tons range. Of the latter, the *Velocity* (1866) and *Ocean Rover* (1867) were fine-lined medium clippers with concave lines at bow and stern up to eight feet above the rabbet. Most of the models had hollow runs but with fuller bodies amidships and slightly convex entrance lines, such as *Amadine* (1866) and *Gitanilla* (1865); but *Deucalion* (1865) and *Southwick* (1865) were somewhat fuller in the entrance. Many of these barques were of composite construction. An earlier vessel was the *British Monarch* (1857) which had the fullest and deepest hull-form of all these models.

Models in the Sunderland Museum of William Pile's ships after 1856 consist of half-models of the *Ganges* (1861) and *Rodney* (1874), both in the clipper category, and a rigged model of *England's Glory* (1869), probably to ⅛-inch scale. The latter represents an iron full-rigged ship of 751 tons, crossing skysail yards on each mast, and having a full poop and topgallant forecastle with a moderately full hull-form and a long parallel body. Unfortunately, it is not known whether the model was built from authentic plans. There is an important survivor of Pile's work in the shape of the *Carrick* which is moored on the Clyde in the heart of Glasgow as the RNVR Club. She was built by Pile in 1864 as the *City of Adelaide* with a tonnage of 791 net, and was given a fine entrance and run.

As regards hull-form, the *Ganges* was slightly more convex in the entrance and run than Pile's tea clipper *Maitland* and she was more kettle-bottomed with very rounded bilges and the maximum beam about 7ft above the keel rabbet. It may have been that Pile's other ships in the sixties and seventies were a variation between these two. On none of his designs is there steep deadrise.

By the end of 1862, William Pile had built 76 vessels of wood; a further 9 vessels were built in the 'Low Yard' at Sunderland between 1860 and 1863. Iron shipbuilding began in 1861 with the *Ganges*, built for James Nourse, and composite construction was later adopted. My data on the ships built comes from a list kept by Thomas C Stamp who was Pile's cashier and later a shipowner.[35] In this list, the iron and composite ships are listed separately, the information consisting of yard number, name, date of launch and owner. *Sophie Joakim*, launched March 1864 for John Willis, was yard number 22, but then the number system jumps by 100 so that the next vessel, *City of Adelaide*, launched in May 1864 for Devitt & Moore, is given as no 123. Making a deduction of 100, the total number of iron and composite ships listed is 133. Out of these, no 142 was not built and the entry for no 187 is left blank. The steamers totalled 43 but it may be that some vessels not identified as such may be steamers. There was one schooner. Pile was in partnership with Richard Hay from 1861 for six years; in 1863 they employed 2000 men and had eight building slips. William Pile died in 1873 and his yard (which was on the site of Joseph L Thompson & Sons) was sold for the benefit of his creditors, but the *Rodney*, which was under construction, was completed by friends and was launched in 1874.

John Pile, William's brother, began shipbuilding at West Hartlepool in 1853 and three years later took Joseph Spence into partnership making the firm Pile, Spence &

Co. They constructed many fine sailing ships and steamers, and their first iron vessel was launched in 1855. The last wooden ship was probably the barque *Orilla* of 1858. They were very enterprising, building their own blast furnaces and rolling mills, had a foundry for castings and a separate yard for iron spars. About 1857 the South Yard and graving dock were opened. They also ran a line of steamers. Unfortunately, they became one of the casualties when the London house of Overend Gurney & Co failed in 1866 and they were forced into liquidation, each part being sold off separately.[36]

The changeover from wood to iron on both the rivers Wear and Tyne was most marked in the years 1860-1864, and this in spite of the number of small yards operating on the Wear where the construction of wooden vessels on speculation was the tradition. On the Tyne, many yards started building in iron and several of these were opened by engineers rather than by shipbuilders. Wigham Richardson was an engineer and Swan built his first steel vessel in 1859.[37]

A typical Sunderland wooden ship illustrated here is the *Medusa* which was built in 1862 by W Briggs & Son (figure 208).

OTHER SHIPBUILDERS IN GREAT BRITAIN

At Annan, on the Solway Firth, Benjamin Nicholson had interspersed the extreme clipper form with full-bodied hulls, but his last clipper was the *Mansfield*, built in 1861. This can be determined from the surviving builder's half-models which were referred to in some detail on page 199 of *Fast Sailing Ships*; a list of the ships he built was also given. Of those ships the following were clippers: *Annandale*, *Queensberry*, *Shakspere* and *Mansfield*. Of the others, the *Elizabeth Nicholson*, built in 1863 of 904 tons, was a medium clipper, but *Burns* (1853 of 363 tons), *John Nicholson* (1859 of 685 tons), *Burnswark* (1862 of 323 tons) and *Sarah Nicholson* (1865 of 934 tons) were all cargo carriers.

From lines taken off *John Nicholson*'s half-model, it can be seen that she has a stem that rounds up with the same profile as the extreme clipper *Annandale* and also a midship section of similar shape although there is no hollow garboard. There the similarities end because the *John Nicholson* has a short convex entrance, approximately 35 feet of parallel body amidships which turns abruptly into a short run that is concave in the lower body but convex above. There is a round stern with a surprisingly shallow transom and very little sheer. Unfortunately, the dimensions of the half-model are smaller than the vessel as built. Assuming a ¼-inch scale, the model gives 147ft 6in × 25ft 6in × 17ft 0in whereas the actual vessel measured 177.6ft × 29.4ft × 18.0ft. Although one cannot tell what the hull-form of the finished ship was like, it is probable that the ends were longer but it is almost certain that the parallel middle body was retained.

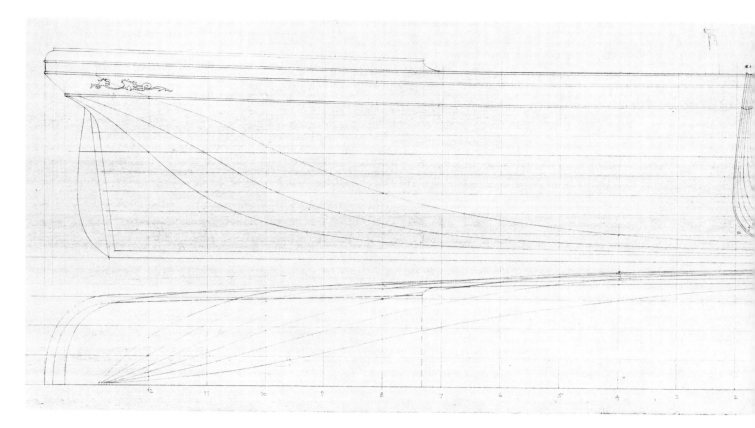

Fig 203. Ganges. *Lines plan drawn by the author from lines taken off builder's half-model in Sunderland Museum. Built of iron at Sunderland in 1861 by William Pile with measurements of 192.0ft × 33.2ft × 20.6ft and 839 tons. No reconstruction, but my drawing remains in pencil.*

Fig 204. *The* Rodney *in drydock c1896 after her last voyage under British colours; her figurehead and trail boards had been torn off in a gale. She was built in 1874 in William Pile's yard as described in the text. The iron plating shows clearly here. (Cyril L Hume)*

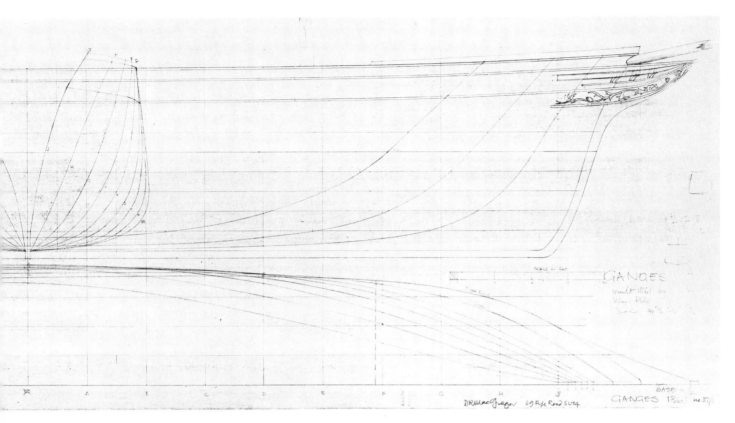

Fig 205. White marble bust of John Pile, photographed in William Gray Museum, West Hartlepool. (Author)

Fig 206. The Baron Blantyre *was built at Sunderland in 1873 by Watson and had a length of 257ft and a tonnage of 1623. James MacCunn of tea clipper fame undoubtedly had efficient and fast sailing ships built and the three 'Barons' were good examples.* (Colin Denny Gallery)

Fig 207. *Built for the New Zealand Shipping Co by Palmer's at Newcastle, the* Otaki *was launched in 1875 with a tonnage of 1014 net. Here she is completely becalmed and the falls that are hanging from the davits which have been swung out show that she was photographed from one of the ship's boats.* (Nautical Photo Agency)

An oil painting of the *John Nicholson* in the possession of the late Dr R C Anderson suggests that she was flush-decked with deep single roller-reefing topsails and a skysail only on the mainmast. In 1862 she sailed out to Hong Kong from Cardiff in 105 days with 923 tons of coal. Between 1863 and 1875 she earned an average of £3 5s 4d per gross ton per annum before voyage expenses were deducted. The average for eleven ships in the Nicholson fleet in the same period was £3 11s 4d.[38]

The town of Annan, near to where the ships were built was a 'quiet country town' and when describing the launch of the *Elizabeth Nicholson* in 1863, the local reporter comments rather smugly that 'the successful launch . . . for one day at least, had given Annan a glimpse of active commercial life . . . '.[39]

Across the Solway Firth in north-west England, the Whitehaven Shipbuilding Co, situated in the town of that name, built nine sister ships in the years 1871-75. They are compared here:

Fig 208. Heeling to the breeze, the Medusa *is clewing up her lower topsails and lowering her outer jib as the tug ranges along her port side to take her in tow. She has a deck load of timber and is owned in Mandel. Some of the crew are mustered on the forecastle head where they have unshipped the railing in way of the anchors which have been hung over the ship's side ready for letting go. The starboard anchor cable can be seen shackled on and led through the hawse pipe and a fish tackle has been rigged from the fore topmast to help shift the anchors. The* Medusa *was built at Sunderland in 1862 by W Briggs & Son and measured 161.0ft × 33.6ft × 21.1ft and 848 tons. The photographer was G A Schenley. (Nautical Photo Agency)*

COMPARISON OF NINE IRON SHIPS BUILT BY WHITEHAVEN SHIPBUILDING CO

Name	Date	UD tons	Net tons	Dimensions
Patterdale	1871	1166	1200	224.3ft × 36.0ft × 21.9ft
Wasdale	1872	1174	1200	227.7ft × 36.3ft × 22.0ft
Eskdale	1873	1178	1220	225.5ft × 36.2ft × 22.1ft
Greta	1874	1158	1190	226.0ft × 36.2ft × 21.9ft
Angerona	1874	1180	1215	
Candida	1875	1181	1222	
Grasmere	1875	1180	1246	226.0ft × 36.1ft × 22.1ft
Rydalmere	1875	1180	1246	
Silverhow	1875	1181	1221	

Basil Lubbock draws attention to the similarity of these nine ships which the registers confirm, as do the identical dimensions of the last five ships.[40] I have not come across any lines plan of them although I traced a sail plan of *Greta* in the Whitehaven Public Library and Museum.

Henry Iredale was fully conversant with the *Wasdale* because he compares her sail plan to that of the *Shenir* in a letter to Alexander Stephen & Sons dated Carlisle, 19 January 1876. The relevant sentences read:

The spar draft [of *Shenir*] I have closely examined having before me the spar draft of the *Borrowdale* and *Wasdale*, and notwithstanding I have increased upon your plans, I have kept within those of these ships, which are 100 tons smaller. Your plans seem very small particularly the yards and lower yards. I should give a 950 tons ship 73 [ft] lower yards.[41]

The *Borrowdale* was built in 1868 at Liverpool by W H Potter & Co with dimensions of 226.4ft × 36.4ft × 22.0ft and tonnages of 1368 UD and 1197 net. At the same time that these nine sisters were being built in Whitehaven, Potter was turning out four ships with almost identical measurements for the Newton's 'Dale Line', namely the *Ennerdale* and *Langdale* in 1874, and the *Grisedale* and *Mitredale* in 1875. Could it be that Henry and Peter Iredale had been called in to advise the respective owners or builders? The *Borrowdale* was the first of all these vessels and the nine Whitehaven ships, at least, are all said to have been based on her design.[42] Incidentally, one must echo Henry Iredale's comments on the smallness of Stephen's sail plans when compared to most other ships.

Fig 209. The Candida *at Sydney; her dimensions are given in the text.* (Nautical Photo Agency)

The sail plan of the *Greta* shows that the mainyard overlaps the foreyard and the crossjack yard by some 10ft each, and that the main lower topsail fills the space between the sails on the fore and those on the mizzen. The fore- and mainyards are 80ft long and the lower topsail yards 70ft. Presumably all the other eight Whitehaven ships had somewhat similar sail plans. The headsails on *Greta*'s plan are cut according to the pattern that was being adopted in the 1870s in which the low-cut foot disappeared and the clew was raised; in these sails the

cloths ran parallel to the foot or the leech and were joined by a seam at right angles to the luff.

But ten years earlier another Whitehaven shipyard was closing down. It was 1865, and Brocklebank's last wooden ship, the *Mahanada* had just been launched and the firm had decided to add only iron ships in future. So the stocks were sold off at the end of August. Their first iron ship had been built at Belfast by Harland & Wolff in 1863 and was of 1352 tons. Between then and the end of 1875, six more iron full-rigged ships were added to the fleet, and the size rose to that of the *Majestic* built in 1875 with a tonnage of 1884.

It would be interesting to learn whether the plans of the *Formby* were published elsewhere prior to their appearance in Professor Rankine's book in 1866. This remark is prompted by an examination of the plan at the National Maritime Museum, Greenwich, of the ship *British Nation* which was built in 1865 at Dublin by Walpole, Webb & Bewley with very similar dimensions, and with the same flat-floored midsection and wall sides. Of 1302 tons net, 1199 under deck, and dimensions of 216.9ft × 35.2ft × 22.9ft, the plan shows her carrying double topsails and a main skysail but with a smaller sail area than the *Formby* as the yards on her mainmast do not overlap those on the foremast, and barely overlap those on the mizzen. There is a curious arrangement of head sails: a fore topmast staysail and inner jib from the fore topmast, an outer jib on the topgallant stay and a flying jib on the royal stay with the tack right down on the

Fig 210. Figurehead of the Borrowdale, *photographed at Bristol by W A Sharman. The right forearm of the figurehead seems to be missing and both carving and figurehead need a coat of paint at least.* (MacGregor Collection)

Fig 211. Greta. *Sail and standing rigging plan traced from original plan in Whitehaven Public Library & Museum. Built of iron at Whitehaven in 1874 by the Whitehaven Shipbuilding Co with measurements of 226.0ft × 36.2ft × 21.9ft and 1190 tons net. Colours on sail plan: white — lower masts, doublings, mast heads, bowsprit, yards, sheer strake, boats, ventilators, hull below LWL; varnished brown — topmasts, topgallant and royal masts, jibboom, gaff, boom, deck fittings on poop; green — capstan on forecastle; white and gold — stern decoration; black — hull above LWL; red — sheer strake to boats. Probably later converted to barque rig as jib-headed mizzen topsail drawn above spanker and 3 larger staysails from mizzen, all in pencil; flying jib and skysail also crossed out in pencil. This reproduction is faint because my tracing has never been inked in.*

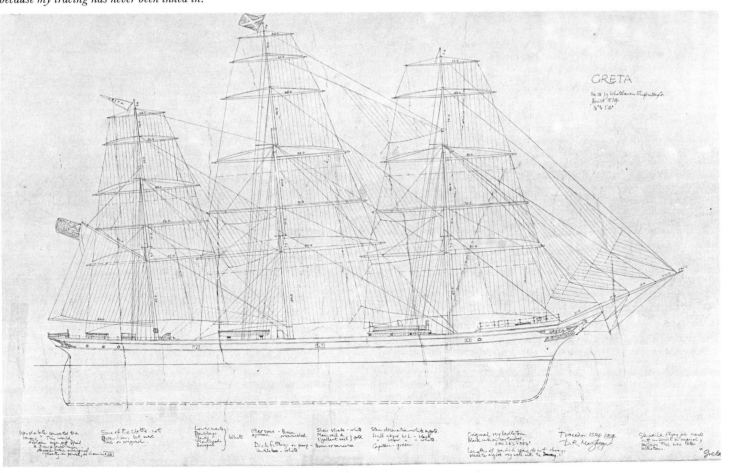

jibboom, so that it is not a jib-topsail. On deck there is a full height poop extending forward of the mizzen, a topgallant forecastle containing ten double bunks, while on the main deck there is the usual layout.[43]

The *British Nation*'s flat floors were probably dictated by her owners who were the newly-formed British Shipowners Co of Liverpool, of whom James Beazley was the managing director. The names of nearly all the ships of this firm began with the word 'British' and in the years 1864-67 they placed orders for twelve iron full-rigged ships with yards in Liverpool or Ireland and all were in the 1200-1300 tons range.[44] Basil Lubbock declared that the *British Peer* (1865) was the fastest ship in the fleet until the appearance of the *British Ambassador*[45] and this is to some extent confirmed by her dimensions, because although she was 2ft longer and 1ft deeper than *British Nation*, her under deck tonnage was 33 tons less, thus indicating a finer hull-form to compensate for the difference.

British Ambassador was celebrated for a mainyard 108ft long and although Basil Lubbock has reproduced a

1 *Fig 212. This ship in distress has been identified from the letters 'Un' in the top right-hand corner as the* Underley *which went ashore near Luscombe, Isle of Wight, in late September 1871, during a violent south-east gale. She was bound for Melbourne with 30 emigrants and general cargo and efforts to tow her off proved useless, so she was abandoned. She had been built of iron at Lancaster in 1866 by the Lune Shipbuilding Co with dimensions of 225.0ft × 37.1ft × 23.0ft and 1292 tons net. The ship was in charge of the pilot at the time. There is no evidence of stunsail boom irons on the yards; but on the other hand the yards are all long, especially the lower yards, and so she must have been able to set a large area of plain canvas. Of the vessels alongside, there is a pole-masted ketch with leeboards. Gould has a broadside photograph of the ship off Gravesend with a main skysail mast. (Osborne Studios)*

2 *Fig 213. The* Wennington, *of 882 tons, fitting out at the yard of the Lune Shipbuilding Co, Lancaster, in March 1865, seen from the Salt Ayre side of the river. She was the first iron ship built at Lancaster. From this photograph can be seen the proportion of masts and yards to that of the hull. The* Underley *came from the same yard. (Richard M Cookson)*

3 *Fig 214. The* Star of Bengal *photographed at Port Pirie, South Australia, in 1896 after she was cut down, ie had her sail plan reduced in size by getting her spars shortened. It should be noticed that her lower and topmasts are in one piece and that she was built like this in 1874 by Harland & Wolff at Belfast. (Arthur D Edwardes)*

Fig 215. *The* Star of India, *built at Ramsey, Isle of Man, in 1863 as the ship* Euterpe *is now preserved at San Diego, California. This photograph shows the restoration of her masts in the early 1960s, with the fore- and mainmasts propped up on the quayside. The wooden topmasts have been sent down: the topmast cap is on the right; next come the iron spreaders and crosstrees, and then the wooden trestletrees; the parral for hoisting the upper topsail yard is close against the iron lower mast cap; the paint is peeling from the iron lower mast. The scale is provided by the men.* (Photograph by Karl Kortum)

Fig 216. *Foot of the mainmast aboard* Star of India *in 1961 as master rigger John R Dickerhoff, works on hanging off the mizzen stay so that the mainmast can be hoisted out. The wording on the pump flywheel reads: 'John Wilson & Co Liverpool'. The fife rail is on the left.* (Photograph by Karl Kortum)

Fig 217. A product of Thomas Royden & Sons of Liverpool was the British General *which they built in 1874 with a tonnage of 1754 net. Here she can be seen towing up the Avon to Bristol with one paddle tug ahead and another alongside.* (MacGregor Collection)

photograph of her half-model, enquiries have failed to discover its whereabouts. The model shows a very cut-away forefoot and suggests a sharp and concave entrance and run; there is also a considerable sheer. This suggests she had a clipper's characteristics and she was evidently a fast vessel. Potter & Hodgkinson of Liverpool also known as W H Potter & Co built her in 1873 of 1794 tons net, 1737 tons UD and with dimensions of 262.0ft × 41.9ft × 23.8ft.[46]

Amongst many other shipyards at Liverpool which were turning out fine ships, it is worth mentioning the iron barque *Huddersfield* which W C Miller built in 1863. She was unique in having an iron deck constructed on Harland's patent. In 1864 she was lengthened 25ft which gave her dimensions of 179.6ft × 28.2ft × 15.8ft and 573 tons net. The lower, topmast and topgallant masts, as well as the lower and double topsail yards were all of iron, but the contemporary description that they were 'all in one' leaves one in doubt as to whether each spar was rolled from a single iron sheet, or whether the masts were in fact poles without doublings.[47]

On the Thames, the biggest iron sailing ship built in the sixties was the *Centaur*, constructed by the Millwall Ironworks & Shipbuilding Co in the same yard in which J Scott Russell built the *Great Eastern*. She was launched in 1864 of 1571 tons net and gross. Next to her in size comes the *Carlisle Castle*, built by R & H Green at Blackwall in 1868 of 1545 tons gross and 1458 net. In 1875, Green's built a larger iron ship of 1857 tons net and 1852 tons UD named *Melbourne*, with dimensions of 269.8ft × 40.1ft × 23.7ft. She was renamed *Macquarie* in 1888 and became best known under this name, a fact which was also due to the splendid photographs taken by Captain Corner when he was in command in the years 1897-1903. Green's ships were superbly fitted out and proved to be fast medium clippers much liked by their passengers.

Composite shipbuilding in Great Britain came to an end for square-rigged vessels in the seventies: the last such craft were almost certainly the barques *Helena Mena* of 673 tons, built by Robert Thompson jnr at Sunderland, and the *India* of 974 tons, built by Alexander Stephen & Sons at Glasgow. Both were constructed in 1876. A three-masted schooner built in 1876 by R Napier & Sons, Glasgow, and named *Canopus*, is also claimed to have been built as a composite, but *Lloyd's Register* and the *Liverpool Underwriters' [Red] Register* both show her to have been built of iron.[48]

After 1875, wooden shipbuilding in Great Britain was confined to the rigs of barquentines, brigantines and schooners, with an occasional barque, but in other parts of the world where forests were readily accessible or where iron plates and angles were expensive, wooden shipbuilding continued.

Fig 218. Another ship from a Liverpool yard forms this fine action picture of sails being clewed up, presumably before being taken in tow by a tug. She is the Chilean barque Cristobal Solar *ex-*Talisman, *ex-*Cursetjee Furdoonjee, *which Thomas Vernon & Sons launched in 1864 with a tonnage of 1199 net. (Nautical Photo Agency)*

Fig 219. Two iron ships built at Chester by Cox & Miller for James Beazley seen in the painting by Samuel H Wilson. On the left is the Robinson Crusoe *(built 1862 of 1164 tons) and the right the* Roodee *(built 1863 of 1036 tons). Presumably some actual incident is recorded by the artist, although why neither ship has her royal yards crossed is unknown. Both ships carry trysail gaffs on fore- and mainmasts; the ship on the left has Cunningham's roller-reefing topsails while the other has double topsails on two masts. Photographed from painting in the offices of Gracie, Beazley & Co, Liverpool.*

Fig 220. The Centaur *of 1864 with the yards removed from her mizzen as a measure of economy but with the old topmast and topgallant mast still aloft and a topmast gaff added. The main skysail yard has not been removed. The large house abaft the mizzen may not have been original; at least it would have been unusual for a ship of 1864. (Nautical Photo Agency)*

Fig 221. The Macquarie ex-Melbourne *under sail, probably photographed from the starboard lifeboat. The bumkin for the fore braces is outside the hull in the foreground.* (Nautical Photo Agency)

Lloyd's Register of British and Foreign Shipping.

ESTABLISHED 1834.

No. *9223*
2582

No. 2, White Lion Court, Cornhill,

London, *18th March* 187 *3*.

These are to Certify That the

Barque "Cornhill" of *Sunderland,*
Richard Wigzell Master, *339* Tons,

bound to *the Mediterranean* has been surveyed

at *Cardiff* by the Surveyors to this Society,

and reported to be, on the *12th March, 1873,*

fit for the conveyance of dry and perishable Cargoes to and from all
parts of the World, and that she has been CLASSED on the List of
Ships of the SECOND DESCRIPTION of the FIRST CLASS, and entered

No. *790,* in the REGISTER BOOK of this Society, A/ in red.

Specially Surveyed 1869 - 5 Years.

Witness my hand,

Charge *5/.*

Chairman
of the Committees of Classification.

B. Waymouth
Secretary

Fig 223. Here is an even older ship which was photographed in the River Medway at Chatham in 1876. She is the Soblomsten, built at Arendal in 1807; in 1877 she was owned there and had a tonnage of 308. She has nothing above her topgallants but she has stunsail booms rigged on her foreyard (below the yard). There is a bentinck boom, a wooden stock anchor, and the jibboom has been hauled inboard with the heel triced up to the fore stay. She appears to be flush-decked; a more modern addition is the wheel house. (Nautical Photo Agency)

Fig 222. The seas were still crowded with old vessels and this form issued by Lloyd's Register in 1873 classes the Cornhill as fit for carrying cargoes at the age of 26 years. (MacGregor Collection)

1 *Fig 224. The* St Paul *fitting out at Chapman & Flint's yard in Bath, Maine, shortly after being launched in September 1874. She was a wooden ship of 1824 tons with dimensions of 228.0ft × 42.0ft × 27.5ft and carried a skysail on the mainmast. At one stage, she was fitted with double topgallants. She could load 2800 tons of wheat.* (National Maritime Museum, San Francisco)

2 *Fig 225. Hull of the* Lucile *hove down so that the copper sheathing could be repaired by men working on stages along her side. She was built in 1874 at Freeport, Maine, and the inside of the ship was strengthened and the masts shored up to take the strain.* (National Maritime Museum, San Francisco)

3 *Fig 226.* James A Borland. *Lines plan reproduced from* Plans of Wooden Ships *by William H Webb. Built at New York in 1869 by William H Webb with measurements given on the plan of 143ft 0in length on deck, 32ft 0in moulded breadth, 18ft 10in depth of hold, and 750 Custom House tonnage. Webb comments on the plan: 'Built for the general freighting business, proved an excellent sea-boat, was a fair carrier, good sailer and desirable class of vessel for the business for which she was intended, gave great satisfaction, was the last vessel BARQUE RIGGED built in the port of New York . . .'.*

SHIPBUILDING IN AMERICA

The American merchant marine suffered a severe decline in the tonnage engaged in foreign trade as a result of the Civil War (1861-65), the total of 2.5 million tons on the eve of its commencement having declined to 1.5 million tons five years later. By the end of the war, less than one-third of American foreign trade was carried in American ships and this total was to fall throughout the remainder of the century. Shipbuilding for ocean trade in the southern Atlantic ports decreased rapidly after 1865 but New England continued to attract some orders although it was in Maine that the bulk of the shipbuilding took place for deepwater vessels. One reason for the decline was the rise in shipbuilding costs by at least 50 per cent which made it cheaper to buy Canadian softwood ships or British and European iron vessels. High tariffs on the import of goods used in ship construction were presumably levied to encourage native industries, but

2

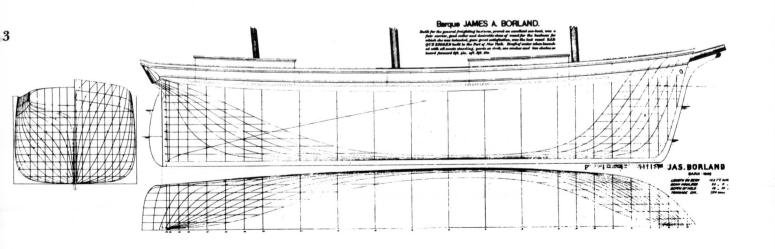

3

Barque JAMES A. BORLAND.

JAS. BORLAND
BARK - 1866

they resulted in the continuation of wooden shipbuilding rather than the expansion of iron construction.[49]

An analysis of wooden shipbuilding in America was carried out by Frank W Thober and published in *Log Chips* and it is summarised as follows:[50]

In 1870, 40 square-riggers were built comprising 17 ships, 20 barques and three barquentines with a total tonnage of 38,326. Of these, Maine accounted for 24 vessels.

In 1875, 79 square-riggers were built comprising 36 ships, 24 barques and 19 barquentines with a total tonnage of 81,220. Of these, Maine accounted for 54 vessels and Massachusetts for 13.

Basil Lubbock, quoting Bates' *American Marine*, states that on average 90 square-riggers per annum were built in the years 1865-70 but the sudden drop by Thober's figures suggest that different sources were used to compile these totals.[51] Square rigged vessels had almost entirely disappeared from the American coasting business by 1865 but the export of grain from California gave employment to American and British ships. For this trade and other deep-sea work, American builders developed a class of medium clippers in the 1000-2000 tons range, constructed entirely of wood but well-built and equipped and able to shift large cargoes in an economical manner and yet at a reasonable speed. With many built in the 'Down East' state of Maine, they became nicknamed 'Down Easters'.

Bath, Maine, was one of the principal building centres in America, and one of the builders, Houghton Brothers, gave a list of costs to build a ship of white oak and pitch pine with iron bolts at $60 per ton in 1855, $70 per ton in 1865, and $45 per ton in 1880. It was estimated that a large schooner would cost $53 per ton at Bath in 1880. At a rate of exchange of $5=£1, the cost of a wooden square-rigger works out at £21. It is not stated if this

Fig 227. The Sarah *running before a fine quartering breeze under topsails and foresail. Her deckhouses look absurdly large but she was only of 558 tons gross, having been built at Stockton, Maine, in 1871.* (Peabody Museum, Salem)

Fig 228. Photographed at her moorings in Calcutta in 1870 when only two years old, the Augusta *still has the trappings of a new ship of the sixties with all her stunsail booms aloft, with the exception of the fore topgallant yard, although the boom irons are fitted. Beyond is one of Donald Currie's ships, identifiable by having the black ports 'upside down'. I am grateful to Andrew Nesdall for this photograph and for data on Currie's ship.* (Andrew Nesdall)

includes the complete outfit of all the cabin and bosun's stores etc.[51]

There were some well-known ships built before 1875 such as the second *Sovereign of the Seas* (1868 of 1502 tons) by Donald McKay, and the *Glory of the Seas* which he built the following year and which proved a masterpiece as a medium clipper; then there was the *Great Admiral* (1869 of 1576 tons), the *Three Brothers* ex-PS *Vanderbilt* (converted to sail in 1873), and the *St Paul* (1874) which achieved notoriety as a hell-ship in the eighties.

In 1874 an important ship was built at Kennebunk, Maine, that was the precursor of a whole range of vessels. This was the *Ocean King* which was a four-masted barque

– a rig that was shortly to be adopted by many maritime nations. Admittedly, she was not the first to be so rigged but the first when economy was the watchword. She was a large vessel for her date with measurements of 250.5ft × 42.3ft × 30.1ft and a tonnage of 2526 register. She carried skysails on fore, main and mizzen masts and had steel wire rigging. The length of her mainyard was 86ft. She was not a fast sailer, her average passage to San Francisco from New York being 145 days.

Wooden ships built in Canada were still being purchased in Great Britain during the 1860s and early seventies. From 1870, Nova Scotia took the lead in shipbuilding, followed by New Brunswick, with Quebec third and Prince Edward Island fourth. The peak year for shipbuilding in the Maritime Provinces was 1874 when 490 vessels with a total tonnage of 183,101 were built.[52]

Fig 229. Another ship photographed with stunsail booms rigged is the
Seminole *which was built at Mystic, Connecticutt, in 1865 with
dimensions of 196.0ft × 41.5ft × 25.0ft and 1439 tons. She cost
$125,000 or £25,000 at the exchange rate of those days. She had a big
sheer and a highly steeved bowsprit; there are stunsail booms on both fore
and main topgallant yards.* (National Maritime Museum, San
Francisco)

DISMASTING OF LARGE IRON SAILING SHIPS

In the preceding sections of this chapter frequent
reference has been made to the splendid and lofty iron
sailing ships completed in the first half of the seventies,
but one aspect only lightly touched upon is the frequent
dismasting that took place in the years 1873-74. Many of
these ships were on their maiden passage when such a
disaster took place and altogether great publicity was
accorded these events in the maritime world. It was
reminiscent of the dismastings that occurred to the early
heavily-rigged American clippers at the beginning of the
1850s when they sallied forth bound for California with
their lofty masts and clouds of canvas. Having wooden
masts and hemp rigging they were often able to set up jury
spars and renew the rigging while at sea, but the medium
clippers of 1873-74 had hollow metal masts and steel wire

Fig 230. Donald McKay's last ship was the Glory of the Seas, *seen here in her prime at a San Francisco wharf c1877. She was built at East Boston in 1869 and measured 240.2ft × 44.1ft × 28.0ft and 2009 tons net. She could load about 3000 tons of dead weight cargo and 3300 to 3600 tons of coal. Although not a clipper, she made a run of 96 days between New York and San Francisco in 1873-74. Her made-masts can be clearly seen and she carried skysail at the mainmast only. (National Maritime Museum, San Francisco)*

rigging which required dockyard skills and equipment for renewal. Lloyd's Register of Shipping was sufficiently concerned about the problem as to issue a special report dated 2 December 1874, signed by the chief surveyor and two assistants. *The Times* reprinted this in full on 14 December 1874 and the *Nautical Magazine* of March 1875 (volume XLIV, no III) carried two articles on the matter. Lloyd's Register later conducted 'mathematical investigations' on the whole problem and came up with a lengthy book of 185 pages and copious appendices, including spar dimensions of 82 vessels, but their initital report of 1874 formed the foreword. This covers the matter in some detail and discusses the entire field of masting, rigging, loading and handling these ships so that it seems sensible to reprint the original 1874 Report in full (follows on p182).[53]

Fig 232. Aboard the St Paul *between the main hatch and the break of the poop, officers and petty officers pose for a photograph. The second mate is wearing the dark shirt and to the right is the first mate, Robert Dunn. There is a massive white-painted fife rail on the foreside of the mainmast, and abaft the mast are the iron flywheels of the Adair pumps, now preserved in the 'tween decks of the* Balclutha. *Then comes a capstan with the bars in place, followed by the after hatch and the break of the poop. With a breadth of 42ft, the decks look very wide. The built wooden masts with their iron hoops can be clearly seen. (National Maritime Museum, San Francisco)*

Fig 231. Rigged down in her old age as a salmon cannery or a cold store for fish, the 'beauty and mystery' of the Glory of the Seas *remains. After being laid up she was finally burned for her metal on the beach near Endolyne, Washington, in 1923. (National Maritime Museum, San Francisco)*

2

1 *Fig 233. A starboard quarter view of* St Paul *under sail when registered in Seattle, where she spent 23 years as a 'salmon packer' from 1903. In this picture the mizzen royal looks too short for its yard.* (National Maritime Museum, San Francisco)

2 *Fig 234. There were two Canadian barques with the name of* Fairy Belle *both of which were registered at Liverpool in the 1880s, but the author, F W Wallace, identified this one as being built at Clifton, New Brunswick, in 1863. (See his* Record of Canadian Shipping, *page 103). This barque, hauled out at Dover to be re-caulked, had dimensions of 139.0ft × 30.1ft × 17.6ft and a tonnage of 519; she had a raised quarterdeck. She is not copper sheathed and does not have outside channels. Copied from old picture postcard.* (MacGregor Collection)

3 *Fig 235. A good example of a heavily-sparred iron ship is contained in this photograph of the* Hoghton Tower *with double topgallant yards on each mast and a long jibboom. The lower masts were composed of iron plates and the topmasts of steel ones. The main lower yard has been cockbilled to do duty as a derrick and looks a long spar. She was built at Birkenhead in 1869 by G R Clover & Co with dimensions of 247.0ft × 40.1ft × 23.7ft and a tonnage of 1589.* (Cyril L Hume)

3

THE DISMASTING OF LARGE IRON SAILING VESSELS.

Remarks by the Chief Surveyor and his Assistants

In accordance with the Secretary's minute, to report on the letter received from Lloyd's Agency at Melbourne, relative to the causes of several sailing ships having recently been dismasted, the following remarks are respectively submitted for the consideration of the Committee:-

It is known that eleven vessels have been dismasted within the last twelve months. Of these, nine were new vessels exceeding 1500 tons, on their first voyage, and built by experienced builders in different parts of the country, including Liverpool, the Clyde, the Tyne, and the Wear. Seven of the vessels dismasted were bound for Australia; the remainder being bound for ports in the East, except one, bound to San Francisco.

The most remarkable feature in connection with these disasters is the number of large new iron sailing vessels dismasted on their *first* voyage. The list of dismasted vessels, so far as we have been able to learn, comprises the following:

Ship's Name	Tonnage	Date of Build
Loch Ard	1693	1873
Ditto (second time)	1693	1873
John Kerr	1864	1873
Cambridgeshire	1766	1873
Chrysomene	1835	1873
Loch Maree	1657	1873
British Admiral	1808	1873
Norval	1503	1873
Rydal Hall	1864	1874
Duchess of Edinburgh	1766	1874
Dallam Tower	1499	1866
Rooparell	1097	1868

The causes assigned by the Melbourne Surveyors are:-

1st That the vessels were overladen.
2nd That the stowage of iron was too low, thus making the vessels too laboursome.
3rd That the vessels were overmasted, the masts being too taut, considering the spread of rigging and weight of yards.
4th That sufficient care had not been taken in staying the masts, or in the strength of head gear.
5th That the masts were not stiff enough at the deck, and in one case that the material and workmanship were defective.

The subject is one to which we have devoted much thought and attention, and we have been endeavouring for some time to obtain as much accurate data in reference to it as possible. Calculations are also in hand at the present time, which it is hoped may throw some valuable light on the subject, and the results obtained will be laid before the Committee at the earliest moment possible.

The causes alleged by the Melbourne Surveyors are stated generally, without a direct reference to particular ships, so that it is impossible to test rigidly their accuracy, or to ascertain whether in their opinion all the causes specified by them apply more or less to all the vessels dismasted, or whether some apply to one vessel and some to another. It appears however as if, except in the matter of material and workmanship, the causes alleged are applied generally.

With reference to the first cause assigned by one of the Surveyors, *viz*, that the vessels were overloaded, it is known that in some of the vessels, this could not have led to the disaster, as they were not deeply laden. It is at the same time highly improbable that the amount of cargo carried in the other ships was excessive, in view of the fact that no class of vessels are loaded with greater uniformity, as to height of freeboard and surplus buoyancy, than these large sailing ships outward bound.

1 *Fig 236. The* Loch Ard *was dismasted twice on her maiden passage and yet this photograph, taken off Gravesend on 2 March 1877 only four years after she was built, does not suggest an over-masted ship, so the dismastings must have occurred due to defects in other ways. Her fore and main lower yards were 87ft long, which were 4ft shorter than the* Lammermoor *of roughly similar tonnage. But the latter did not have such long topgallant and royal yards. Barclay, Curle were her builders and gave her a length of 262.7ft and 1624 tons. (Nautical Photo Agency)*

2 *Fig 237. Another ship dismasted at this time was the* Chrysomene *here seen as the* Clevedon *later in her life, with her spars undoubtedly cut down. Potter & Hodgkinson of Liverpool launched her in 1873 with a tonnage of 1778 net, and fore and main yards 90ft long. (Nautical Photo Agency)*

3 *Fig 238. This painting gives an impression of what could happen in a squall when lanyards gave way or stays parted. Sometimes falling spars damaged the rigging lower down and resulted in a complete dismasting. This picture signed by Woolston Barratt of Newcastle, New South Wales, shows the* Gladstone *later in her life after being cut down to a barque. She had been built of iron by McMillan at Dumbarton in 1873 with the name of* Francisco Calderon *for owners in Sydney. Tonnage was 1159 net. (Maritime Museum, Kronborg, Denmark)*

Fig 239. Two names can be made out on the bows of this ship: the second is Stuart *and I suggest the first is* Peter. *The* Peter Stuart *was another of McMillan's iron clippers having been built in 1868 at Dumbarton with measurements of 234.0ft × 38.9ft × 23.0ft and 1447 tons net. Her fore and main yards were each 87ft long and she could carry skysails on each mast. She appears to have a long white house aft presumably set in a raised quarterdeck. She is no 50 in the Lloyd's* Register *Report on Masting (table 1). (Robert A Weinstein)*

Fig 240. Described on page 4 of Lloyd's Report on Masting *as the manner in which the mainmast of an unnamed ship — none of the cases have named vessels attached to them — settled on the keelson after the ship had made several voyages, and the builder had built several ships in like manner. A new main stay had been fitted prior to the voyage in question, and in a gale the angles of the keelson buckled so that the mast sank causing the rigging to become slack and allowing the mast to move about. Its rigging was therefore cut away which brought down not only the mainmast but all the others.*

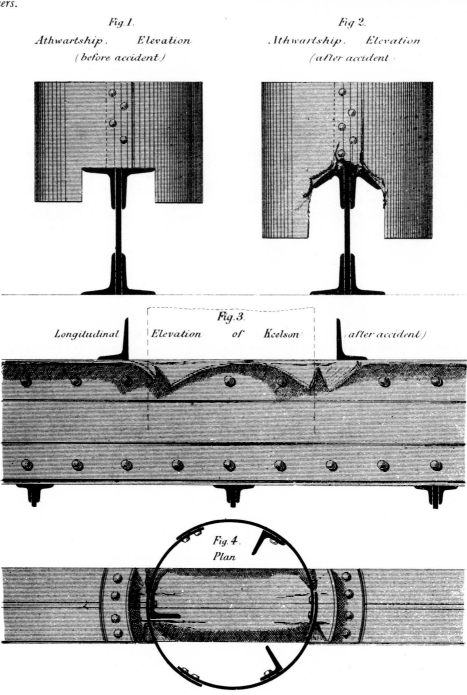

Fig.1.

Athwartship. Elevation
(before accident)

Fig 2.

Athwartship. Elevation
(after accident)

Fig.3.

Longitudinal Elevation of Keelson (after accident)

Fig. 4.
Plan

The second cause alleged appears to be of far greater weight and importance, *viz*, that, in some instances, by injudicious stowage, excessive stability was produced, thus causing violent rolling and undue strain upon the masts and rigging. This is rendered probable from the fact that the form of modern sailing ships is one conducive to great stability, and their being very heavily rigged and intended for high speeds make it almost certain that any error of stowage, at least on the first voyage, before any experience had been acquired with the vessels for guidance, would be in the direction of excessive stiffness.

High speeds have been aimed at almost universally in the largest modern sailing ships, and to obtain it, great rise of floor and great spread of sail are resorted to, almost of necessity. Great rise of floor, even with the ordinary proportion of beam and depth, produces great stiffness in the vessel due to her form alone; but in addition to this the beam is now somewhat increased in relation to the depth in order to retain the same displacement; – and that many of these vessels have great initial stability is apparent from the fact that they are able to shift, when light, without ballast, in spite of their heavy equipment and great top weight. This great stability of form, however, need not of necessity lead to heavy rolling at sea when the ship is loaded, provided the circumstances be properly recognised, and the heavy weights be accordingly not stowed too low down. It is well known that a vessel having little stability of form might be loaded so as to have excessive stability and be very laboursome; whereas, on the other hand, a vessel possessing great stability of form might be loaded so as to be a tender vessel, scarcely able to stand up under her canvas. Without elaborate calculations, or practical experience of her qualities, it is impossible to stow a vessel so as to obtain the desired amount of stability with precision on her first voyage; and although when a vessel's qualities become known, the stowage can be, and is generally, regulated with a tolerable amount of success, yet, with a comparatively new vessel of great size, and having, to some extent, a new form and proportions, a considerable margin exists for errors of stowage. And the more the value attached to speed, and the heavier the rig, the more caution is likely to be exercised at first to keep the weights low down – thus causing greater liability to excessive stiffness. It is stated by the Melbourne Surveyors – and it is well known that such has been the case – that heavy weights, such as iron *were* stowed low down. This, if sufficient in quantity, might have caused excessive rolling to such an extent that the momentum produced by the great height and weight of the masts and yards might have made the strain greater than any ordinary means of securing or staying the masts could provide against.

With reference to the third cause assigned – *viz*: That these ships were overmasted in relation to the strength and spread of rigging. It is considered that this is a matter of great moment, and one to which sufficient attention has scarcely been directed hitherto. The fact that these modern iron sailing ships possess sufficient strength and stability to carry very great areas of sails and attain high speed has led to the masts and yards being much increased in length and consequent weight. Added to this, the fitting of double topsail and top-gallant yards has added still further to the top weight, and from their great height materially increased the strain. At the same time, instead of the greatest possible spread of rigging being obtained to compensate for these additions to the strain, the shrouds are secured on the inside of the vessel, whereas formerly in large sailing ships (and in the Government service still) guard boards or channels were fitted, which admitted of the shrouds passing outside of the rails.

Other causes might be assigned under this head, tending to show that the increased magnitude of the strains in these recent loftily-rigged vessels has scarcely been fully realised; that the quality of the rigging and of the iron in the masts has not improved; and that the increased difficulties of setting up the rigging of large vessels, especially during the first voyage, have scarcely been satisfactorily overcome, or sufficiently attended to, and unequal strains have thereby been brought on the shrouds. In the largest and swiftest unarmoured cruiser in HM Service, the *Inconstant*, which has seen much service since 1868, and carries a great spread of canvas, the height of the lower masts and length of lower yards are somewhat less than those of some of the modern mercantile sailing ships; but the means of supporting them are much superior to those adopted in the ships referred to. In the first place the spread of the shrouds the *Inconstant* is 50 feet, whereas in the recent large merchant sailing ships, it does not exceed 40 feet, and the shrouds are larger and more numerous, and the lower masts are of greater diameter. On the other hand, it might be said that data more directly applicable to the subject are furnished by large merchant sailing ships, with no greater spread of shrouds than 40 feet, which have sailed successfully. But it is greatly to be feared that many recent disastrous cases show that additional strength is needed generally in the masts and standing rigging, as well as greater care in the fittings, in order to enable vessels of this magnitude to pass successfully through the heavy gales to which they are sometimes exposed.

Another cause assigned, *viz*: That the masts were not strong enough at the deck, does not possess that weight which it would have if it could be shown that the masts actually broke at the wedging; it should be remembered that the masts are usually doubled at the deck. But it is known that in some cases the masts broke between decks. And in view of this it is worthy of attention whether the advantage gained by wedging at the upper, as well as the lower deck, and thus practically reducing the length of unsupported masts by 7 or 8 feet, is not of sufficient importance to commend itself for more general adoption in these iron ships, where sufficient strength can be given by plating, or by fitting diagonal tieplates on the beams, to prevent the deck or the topsides straining, and the cargo being damaged therefrom. It may be pointed out that this will be still further facilitated by the provision in the amended Rules, that all the reverse frames should extend to the gunwale in large sailing ships, thus affording additional transverse strength to the topsides.

It is also urged by the Melbourne Surveyors that sufficient care had not been taken in fitting the head gear to provide adequate strength; and the material and workmanship are said to have been, in one case, defective. It appears certain that, in several vessels, the first part of the rigging to give way was the head gear; and the carrying away of bowsprit and jib-boom supports at the beginning of the disaster, has been attributed to bad workmanship or material. There can be no doubt that in the rigging of a ship, where all the parts depend so much on the support obtained from each other, the workmanship and material throughout should be of the best possible description, and particular regard should be paid to every detail. There are some doubts whether this has been sufficiently attended to, and these will, perhaps, be further confirmed when the details of the disasters are more fully known. In cases where particulars have been ascertained, it has appeared from such observations as could be made by those on board, under the difficulties of the situation, that some slight security was first found to give way, either an eye-bolt, or a stay, and that other parts being attached to, or depending on this, next broke adrift, and thus causing a *gradual* breaking up of the supports, and not a sudden carrying away of any large spar, or of the whole of the

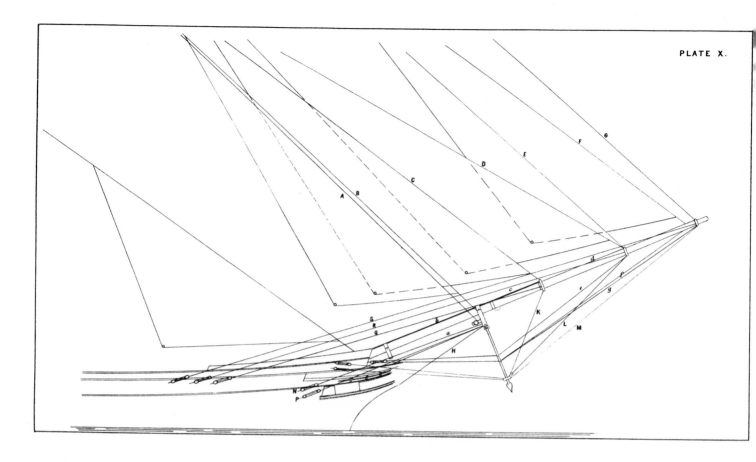

PLATE X.

Fig 241. This diagram of the headgear for a ship of 1600 tons appears as plate X in the Lloyd's Report. The following is from page 141 of the text and gives the sizes of spars and rigging. The lower case letters in the left column of the table are those of the stays continued below the jibboom. 'The bowsprit is 42 feet total length and 26 feet outboard. It is of iron 32½ inches in diameter, composed of four plates in the round ⁸/₁₆ inch thick, and is fitted with a diaphragm plate ⁹/₁₆ inch thick for a length of 12 feet attached at each edge by a single angle iron 4½ × 3½ × ⁸/₁₆, and there is besides an angle iron on each side.

'The jib-boom is of Oregon pine 18 inches diameter reduced to 14 inches, having a total length of 53 feet, and being 12 feet 6 inches long from the outside of bowsprit cap to inner hounds, and 18 feet long from the inner to the outer hounds. The length of the flying jib-boom outside of the outer jib-boom hounds is 16 feet, and the diameter of the same is 10 inches.

'The sizes of the rigging are as follows:-
'TABLE XXIX — SIZES OF HEAD GEAR OF 1,600-TON SHIP.

		Inches
Aa	Fore topmast stay, iron wire rope	4½ circumference
Bb	Fore topmast staysail stay, iron wire rope	3½ circumference
Cc	Inner jib stay, iron wire rope	3¾ circumference
Dd	Outer jib stay, iron wire rope	3½ circumference
Ee	Fore top-gallant stay, iron wire rope	3½ circumference
Ff	Flying jib stay, iron wire rope	3 circumference
Gg	Fore royal stay, iron wire rope	2½ circumference
H	Bobstay, iron bar	3 diameter
KLM	Martingale iron chains	¾ diameter
NP	Bowsprit shrouds chains	⅞ diameter
QR	Jib guys, iron wire rope	3¾ 3½ circumference
S	Flying jib guy, iron wire rope	3 circumference

'The chief strains which the bowsprit and head gear proper of a ship have to withstand arise from the tension of the stays attached to the bowsprit and jib-boom, and from blows of the sea, the motions of the ship, and the over-hanging weights.'

securities at once. From this it has been argued that the recent disasters have, for the most part, been due to local causes, and that if sufficient attention be paid to these details, similar disasters in the future might be avoided. On the other hand, it cannot too strongly be urged, that if a vessel is overmasted for the spread and strength of the rigging and supports, and she has in addition a tendency to violent rolling sufficient to dismast her, the supports might and probably would give way in detail, and yet no amount of attention to detail *alone* would cure the evil.

As before stated, too much attention cannot be devoted to all parts of the rigging, and it is considered that all eye-bolts and hoops, intended to bear heavy strains, should be of a special superior quality of iron, and that the bar iron from which these fittings are to be made should, in ships intended for classification, be specially examined, and samples submitted to tests by the Surveyors, as the safety of the rigging throughout must necessarily depend greatly upon these parts.

At the same time, the larger questions involved, relating to the stowage and stability of these large sailing ships, and the general strength of the masts and spars themselves, together with the strength and arrangement of their stays, shrouds, and other principal supports, are of the utmost importance, and require the fullest investigation.

A full investigation is the more necessary, as a tendency is apparent to attribute dismasting to a mere question of the proportion of beam to depth in the vessel, without regard to rise of floor and form, or strength of the masts and rigging; whereas, with the same beam and depth, an ordinary vessel might be made either full or fine, stiff or tender, and the proportion of beam to depth remain unaltered. When the calculations now in hand have been completed, and the facts and particulars of the recent diasters have more fully reached us, a definite statement of the results arrived at will be submitted for the Committee's consideration. It is already known, however, that the masts and yards for these large ships scarcely if ever exceed the strength provided in the Committee's 'Tables of Suggestions' for their sizes; and they are frequently of less strength. In view therefore of recent experience, it is respectfully submitted that it appears advisable that these Tables which have been prepared with great care, should no longer be regarded as 'Suggestions', but should be enforced as 'Rules' for Ships intended for Classification, and in those cases where it is desired to deviate from the Tables, sketches and particulars of the masts and yards should be submitted for the approval of the Committee.

It is also submitted that a scale should be framed, for the Committee's consideration, showing the minimum sizes and number of shrouds and principal stays which should be required. And in view of the few particulars relating to the masts, yards, and rigging given on the First Entry Reports of Sailing Vessels, a 'Form' for Masts, etc, should, it is thought, be prepared, to be filled up by the Surveyors, showing the particulars of rig in *detail*, and attached to the First Entry Report, as is the case with regard to the engines and boilers of steamers.

Among the proposals recently made to diminish the strain on the masts and rigging, while retaining the present great spread of canvas and high speed are:- to spread the canvas over four masts instead of three, as at present, thus enabling the height to be reduced: and to return, as it is intended to do in one or two known cases, to the old system of fitting channels of sufficient breadth to admit of the shrouds passing outside the rails, and thus affording greater spread to the rigging. A point which recent experience has shown to be of the first importance is a more adequate security for the bowsprit and jib-boom than has sometimes been afforded. It is considered that the modern practice of fitting single-bar bobstays is objectionable, unless they be made of much larger diameter than is now general; or otherwise, not less than two bars or chains should be fitted to these large bowsprits, and great care should be exercised to ensure the eye-bolts, or shackles to which they are attached, being of superior quality, and sufficient in size and well fitted, as it is known that these fittings have been found to fail.

In conclusion, we would venture to add that after all the precautions above suggested have been adopted, much will still depend upon the skill and judgement of those in command of these large vessels to prevent similar accidents. The inducement to make quick passages is fostered where so many similar ships are engaged on the same voyage, and there can be little doubt that a spirit of emulation often induces captains to carry on with a full spread of sail long after it is safe and prudent to do so.

Formerly a limit was provided to the amount of sail that it was considered right to carry in any particular weather, by the straining, as well as by the heeling of *wooden* vessels. In a modern iron ship no such straining is visible, and if the vessel is excessively stiff, and does not heel much, no direct warning is conveyed until something gives way aloft, or until it has become so late that, with the limited number of men available, sail cannot be shortened in time to relieve the masts and rigging.

It is respectfully submitted that should the Committee approve the above recommendations, to make the present Tables for masts and yards a part of the Rules, and to specify the minimum sizes and number of shrouds, etc, and to have a 'Form' prepared for details of masts, yards, etc, much good will be effected. And this, together with the great interest awakened by the number of recent disasters to large sailing ships, and with the experience thus gained by the Surveyors, Builders, and Masters, will it is hoped lead to greater

precautions being taken, both in the fitting out and the navigation of these large ships, and thus tend to prevent a repetition in the future of such deplorable casualties.

B MARTELL
Chief Surveyor
H J CORNISH
W JOHN
Assistants to Chief Surveyor

2nd December, 1874

The main text of the later report was full of observations, recommendations and calculations concerning strains on masts and rigging. In an interesting sideline the report discusses masting rules according to various authorities:

It is found impossible to arrive at any sound conclusion as to the extent of masting in modern compared with early ships by any application of the rules given in books on masting, because sailing ships are longer in proportion to their depth and breadth than formerly, and rules which used to be applied almost universally are now utterly impracticable. Chapman gives the height of the lower mast for a trading ship as from 2½ to 3 times the breadth, and the mainyard more than half the length of the ship. In no modern ship is the size of the spars nearly so large as these rules indicate, as seen from the fact that this would give a mainyard of 120 or 130 feet long instead of from 90 to 100 feet, the maximum now fitted. Another rule, given by Fincham, was to make the length of the mainmast equal to half the sum of the length of the lower deck and the extreme breadth, and to make the mainyard seven-eighths of the length of the mainmast. This would give for a modern ship the absurd length of 150 feet and 131 feet for the mainmast and mainyard respectively. It was in fact a recognised practice not only in this country but in France, Sweden and in other countries abroad about the beginning of this century, to make the length of the mainyard somewhat more than half the length of the ship, and the topgallant yard about half the length of the mainyard, although in some authors the mainyard is determined to be 2⅛th times the breadth of the ship. The latter measurement would more nearly correspond to the present practice, but it can scarcely be taken as a criterion of any value. In fact, any comparison between the dimensions of masts and yards in the present day with the rules adopted in former times only shows how fallacious fixed rules might soon become when applied to ships changing in form and proportions, and developing into different types.[54]

Later on there are comments on the increasing popularity of double topgallant yards and the fear that the additional weight aloft was one of the causes of dismasting, as a result of which some vessels reverted to single topgallants. In some cases, masts were also reduced in height and yards shortened, but the report remarks that other vessels continued to sail safely whilst continuing to set their original large suits of sails on lofty masts.[55]

The general conclusion is lengthy but in essence it confirms the observations made in 1874. It is a pity there are not more details of masts and spars of the kind to be found in Middendorf's book on masting and rigging, published in 1903.[56] However, the Appendices do include full spar dimensions of 82 ships, and although unnamed, it is possible to identify all but two of them by means of the data given *viz* rig, date of build, under deck tonnage, register dimensions. Thanks to Roderick Glassford and the late John Lyman the identification is almost complete

Fig 242. County of Cromarty. *Sail plan photographed from original when in possession of the builders, Barclay, Curle & Co. Built of iron at Glasgow in 1878 with dimensions of 267.3ft × 38.8ft × 23.7ft and 1644 tons net. She stranded on the Brazilian coast on her maiden voyage. Altogether six four-masters were built by Barclay, Curle in the years 1875-78.*

and our joint conclusions are given here in Appendix VI.

The Lloyd's Register report on dismasting put forward the suggestion that four masts of a lower height might be employed to replace three loftier masts, and this is just what the Glasgow shipbuilders, Barclay, Curle & Co, did when constructing a new iron ship for J & R Craig. A Glasgow newspaper described how it came about:

> From the number of large-sized vessels that have been built of late years, necessitating heavy masts, yards, and sails, and the dismasting of so many of them, in some cases twice in a single voyage, entailing a serious loss on shipowners and underwriters, it occurred to Mr Ferguson, of Messrs Barclay, Curle & Co that, by adopting four instead of three masts, and thus reducing the size of the spars, while retaining all the canvas necessary for propulsion, a great improvement would be made; and, in submitting this new rig to the Messrs Craig, they decided on giving it a trial, and it must be gratifying to the builders to know that the first ship thus fitted out by them proved in every respect all that could be desired, and gives confidence to shipowners to adopt a rig thus so successfully inaugurated.[57]

This ship was christened *County of Peebles* at her launch in 1875 and was the first four-masted full-rigged ship, if we except the French privateer *L'Invention* of 1801 and a

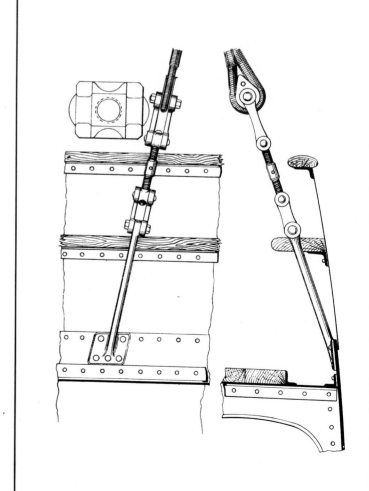

preliminary design for HMS *Warrior*. She was followed by about fifty other four-masters whose claims to this distinction have been verified by John Lyman.[58] There is a pencil draft for a plan of the *County of Peebles* as a conventional three-master, so it is obvious that her design had progressed a short way before the idea of four masts was first mooted. She measured 266.6ft × 38.7ft × 23.4ft and 1614 tons net register. As a four-masted ship, nothing was carried above royals and the topgallants were not divided; on the jigger there was a single topsail. On a sail plan of her almost similar sister-ship, *County of Cromarty* (1878), lower, topmast and topgallant stunsails are drawn on the foremast. A comparison between the sail area of *County of Peebles* and *Mermerus* assigns 30,610 feet to the former and 34,997 feet to the latter.[59]

It was soon found that a fore-and-aft rigged jigger mast was equally effective and more economical to maintain, so that the yards were dispensed with and the modern four-masted barque had arrived. The first of these was the *Tweedsdale* (1877) which came from the yard of Barclay, Curle & Co and measured 1403 tons net. This became a very popular rig throughout the remainder of the nineteenth and the early twentieth centuries. Prior to the

launch of the *Tweedsdale*, several other four-masted barques had made their appearance, some of which have already been described: *Columbus* (1824), *Baron Renfrew* (1825), Donald McKay's monster clipper *Great Republic* (1853), and *Ocean King* (built 1874 at Kennebunk, Maine, of 2526 tons).

A form of rigging screw had been used in 1836 on the schooner *Marshall* and in other vessels of about this time but its use appears to have lapsed until the 1870s when it came into its own for setting up the rigging of the new breed of large iron sailing ships.

As bulk carriers of less than one thousand tons became increasingly uneconomic propositions to operate, so the yards which had built square-rigged ships below this size had either to enlarge their premises and their ideas or go out of business. Some, it is true, continued by building schooners, sloops and yachts, and taking on repair work, and in many smaller seaports the shipbuilding business dwindled to such proportions.

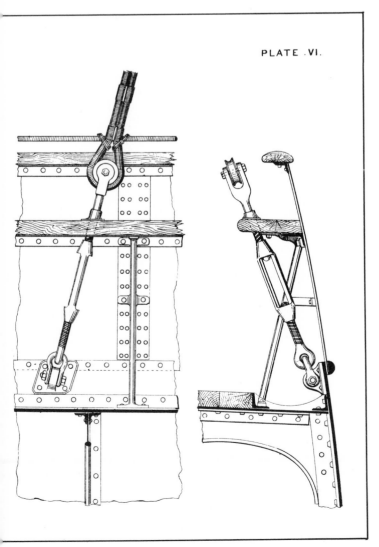

PLATE · VI ·

Fig 243. Two methods of setting up the rigging for shrouds and topmast backstays by the use of rigging screws. Reference is made to Plate VI on page 57 of the Lloyd's Register Report on Masting but no indication is given from which shipyards the two methods emanated.

189

6

SMALL SQUARE RIGGERS AND FORE-AND-AFT
1865-1875

INTRODUCTION

Although brigs continued to be built throughout the period now under discussion, they were being replaced by schooners and brigantines in all parts of the British Isles, particularly on the south and south-west coasts, although on the north-east coast the brig remained as the most popular rig for many years. The growing popularity of the barquentine with its more economical rig made it a suitable replacement for the small barque. All types were employed in coasting and deep-sea work: the brigs from the north-east coast of Great Britain traded to the Baltic and also carried coal to southern ports, but from other districts they were mostly engaged in ocean trade; the schooners and brigantines were employed in every form of home trade in addition to ranging the oceans of the world. Size was no obstacle and vessels of under 100 tons regularly crossed the Atlantic, entered the Mediterranean, or traded to South America and West Africa. The vast majority of these brigs and schooners were constructed of wood, and although a number were built of iron, only a handful were of composite construction.

SOME BRIGS COMPARED

A sail plan in the Whitehaven Public Library and Museum of an unnamed brig, reproduced in figure 246, provides a good example of a wooden vessel of this rig that was suitable for world-wide trade. The hull on the plan scales 104.5ft register length and 13.5ft depth of hold at $\frac{1}{4}$ inch scale. This plan appears to have been prepared by or for the sailmaker and spar maker, because the sails and spars look to be accurately drawn to scale, whereas the hull is of a more primitive character. Yet it indicates the deck fittings well in pure elevation, apart from the inevitable attempt at showing the wheel in perspective – a foible which no provincial ship draughtsman could resist. The hull structure is capably portrayed, the beams and iron knees faithfully rendered and, other than the undoubted thinness of the stem, the hull can probably be relied on to indicate a typical vessel of the period. The watermark on the plan is dated 1864 and several brigs can be considered as possible candidates.

First, let us compare her with other locally-built brigs of her size. The Whitehaven builders of the sixties consisted of Hugh Williamson, who built fourteen vessels between 1851-70; Lumley Kennedy & Co, whose yard closed down after building the brig *Erato* in 1864; Shepherd & Leech, who took over the latter's yard; and T & J Brocklebank. The latter firm only produced two brigs in the fifties and sixties, and both were twenty feet shorter than the one illustrated here. Lumley Kennedy can also be dismissed as a possible builder, because of the date when he closed down his yard.

Continuing the comparison of size, Hugh Williamson launched the brig *Jane Williamson* in March 1870 with measurements of 105.0ft × 24.2ft × 13.0ft and 188 tons net. Her builder was listed as the owner and she classed 10 A1. She could be regarded as a suitable candidate as two dimensions fit almost exactly – the breadth of the brig in the drawing being impossible to determine – if it were considered likely that she would have been equipped with roller-reefing single topsails as late as 1870. This seems a fairly remote possibility and is one obstacle to naming the plan *Jane Williamson*. The next most likely candidate is another brig launched by Williamson, the *Ellen Ashcroft*, built in 1866 with measurements of 102.8ft × 23.8ft × 13.0ft and 189 tons. It is possible that she could have been fitted with roller-reefing topsails, but the hull length is two feet too short.

On the other side of the Solway Firth, Benjamin Nicholson launched a brig in 1864 named *Solway Queen* of similar length to the brig in question, and as Annan-built ships were towed to Liverpool for fitting out, it is conceivable that the *Solway Queen* might have been taken to Whitehaven or that a Whitehaven sailmaker was supplied with this plan for cutting out the sails. The *Solway Queen* measured 104.9ft × 23.4ft × 14.2ft and 216 tons, and classed 13 A1; she was owned at Liverpool and traded to South America.

Now let us consider the style of draughtsmanship of the plan in figure 246 which has an important bearing on the case. There is a strong resemblance in style between this plan and that of a longitudinal section in the Brocklebank archives of their barque *Petchelee* (1850). In the period 1850-70 no Brocklebank-built vessel approximates to the

Fig 244. The Trusty *was built at Bridport in 1872 by Cox with dimensions of 101.6ft × 23.4ft × 12.6ft and 155 tons net. She was owned by J Munn & Co and employed in the North Atlantic trade.* (David Clement Collection)

Fig 245. This actual photograph of the Trusty *compares favourably with the artist's portrait of her. There is a wheel house aft, and a long overhang to the stemhead; the knightheads are white and prominent; and there are stunsail booms on top of the foreyard. The name of 'R.T. Parsons, Harbour Grace, Newfoundland' appears on the bottom of the photograph.* (David Clement Collection)

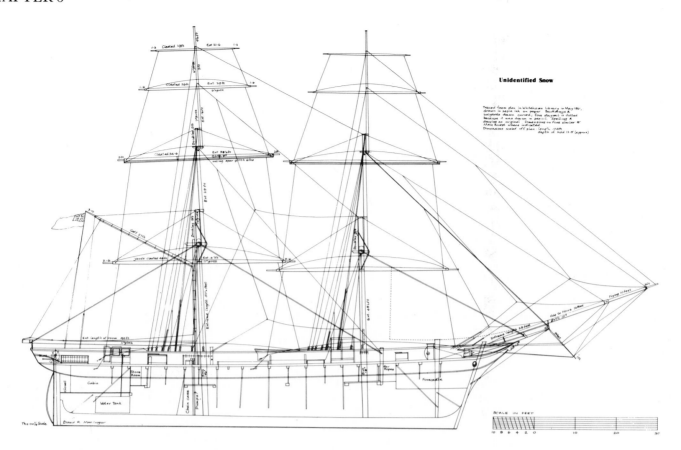

Fig 246. Unidentified Snow. *Longitudinal section with sail and standing rigging plan redrawn from plan traced in Whitehaven Library & Museum. Dimensions scaled off plan: length 104ft; depth of hold 13.5ft approx; beam impossible to determine. Fore staysail drawn dotted because it is in pencil on original. See text for ways of identification.*

required length so that the plan obviously does not represent any product from this yard, but it could have been drawn by a person who worked in this yard, such as Joseph Shepherd who had been their foreman and who began shipbuilding on his own account in 1865 under the name of Shepherd & Leech. Shepherd must have left because Brocklebank's closed their yard. Longitudinal drawings showing masts in position and yards crossed, as well as some deck fittings, principal timbers and iron knees, are sufficiently unusual to demand special attention, as in the present case.

It must also be observed that not only has the brig's plan got new positions indicated in blue crayon for each mast – 12in forward for the foremast and 3ft 6in forward for the mainmast – but also two centrelines in red suggesting the positions for stepping the main and mizzen masts of a barquentine. Here again, Shepherd & Leech are the only Whitehaven builders to produce barquentines, namely the *Chrysolite* and *Beckermet*. It accordingly seems most likely, from present evidence, that this plan emanated from Joseph Shepherd and that it indicates, if not an actual vessel, then the type of deck fittings, hull construction, masting and rigging put into his ships. A sail plan of the *Chrysolite* appears in figure 296 and is discussed later in this chapter under the section on barquentines. The following list of ships built by the firm was compiled with the assistance of Daniel Hay, Borough Librarian at Whitehaven.

SHIPS BUILT BY SHEPHERD & LEECH OF WHITEHAVEN

All built of wood

Date	Name	Rig	Tons	Dimensions	Comments
1865	*James Davisdon*	bk	216	107.0ft × 23.2ft × 14.0ft	Yard no 1 bkn 1883-4
1865	*Ann Humphreys*	bg	174	97.0ft × 22.4ft × 12.8ft	bgn 1874
1866	*Elizabeth Kelly*	bgn	168	83.9ft × 21.2ft × 12.3ft	
1867	*Ann Middleton*	bg	180	98.3ft × 22.7ft × 12.9ft	
1867	*Pearl*	sch	122	82.6ft × 20.3ft × 11.2ft	Yard no 5
1868	*Miriam*	bgn	126	83.8ft × 21.1ft × 11.2ft	Yard no 6
1869	*Chrysolite*	bkn ex-bgn	158	95.6ft × 21.6ft × 12.0ft	Yard no 7 later 3-mast schooner
1870	*Sea Mew*	trawler		?	
1871	*Beckermet*	bkn	229	107.1ft × 23.1ft × 12.9ft	

The remaining eight vessels built 1872-79 were trawlers and yachts

It will be noted that none of the vessels agrees too closely with the particulars of the unnamed brig.

The lines plan of *James Davidson* appears in figure 102, and so it becomes possible to build up some idea of the type of craft being produced by this small yard, as many of the other vessels were undoubtedly variations on the *James Davidson*'s design.

Examining the sail plan of this Whitehaven brig in more detail, it is obvious from dimensions written on the original that, with the exception of the lower masts, the masts and yards of the foremast are identical in length to those of the mainmast; but at 50ft 6in the main lower mast is two feet longer than its equivalent on the fore. The topsail yards are dimensioned as 38ft 6in but scale 39ft 6in and are fitted with roller-reefing gear. Roller reefing topsails were frequently cut with hollow leeches to ensure that when the sail was close-reefed it did not extend beyond the yardarm hoops which supported the revolving yard, otherwise there would have been a most frightful tangle. In this plan the leeches are given far less gore than

Fig 247. The Teazer *close-hauled off Sandy Hook makes a dramatic picture with her single topsails, long trysail boom and fidded flying jibboom. Compare her with the sail plan in figure 246. (Peabody Museum, Salem)*

normal thus making the head unusually long, which in turn gives the brig a big area of square canvas. No lower staysails are shown nor a main royal staysail, but the luff of those included extends high up on the stays. No dimensions are given for the trysail mast, either for length or diameter. Strictly speaking, to be classed as a snow she should have no trysail boom, a condition rarely fulfilled by the middle of the nineteenth century, although the *Belle of the Clyde* complies with it (figure 98). As the Whitehaven brig has a span led to the peak of the gaff, instead of a halliard, it must have been intended either to brail in the sail or to fit hoops on the gaff.

The deck layout is standard and the fittings require no comment. The occasional hold beams are only decked-over in way of the masts and no hold beams are indicated beneath the floor of either forecastle or after cabin. The deck beams are obviously incomplete: another three could be added aft and one more at the forward end. Excluding the carlings at the main hatch, this would give her twenty-one deck beams or a similar number to those possessed by the *Solway Queen*, according to the Lloyd's Register survey report. The latter allots to *Solway Queen* a longboat and one other boat, and two iron pumps. Heavy timbers were employed in her construction: the scantlings of the keel were 13½in × 14in moulded; the keelson was

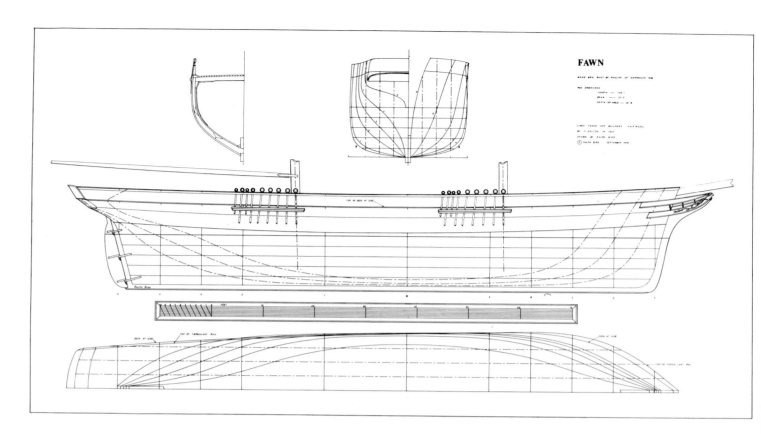

FAWN

WOOD BRIG BUILT BY PHILLIPS OF DARTMOUTH, 1868

REG DIMENSIONS

LENGTH — 108.1
BEAM — 21.3
DEPTH OF HOLD — 12.8

LINES TAKEN OFF BUILDERS HALF MODEL
BY F DALTON IN 1962
DRAWN BY RALPH BIRD
© RALPH BIRD SEPTEMBER 1979

Fig 248. Fawn. Lines plan drawn by Ralph Bird from lines taken off builder's half-model by P Dalton in 1943. Built of wood at Dartmouth in 1866 by Phillips with dimensions of 109.1ft × 23.2ft × 12.9ft and 211 tons. Later, net tonnage given as 192, and when owned at Ramsgate by 1900, net tonnage is 178 and rig altered to brigantine. Trailboards, figurehead, masts and LWL as on model. Reconstruction by Bird: main boom; channels, chainplates and deadeyes; cross-section.

Fig 249. This rig of the Sarah was commonly described as 'brig' in the nineteenth century even though a 'snow' or trysail mast is fitted. But a snow should not have a main boom and there is a long one here. See the text for description; she could well be laid-up here. (The late H O Hill)

similar; the floors were 10½in × 11in moulded; and six pairs of 4in × ⅝in iron plates were let in diagonally on the outside of the frames. Such sizes would also apply to the Whitehaven brig.

The photograph of the brig *Teazer*, reproduced here in figure 247, bears a striking likeness to this Whitehaven brig. It is a remarkable photograph because it portrays a vessel with single topsails set – topsails which are actually Cunningham's patent, and the travellers down the centre of the sails are just visible. She measured 293 tons and was built at Dartmouth in 1858 by W Kelly and owned by W Cuming & Co of Plymouth, who placed her in the South American trade. The *Teazer* might have had a hull-form somewhat like this lines plan of the brig *Fawn* which Phillips built at Dartmouth in 1866 of 211 tons. At first she traded to South America. This plan shows a combination of good capacity and fine sailing abilities, and I am grateful to Ralph Bird for providing it.

An excellent illustration of the hull-form of a wooden brig is afforded by a photograph in the collection of the late H Oliver Hill, which shows the brig *Sarah* on the grid at Littlehampton, probably when under the ownership of Captain Robinson of that port. This brig was built by May at Kingston, a district of Shoreham, Sussex, in 1862. She measured 110.0ft × 23.0ft × 11.6ft and 185 tons. The photograph shows the run of the planking to best advantage, the Plimsoll mark, and the general contours of the hull. When launched, the *Sarah* would have had single topsails and the topgallant masts would have been twice as tall to permit royals to be set on each mast; stunsails would also have been carried as a matter of course. By the end of the nineteenth century, first the fore royal would have been lopped off and than the main royal, and the topgallant masts would have been shortened simultaneously. The yards might also have been reduced in length, or when a new sail was required it would possibly have been given one less cloth in the head.

The sail plan of the brig *Mary* in *Merchant Sailing Ships 1815-1850* (figure 46) illustrates just such a cut-down brig. She was built in New Brunswick in 1831 of 109 tons register and this sail plan was prepared in 1872 by William Kennaugh, the Whitehaven sailmaker. Her bowsprit is the traditionally massive stick of the early nineteenth century and she has no fore trysail gaff, but otherwise the rig and spar proportions are identical to the *Sarah*.

As the vessels grew older, changes in rig become too numerous to mention, but two specific cases illustrate what could happen to brigs. The brig *Hannah Douglas* built at Llanelly in 1864, was converted to a brigantine in 1870, and a sail plan in the Whitehaven Public Library and Museum has the alterations superimposed on the existing layout: the foremast is unchanged, but the mainmast is moved seven feet forward, giving a main boom 46ft long; a new and longer main lower mast is required, and also a longer main topmast; the stays leading forward to the foremast are re-positioned, and larger staysails are drawn on them.

The other case is better known and concerns the *Waterwitch*, built at Poole in 1871-72 by Thomas Meadus. She began life as a brig with double topsails and royals on each mast, but within six months of her launch a change of ownership brought about the loss of the fore royal and stunsails, and the fitting of a bentinck boom to the fore course. In 1884 she was re-rigged as a barquentine as a measure of economy and in the following manner: the foremast was re-stepped and its yards were replaced with those from the main; the mainmast was removed and a new fore-and-aft mainmast and mizzen were fitted. Under this rig she sailed in the British home trade until 1936.[1]

A view of brigs in the River Nene at Wisbech, taken in 1856, shows the difficult and unpleasant conditions under which trade existed there. The great rise and fall of the tide combined with muddy, sloping banks resulted in sewer-like conditions at low water, and placed severe strain on the hulls. Only heavily-built, flat-bottomed vessels could withstand such usage year after year, which is why many brigs were thus constructed and why many achieved such longevity. The only brig in this photograph capable of carrying two royals is the Portuguese *Amelia*, whose hull-form is noticeably different to the British vessels.

Brigs and brigantines built on the Continent usually retained both royals when the British craft had had theirs removed for the sake of economy. The absence of a fore royal gave rise to the expression: 'No fore royal, no morning coffee'. They also possessed a large house built on the deck abaft the mainmast to accommodate the master, officers, steward, saloon and sail room, thereby increasing the cargo capacity of the hold by a like amount. But the crew normally berthed in a forecastle situated below deck in the traditional manner, right up in the bows, with little light or air. Such brigs also had more sheer than their British counterparts. In European waters, the Baltic and Mediterranean remained the last havens for brigs.

Fig 250. *Brigs photographed in the River Nene at Wisbech by Samuel Smith on 30 August 1856. Reading from left to right they are the Portuguese* Amelia, *with timber from Quebec;* Craggs *(nil L.R. 1856-57);* Vigilant *(built 1853 at Sunderland 226 tons). No others named.* (Wisbech Museum)

BRIGANTINES

Most brigantines in the second half of the nineteenth century were notable for the variety of staysails set from the mainmast. Three, four or five might be set, and they were often four-sided and of curious shapes, according to the whim of the local sailmaker. Sometimes the foot was rounded into the leech so that it was difficult to determine where they met. William Kennaugh of Whitehaven was one who favoured this as may be seen in the sail plan of the barquentine *Chrysolite* (figure 296)). The lower, middle and topmast staysails on the mainmast are four-sided but the topgallant staysail is triangular. The foot of the main middle staysail, although rounded, runs roughly parallel with the stay. This last feature occurs in the brigantine *Juan de la Vega*, built in 1871 by Alexander Hall & Sons, only in this case the foot is straight and the nock extends for practically the full drop of the fore course. Her main topmast staysail is also a big sail with a leech of 39ft 6in, foot 23ft 0in, nock 5ft 0in and luff 43ft 0in. Barquentines and jackass barques likewise employed this multipilicity of staysails between the main- and foremasts, but few brigs did so.

In a photograph taken about 1888 by Beken of Cowes of the schooner yacht *Hilda*, there is a brigantine on the left of the picture which is setting no less than five staysails from her mainmast: only the lower staysail is triangular and sheeted to a boom; all the others are four-sided and two of them hoist to the head of the main topmast. In addition, a flying jib is set like a jib-topsail and the topmast studdingsail boom on the foreyard is still rigged out. Her nationality is uncertain, but there is no large deckhouse aft – something that would automatically proclaim her as a foreign ship.

The 189-ton brigantine *Sensation*, built in 1865 at Rye by Hoad Brothers, had a very similar rig to judge from a sail plan in the National Maritime Museum, Greenwich: the main lower staysail was sheeted to a boom, and the main middle, topmast and topgallant staysails were all four-sided. There appears to be some form of jackstay from the hounds of the fore topmast to the afterside of the top to take the nock of the main topgallant and topmast staysails. Ralph Bird has redrawn this plan and reconstructed the standing rigging from deadeyes drawn faintly in pencil (figure 256).

The fact that a brigantine was not classed as a square-rigged vessel in the Merchant Shipping Acts, whereas a barquentine was, permitted masters holding a fore-and-aft ticket to take command of the former, thus perpetuating the brigantine rig at the expense of the barquentine.

Many of the wooden brigantines in active trade towards the end of the century were elderly, hard-worked vessels, with reduced canvas and much-repaired hulls. These wooden hulls suffered severely in contact with the iron sides of small coasting steamers when jammed together in some dock, such as the narrow basin at Charlestown, where vessels of all types and nationalities went to load china clay.

In the United States of America, some shipowners continued to order brigantines for the West Indies and trans-Atlantic trades, and the abandonment of square sails was brought about by the rising cost of hiring seamen and the substitution of a rig which fewer men could handle. Howard I Chapelle has observed that 'the brigantine was replaced by the three-masted schooner which benefitted more by use of steam winches' in handling sail than did the barquentine. The lines plan of the brigantine *J.W. Parker*, built at Belfast, Maine, in 1874, which he reproduces and comments on in the same section, is very similar in hull-form to the *James Davidson*, the chief differences being that the English barque is deeper in proportion to her length, and also narrower.[2]

In Canning, Nova Scotia, Ebenezer Bigelow was building a variety of craft in the 1850s and 1860s, until the yard was taken over by Ebenezer Cox in about 1870. A few surviving sail plans include the brigantines *Fred Clark* (1865) and *Spring Bird* (1868), and a copy of the former is shown in figure 258. The *Spring Bird*, of 176 tons, had a register length as scaled off the plan of 96ft, or nine feet longer than *Fred Clark*. Nevertheless, the length of the latter's foreyard (54ft 4in) is only 2ft 4in shorter than in *Spring Bird*, and the height of both sets of masts from deck to truck is approximately similar. *Fred Clark* has therefore a larger sail area in relation to hull profile, and a note on her plan states: 'This vessel was considered by the captain after proving her to be perfect both in Hull and Sparring'.[3]

Yards in Prince Edward Island also favoured the brigantine and the painting of the *Edna* shows a typical vessel of this period. Five square sails on the foremast, four large staysails between the masts, a big gaff mainsail and three or four headsails formed the typical rig. The *Edna* has a jollyboat stowed inside her long boat on deck, and her deck layout corresponds closely with brigs and brigantines built in the British Isles. She was built in 1871 by John Lefurgey at Summerside and measured 104.0ft × 24.5ft × 12.8ft and 190 tons, and classed 7 A1.

Another of Lefurgey's vessels was the *Raymond*, built as a brigantine in 1876 and of practically identical dimensions to *Edna*, suggesting she was from the same set

Fig 252. The brig Ida *ready for launching at Nyborg, Denmark, in 1868. Of 201 tons, she is to be launched bow-first, a method that was employed in many European countries outside Great Britain. (Maritime Museum, Kronborg, Denmark)*

Fig 253. A brig under single topsails hove-to off Gravesend c1870 as seen across the bows of the Blackwall frigate St Lawrence. *This is an enlargement from a small portion of a Gould negative which is somewhat spotty. The brig's jibboom has been run in along the bowsprit; she has a trysail mast, but also a boom; and there are long mast heads painted white. There appears to be no fore royal, but there is a suggestion that a main royal has been lowered on the foreside of the main topgallant, a practice occasionally adopted with smaller square sails, because the top of a spar is just showing above the main topgallant yard. (National Maritime Musuem, Greenwich)*

Fig 254. A brigantine leaving Ramsgate harbour illustrating the four-sided staysails set between the masts. The throat halliards of the mainsail have been hauled up and now it is the turn of the peak halliards. No name was attached to this photograph but the letters on the hull just below the tack of the foresail could read Fawn. A lines plan of this vessel appeared in figure 248 and she was owned at Ramsgate in 1900. Copied from an old photograph in Ramsgate Central Library.

Fig 255. *The brigantine* Rose Bud *flying her code flags VQTF. She was built at Fowey in 1865 by Nickels with a tonnage of 160 and a length of 101.5ft for the Mediterranean trade.* (Paul Mason Gallery)

Fig 256. Sensation. *Sail plan redrawn by Ralph Bird from builder's plan in the National Maritime Museum, Greenwich. Built of Wood at Rye in 1865 by Hoad Bros with dimensions of 100.3ft × 23.6ft × 12.8ft and 189 tons. She only classed 5 A1. Reconstruction: shrouds, backstays and chainplates.*

Fig 257. *The British brigantine* Coila *entering the harbour of Port-en-Bessin, Normandy, just north of Bayeux, probably with a cargo from Llanelly in south Wales. Originally a brig, she was built at Brucehaven, Fife, in 1871 by Whitehead for the South American trade and had a tonnage of 164 net and a length of 97.8ft. Copied from a picture postcard.* (MacGregor Collection)

Fig 258. Fred Clark. *Spar and sail plan reproduced from builder's plan in possession of John Bigelow. Built at Canning, Nova Scotia, in 1865 by Ebenezer Bigelow with a length of 105ft. Not listed in Lloyd's Register. I am grateful to John Bigelow for permission to use this plan.*

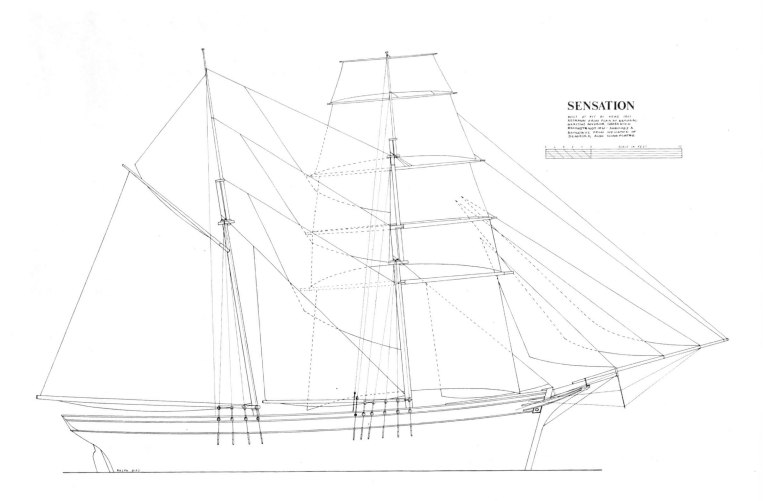

SENSATION

A✝D   6. - PORT-en-BESSIN
Navire de commerce entrant au Port

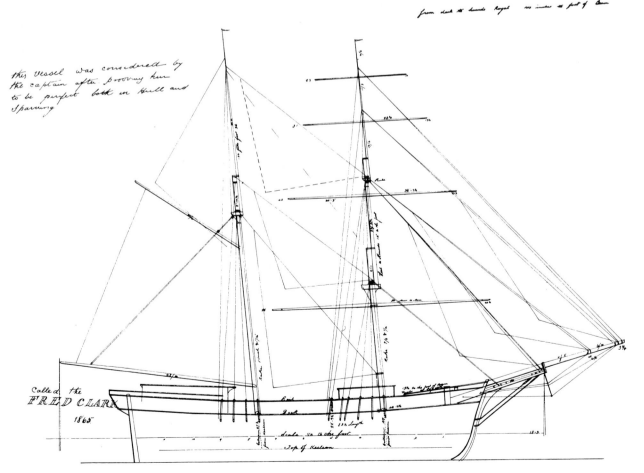

Fig 259. The brigantine Edna *under full sail from the oil painting by J Fannen dated 1885. All the spars are varnished with yardarms, caps and mast hoops white; the bulwarks are white inside with the main rail painted yellow; the boats are blue inside and the galley roof is green. See text for measurements and other data.* (Private Collection)

of moulds. Her tonnage was 188, and like the *Edna* she was first registered at Swansea. Later she became a barquentine and survived the Second World War under the name of *Lady Quirk*, being abandoned on the shore at Leigh-on-Sea, Essex, after serving as the local sailing Club's headquarters. She had a square stern, a heavy vertical stem carrying a female figurehead, and a slab-sided hull with full ends. A gaff mainsail made for her at Falmouth between the wars has dimensions of 29ft 4in luff, 41ft 9in leech and 23ft 6in foot; the head scales 25ft 0in. The *Aneroid*, built on Prince Edward Island in 1874 by David Ramsay, as a brigantine of 210 tons, was still sailing out of Bideford in the 1920s.[4]

SMALL BARQUES AND THE *BELLE OF LAGOS*

By 1865 there were very few full-rigged ships of under 250 tons being built in Europe or North America, because economic conditions meant that this once-popular size could equally well be propelled by a vessel rigged as barque, barquentine or even brigantine. The employment of fewer seamen and the upkeep of less rigging and spars all meant that running expenses were reduced. An example of one of these full-riggers has been preserved at Mystic Seaport in the shape of the *Joseph Conrad*, formerly the Danish training ship *Georg Stage*, which was built in

1882 and measures 100.8ft × 25.2ft × 13.2ft and 203 tons. Such an exquisitely-proportioned ship is shown to be small by the size of her lifeboats and of the people aboard her.

Many barques in the 250-300 tons range and others of lesser size continued to be built throughout the world, and their hulls and deck arrangements were little different from full-rigged ships. The following names have been compiled from the building lists published by John Lyman in his indipensable periodical *Log Chips*. No lists covering the year 1875 were compiled for French or German ships.

SHIPS OR BARQUES OF LESS THAN 300 TONS BUILT IN 1875

GREAT BRITAIN[5]
(East Coast of Scotland excluded)

Name	Material	Rig	Gross tons	Builder
Bayadere	wood	bk	212	Gibbon & Son, S Hylton,
Belle of Benin	iron	bk	299	Gulston, Sunderland Sunderland
Rhoda	wood	bk	265	John Johnson, Bideford
Wild Wave	wood	bk	251	Croft, Liverpool
Carpasian	wood	bk	299	A Weir, Ayr

NETHERLANDS[6]
(The smallest barque was the *Bima* of 411 tons. They only smaller square-rigger was the brig *Amerika* of 270 tons built at Rotterdam.)

DENMARK[7]

Cecilie	wood	bk	251	S Boas, Rudkøbing

(Only one other square-rigger was built this year, a barque of 475 tons.)

USA[8]

Columbia	wood	bk	304	Charles M Miner & Son Madison, Conn.

(The smallest full-rigged ship was 1050 tons and the smallest barquentine was 223 tons.)

Fig 260. The white-hulled Belle of Benin *was built at Sunderland in 1875 by Gulston and had a tonnage of 285 net. She was in the same trade as the* Belle of Lagos *but owned by T Harrison & Co. Source of picture unknown.*

Fig 261. There are several good photographs of the Wild Wave, *probably due to the fact that she was still sailing out of Tasmanian ports until 1923 when she was wrecked. She was built at Liverpool in 1875 by Croft for J Fisher of Hobart and measured 119.1ft × 27.1ft × 12.8ft and 237 tons net. She might have carried royals when first built. (David Clement Collection)*

There are a number of photographs in existence illustrating these small square-riggers, and one in the National Maritime Museum, Greenwich shows the *Garstang* lying in the Torridge at Bideford opposite the town quays on the side known as East-the-water. This picture indicates little deadrise and a short convex entrance, but there is a longer run with some concavity; there is the suggestion of a bilge keel amidships and also some bottom sheathing. The foremast protrudes from a small deckhouse which is an unusual feature, but perhaps by moving the house forward, sufficient room was formed for stowage of the longboat between the after end of the deckhouse and the mainmast.

A half-model to ¼-inch scale of the small barque *Planter*

is in the possession of Bideford Public Library, and has similar features to the *Garstang*. The *Planter* was built in 1871 by George Cox & Son at Cleavehouses, below Bideford, and measured 124.7ft × 25.0ft × 12.9ft and 267 tons. A label on the back of the model's baseboard reads: 'Designed by Thos Sanders and built at Cox's Yard, Cleavehouses; H Sanders, Bridge Buildings, Bideford'. Thomas Sanders' influence in matters of naval architecture in Bideford shipyards is at present unknown;

in 1835 the snow *Margaret* was built at Sea Locks above Bideford, beside the basin of the Rolle Canal, by one Thomas Sanders; in 1855 he designed the cutter *Lassie* which George Cox built.

In contrast to these wooden ships, iron construction enabled longer hulls to be built, and the greatly reduced shell thickness permitted bigger capacity even when the overall dimensions were unchanged. An example of such a small vessel, eleven tons bigger than *James Davidson*, is

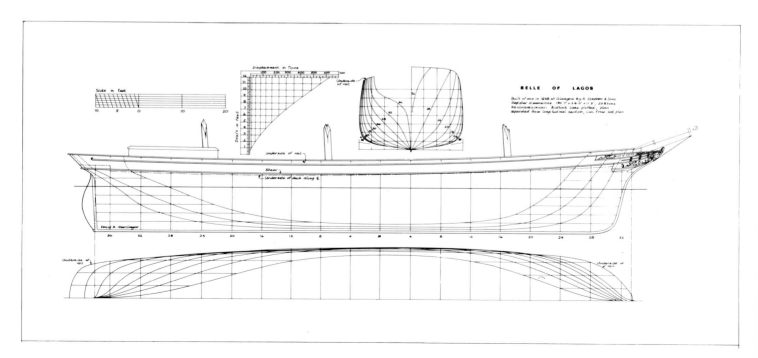

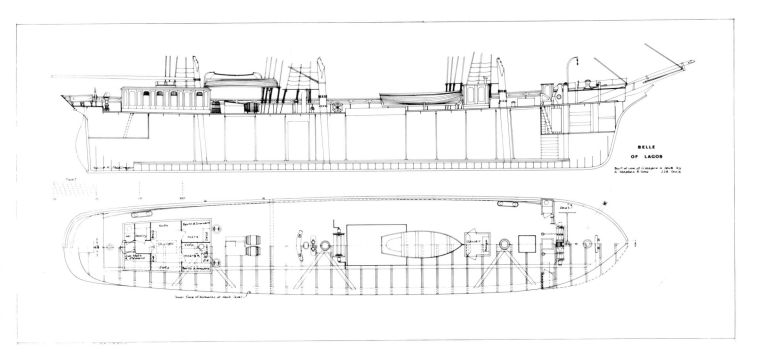

Fig 262. The small Danish barque Faveur *was built at Flensburg in 1863 with a tonnage of 272; she disappeared in 1875. Here the crew are on the foreyard, probably bending the sail. (Maritime Museum, Kronborg, Denmark)*

Fig 263. Belle of Lagos. *Lines plan redrawn from tracing of plan in builder's possession. Built of iron at Glasgow in 1868 by A Stephen & Sons with dimensions of 130.7ft × 24.0ft × 11.3ft and 228 tons. Reconstruction: buttock lines plotted; LWL from sail plan.*

Fig 264. Belle of Lagos. *Longitudinal section and deck plan redrawn from tracing made of builder's plan. Reconstruction: cathead added; break of forecastle; main rail drawn on deck plan.*

afforded by the *Belle of Lagos* which was built in 1868 by Alexander Stephen & Sons at Kelvinhaugh, Glasgow, for George Eastee of Liverpool. The plans are redrawn from copies of the builder's plans and are reproduced in figures 263 and 264. Her register measurements are 130.7ft × 24.0ft × 11.3ft and 228 tons; the contract price of £3900 gave her builder a clear profit of £69. The builder's drawing is one long sheet containing the body plan, longitudinal section, half-breadth plan and deck plan all at ¼-inch scale, the sail plan at ⅛-inch scale, and the constructional midship section at ½-inch scale.

The lines have little deadrise, with firm bilges and the maximum beam kept low, from whence the sides tumble home all the way to the rail. Considerable hollow is worked into both entrance and run where they meet the stem and sternpost, but this is to be found in the hulls of many iron ships. The midsection is placed forward of the middle point of the load line so that the run is 10ft 6in longer than the entrance; the latter is convex apart from the short hollow where it turns into the stem, but the run is finer and more concave. The finished result is a pleasing hull-form that is fairly shallow. She was obviously

influenced by the iron snow *Belle of the Clyde* (figure 96), built three years earlier by Stephen for the same owner, which has similar deadrise and entrance, but a fuller run.

The deck arrangements show *Belle of Lagos* to be virtually flush-decked apart from a low, short anchor deck forward on which a capstan is mounted, and a platform aft for the helmsman to stand on. Instead of a raised quarterdeck which would have been expected in a vessel of her size, she has a house standing on the deck with the mizzen passing through it; this is one of the few plans to show such an arrangement although it was a common enough feature in small vessels. Barclay, Curle & Co's small iron barque *Orange Grove* (1861) had a similar arrangement. If such a house is surrounded on all sides with a raised quarterdeck it becomes an 'Aberdeen house' of the type to be found in such ships as *Cutty Sark* and *Thermopylae*. In *Belle of Lagos* this house only accommodated the master, first and second mates, and the steward. The crew's quarters were entered through a scuttle close abaft the windlass, but little light or air can ever have penetrated. There is no lower deck nor any lower deck beams. This deck layout can be taken as suitable and typical of any small square-rigger whatever may be the materials of construction, and the position of the various standard elements – windlass, winch, hatchways, fife rails, mooring bitts, pumps, water casks, harness casks, binnacle and heads – does not deviate from the normal.

As regards the sail plan, the hull looks rather long for the height of the masts, and there seems to be a shortage of staysails on the main and mizzen, but this is all the builder's plan indicates. Fortunately, the stunsail booms are reasonably long. No main topmast stunsail is carried, which was a practice that was being adopted by the close of the sixties, as this sail frequently blanketted those on the foremast.

The photograph in the frontspiece of the 230-ton

barque *Natal Queen* (1866), seen under sail, shows one of these small square-riggers to good advantage, but the size of the man on the royal yard footropes indicates the relatively diminutive size of everything aboard. In spite of this, these small ships regularly engaged in the same trade as vessels treble their size and thought nothing of voyages to distant ports. By 1900 they might be considered on the small side, but seventy-five years earlier ships of 200 to 300 tons formed the bulk of the nation's carrying trade, and this changing outlook on size was symptomatic of the rapidly changing shipping industry.

WILLIAM H NEVILL OF LLANELLY[9]

This yard operated from 1863-74 and built entirely in iron. There were three building berths together with rigging and sail lofts, and the ironwork was produced by William Nevill's brother, Richard, who also built engines and boilers for the steamers. Twenty-five sea-going vessels were produced in the yard as well as three tugs and some harbour craft. The sea-going craft comprised the following, the figures in brackets giving the net tonnage and date of building:

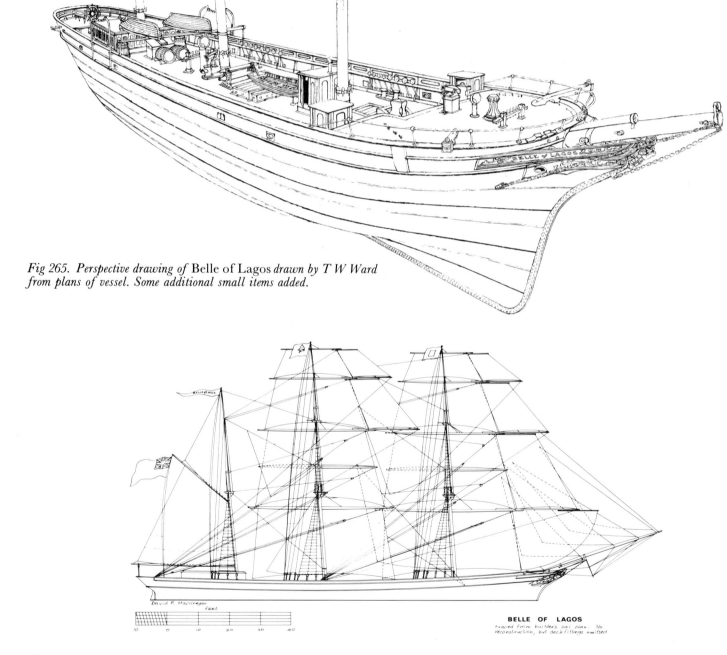

Fig 265. *Perspective drawing of* Belle of Lagos *drawn by T W Ward from plans of vessel. Some additional small items added.*

BELLE OF LAGOS
traced from builder's sail plan. No reconstruction, but deck fittings omitted

Fig 266. Belle of Lagos. *Sail and rigging plan redrawn from tracing made of builder's plan. No reconstruction, but deck fittings omitted as were the dimensions written on spars.*

Fig 267. The Isle of Beauty *in the Bay of Naples, attributed to the Italian artist G G Ianni. She was built at Sunderland in 1865 by J Metcalf and had a tonnage of 286 net. Although setting no royals, the topgallants are fairly deep and so are the topsails; the latter are roller-reefing to Colling & Pinkney's patent. She would appear to be flush-decked. There must have been many barques and brigs afloat which carried nothing above their topgallants, even when new. (Colin Denny Gallery)*

BARQUES	*Oliver Cromwell* (415 tons 1864), *Towy* (324 tons 1866), *Blonde* (329 tons 1866), *Brunette* (333 tons 1866), *Hinda* (476 tons 1869), *Grijalva* (222 tons 1874).
BARQUENTINES	*Jampa* (194 tons 1872; may have been jackass barque), *Gertrude* (243 tons 1874).
BRIGS	*Premier* (220 tons 1863), *Ann* 271 tons 1864), *Rachel* (272 tons 1865), *Betsey* (272 tons 1865), *Concord* (278 tons 1865), *Louisa* (280 tons 1869), *Marie Ange* (295 tons 1870; L.R. calls her 'BK').
BRIGANTINES	*Burry* (194 tons 1868), *Cymro* (188 tons 1871).
SCHOONERS	*Naiad* (149 tons 1867), *Quadroon* (160 tons 1867), *Merlin* (65 tons 1867), *Bess Mitchell* (98 tons 1871), *Johanna* (148 tons 1872), *C.A.* (86 tons 1872).
STEAMERS	SS *Cambria* (79 net, 134 gross tons 1866), SS *Llanelly* (163 net, 304 gross tons 1867).

Many of the vessels were built to carry metal ores: copper from South America, iron from Spain, or tinplate in coasting trades, and so they would be fitted with a trunk in the hold. Others carried coal, and Robert Craig has called the *Louisa* and *Marie Ange* 'possibly the fastest sailing colliers employed in Great Britain' in the carriage of coal from Wales to St Malo.[10] They were owned in Jersey and could shift almost 500 tons each. The *Oliver Cromwell* was the only vessel described contemporaneously as a 'clipper'.

The shipyard was at its busiest between 1864 and 1867. Without an examination of plans or half-models, none of which have survived, it is impossible to say if there was a standard model used, but the similarity in register dimensions suggests this was possible. For instance, the brigs *Betsey* and *Concord* measured 125.3ft × 23.9ft × 14.4ft and the *Rachel* was only slightly different. The dimensions of the *Brunette* – 134.3ft × 24.9ft × 14.7ft – were an average for the barques *Towy* and *Blonde*. The brigantines *Burry* and *Cymro* were built on the same lines. The *Grijalva* is described further in the section on jackass barques and her portrait is reproduced in figure 302.

In the matter of costs, there is always a difference between the actual cost price and the contract price, due to the profit element. Robert Craig has estimated that £17 per ton gross was the average cost to build in the yard, although the brig *Concord* was as low as £16 3s 3d and the *Grijalva* cost £20 11s on a gross tonnage of 234.

Harvey & Co of Hayle built both sail and steam ships from 1788 to 1893 and in iron from possibly 1805. Schooners and brigantines were built in wood but also in iron, beginning with the brigantine *Henry Harvey* in 1857. Two more iron brigantines were built before 1875: the *Penair* in 1862 and the *C.H.S.* in 1863. There were two iron schooners: *Riviere* (1861) and *Margaret* (1866). Five composite vessels were built in the years 1865-68: two brigs, one brigantine, one three-masted schooner and one two-masted schooner.[11]

SCHOONERS

Fig 268. W A Sharman photographed the Parton *sailing down the Usk from Newport bound for Ireland. She was a schooner of 115 tons, 81.9ft long, which had been built by Nicholson at Annan in 1866; she was then owned at Whitehaven by Burnyeat. The main topsail looks too small and the flying jib has not yet been sheeted home.* (MacGregor Collection)

Fig 269. Another of Sharman's photographs shows the Mary & Gertrude *lying at Bridgwater and illustrates her hull-form and deck fittings. The stern tapers into a neat round and she sits squarely on the mud without heeling too much. Ferguson & Baird built her at Connah's Quay on the River Dee in 1867 with dimensions of 78.0ft × 20.7ft × 9.7ft and 93 tons net.* (MacGregor Collection)

Fig 270. This picture of the Little Minnie *on the port tack in Mount's Bay portrays a typical British schooner of this date. She was built at Padstow in 1866 by Willmett under the name of* Minnie, *but was renamed about 1890 when John Stephens acquired her. When built she probably had a bowsprit and jibbom; also single topsail and a topgallant.* (The late H O Hill)

The type of schooner design illustrated in plans of the *Express* of 1860 (figure 117) was a transitional one, embodying features found in other types of craft: a midship section from a brig or small square-rigged ship; a fair amount of drag; masts closely spaced which were reminiscent of a clipper schooner; a shallow-draught hull. From lines taken off a half-model of the three-masted schooner *Dairy Maid* which Matthew Simpson, builder of the *Express*, produced at Glasson Dock in 1867, it can be seen that the sides between the turn of the bilge and the sheer strake were flatter than in the *Express* and the drag aft had almost disappeared. The stern was now rounded on plan.[12]

Two-masted schooners continued as popular as ever, and they were invariably lofty vessels with a single square topsail and topgallant, and a large gaff mainsail surmounted by a jackyard topsail. There were usually four headsails. On a sail plan of the schooner *Emily Burnyeat*, built in 1862, lines are pencilled showing how she could be converted into a brigantine. This must have occurred about 1875.[13]

The schooners built in south-west England were of a different style with sharp convex entrance lines but fine

Fig 271. The stern of Amanda with her crew. She was built a year later than the Minnie, pictured under sail in figure 270, and by the same builder. They must have been almost sisters as the dimensions are virtually the same: net tonnage was 87 in each case; Amanda's dimensions were 82.7ft × 21.3ft × 10.1ft while Minnie's were 82.0ft × 21.2ft × 10.2ft. Both had square sterns. (R H Gillis Collection)

concave runs, and many had a big overhang to their counters. They were fast vessels and probably owed much in their design to the cutter form of hull. Many of these schooners had been built for the fruit trade, but as it was taken over by steamers in the sixties they were forced to look elsewhere for their livelihood, and many were soon voyaging to the Baltic or the Mediterranean and across the Atlantic.

It was in the 1870s that the schooner became firmly established as the most useful rig for smaller vessels in the

Fig 272. The decayed hulk of the Millom Castle *in the 1960s, looking forward from the main hatch. The steel tabernacle was a recent addition.* (Author)

Fig 273. The author digging a trench through the mud and debris on the inside of the Millom Castle *in order to take offsets.*

home trade and soon in much of the north Atlantic. The hulls became longer and somewhat fuller amidships, although few were built with any real parallel middel body, and whether they were given two or three masts, the square canvas on the foremast was always retained.

One type of British schooner had a double-ended hull with the wales finishing on the sternpost and the rudder mounted outside, so that there was no overhanging counter, but the bulwarks flared out above the sternpost. This was generally known as an 'Irish Sea stern'. The after body was formed with cant frames like the fore body and this gave it great strength and long life. Plans of such a craft, the *Millom Castle*, appear in figures 274 and 275. In 1960 I discovered this schooner deeply embedded in the mud of the Lynher River, Cornwall, and although I could not find a name on her, Cmdr H Oliver Hill identified her. Eighteen years later, Ralph Bird and I took off her lines from inside, the hull having sunk four feet into the mud. This necessitated digging trenches through the mud, coal and tangled wreckage lying inside, and then making suitable allowance from the offsets taken to produce a set of lines to the outside of the external planking. The Lloyd's Register Survey Report gave the plank and frame thickness. It also indicated her massive construction and the wood used: frames of oak; external planking and ceiling of pitch pine; keelson and rider keelson, each in one length without scarphs, of pitch pine; most of the sixteen deck beams of larch; deck planking of yellow pine. She had been built in 1870 at Ulverston, Cumberland, by William White with measurements of 81.2ft × 20.6ft × 9.5ft and a net tonnage of 84 (in the 1870s). She was built to carry heavy cargoes of coal and iron ore from the Lancashire and Cumberland mines.

A sail plan has been reconstructed by Ralph Bird from a broadside photograph and from sail plans of contemporary schooners but so far no deck plan has been attempted. She forms a good example of a round

bottomed, full-ended schooner built for survival and hard work.

Another schooner whose lines I took off was the *Rhoda Mary* whilst she was lying in the River Medway near Hoo as an abandoned hulk, sunk in the mud and filling with every tide. Basil Greenhill assisted me and I drew out the lines and also reconstructed the deck layout and the sail plan. This was all in the years 1949-52. Thirty years later I decided to attempt a reconstruction of the sail plan to show how she might have looked when originally built as a two-masted schooner in 1868. I left the mainmast in the same position it occupied as a three-master and merely removed the mizzen; I assumed that the main topmast was the original length and so increased the length of the fore topmast to match it. This gave sufficient height to draw in a topgallant above a single topsail. This schooner was constructed at Yard Point, Restronguet Creek, off the Truro River by John Stephens, whose foreman, William Ferris, made the bracket half-model, which determined her design. She had measurements of 101.21ft × 21.9ft × 11.0ft and 118 tons net. From her lines plan it can be seen that she has an easy entrance and a long concave run; the bilges are very rounded, but there is no tumblehome. She had the reputation of being a fast vessel with power to carry sail and was steered with a tiller for much of her life. She was converted to a three-masted schooner in 1898.[14]

Another example of a Cornish schooner can be had from a lines plan in the Science Museum, London, of an unnamed vessel built at Mevagissey and drawn to show her port side. She has a register length of 95ft and all the characteristics of a West Country schooner with two masts, and is very similar in hull-form to the *Rhoda Mary*, but with considerably more sheer. Other dimensions scaled off the plan give a moulded beam of 21ft and approximately 10ft depth of hold. The bulwarks are 3ft high, and the two masts are spaced close together.[15]

Although shipyards producing iron hulls would

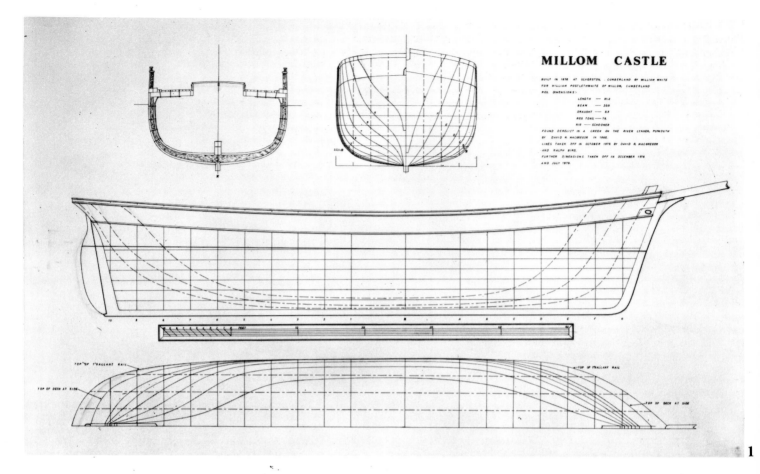

MILLOM CASTLE

BUILT IN 1870 AT ULVERSTON, CUMBERLAND BY WILLIAM WHITE
FOR WILLIAM POSTLETHWAITE OF MILLOM, CUMBERLAND
REG. DIMENSIONS:

LENGTH — 91.2
BEAM — 20.8
DRAUGHT — 9.5
REG TONS — 75
RIG — SCHOONER

FOUND DERELICT IN A CREEK ON THE RIVER LYNHER, PLYMOUTH
BY DAVID R. MACGREGOR IN 1960.
LINES TAKEN OFF IN OCTOBER 1975 BY DAVID R. MACGREGOR
AND RALPH BIRD.
FURTHER DIMENSIONS TAKEN OFF IN DECEMBER 1976
AND JULY 1978.

1

2

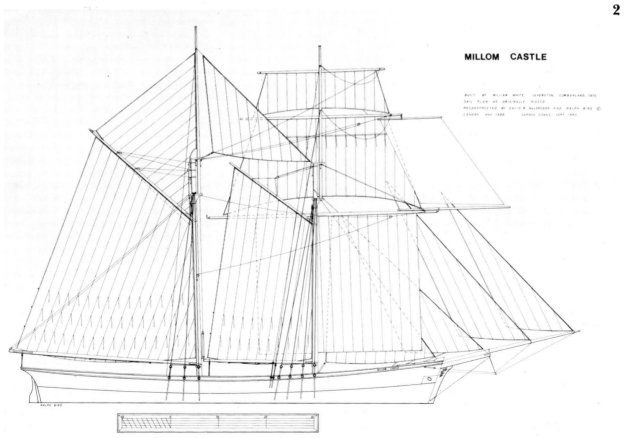

MILLOM CASTLE

BUILT BY WILLIAM WHITE, ULVERSTON, CUMBERLAND, 1870.
SAIL PLAN AS ORIGINALLY RIGGED.
RECONSTRUCTED BY DAVID R. MACGREGOR AND RALPH BIRD ©
LONDON MAY 1980.   CARNON DOWNS, SEPT 1980.

1 *Fig 274.* Millom Castle. *Lines plan and midship section drawn by Ralph Bird from lines taken off vessel to inside of ceiling by himself and the author in 1978. Built of wood at Ulverstone, Cumberland, in 1870 by William White with measurements of 81.2ft × 20.6ft × 9.5ft. When built the Lloyd's Register survey report gave the under deck tonnage and gross tonnage as 91.27; in the 1870s the net tonnage was 84. Reconstruction: bulwarks at stern, rudder, outside form of hull below bilge, LWL, shape of fore foot. Note: word 'Draught' in list of dimensions should read 'Depth of hold'.*

2 *Fig 275.* Millom Castle. *Sail and rigging plan reconstructed by Ralph Bird with suggestions by the author. Sources: painting by R Chappell, photographs of vessel, sail plans of contemporary schooners.*

3 *Fig 276. Watercolour by Reuben Chappell of* Millom Castle. *The galley is close abaft the mainmast and she is steered with a tiller. Her deck plan could have been broadly similar to that of the* Express *in figure 117.* (T W Belt)

4 *Fig 277.* Rhoda Mary. *Lines plan drawn by author from lines taken off vessel to outside of plank by Basil Greenhill and himself in 1949-51. Built of wood on Restronguet Creek, near Truro, in 1868 by John Stephens with measurements of 101.2ft × 21.9ft × 11.05ft and tonnages of 129.68 under deck and 118 net. Reconstruction: rudder, figurehead, keel below rabbet. It may be that she is of too sharp hull-form to warrant inclusion here, but she does provide an example of a Cornish schooner.*

undoubtedly build the vessels from plans drawn by a naval architect or his draughtsman, it was rare for smaller yards which built only in wood, to do so. They would obtain all measurements necessary for the hull from a half-model. These half-models were the medium by which a builder transferred his ideas into three dimensional form, and then enlarged them by way of the mould loft into the frames and hull of a vessel. Some builders of iron ships still found it desirable to design a half-model before any drawings were made and then with the aid of this model the lines plan could be drawn. Alexander Stephen jnr was one of these and his diary

3

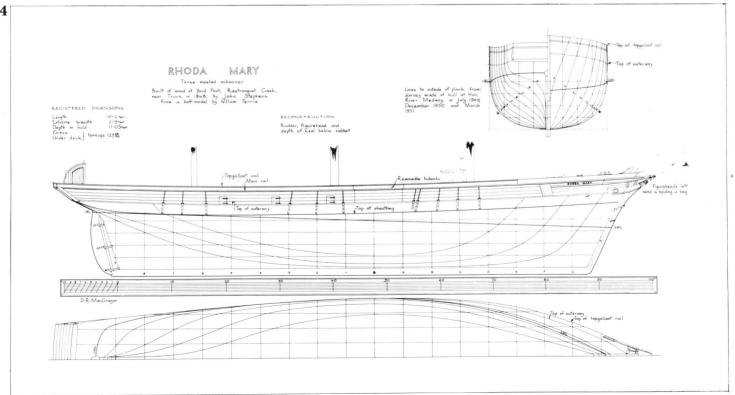

4

RHODA MARY
Three masted schooner
Built of wood at Yard Point, Restronguet Creek,
near Truro, in 1868, by John Stephens
from a half-model by William Ferris

REGISTERED DIMENSIONS
Length   101·2 feet
Extreme breadth   21·9 feet
Depth in hold   11·05 feet
Gross   } tonnage 129.68
Under deck }

RECONSTRUCTION
Rudder, figurehead and
depth of keel below rabbet

Lines to outside of plank from
survey made of hull at Hoo,
River Medway, in July 1949,
December 1950 and March
1951

D. R. MacGregor

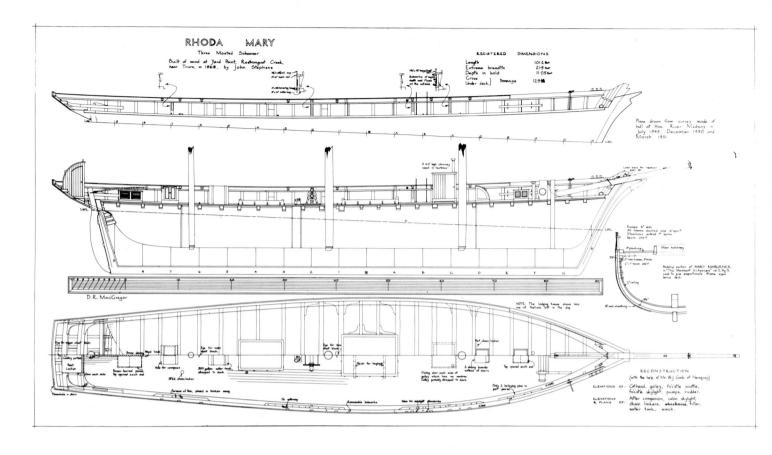

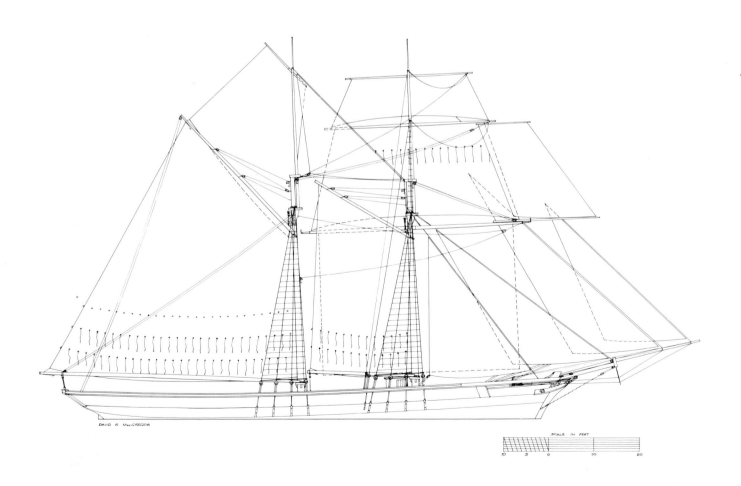

records time spent on carving half-models. Such models were also utilised to show a client or possible purchaser what the shape of the hull would be like and also to plot the size and position of the plates on an iron hull. From research undertaken, a few builders of schooners are known to have drawn plans which may have been employed in the design stage: James Geddie at Garmouth has already been mentioned; so has Robert Harrison who apparently drew the plans for J & J Hair of Newcastle; a plan by James Gray of Newhaven is known; there are the assorted plans collected by Walter Lisslie of Appledore; the Science Museum, in addition to the Geddie drawings, has two undated lines plans of unnamed Mevagissey schooners, one of about 1840 and the other of the 1860-75 period as described above; at Barrow, Richard Ashburner was a trained naval architect and designed his schooners on paper. But the mass of schooner builders did not use plans, still less could they draw them.

By contrast, sailmakers habitually drew plans and could read them, for which reason profiles of many vessels have survived. One such plan is of the Danish-built *Phoenix*, which is drawn with double topsails and a topgallant, as well as two stunsails. This plan in figure 282 is typical of the schooners being sent afloat on the Continent.

In New England, the topsail schooner had gone out of fashion in the mid-fifties, and the fore-and-aft coasting schooners were shallow draught vessels by British standards, with much greater beam. Plans of them in *The National Watercraft Collection*, as drawn by Howard I Chapelle, generally show hulls with a clipper bow,

Fig 278. Rhoda Mary. *Longitudinal section, deck plan and bulwark elevation reconstructed from measurements taken of vessel at Hoo 1949-51. Bulwarks and deck beams still in position and reconstruction based on these; also on photographs of schooner and other similar vessels.*

Fig 279. Rhoda Mary. *Sail and rigging plan reconstructed by the author as described in the text. Since this plan was finished in June 1982, a painting has come to light showing her as first rigged in 1883 and reproduced here in figure 280. I was glad to note that my reconstruction was generally correct although the mainsail did not have quite such a high peak.*

Fig 280. Oil painting by C S Trout of Rhoda Mary *entering Falmouth in June 1883, according to signature and inscription along bottom. No stunsail booms are drawn nor is there a flying jib set, although the stay is there. Reproduced by courtesy of Mr Webster.* (Colin Denny Gallery)

headrails and trail boards, a poop which is level with the rail, abaft the mainmast, and in the centre of this poop the top half of a large house, the bottom of which was presumably standing on the main deck. They had square sterns and invariably a big drag aft.[16]

By 1865, the three-masted schooner was a well-established rig in America but the employment of any square canvas was rare. These schooners, like their British counterparts, were longer versions of the two-masted rig and had two basic hull-forms: either they were deep-hulled vessels; or else they were of shallow draught with a centreboard. A plan of the former, drawn by Howard I Chapelle, shows the *William F Frederick* which was built in 1874 by C P Carver & Co at Belfast, Maine, with dimensions of 135ft 10in moulded length at rail, 30ft 6in moulded breadth, 15ft 0in depth of hold and 430 tons register. She was thus much bigger than the usual

British three-master, having flat floors, a short convex entrance and a longer concave run, but with little drag. The spar dimensions were as follows:[17]

Foremast	76 ft	Fore boom	35 ft
Mainmast	77 ft	Main boom	35 ft
Mizzen mast	78 ft	Mizzen boom	53 ft
All topmasts	50 ft		
Bowsprit	34ft	Bowsprit length outside stem rabbet	22ft

Jibboom outside bowsprit cap 30ft
[No length of mast doublings given nor lengths of gaffs.]

By the end of the seventies, two-masted schooners ranged in size from 100-250 tons, and three-masters up to 750 tons. It was only on the Great Lakes that any square canvas was to be seen, and the schooner rig completely monopolised the coasting trade, the employment of barquentines, barques and ships being restricted to ocean voyages. In 1875, forty-eight three-masted schooners were built on the east coast of the United States of which only one, the *William E. Clowes* of 438 tons, carried any square sails.[18] On the Pacific coast, twelve three-masters had been built between 1866 and the end of 1875, and only one, the *Pio Benito* of 1873 had any square canvas, although the *Joseph Perkins* of 1875 might have had some, as some accounts describe her as a barquentine.[19]

THREE-MASTED SCHOONER *METERO*

It was only after about 1875 that rigs became more standardised, but before then there was continual variation and experiment in hull-form and rig which

Fig 281. An engraving from the Illustrated London News *entitled 'Short Handed', presumably because of the girl helping to man the pumps, was painted by Lionel Smythe. It appeared in the issue of 26 December 1874 and illustrates a schooner's decks abaft the main hatch with a helmsman at the tiller.* (Ronald H van den Bos)

Fig 282. Phoenix. *Sail plan reproduced from original loaned by Frode Holm-Petersen. Built at Svendborg in 1873 by J Ring-Andersen and of 122 tons.*

Fig 283. Bows of the brigantine Thule *of Pataholm, Sweden. She was probably the brig listed in the* Bureau Veritas Repertoire General *of 1877 as built in 1855 at Grimstead and of 287 tons. The heavy whisker booms to spread the bowsprit rigging are very prominent.* (Maritime Museum, Kronborg, Denmark)

Fig 284. Stern view of the Groninger galjoot Boukje *in the Oosterdok, Amsterdam. The rig is similar to a British schooner but the stern has no wing transom; the wale is taken to the sternpost and there is an 'outside' rudder, the tiller of which passes over the top of the bulwarks, and the washboard is stopped short to give it free passage. The two square stern windows complete the picture. On the right are a schooner (nearest) and a brigantine. (Ronald van den Bos Collection)*

tended to produce many interesting results, one of which was the fitting of yards to the main topmast of a three-masted topsail schooner. Examples have already been given in Chapter Four of schooners with topsail yards on both fore- and mainmasts (figures 122 and 123). Earlier still, they were illustrated in *Merchant Sailing Ships 1775-1815*. These schooners were in use in British, European and American waters.

The few named examples of three-masted two topsail trading schooners which have been discovered have all conformed to the type of sail plan shown in figure 287. This is assumed to represent a projected plan of the *Metero*, built in 1866 by Alexander Stephen & Sons, because the plan was found in the shipbuilder's plan store rolled up amongst the drawings of this particular schooner, and the hull profiles of the two vessels correspond exactly. This projected plan was drawn in

pencil on cartridge paper and has been traced from the original without any reconstruction. There are many points of interest on the plan: the hollow leeches to the topsails suggest roller-reefing gear although it is unlikely that the topgallant sails would have been so fitted; the area occupied by the square sail on the foremast indicates that it could be shifted on the yard to the weather side, which is normal practice on schooners; the lead of the topping lifts and gaff halliards is actually given. This rig is really little different from that of a 'barquetta' or jackass barque. The *E.S. Hocken*, built at Fowey in 1879, also began life with a rig like this projected one.[20]

But as built, the *Metero* was a conventional three-masted schooner in rig, although in hull-form she was of composite construction with great beam for her depth as can be observed in her plan. She was fairly full in the ends and must have had good stowage capacity. The measurements written on her plan are: 120.0ft length between perpendiculars, 26.0ft breadth extreme; 9.0ft depth in hold on top of floors; 191.03 register tons and $375^{37}/_{94}$ tons BM. Some of the calculations are written on the plan thus:

	154 tons of coals
	20 tons of pig iron
	5 tons of machinery
	10 tons of stores
Weight of ship with cargo of	189 tons
Weight of hull & fittings	176 tons
	365 tons in fresh water
Draught was 7ft 10in forward and 8ft 6in aft	

The contract price was £3600 and dated 21 February 1866 for a schooner not exceeding 200 tons register to class 9 A1 and to be delivered within four months. She was launched on 8 June 1866 having been built to the order of J Hainsworth of Liverpool who ordered a barge at the same time. She stranded south of Valparaiso at the end of the same year or early the next and became a total loss.[21]

Other three-masted schooners built by Stephen's consisted of an auxiliary one launched in the same year as *Metero*, 1866, and two others for a French firm built after 1875.

J & W A UPHAM OF BRIXHAM

The principal builders in the Devon port of Brixham were S Dewdney & Sons; Furneaux; and J & W A Upham. All built schooners amongst other vessels, and an examination of Upham's yard book illustrates the type of vessels constructed and their cost. I am very grateful to John Holman, Upham's manager, who made the book available to me in 1963. Yard no 1 had her keel laid in 1856, but some earlier vessels listed in the front consisted of the barque *Refuge* (1855), the brigs *Nonpareil* (1837) [or should it be 1852?] and *Thermanthus* (1853), the schooner *Jane Smith* (1847), three trawlers and two yawls.

Between 1856 and 1875, forty-nine vessels of the following classes were built: 14 sloops, 7 ketches, 24 schooners, 3 brigs and 1 barquentine. After 1875, only one more schooner was built, the *Mistletoe* in 1876; and only one more barquentine, the *Silver Lining* in 1881; all the

remaining vessels were sloops, ketches or trawlers.

The brigs consisted of the *Fearless*, launched in 1857, of 240 tons at £10 10s per ton old measurement to class 12 A1; the *Czarowitz*, launched in 1866 of 254⁵²⁄₉₄ tons at £9 10s per ton; and the *Neptune's Car* launched in 1870, of 305 tons at £9 per ton.

The first barquentine was the *Florence*, no 48, termed a '3 mast brigantine' and launched in 1875 at a cost of £2859 12s with a gross tonnage of 226.

No three-masted schooner appears to have been built but some of the two-masters ranged up to 200 tons. The practice of employing builder's measurement tonnage in the yard book produced some apparently large tonnages, the biggest of which was 273 for the schooner *Madcap* built in 1871. Her equivalent net register was 200 tons with dimensions of 117.0ft × 24.3ft × 12.9ft, and she seems to have been the biggest schooner built in this yard. The total cost was £2529 9s to class 13 A1.

On several occasions it would appear that a series of schooners were built from the same moulds, when the basic yard dimensions are identical. For instance, between 1862 and 1864 the *Queen of Clippers*, *Welcome*, *Torbay Lass* and *Via* were all built with 84ft keel, 21ft beam and 12ft depth of hold, giving 177 tons om. Then again between 1873 and 1876, the *Silver Stream*, *Bella Rosa* and

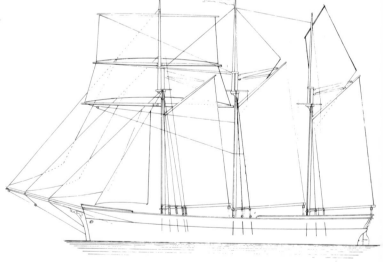

Mistletoe were all built with 94ft keel and fore rake, and 22ft beam, giving 208 tons om. Prices for schooners to class 10 or 12 A1 which had been £10 10s per ton in 1857-58 had fallen to £9 in 1861 and ten years later were £9 5s-£9 15s. The outfit comprised in the price is not always given, but in other cases it included 'Hull, spars, boat, forecastle, cabin'.

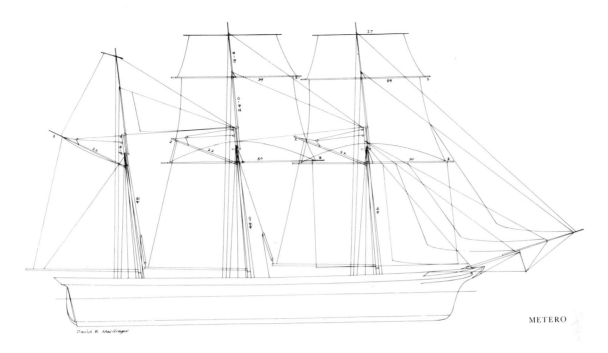

METERO

Fig 285. This tern or three-masted schooner named Jefferson Borden *brought a cargo of oil cake from New Orleans to London in 1875 during which passage there was a mutiny and an 'affray'. The crew consisted of a master, 2 mates, steward, 4 seamen and a boy. She was of 562 tons having been built at Kennebunk, Maine, in 1874. British schooners never approached the proportions of these American wooden schooners. Engraving from* Illustrated London News *15 May 1875.*

Fig 286. Ottawa. *Sail plan reproduced from tracing made by William Salisbury of sailmaker's plan at Glasson Dock. Built of wood at Parrsboro, Nova Scotia, in 1867 by Kelly with dimensions of 90.5ft × 24.7ft × 11.0ft and 143 tons net. Built as a brigantine and converted to a 3-masted schooner between 1907 and 1912. S Vickers of Chester owned her for over 30 years from the early 1870s. She was wrecked in June 1912. The fore upper topsail has vertical leeches which result in a very square sail.*

Fig 287. Metero. *Sail and standing rigging plan redrawn from plan in possession of A Stephen & Sons. Presumably a preliminary design as schooner not built like this. No reconstruction. See figure 288 for sail plan as built.*

Fig 288 (and overleaf). Metero. *Lines, longitudinal section, deck plan and sail plan photographed from the builder's plan when in their possession. Built of composite construction at Glasgow in 1866 by A Stephen & Sons with dimensions on plan of 120ft 0in length between perpendiculars, 26ft 0in extreme breadth, 9ft 0in depth of hold to top of floors, 375$\frac{37}{94}$ tons BM, and 191.03 tons register. Some displacement calculations listed in text. Sail plan drawn here is assumed to be the one she was given.*

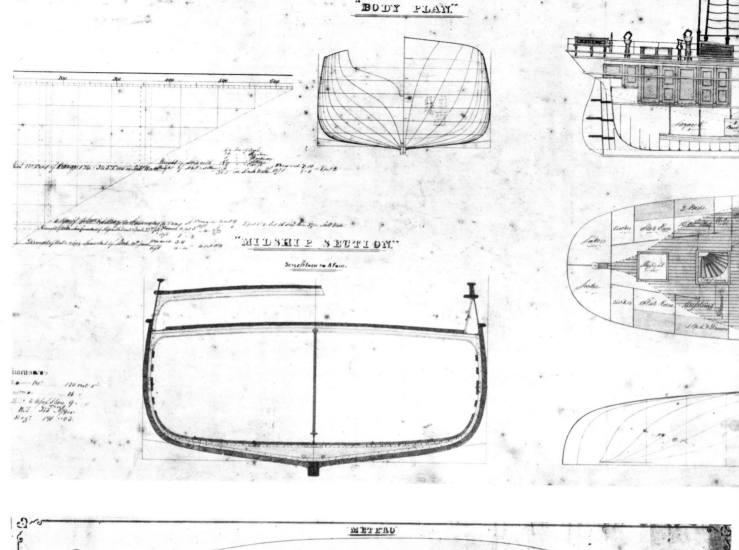

"BODY PLAN."

"MIDSHIP SECTION."

METERO

Fig 289. Metero. Shell expansion plan photographed from builder's plan. The purpose of this is to show widths of planking if laid flat.

The sloops launched at the end of the sixties had dimensions of 50ft keel, 12ft beam and 9ft depth of hold and cost in the region of £400; by the early seventies, the dimensions averaged 55ft × 17ft × 9ft for about the same price. The ketches, of about 70 tons, had a keel of 57ft and cost from £600 to £650. They and the sloops were probably built for use as fishing boats.

The hull-form of Upham's clipper schooners is well illustrated in the lines plan of the *Fling* (1858) which appeared as figure 230 in *Fast Sailing Ships*. The half-model was of the bracket type which this firm employed up to about 1875, and models of the following vessels have survived: *Nonpareil, Fling, Czarowitz* or *Bella Rosa*, and *King of Tyre*. The half-model of the barquentine

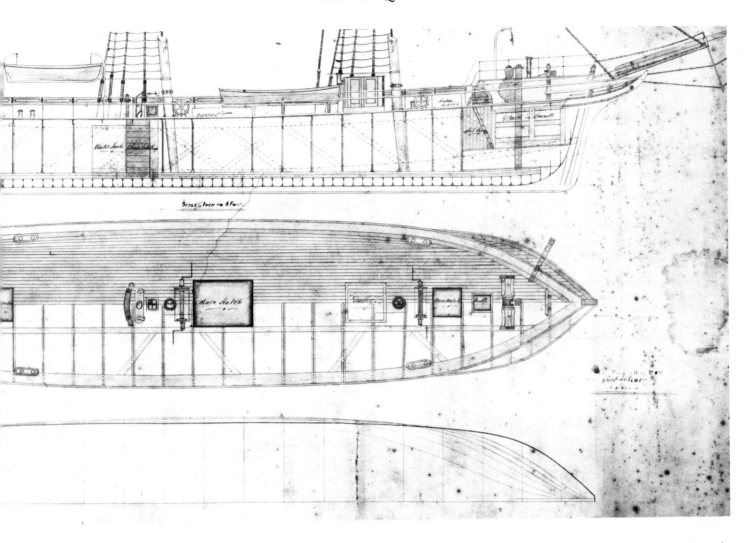

Florence in the Brixham Maritime Museum, however, is of the solid hull variety and is mounted on a rectangular backboard. Both kinds were made at a scale of half an inch to one foot which produces a big model, and all had square sterns. The bracket model of the brig *Nonpareil*, built in 1852, had slightly more deadrise amidships than the *Fling*, but all the other models had flatter floors. These bracket models are now at the National Maritime Museum, Greenwich.

BARQUENTINES

It was in 1867 that James Geddie launched the *Union* at Garmouth and the same year that Alexander Hall & Sons produced the *John Wesley* at Aberdeen, so their relative measurements are of interest:

Union	234 tons 113.4ft × 24.5ft × 14.3ft	8 A1 wood.
John Wesley	238 tons 118.0ft × 23.9ft × 13.5ft	15 A1 composite.

The above figures show the two vessels to be very similar in size, and the lines plan of the *Union* and a builder's model of the *John Wesley*, both now in the Science Museum, London, indicate that the hull-form is approximately similar too, although the *Union* is shorter and a little deeper.

The *Union*'s lines at ⅜-inch scale (figure 291) show a long, fairly shallow-draught hull with fine ends; the entrance is generally convex but some hollow is worked into the hull near the stem, rather as in an iron ship; the run has rather more concavity, but the hull does not taper much as it approaches the stern, which is rounded. There is a fair amount of deadrise with straight floors, slack bilges and vertical sides. The builder's plan has the deck beams drawn but no fittings are indicated, although the positions of the main and after hatchways are obvious from the wider beam spacing at these two places; however, the general arrangement plan could be reconstructed on the basis of the deck beams and the raised quarterdeck which is 21ft long.

The laminated construction of the *John Wesley*'s model suggests that it was made by the builder, and so probably also were the deck fittings. The Science Museum catalogue states that 'the model was rigged in the Museum in 1909, from particulars of her original masts and spars, supplied by her builders', but does not indicate whether they also supplied a rigging plan, although this is now thought to be unlikely.[22]. The lead of the main and mizzen topmast and topgallant stays, and the doubling of all the backstays is most irregular and so the *John Wesley* cannot be considered a reliable model as regards the rigging. The fitting of a fore gaff indicates that the

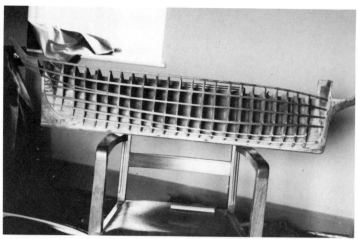

Fig 290. *Bracket half-model photographed at Upham's yard in 1951. Top ribband is at deck level. Thick base-board shaped to correct profile of stem, keel and stern. Curved line from keel to sternpost indicates deadwood, not the rabbet.* (Author)

complete break with a schooner had yet to be made. A photograph of the white-hulled *Craig Ewan* of Peterhead also shows a fore gaff; the fore trysail is both hooped to the mast and hooped to the gaff, which was a common practice in those days. Her single fore topsail was of Colling & Pinkney's roller-reefing pattern.

A fine sail plan of the *Union* (figure 293) accompanied the lines plan and so enables us to gain a good idea of this lovely barquentine. As dimensions are written on the plan against each spar, and as the rigging is carefully drawn, the plan is undoubtedly a shipyard drawing and not a sailmaker's plan. The rigging sizes are taken from the plan and listed in Appendix V. No sail outlines were drawn on the original for any of the staysails, nor was the foot of the fore course or of any of the square sails indicated. The double mizzen stays, one of which leads each side of the mainsail, were fairly common then, but were soon to be superseded by the arrangement seen in the plan of the *Chrysolite* (figure 296) in which the height of the

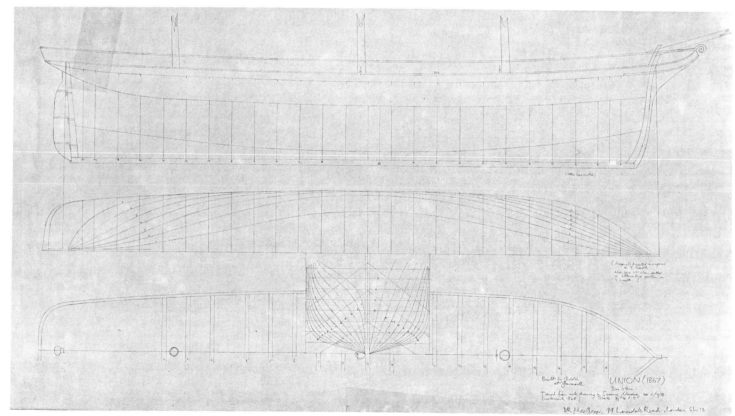

Fig 291. Union. *Lines plan and deck beam plan traced from builder's plan in Science Museum, London. Built of wood at Garmouth in 1867 by James Geddie with dimensions of 113.4ft × 24.5ft × 14.3ft and 234 tons. Projected diagonals omitted and also some waterlines which were dotted on the half-breadth plan.*

Fig 292. The barquentine Craig Ewan *was built and owned in Peterhead and traded to the Baltic. This photograph gives the builders as Carnegie & Matthew and suggests she was built in 1865; but Lloyd's Register has her built in 1868 by Simpson of Peterhead with a tonnage of 191 and a length of 110.0ft. Some of the rigging has almost disappeared in the photograph: from the mizzen topmast head there is a stay to the hounds of the mainmast; from the main topmast head there is a stay to the cap of the foremast; there is no triatic stay; there must have been stays from the fore topgallant mast to the jibboom.* (Peterhead Library and Arbuthnot Museum)

main and mizzen lower masts are made nearly equal, thus permitting a stay to the cap to clear the peak of the main gaff. Obviously there is a source of weakness on the mizzen topmast where this stay is secured, and it is of interest to note that when converted to a schooner, the *Chrysolite* adopted the old practice of double stays from hounds to deck, set up with tackles to permit the lee stay to be slackened.

There are sail plans in the Science Museum, London, of three more Geddie barquentines: the *Zephyr* built in 1869 of 256 tons net; the *Fiery Cross* built in 1872 of 338 tons net; and the *Coronella* built in 1874 of 269 tons net.

For an example of an iron-hulled barquentine there is the *Osburgha* which Alexander Stephen & Sons constructed at their Linthouse yard, Glasgow, in 1875 for William Cook of Dundee. She was contracted for on 31 August 1874 for a price of £19 per ton gross, a clear profit of £1004 being made on her construction. According to *Lloyd's Register*, her measurements were 146.7ft × 26.1ft × 13.0ft with tonnages of 317 underdeck, 357 gross and 346 net register. In hull-form she was not particularly sharp with slight deadrise, and her sail plan indicates that she must have been an attractive vessel with clipper bow and rounded counter stern. There is a triatic stay from the mizzen truck to the main. The forward house contains berths for 4 seamen, 2 boys, a galley and bosun's storeroom; the after house had accommodation for the master, two mates and steward. The forecastle contained nothing and merely provided a raised deck to work the anchors. The panelling to the two deckhouses looked very smart. The mizzen passed through the after house and there must have been a raised deck abaft the house for the helmsman.

The three iron barquentines built at Hayle by Harvey

Fig 293. Union. Sail and standing rigging plan traced from builder's plan in Science Museum, London. Head was incomplete and so that of barquentine Zephyr (1869) was traced to complete hull. The rigging sizes written on the plan are listed in Appendix V.

Fig 294. Osburgha. Sail and rigging plan photographed from original when in builder's possession. Built of iron at Glasgow in 1875 by A Stephen & Sons with dimensions of 146.7ft × 26.1ft × 13.0ft and 346 tons net.

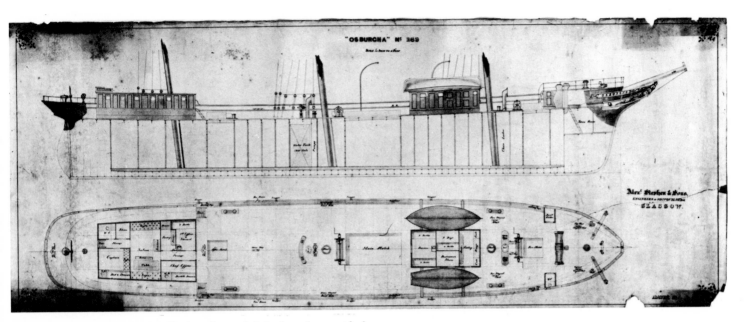

Fig 295. Osburgha. *Longitudinal section and deck plan photographed from original when in builder's possession. The dark portions in the corners are accumulated dust.*

& Co were not constructed until after 1875, but W H Nevill's two have already been mentioned.

Another splendid example of a barquentine may be seen in the sail plan of the Whitehaven-built *Chrysolite* which Shepherd & Leech sent afloat in 1869 (figure 296). Her measurements were given at the beginning of this chapter when she was compared with other ships built by this firm, and it was observed then that her hull-form was likely to have been based on that of the barque *James Davidson*, whose plan is given in figure 102. The sail plan of the *Chrysolite* was traced from the original in the Whitehaven Public Library and Museum. It is drawn at ¼-inch scale on Whatman paper (watermark 1866) in ink, now sepia in colour, and was almost certainly the work of the sailmaker William Kennaugh. The plan illustrates the four-sided staysails set between the main- and foremasts which are to be found in many barquentines and brigantines of the period. Other points of interest are the replacement of the main topsail with a four-sided mizzen topmast staysail; the high angle given to the foot of some of the staysails which was fashionable about this time; the position of the foremost shroud at each mast which is forward of the centreline of the mast; the absence of any bobstay, although one must have been fitted in practice. The barquentine must be floating at her light waterline. The high steeve to the bowsprit is confirmed in a photograph taken when she had been cut down to a three-masted schooner.

William Kennaugh's original plan has been over-written in pencil to indicate how the spars were to be shortened at some later date. This included the replacement of the mizzen staysail with a jib-headed main topsail. It is not known if or when the alterations were made, but between 1887-91 she was sold to Penzance owners who cut her down to a three-masted topsail schooner, and she was photographed as such by J F

Gibson. Amongst the details to be seen in the photograph is the after companionway, located at the break of the raised quarterdeck, with a rounded sliding hatch similar to that on the *John Wesley*.

The Whitehaven sailmaker, William Kennaugh, quoted the sum of £236 12s each for supplying the sails of the two barquentines *Bootle* and *Irton* in 1873, the sails to be 'fitted with rope, leather, galvanised iron thimbles and spectacle clews where required'. These vessels were sister ships of 248 tons net and built of iron by the Whitehaven Shipbuilding Co for a local owner. On one page of his account book, Kennaugh calls them 'three-masted brigantines', and later on the same page refers to them as 'schooners'. His accounts showed that his estimate for the two barquentines totalled £473 4s, and that after deducting the costs of canvas, rope and other materials, and the labour of cutting and making the sails which amounted to £382 8s 6d there would be a 'clear profit' of £90 15s 6d. It appears, however, that he only received the sum of £446 8s 6d for the job, yet still made a handsome profit.[23]

Although the examples described above come from Scotland and north-west England, very similar barquentines were being built elsewhere in the country. J & W A Upham's craft have already been described. At the Bideford Public Library is a half-model of the barquentine *Minnie*, built in 1875 by George Cox & Son of Bideford, and of 161 tons. This shows a hull moderately sharp forward with a good beam and some deadrise. Two other barquentines were built in 1875 in North Devon: the *Lord Tredegar* by Westacott at Barnstaple and the *Ocean Ranger* at Appledore by Cook. Two years before, Cook had built the well-known barquentine *Lydia Cardell* of 225 tons. Two West Country barquentines had intriguing names: at Dartmouth, Phillips built the *Sly Boots* — sometimes spelled in one word — in 1868 and she was

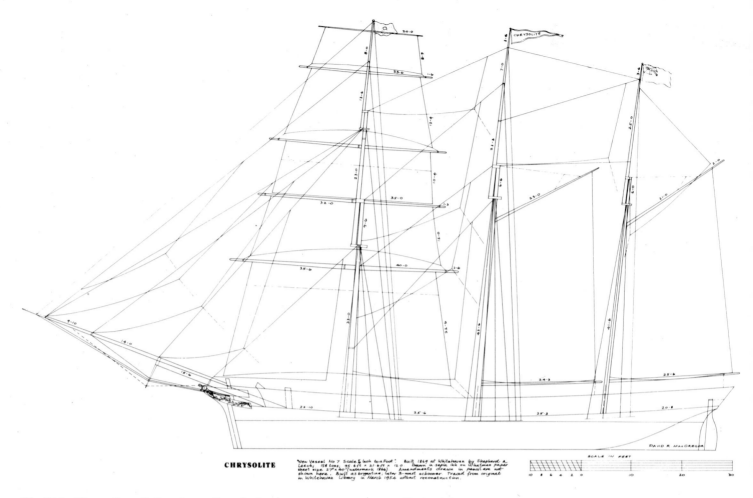

CHRYSOLITE

Fig 296. Chrysolite. *Sail and standing rigging plan redrawn from tracing made of original in 1954. Built of wood at Whitehaven in 1869 by Shepherd & Leech with dimensions of 95.6ft × 21.6ft × 12.0ft and 158 tons. No reconstruction. Converted to 3-masted schooner 1887-91.*

Fig 297. *The* Chrysolite *under sail after conversion from barquentine to schooner as described in the text. The triatic stay between mizzen and main has survived, but now there is a pair of mizzen stays set up each side of the mainsail with a tackle, which was an older practice.* (F E Gibson)

called a 'three-masted brigantine' when offered for sale in 1880; at Hayle in 1870 Harvey & Co launched the *Girl of the Period* which had a prettily painted figurehead.

Illustrations show some of the fine barquentines being built in large numbers on the Continent, while across the Atlantic in the Maritime Provinces of Canada, scores of barquentines were being constructed. A sail plan of a typical vessel is that of the *Vigilant* built in 1877 by John M'Dougall at Dundas, Prince Edward Island. She was of 398 tons, which was larger than British-built vessels. She also had more sheer forward; and aloft she had lengthy topmasts, especially on the mizzen which was as tall as the main.[24]

Fig 298. *The barquentine* May Cory's *yards are fore-shortened and so difficult to discern as she lies on the grid outside the Cumberland Basin, Bristol, with the Clifton Suspension Bridge seen between the masts. This photograph exhibits her hull-form and the shadow of the ladder helps. The copper sheathing shows up light against the dark of the timber planking. She was built at Bideford in 1875 by Johnson and measured 107.8ft × 22.7ft × 11.4ft and had a tonnage of 163 net.* (York Collection, Bristol Museum)

JACKASS BARQUES LISTED

The sail plan of the *Ziba*, built at Aberdeen in 1858 and rigged in this manner, appeared in figure 128, and below are listed some named examples which have been identified from the evidence of paintings, drawings and descriptions. As mentioned earlier, 'barquetta' is the name sometimes given to the rig of jackass barque in the Channel Islands.

PROVISIONAL LIST OF JACKASS BARQUES BUILT AFTER 1855

Date built	Name	Builder	Tons & material	Description of rig and source
1855	*Kelpie*	Hall, Aberdeen	118 wood	Figure 124
1858	*Ziba*	Hall, Aberdeen	465 wood	Figure 128
1859	*Matchless*	Guernsey	241 wood	Reproduced as Figure 222 in *Fast Sailing Ships*.
1861	*Tien-tsin*	W Pile, Sunderland	242 wood	Cunningham's roller-reefing topsails; main skysail mast fidded abaft royal. Watercolour (James Henderson) Collection).
1861	*Amber Witch*	T Valin, Quebec	517 wood	Drawing as Norwegian *Uller*; double topsails on fore; single on main; nothing above topgallants.[25]
1863	*Erme*	Bouker, Salcombe	206 wood	Single topsails; deep foresail; photograph of painting (A E Fairweather Collection).
1863	*Mathilde*	Reuter & Ihms, Kiel	[?]	Royals, topgallants, and single topsails on fore and main; photograph of painting;[26] another painting has no royals and makes her look like 3-mast 2-topsail schooner.[27]
1865	*Empreza*	Hedderwick, Glasgow	250 comp	Double topsails on fore and main; nothing above topgallants; photograph of painting.[28]
1866	*Mirliton*	A Lefebvre, Dunkirk	239 wood	'Baleston' topsails on fore and main; nothing above topgallants; masts in two pieces; spike bowsprit; standing rigging made of iron bars; hull double-ended (see below).[29]
1867	*Nellie*	W Date, Kingsbridge	281 wood	Single topsails on fore and main; photograph of painting (A E Fairweather Collection). Similar to *Mirliton*.
1868	*Alexandre*	A Lefebvre, Dunkirk	235 wood	

Fig 299. *Oil painting of* Unity *inscribed 'Three-mast Brigantine "Unity" of Goole, Capn. G. Calvert, off Leghorn 1872' and it is signed 'L. Renault, Leghorn'. This barquentine was built of wood at Howden, River Humber, in 1871 by Banks with dimensions of 105.6ft × 24.3ft × 12.8ft and 179 tons. Lloyd's Register 1876 has her rig as schooner. The painting shows stunsail booms under the foreyard and large rectangular topsails on the main and mizzen with long head yards, and the hull is made to heel just enough to see the deck fittings.* (Paul Mason Gallery)

| 1874 | *Grijalva* | Nevill, Llanelly | 222 iron | Double topsails on fore; 'Baleston' topsail, and topgallant on main, also main course and hoisting main trysail; (photograph of painting supplied by J D Attwood). Figure 302 |
| 1876 | *Sabrina* | Richardson, Sunderland | 317 wood | Double topsails on fore and main; (photograph 1895 by E A Dingley.[30]). |

Fig 300. *The iron-hulled barquentine* Lake Simcoe *was originally barque-rigged when built in 1871 at Greenock by Robert Steele & Co. She had a length of 152.2ft and a tonnage of 334 net. She has a long spike bowsprit with a dolphin striker and there is a bumkin at the feet of the figurehead to extend the lead of the bobstay. The hull has the grace one would expect from Robert Steele.* (Nautical Photo Agency)

1877	*Calabar*	Potter, Liverpool	305 iron	Topgallant masts fidded abaft topmasts; large gaff mainsail.[31]
1877	*Eboe*	Sister to *Calabar*		
1881	*Zebina Goudey*	Annapolis, Nova Scotia	1087 wood	'Nova Scotia barque with fore-and-aft mainsail'.[32]

Fig 301. *The jackass-barque* Nellie *was built at Kingsbridge in south Devon in 1867 and had measurements of 123.4ft × 25.0ft × 14.4ft and 281 tons and classed 13 A1. It was not an unattractive rig. According to the painting, the fore topsail appears to be a roller reefing sail but the main topsail has a single row of reef points.* (J Fairweather Collection)

There is an interesting engraving of a jackass barque in a book on model yacht building published in the last century, in which the main topsail is of Cunningham's roller-reefing variety with excessive hoist, so that it combines both topsail and topgallant.[33] The *Kelpie*, built in 1855 (figure 124) could easily have been rigged in like manner, although Alexander Hall did not list a main topsail yard for her.

The distinction between a three-masted two-topsail schooner portrayed as setting a square sail below the foreyard, and a jackass barque shown setting a fore course and a fore-and-aft mainsail is often hard to determine, especially from an old painting. This is the very problem concerning the *Mathilde* of Kiel whose appearance differs in two separate paintings. The evidence of *Amber Witch* (1861) is difficult to evaluate as she became the Norwegian *Uller* in 1891 and it is as the latter that the rig is known.

The 'baleston' topsail fitted to *Mirliton* and *Grijalva* was used extensively at Nantes in small vessels to save the weight of double topsail yards. Figure 302 shows it fitted on the *Grijalva*'s mainmast. The 'baleston' was a light yard bent to the after side of a single topsail by means of reef points, but it was not parralled to the mast. It was fitted with lifts,, and the clew lines led to it. Sometimes there was a single brace but this was often omitted. D L Dennis described the rig in more detail in the *Mariner's Mirror*, and there are other references to it in this journal.[34] Apart from its use at Nantes, it was employed in a limited way at Dunkirk and Havre. A clear photograph of an unnamed barque so rigged appears in G La Roërie's *Navires et Marins*.[35]

The *Alexandre*, which was a sister to the *Mirliton*, carried a Bermuda-like sail on her mizzen. Two other barques, claimed to be sister ships to the *Alexandre*, were the *Achille*, built 1870 of 259 tons, and the *Maria*, but these latter two had double topsails. Whether they were also rigged as jackass barques in unknown.

Fig 302. *A jackass-barque with a different rig was the* Grijalva *with conventional sails on the foremast — indeed the foremast was always conventional on a jackass barque — but with a single 'baleston' topsail on the main and a deep topgallant; also a square main course. She was built of iron at Llanelly in 1874 with a length of 118.4ft and a tonnage of 222 net. Both the deckhouses had coved edges where sides and roofs met and the sides look to be of iron. (J D Attwood)*

KETCHES, SLOOPS AND BARGES

A ketch-rigged billy-boy, the *Bluejacket*, is described in Chapter Four and her rig is typical of the ketches to be found on the east and north-east coasts. There is also a useful account of the equipment and handling of the Yorkshire keels and billy-boys which Basil Greenhill has reprinted in *The Merchant Schooners*.[36]

Without her square canvas and ignoring the exceptionally long head to the lower mast, the *Bluejacket* has a typical rig which was being adopted with increasing frequency from the seventies onward. After 1880 it became rare for a ketch to set any square canvas, but a painting or photograph occasionally shows a lower yard crossed, below which a sail could be set on the windward side as in the fine picture reproduced by Basil Greenhill of two ketches racing.[37] When bereft of her square sails, the *Bluejacket* hoisted a jib-headed topsail on the mainmast. Many billy-boys and ketches led the halliards of the flying jib to the main cap, as did the *Rival*, but the photograph

taken of *Bluejacket* at Blakeney in the early eighties shows that she did not then adopt this practice although she might easily have done so under a different master. This arrangement placed less strain on the topmast head in a fresh breeze.

The spritsail barges on the Thames estuary and south-east region were stimulated to improve their equipment and sailing powers by the introduction of barge races, the first of which was held in 1863. The swim-headed bow was gradually being replaced by the round bow and soon after by the more vertical stem; the transom was made broader; the mizzen was stepped well inboard; and square canvas was discarded. Of course the older forms lingered on in existing vessels until the end of the century. At the end of the fifties, some barges set their mainsail and mizzen on gaff and boom, particularly the larger ones engaged in coastal trade.

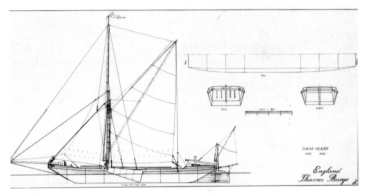

Fig 303. Spritsail Barge. *Sail plan and end elevations drawn by Harold I Chapelle. Unnamed and place of build not specified but employed on the rivers Thames and Medway and adjacent creeks. No flying jib drawn.*

Fig 304. *An unidentified stumpy barge bearing the words 'EAST-WOODS BRICKMAKERS' on the spritsail. She is deeply laden with the bulwarks still above water amidships, which was a common sight. This one has a steering wheel. Photograph by Basil Lavis or a copy negative by him. (MacGregor Collection)*

These 'boomies' as they were called were suitable for all work, and on the east coast replaced the deeper-hulled trading smack. In addition, they could carry as large a cargo as many of the schooners, and their flat-bottomed hulls enabled them to get into many silted-up harbours. Also referred to as 'schooners with the bottom cut off', they were built in Yorkshire, East Anglia, Kent and Sussex, and by 1875 were a well-established form of hull and rig. They usually carried leeboards, and many had a gammon knee under the bowsprit, a rounded counter stern, and crossed one or more yards on the foremast.

The practice continued of building large barge hulls and rigging them with three masts. They were of chine construction with flat bottoms and straight sides, and carried huge leeboards between the fore- and mainmasts. In America, of course, they would have been given centre boards. Although these huge hulls drew little water when light, they could lift a very large cargo, but must have been awkward vessels to sail. George Smeed of Rochester named several after members of his family. The largest was *Esther Smeed*, built at Sittingbourne in 1868 of 494 tons and rigged as a barque with dimensions of 166.0ft × 31.0ft × 16.9ft. Then there was the *George Smeed*, a barquentine of 477 tons gross, built in 1866; next in size

Fig 305. The boomie barge Lothair *was built at Ipswich in 1872 with a tonnage of 108. She was owned at Rye. Her leeboard is just visible on her port side. Her fore yard is being used as a derrick, but her main topmast is missing and so is her jibboom. The inboard clasp for the latter is hinged open on the bowsprit, just above the fiddlehead. (David Clement Collection)*

Fig 306 The West Country smack Mary of Truro *under full sail with her big foresail and loose-footed mainsail. She is deeply laden.* (MacGregor Collection)

was the *Emily Smeed* of 286 tons net, built in 1872 and first rigged as a barquentine with three square sails on the foremast, of which one was a single topsail, and the fore course was set on a bentinck boom. As Smeed is given as her builder, it may be that he built these three. Last of the quartet was the three-masted schooner *Sarah Smeed*, built at Murston near Sittingbourne by Sollitt in 1874 and of 241 tons.[38]

Each major estuary which served the needs of a farming hinterland or an industrial community on its banks, had its own type of barge, but the varieties are too numerous to recite in detail. In the counties of Cornwall, Devon and Somerset, the trading smacks or 'barges' were one such category.

These West Country barges went in three sizes: the smallest was used for lightering and river work and therefore was only of light construction with a large

Fig 307. Mary. Lines and deck layout drawn from lines taken off the vessel to outside of plank by Basil Greenhill and the author in 1948. Built of wood at Devoran, near Truro, in 1875 by Hugh E Stephens with Custom House measurements in 1875 of 49.3ft × 17.5ft × 5.65ft and 25.34 tons net and gross. Reconstruction: tiller, mast winch, bowsprit mounting etc.

hatchway stretching from gunwale to gunwale, covered by tarpaulins, and was propelled by a foresail and gaff mainsail set on a pole mast, or by sweeps and quants if there was no wind. The next size was for river and estuary work with occasional short trips along the coast, and was a scaled-up version of the river barge, but with proper hatchways, raised coamings, side decks and low bulwarks, and possibly the addition of a bowsprit for two headsails. The largest size of 40-50 tons made regular trips along the south and west coasts, and was accordingly of more substantial build with less beam and more draught to improve her windward qualities, and she had a bowsprit and fidded topmast in order to set a good spread of sail, being equipped with smaller hatchways and fittings of the kind to be usually found in a normal short sea trader. All the three types had to take the ground regularly, and load and discharge on beaches and river banks, which resulted in fairly flat floors and well rounded bilges; in particular, the river and estuary barges had to negotiate shallow creeks and were therefore designed with the minimum amount of draught compatible with good sailing qualities. This lack of draught required additional beam to give stability, and some barges had less than three beams to length.

By 1860 some of the large sloops measuring 60 to 100 tons had been broken up or converted into schooners or ketches, and nothing so large was being built any more with just a single mast. In *Merchant Sailing Ships 1815-1850*

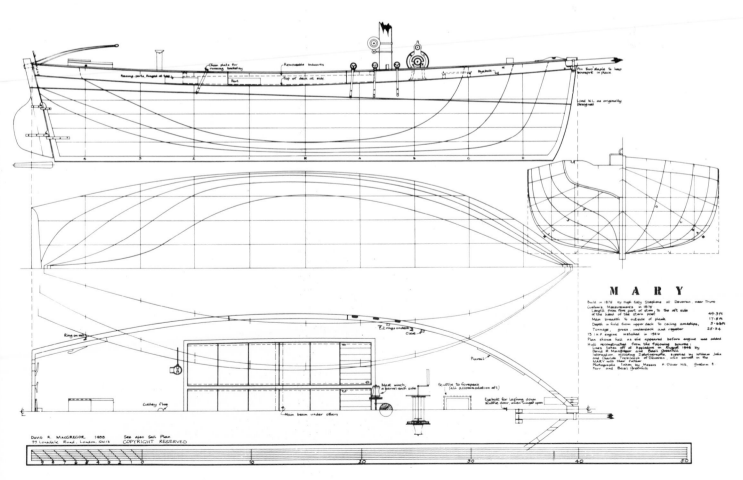

MARY

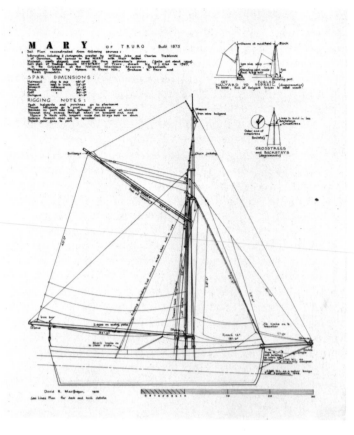

plans of the Whitby sloop *Clio* of 86 tons were given in figures 64 and 65 of those a Leith smack of 173 tons in figures 70 and 71.

The *Mary* was of the intermediate size of a West Country smack with a gross tonnage of 25, and dimensions of 49.3ft × 17.5ft × 5.65ft which gave her only two and three quarter beams to length. She was constructed in 1875 at Devoran on Restronguet Creek, a tributary of the Truro River, in the yard of Hugh E Stephens whose foreman and designer was Charles George, who carved the *Mary*'s half-model in a day. Hugh

Fig 308. Mary. Sail and rigging plan reconstructed by the author. Principal sources: sailmaker's sizes of mainsail, staysail and jib (c1930); photographs and information supplied by William and Charles Trebilcock: plans and photographs of other barges. Recently some older sailmaker's plans have shown that the mainsail was originally higher peaked as confirmed by the picture in figure 306.

Fig 309. Another trading smack or barge but this one trading in the Bristol Channel. She is the Industry of 38 tons gross which was built at Chepstow in 1871 with dimensions of 55.6ft × 16.6ft × 7.4ft. Her foresail is set on a boom and looks a trifle small. The barge must previously have been sailing on the other tack and the crew have not bothered to dip the head yard of the topsail to the port side. She was scrapped in 1931. (York Collection, Bristol Museum)

Fig 310. Boscastle Harbour on the north Cornish coast. The trading smack in the left foreground and the schooner in the centre are described in the text and their relative sizes compared. (R H Gillis Collection)

Stephen's brother, John, had had the fast schooner *Rhoda Mary* built in his nearby yard seven years earlier as well as many other schooners and barges. The lines of the *Mary* were taken off at Appledore in 1948 by Basil Greenhill and myself, and we contributed an article on her to the *Mariner's Mirror* in 1960.[39] The plan, figure 307, shows the characteristics already outlined for this type of barge: small deadrise, slack bilges, no tumblehome, easy convex entrance, very hollow run, enormous beam, and small freeboard. The quarter-beam buttock is almost straight where it crosses the load line and confirms numerous reports of her speed. On deck she has a large hatchway with raised coamings, and the pumps are situated at the after end; there is no wooden windlass but an iron winch instead, which can be used for heaving up the anchor and warping to a quay, and there is also a small cargo winch secured to the after side of the mast.

The *Mary* was originally equipped with a pole mast, a mainsail and a boom that projected six feet outside the transom, a bowsprit, foresail and jib; later a topsail with a long head yard was added, perhaps similar to that set by the smack *Industry* of Chepstow, as shown in figure 309; and finally a fidded topmast was carried. She had a long life and survived to be an Appledore gravel barge after the Second World War.

The photograph of three smacks and a schooner lying in Boscastle Harbour, figure 310, clearly shows that a smack and a schooner could well be of similar hull size. The smack in the foreground is of the largest coasting size and her inevitably huge mainsail would have needed a big crew to handle it. Also visible are her long tiller, high bulwarks, small hatchway, removable bulwark section for discharging or loading cargo, short cargo gaff in position, and after companionway fitted athwartships and entered on the port side. The two smacks on the right of the picture have similar arrangements, and in the right-hand one a two-barrelled dolly winch is visible between the mast and the hatchway. When converted into ketches or schooners, some of the smaller smacks were lengthened by about ten feet, an operation which added a foot or two to the maximum beam.

Many owners found it difficult to adjust their outlook to changing circumstances, and the spreading railways and steamer services began to cut into the long-held trades which they considered indisputably theirs. This was certainly true for the last decade or two of the nineteenth century, but it comes as something of a surprise to learn that a smack was offered for sale in 1860 because the railway was depriving her of her usual trade. This was the *Charlestown* of Fowey, registering 38 tons and carrying 60, which had been such a regular trader between Plymouth and Charlestown that she was familiarly known as the 'Charlestown barge'.[40]

Examples of the Severn trow have already been cited and figure 311 shows the lines plan of the *Wave* which was built by Samuel Hipwood at Gloucester in 1867. A builder's lines plan in the Bristol Museum, dated 1866 and drawn to a scale of ⅝-inch to 1ft, has been used to reconstruct the plan reproduced here. Her register

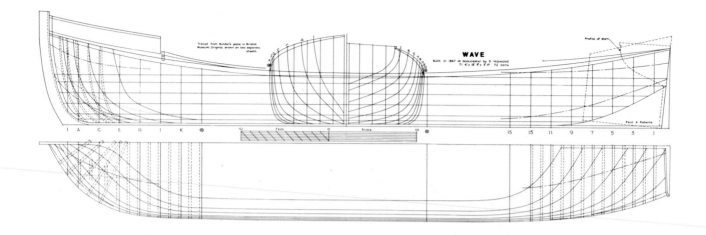

Fig 311. Wave. *Lines plan redrawn by Paul A Roberts from tracing made by the author of plan in the Bristol Museum. Built of wood at Gloucester in 1867 of S Hipwood with dimensions of 71ft 6in × 18ft 9in × 5ft 5in and 72 tons; she was a trow. Reconstruction was to combine plan from two sheets into one.*

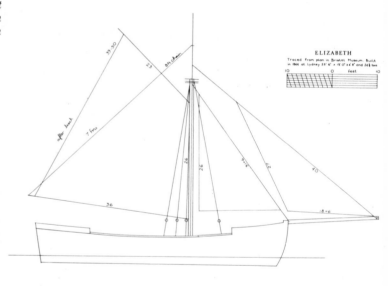

Fig 312. Elizabeth. *Outline sail plan drawn by Paul A Roberts from tracing made by the author from original in Bristol Museum. Built at Lydney in 1844 with dimensions of 55ft 6in × 13ft 0in × 4ft 8in and 24¾ tons. No reconstruction. She was also a trow. Rebuilt by S Hipwood at the end of the 1860s.*

dimensions were 71.6ft × 18.9ft × 5.5ft and 72 tons. The most noticeable features of her hull-form are the big sheer, great beam, flat floors and hard bilge, and long parallel body of 25ft 6in deadflats. She was later turned into a ketch when the big hatchway was partly decked over – an alteration which befell many of the sloops.

Although no sail plan of the *Wave* has survived, Samuel Hipwood was rebuilding the *Elizabeth* in his yard at the end of the sixties and her sail plan (figure 312) indicates the type of single-masted trow then in use. A note on the plan states that the topping lift had eight feet of chain at its upper end and that the total length of rope was seven fathoms. Dimensions of each sail are written on the plan and also the lengths of each shroud. Additional dimensions compare the size of the *Queen*'s mainsail, although she was a ketch, 11ft longer. The *Elizabeth*'s measurements were 55.6ft × 13.0ft × 4.8ft and 24¾ tons. She had been built in 1844 at Lydney by David Davies.[41]

On the River Mersey and adjacent navigable waterways, the local type of barge was known as a 'flat'. It was a flat-bottomed hull with hard bilges, little sheer, a long hatchway, and full ends. Many of the flats had masts that could lower to go under bridges. They were noteworthy for their high-peaked gaff sails, but the sloops only set a mainsail and foresail. Some sailed as coasters to Wales and the Isle of Man.

More specialised books can provide further details of all the barges of the different creeks and tidal estuaries around the coasts of the British Isles, each type bearing its own name and traditions: the keels on the rivers Tyne and Humber; the wherries on the Norfolk Broads; the sailing lighters on the Sussex rivers; the Cowes ketches; the Teignmouth barges – to name a few of the better-known craft.

Fig 313. Ketch Flora *under full sail but also under tow. She was built at Framilode in 1870 with a tonnage of 42 and was still registered at Gloucester in 1911. Photograph by W A Sharman. (MacGregor Collection)*

APPENDIX I

LIST OF SHIPS BUILT BY ALEXANDER STEPHEN & SONS AT KELVINHAUGH YARD, GLASGOW, 1852-1875.

Yard nos and dates of build taken from lists in history of firm; prices taken from Stephen's diaries and letter books which I examined in 1961 when in the possession of the firm.

Date	Material	Rig	Yard no	Name	Tons BM	Tons reg	Lump Sum	Per Ton	Tons for Contract	Profit excluding yard rent etc
1852	wood	S	1	Cyclone	594		?			
1852	iron	S	2	Typhoon	780	965	?			
1853	iron	S	3	Hurricane	1110		£12,270[?] fetched £14,000 in 1855			£1500
1853	iron		4	PS Myrtle	590		?			
1854	iron		5	PS William McCormick	840		?			
1854	iron	S	6	John Bell		1058	?			
1854	iron	S	7	Storm Cloud		907	£16,741 (cost)			
1855	iron	S	8	White Eagle		993	£15,986 asked for her in 1856			
1855	iron	S	9	SS Euphrates	1348		?			
1855	iron		10	SS Semaphore	715		?			
1856	iron		11	PS Blazer (tug)	383		£11,626			
1857	wood	S	12	Tyburnia	1012	962	£20,660			
1856	iron		13	SS Bee	118		£2730			
1857	iron	S	14	Charlemagne	1014		£18,374			
1857	iron		15	PS Prince Albert	544		£19,040			
1857	iron	bk	16	SS Dahome	450		£12,000			
1858	iron	S	17	Sea Queen	$775\frac{3}{4}$		£11,250			
1858	iron	bk	18	Edmund Preston	$436^{54}/_{94}$			£15 10s	412 BM	
1859	iron	S	19	City of Lucknow	859			£13	$859^{66}/_{94}$	
1859	iron	bk	20	Carnatic	565			£15 15s	565 BM	
1859	iron	sch	21	Angelita	134		£1850			
1860	iron	S	22	Clyde	1044		£18,792		1044 BM	nil
1859	iron	S	23	City of Madras	967			£13	$965^{57}/_{94}$	£1093
1859	iron		24	SS Cora Linn	234		£2400 without engines		234 BM	
1860	iron		25	SS Ailsa craig	234		£2460 without engines		234 BM	
1860	iron	-	26	Dredger	240		£2490			
1860	iron	S	27	City of Calcutta	967			£13 12s 6d	$965^{57}/_{94}$	£800
1861	iron		28	SS Coringa	765		£24,680[?]			
1861	iron	sch	29	Mexico			£2750		187 BM	
1861	iron	bk	30	Ismay	447			£16 5s	447 BM	
1861	iron	bk	31	Dunniker	450		£7256			
1861	iron	S	32	Wave Queen	775		£12,500	£16 2s 2d		
1862	iron	S	33	City of Bombay				£13 5s	967 BM	
1862	comp	S	34	John Lidgett				£18 18s	751 BM	
1862	comp	S	35	Arima	683		£11,800		683 BM	
1863	iron	S	36	City of Cashmere	967		£13,300		$965^{40}/_{94}$	£1487
1862	iron	brig	37	Belle of the Mersey	229			£15	229 BM	
1862	iron	bk	38	Black Watch	524			£16 7s	$524^{28}/_{94}$	
1863	iron	bk	39	Glencoyn	454			£16 15s	$452^{65}/_{94}$	
1862	comp	bgn	40	Arriero	216			£17 10s	$216^{80}/_{94}$	
1863	iron	S	41	Severn	$775^{5}/_{94}$		£13,500			£1685
1863	comp	S	42	SS Sea King		790	£25,540 £28,475=cost		1104 BM	£3267
1863	iron	S	43	Bothwell Castle	$638^{92}/_{94}$		£8800			£1726
1863	comp	S	44	Eliza Shaw		696	£15,400		$800^{10}/_{94}$	£3300
1863	iron	bk	45	Pembroke Castle	$452^{65}/_{94}$		£7300			£1598
1863	iron	bgn	46	Zircon	216		£3600			£712
1863	iron	S	47	Woosung	$774^{85}/_{94}$		£14,000			£2369
1863	iron		48	PS Fergus	$553^{12}/_{94}$		£12,200			£3500
1864	iron	S	49	City of Lahore	$965^{40}/_{94}$		£13,000			£1939
1864	comp	S	50	Hoang Ho	$660^{56}/_{94}$		£13,000			£2059
1864	comp	S	51	Janet Ferguson	$605^{65}/_{94}$		£10,000 hull and spars			£1813
1863	iron	sch	52	PS The Dare	$553^{12}/_{94}$		£12,860 £4720 for engines incl			£3500
1864	comp	S	53	Gossamer	$800^{10}/_{94}$		£16,000		800	£2875

Date	Material	Rig	Yard no	Name	Tons BM	Tons reg	Contract price Lump sum	Per ton	Tons for contract	Profit excluding yard rent etc
1864	comp	S	54	*Mofussilite*	$1043^{76}/_{94}$		£22,000			£3000 estimated
1864	comp		55	ps *Luzon*	$591^{13}/_{94}$		£15,100			£1300 estimated
1864	iron	S	56	*Lucerne*	615		£10,300			£900 estimated
1864	iron		57	ps *Lake Ontario*	635			£22 taken apart & shipped out in pieces		£698
1864	iron		58	ps *Bay of Kandy*	615			£22 taken apart & shipped out in pieces		£530
1864	iron	S	59	*Copernicus*	$658^{23}/_{94}$		£11,250			£1246
1864	iron		60	ss *Spartan*	$421^{39}/_{94}$		£6650 without engines			£1093
1864	iron		61	ss *Clara*	$345^{71}/_{94}$		£5800 without engines			£1400
1864	iron	S	62	not built	$1166^{32}/_{94}$		£20,600			-
1864	iron	S	63	*Newton*	$658^{23}/_{94}$		£11,250 sister to no 59			£1222
1864	iron		64	ss *Roma*	$615^{2}/_{94}$		£9304 hull only			£263
1865	comp	S	65	*Leon Crespo*	704			£16 19s 6d	$703^{91}/_{94}$	£2069
1865	iron	bk	66	*Tocopilla*	$506^{8}/_{94}$			£19	506	£1097
1865	comp	bk	67	*Carmelita*	$617^{3}/_{94}$			£19[?]		£2270
1865	iron	3 sch	68	ss *Hibernia*	$1492^{52}/_{94}$		£26,125 for hull & spars			£95
1865	iron	-	69-80	12 barges	155		£1305 each			-
1865	iron	bk	81	ss *Zeta*	713		£13,500 excl ore trunk & condenser			£1515
1865	iron	brig	82	*Belle of the Clyde*	$249^{19}/_{94}$		£3900			-
1865	comp	bk	83	*Fusi Yama*	618 approx			£18 10s	618 BM	£632
1865	comp	bk	84	*Kappa*	$545^{70}/_{94}$			£19 10s	BM	-
1865	comp	S	85	*Rohilla*	$1043^{76}/_{94}$			£19 15s	1043 BM	£3337
1865	iron		86	ss *Valetta*	$615^{2}/_{94}$		£9364 hull only similar to no 54			£1635
1865	iron		87	ss *Sarah Garcia*	$421^{39}/_{94}$		£8400 hull & engines			£729
1865	iron		88	ss *Venezia*	$615^{2}/_{94}$		£9364 hull only similar to no 86			£1700
1866	iron	bk	89	*Mineiro*	$537^{1}/_{94}$			£16 8s 6d	535 BM	£1635
1866	comp	S	90	*William Davie*	$876^{62}/_{94}$			£18	830 reg	£1560
1866	iron		91	ss *Columbia*	$1551^{42}/_{94}$		£27,780 hull & spars similar to no 68			£2370
1866	iron		92	ss *Osaca*	$637^{54}/_{94}$		£8350 without engines			£512
1866	comp	3 sch	93	ss *Thomas Roys*	$296^{47}/_{94}$		£6300			-
1866	iron		94	ps *Topsy*	$360^{29}/_{94}$			£16 10s without engines		-
1866	iron	S	95	*Abeona*	$1053^{75}/_{94}$			£16 5s	996 gr	£1365
1866	iron		96	ss *Arcadia*	$699^{1}/_{94}$		£10,5000			£882
1866	comp	3 sch	97	*Metero*	$375^{37}/_{94}$		£3600			-
1866	iron		98	barge	$27^{13}/_{94}$		£170			£100
1867	iron	bk	99	*Annie Story*	$618^{8}/_{94}$			£15 15s	reg	£430
1867	iron	bk	100	*Pacific*	$447^{29}/_{94}$			£16 5s	reg	£624
1867	iron	S	101	*Humboldt*	$713^{28}/_{94}$		£20,860 for 2 ships incl double topsails			£1741
1867	iron	S	102	*Reichstag*	$713^{28}/_{94}$					£1726
1867	iron		103	ss *Europe*	$1551^{42}/_{94}$		£25,990 sister to no 91			£2169
1867	iron		104	ss *Hannah Simons*	$712^{67}/_{94}$		£12,650 engines incl			£1740
1867	iron	S	105	*Grace Gibson*	$575^{27}/_{94}$		£9,000			£894
1868	comp	S	106	*Omba*	$889^{77}/_{94}$			£17 5s	820/830 reg	£2257

Date	Material	Rig	Yard no	Name	Tons BM	Tons reg	Contract price		Tons for contract	Profit excluding yard rent etc
							Lump sum	Per ton		
1868	iron	bk	107	*Annie Richmond*	$693\frac{73}{94}$			£15 15s	600 reg max	£1443
							sister to no 99			
1868	comp	bk	108	*Mary Moore*	$618\frac{12}{94}$			£17 9s	reg	£705
1867	iron	bk	109	*Annie Main*	$538\frac{1}{94}$			£15 17s 6d	500 reg max	-
1867	comp	S	110	*Forward Ho!*	$1014\frac{18}{94}$			£17 15s	approx 900 reg	£2865
1867	iron	bk	111	*Limari*	$612\frac{32}{94}$			£16 11s	600 reg max	£1310
1867	comp	S	112	*Rona*	$635\frac{52}{94}$			£18 2s 6d	reg tons	£1843
1868	comp	bk	113	*Lizzie Iredale*	$773\frac{85}{94}$			£17 7s 6d	approx 680 reg	£1583
1867	iron	2 sch	114	*Janette*	$135\frac{53}{94}$		£1650			-
1868	iron	S	115	*Centurion*	$1296\frac{63}{94}$			£14 14s	reg	£2041
1868	iron	S	116	*Comadre*	$850\frac{55}{94}$			£15 10s	reg	£1163
1868	comp	S	117	*Malacca*	$660\frac{25}{94}$		£10,600			£1141
1869	comp	S	118	*Singapore*	$716\frac{27}{94}$			£17 2s 6d		£1229
1868	iron	bk	119	*Clydevale*	$537\frac{1}{94}$		paid over 3 years; bldr to get mortgage on ship × £3000 COD.			£1053
1868	comp	S	120	*St Kilda*	$941\frac{6}{94}$			£17 17s 6d	868.68 gross	£2015
1868	iron	bk	121	*Belle of Lagos*	$338\frac{80}{94}$		£3900			£69
1869	iron	bk	122	*Atlantic*	$537\frac{1}{94}$			£16 10s	gross	£1086
1869	iron	bk	123	*Caroline*	$700\frac{5}{94}$			£14 13s 9d	700 reg	£1385
1869	iron	bk	124	*Antonia*	$700\frac{5}{94}$			£14 13s 9d	700 reg	£1241
1869	comp	S	125	*City of Hankow*	$1367\frac{65}{94}$			£12 17s 6d hull & spars	1200	£231
1869	iron	S	126	*Kildonan*	$727\frac{62}{94}$			£14 8s 9d	660 reg	£511
1870	iron	S	127	*City of Sparta*	$1296\frac{63}{94}$			£11 19s[?] hull & spars?	1200	?
1869	comp	S	128	*Norham Castle*	$848\frac{57}{94}$			£16 11s [or 15s]	700	£65
1869	comp	S	129	*Brechin Castle*	$1046\frac{56}{94}$			£16 10s	900	£956
1869	iron	S	130	*Friedeburg*	$751\frac{56}{94}$ }		£19,000			£1017
1869	iron	S	131	*Lammershagen*	$848\frac{57}{94}$ }					£1057
1869	iron	bk	132	*Armin*	$848\frac{57}{94}$		£11,100			£1059
1869	iron	bk	133	*Henry Sempe*	$538\frac{1}{94}$			£15 8s	500	£550
1869	comp	3 sch	134	ss *Diana*	$251\frac{3}{94}$		£5335			£617
1869	iron		135	ss *Anglia*	$1915\frac{65}{94}$		£24,490			?
1869	iron	bk	136	*Otago*	$447\frac{24}{94}$			£16	gross	£222
1870	iron	S	137	*Sydenham*	$1107\frac{32}{94}$			£14 14s	under deck	?
1869	iron	sch	138	*Aurora del Titicaca*	$24\frac{42}{94}$		£685			£236
1869	comp	brig	139	ss *Tszru*	$411\frac{35}{94}$		[not stated]			£2192
1870	iron	S	140	*Maggie Trimble*	$850\frac{55}{94}$			£14 12s 6d	under deck	£2192
1869	iron		141	ps *Countess of Kelly*	$133\frac{60}{94}$		£1720 engines incl (cost £700)			?
1870	iron	bk	142	*Valentine & Helene*		638	[unknown]			[unknown]
1870	iron	bk	143	*Virginia*		853	[unknown]			[unknown]
1870	comp	bk	144	*Lima*		831	[unknown]			[unknown]
1870	iron	brig	145	ss *Athol*		1082	[unknown]			[unknown]
1870	iron		146	ss *Shiraz*		867	[unknown]			[unknown]
1870	iron	sch	147	ss *Alert*		521	[unknown]			£748

LIST OF SAILING SHIPS BUILT BY ALEXANDER STEPHEN & SONS AT LINTHOUSE YARD, GLASGOW, 1870-1875.

Note: Out of 44 ships built in these 6 years, 26 were steamers, although only one steamer was built in 1875.

Date	Material	Rig	Yard no	Name	Tons BM	Tons reg	Contract Price Lump sum	Per ton	Tons for Contract	Profit excluding yard rent etc
1870	iron	bk	149	*Canopus*	912^{92}/94		£12,300			£1629
1871	iron	bk	157	*Anna*	848^{57}/94		£11,450			£1076
1872	iron	bk	159	*Josefa*	848^{57}/94		£11,450			£444
1872	iron	bk	162	*Belle of the Niger*	398^{88}/94		£5700			£209
1874	iron	bk	176	*Germania*	?		£16,300			?
1874	iron	bk	177	*G. Broughton*	?			£19 10s	under deck [=779]	?
1874	iron	bk	178	*Britannia*	?		£16,000			?
1875	iron	S	180	*Airlie*	1647			£16 12s 6d	gross	£4177
1875	iron	S	181	*Camperdown*	1647			£16 12s 6d	gross	£4808
1875	iron	S	182	*Panmure*	1647			£16 12s 6d	gross	£5340
1875	iron	bkn	183	*Osburgha*	447^{29}/94			£19	gross	£1004
1875	iron	bk	184	*Picton Castle*	618^{2}/94			£17 7s 6d	gross	£605
1875	iron	bk	185	*Lord Clyde*	618^{2}/94			£17 7s 6d	gross	£645
1875	iron	bk	186	*Llewellyn*	557^{12}/94			£17 5s		£341
1875	iron	S	187	*Amana*	1436^{59}/94			£17	gross	£4600
1875	iron	bk	189	*Lady Penrhyn*	897^{72}/94			£17	under deck	?
1875	iron	bk	190	*Martha Fisher*	912^{5}/94			£16 10s		?
1875	iron	bk	191	*Primera*	639	£10,000		If below 600 tons deduct tons @ £16 10s, vice versa if above.		£961

APPENDIX II

LIST OF IRON SHIPS BUILT BY ROBERT STEELE & CO, GREENOCK, UP TO THE END OF 1875.

THIS LIST KNOWN AS THE 'IRON BOOK' AND BEGINS AT YARD NO 1.

Copy made in 1954 from original loaned me by the late James Steele.

Yard no	Date launched	Name	Tonnage	Rig of sailing ships
1	Sept 1854	ss *Beaver*	383 BM 266 reg	
2	Feb 1855	*City of Madras*	823 BM 914 reg	S
3	Apr 1855	ss *Plover*	549 BM 382 reg	
4	Jun 1855	*City of Quebec*	775 BM 664 reg	S
5	Jul 1855	*City of Dublin*	823 BM 814 reg	S
6	Aug 1855	ss *Mangerton*	598 BM 364 reg	
7	Jan 1856	*City of Tanjore*	823 BM 799 reg	S
8	Mar 1856	PS *Inca*	343 BM 230 reg	
9	Aug 1856	ss *Dom Affonso*	311 BM 240 reg	
10	Sep 1856	PS *Panther*	754 BM 442 reg	
11	Sep 1856	cargo float	600 BM -	
12	?	ss *Dom Pedro*	311 BM 244 reg	
13	Apr 1857	ss *Scotia*	1197 BM 1021 reg	
14	Jun 1857	ss *United Kingdom*	1230 BM 1067 reg	
15	Aug 1857	*City of Canton*	881 BM 909 gr	S
16	Apr 1858	ss *Palestine*	1381 BM 936 reg	
17	Sep 1858	PS for R.Ganges	1346 BM -	
18	Nov 1858	cargo float	680 BM -	
19	May 1859	cargo float	871 BM -	
20	Jun 1859	cargo float	871 BM -	
21	Dec 1859	ss *Canadian*	1801 BM 1310 reg	
22	Mar 1861	ss *City of Hankow*	430 BM 241 reg	
23	Aug 1861	ss *St George*	1424 BM 1141 reg	
24	May 1861	dredger	271 BM -	
25	Apr 1862	*Circe* (of steel and iron)	127 BM 71 reg	sch yacht
26	Apr 1862	ss *Sarah*	285 BM 161 reg	
27	Jun 1862	*Reverie*	39 BM 24 reg	sch yacht
28	Jul 1862	*E. Shun*	327 BM 288 reg	sch
29	Sep 1862	*Silvercraig*	488 BM 491 reg	bk
30	Nov 1862	*King Arthur*	736 BM 700 reg	S
31	Jan 1863	*Waverly*	958 BM 1000 reg	S
32	Aug 1863	ss *Peruvian*	2129 BM 1908 reg	
33	Mar 1863	*Tuh Shing*	327 BM 275 reg	sch
34	?	iron barge	-	-
35	?	ss *Barwon*	421 BM 311 reg	
36	Apr 1863	ss lighter	776 BM -	
37	Dec 1863	*Taeping* (comp)	850 BM 757 reg	S
38	Feb 1864	*Lady Palmerston*	1212 BM 1247 reg	S
39	Sep 1864	*Redgauntlet*	1044 BM 1073 reg	S
40	Sep 1864	*Arundel Castle*	1056 BM 1042 reg	S
41	Jul 1864	ss *Moravian*	2311 BM 1598 reg	
42	Oct 1864	*Knight of Snowdoun*	665 BM 656 reg	S
43	Nov 1864	*Lord of the Isles*	665 BM 656 reg	S
44	Mar 1865	*Tantallon Castle*	1104 BM 1057 reg	S
45	Jul 1865	*Aglaia*	47 BM 31 reg	sch yacht
159	Jul 1865	*Sir Lancelot* (comp)	1058 BM 886 reg	S
		[this yard no appears to be transposed from the list of wood and composite ships, although no 159 in that list is *Albert Victor* launched Aug 1864]		
46-51	Oct 1865	6 hopper barges	- -	180ft long
58	?	iron bow for hooper barges	-	
52	Jan 1866	*Ravenscrag*	1231 BM 1263 reg	S
53	Jun 1866	*Janet Cowan*	1231 BM 1278 reg	S
54	Sep 1866	*Gryfe*	1056 BM 1073 reg	S
55	Dec 1866	*City of Athens*	1190 BM 1199 reg	S
56	Feb 1867	*Pomona*	1190 BM 1196 reg	S
57	Apr 1867	*Fleetwood*	665 BM 650 reg	S
59	Sep 1867	*Ardgowan*	1267 BM 1283 reg	S
60	Feb 1868	*Cartsburn*	1232 BM 1257 reg	S
		[First ship in Iron Book to have a deduction in tons for crew space]		
61	Apr 1868	*Walter Baine*	944 BM 898 reg	S

Yard no	Date launched	Name	Tonnage	Rig of sailing ships
62	Jun 1868	*Ralston*	864 BM 815 reg	S
63	Jul 1868	*Hartfield*	864 BM 815 reg	S
64	Aug 1868	*Assaye*	1328 BM 1281 reg	S
65	Sep 1868	*Parsee*	1328 BM 1281 reg	S
66	Oct 1868	*Araby Maid*	903 BM 837 reg	S
67	Dec 1868	*Lake Superior*	1368 BM 1274 reg	S
68	Mar 1869	*Halcione*	887 BM 843 reg	S
69	Nov 1869	ss *Scandinavian*	2579 BM 1701 reg	
70	Oct 1869	*Cathcart*	1404 BM 1387 reg	S
71	Nov 1869	*Ladyburn*	1513 BM 1431 reg	S
72	Jul 1869	*Arethusa*	1328 BM 1272 reg	S
73	Jun 1870	ss *Palatine*	449 BM 192 reg	yacht
74	Mar 1871	ss *Samaritan*	3235 BM 2316 reg	
75	Feb 1872	ss *Polynesia*	3517 BM 2032 reg	
76	Jul 1871	*Lake Simcoe*	408 BM 350 reg	bk
77	Jun 1872	ss *Circassian*	2877 BM 1484 reg	
78	?	iron barge	551 BM -	
79	Apr 1873	ss *Brimschweig*	2652 BM 2085 reg	
80	Sep 1873	ss *Numberg*	2652 BM 2085 reg	
81	Jun 1874	ss *Sardinian*	3537 BM 2577 reg	
82	Nov 1873	*Hesperus*	1889 BM 1777 reg	S
83	Jul 1874	*Eurydice*	1678 BM 1465 reg	S
84	Sep 1874	*Aurora*	1889 BM 1768 reg	S
85	Nov 1874	*Orpheus*	1677 BM 1462 reg	S
86	Dec 1874	*Niobe*	1677 BM 1469 reg	S
87	Apr 1875	*Bannockburn*	1921 BM 1675 reg	S
88	Jun 1875	*Lady Ruthven*	1802 BM 1591 reg	S
89	Jul 1875	*Bencleuch*	1555 BM 1350 reg	S
90	Sep 1875	ss *Zingara*	535 BM 263 reg	yacht
91	Jun 1875	ss *Cuba*	337 BM 112 reg	barge
92	Nov 1875	ss *City of Santiago*	1906 BM 1296 reg	
93	Nov 1875	*Deveron*	1377 BM 1256 reg	S
94	Nov 1875	*Aline*	765 BM 718 reg	bk

NOTE: The last ship in the Iron book is no 130 *Inveruglas* launched Sept 1883.

Of the ships listed as built of wood and composite after 1850, 49 were wood and 15 were composite, and the yard nos ran from 114 of ss *Asia*, launched in Jan 1850 to no 177 of *Garrion* launched in April 1871. This latter was the last in this part of the list.

APPENDIX III

LIST OF SHIPS BUILT BY WILLIAM PILE AT SUNDERLAND

List incomplete for wooden ships, only beginning with No 52 or 1857/1858. List complete for iron and composite ships from 1861 to 1873. It is conceivable that ships laid down but not completed at Pile's death are not included.

Original from which this was copied was a small notebook, kept by Thomas Collie Stamp, first cashier to Williaim Pile and later a shipowner. Notebook loaned me by T C Stamp's great grandson, J G M Stamp of Newcastle.

The *Rodney* was built in March 1874, being completed by friends. She is not in the list. The same may apply to other ships. I am grateful to Peter Barton for suggesting corrections to the spelling which have been added in square brackets, and also for other comments.

WOOD SHIPS

Yard no	Name	Launched	Owners
52	*Clarence*	23 Jan 1858	
53	*Dunlorlain* [or *Dunorlan?*]	17 Sep 1857	
54	*Standard*	Jan 1858	John R Kelso

Yard no	Name	Launched	Owners
55	*Reullura*	25 Feb 1858	
56	*Glendower* [or *Glendoveer*]	12 Jun 1858	
57	*Integrity*	20 Nov 1857	
58	*Star of Ere* [L R has *Star of Eve*]	10 Aug 1858	
59	*Newcastle*	5 Jan 1859	
60	*Sir Geo Gray*	26 Sep 1859 Launched as *Fiery Cross*	
61	*Westbury*	Sailed about 25 Jun 1859	
62	*Queen of the Ocean*	23 Jan 1860	
63	*Cubana*	23 Feb 1860	
64	*Ocean Belle*	26 Sep 1859	Due to be launched same day as no 60, but owing to slight mishap was launched next day. Named *Ocean Bride* (Middlesborough Weekly News Oct 1859)
65	*Malabar*	May 1860	
66	*Zeus*	Jan 1860	
67	*Alfred Hawley*	1860	
68	*Eliza Blancho* [or *Eliza Blanche?*]	1861	
69	*Kelso*	13 Feb 1861	John R Kelso
70	*Herald*	16 May 1863	John R Kelso
71	*Glenaros*	19 Sep 1861	
72	*Tinen Tsin* [or *Tien Tsin?*]	23 Jul 1861	
73	*Lord Warden* [or *The Lord Warden?*]	15 May 1862	Richard Green
74	*Queen of the Age*	7 Nov 1862	Henry Ellis
75	*Arab Steed*	18 Feb 1863	Thos B Walker
76	*Colorade*	12 Sep 1862	John Hay

LOW YARD

(This is another yard heading for ships built at a different yard)

No	Name	Launched	Owners
1	*Forth*	8 May 1860	R Devereux
2	*Onward*	Sep or Oct 1860	J Galley & Co
3	*Quercus*	27 Apr 1861	Richard Iliff
4	*Aquila*	6 Nov 1861	S W Kelso
5	*Deerfoot*	16 Apr 1862	John R Kelso
6	*Chanticleer*	24 Sep 1862	John R Kelso
7	*Sarah*	21 Mar 1863	Joshua Brothers [brig; iron & wood frames; experimental; Biennial Survey (LR 1868)]
8	*Golden Fleece*	11 May 1863	Henry Ellis
9	*Sea Ripple*	Sep 1863	[LR, 1868 gives builder as Gardner, Sunderland]

IRON AND COMPOSITE SHIPS

No	Name	Launched	Owners
1	*Ganges*	9 Jul 1861	James Nourse
2	*Wisbeach* ss [or *Wisbech?*]	8 Jun 1861	Richard Young
3	*Stettin* ss	19 Sep 1861	J Richardson & Sons
4	*Caldera*	5 Nov 1861	N J Madge
5	*Cape City*	7 Sep 1861	Henry Ellis

Yard no	Name	Launched	Owners
6	Charente ss	29 May 1862	H I M Napoleon III
7	Lord Royston ss	1 Jan 1862	Richard Young
8	Gazelle ss	12 Mar 1862	Killick & Martin
9	Sir H.V. Barkes ss	13 Aug 1862	Killick & Martin
10	Miriain / Silas Marineo ss	10 Jul 1862 [sic ss crossed out]	J Richardson & Sons
11	Herradura	26 Aug 1862	H J Madge
12	Aunt Lizzie	25 Oct 1862	Thos Scott
13	Cubaria [or Cubana?]	6 Dec 1862	John Hay
14	Canada	3 Jan 1863	Mr Douglass
15	Trevelyan	2 May 1863	G D Tyser
16	Santon	4 May 1863	Mr J Watson
17	Ocean King	17 Jun 1868	Thos Bell & Co
18	Beth Shan	20 Jul 1863	Mr Brass
19	Berer [or Berar?]	16 Sep 1863	G D Tyser
20	Himilaya	26 Nov 1863	G D Tyser
21	Queen of the East	23 Jan 1864	Henry Ellis
22	Sophie Joakim	9 Mar 1864	John Willis
123	City of Adelaide	7 May 1864 [sic order of yard no]	Devitt Moore
124	Howrah	4 Jun 1864	G D Tyser
125	Smack Belle	7 May 1867	P W Pile & Co to recokon for this number
126	Mula ss	16 Jul 1864	Reynolds Mann & Co
127	Ellen Constance ss	4 Oct 1864	R T Buck
128	Memphis (ss) / Louis David	28 Jan 1865 [sic, in line given to Cleopatra]	David Verbist & Co
129	Cleopatra ss	8 Jul 1865	Temperley, Corter & Co
130	Thurso	8 Jun 1864	Sir John Pirie Bart
131	St. Leonards	19 Sep 1864	Mr Douglass
132	Coral Nymph	1 Dec 1864	John Hay
133	Star of the West	11 Jan 1865	A Pardew
134	Star of the East	11 Feb 1865	A Pardew
135	Queen of the South	28 Nov 1864	Henry Ellis
136	Queen of the North	8 Apr 1865	Henry Ellis
137	Corra Linn ss yacht	27 May 1865	John Hay
138	Maitland	2 Dec 1865	John R Kelso
139	Star of the North	24 Aug 1865	A Pardew
140	Star of the South	7 Oct 1865	A Pardew
141	St. Vincent	22 Jul 1865	Devitt Moore
142	Not built	-	-
143	Cotopaxi	21 Nov 1865	John Hay
144	Tongoy	3 Feb 1866	H J Madge
145	Serena	16 Jun 1866	H J Madge
146	Caradoc ss	31 Jan 1866	Graydon & W Hay
147	Thetis ss	29 Mar 1866	Ryde & Co
148	Harmodius	6 Mar 1867	Henry Walker
149	Ethel	31 Mar 1866	Tonwick & Co
150	Charles Howard	24 Nov 1866	Ryde & Co
151	Carnatic	22 Jan 1867	J J Wait
152	Undine	28 Sep 1867	John R Kelso
153	Westbury	20 Apr 1867	T B Walker
154	Canaradze [Canaradzo L R '70]	6 Jun 1867	John Hay
155	Callisto	9 Jan 1868	John Hay
156	Jumna	17 Aug 1867	Capt Nourse
157	Poonah	28 Oct 1867	G D Tyser
158	Queen of the West	26 Sep 1867	Henry Ellis

Yard no	Name	Launched	Sailed	Owners
159	Plover (sch)	13 Aug 1867		J & S Park
160	South Australian	24 Feb 1868		Devitt & Moore
161	Rhone ss	8 Feb 1868		Ryde & Co
162	Richard Cobden	11 Mar 1868		Ryde & Co
163	Dacre ss	11 Jan 1868		J & S Todd & J Nicholson Jn
164	Ivanhoe	9 May 1868		Wilson & Bell
165	Syria	8 Jun 1868		James Nourse
166	Arcot	8 Jul 1868		G D Tyser
167	Decapoles	22 Aug 1868		T B Walker
168	Chacma	31 Aug 1868		John Hay
169	Cerastes	6 Oct 1868	19 Oct 1868	John Hay
170	Lacydon ss	22 Jul 1869	22 Sep 1869	Ryde & Co
171	Hawksbury	17 Nov 1868	9 Dec 1869 [sic, but surely should be 1868]	Devitt & Moore
172	L'Imperatrice	28 Jan 1869	23 Feb 1869	A Pardew
173	Deerhound	13 Jan 1869	10 Feb 1869	J R Kelso
174	Fingoe	11 Feb 1869	1 Mar 1869	Henry Ellis
175	England's Glory	2 Mar 1869	24 Mar 1869	Peter Smith
176	Runnymede	25 Mar 1869	8 Apr 1869	Jas Alexander
177	Golden Fleece	13 May 1869	5 Jun 1869	Henry Ellis & Co
178	Annie	26 Apr 1869	8 May 1869	J J Holdsworth
179	Osaka	12 Jul 1869	27 Jul 1869	Killick & Co
180	Ariadne	9 Oct 1869	10 Nov 1869	Ryde & Co
181	Miako	15 Apr 1869	22 Apr 1869	Killick Martin & Co
182	Langstone	10 Jun 1869	26 Jun 1869	H Ellis
183	British Empire	23 Sep 1869	6 Nov 1869	G Duncan
184	Marmion ss	4 Jan 1870	5 Feb 1870	Kelso & Bell
185	Evora ss	31 Jan 1870	19 Mar 1870	Ryde & Co
186	Berean W & I	24 Aug 1869	4 Sep 1869	T B Walker
187	[left blank]			
188	Corinth W & I	19 Apr 1870	9 May 1870	T B Walker
189	Laira	5 Mar 1870	7 Apr 1870	R Hill
190	Galatea ss	8 Nov 1870	11 May 1871 from Shields	Ryde & Co
191	Excelsior ss	28 Jul 1870	6 Sep 1870	J & J Wait
192	Express ss	29 Mar 1870	30 Apr 1870	Banks & Mitchell
193	Vanguard ss	8 Dec 1870	1 Feb 1871	J R Kelso
194	Corisande ss	2 Jun 1870	13 Sep 1870	John Hay
195	Polino ss	31 Aug 1870	18 Oct 1870	D G Pinkney
196	Blyth ss	16 Jun 1870	19 Jul 1870	Jas Hunter
197	Dale ss	9 Jan 1871	8 Mar 1871	P Dale & Co
198	Oriental ss	6 Feb 1871	10 Apr 1871	S W Kelso & Co
199	Ariadne ss	17 Aug 1870	19 Oct 1870	Pile & Co
200	Hyperior ss	23 Feb 1871	16 May 1871	H Ellis & Co
201	Fawn ss	17 Aug 1870	17 Sep 1870	Stamp & Co
202	Clifford ss	22 Apr 1871	22 Jul 1871	P Dale & Co
203	Olympias ss	6 Jun 1871	4 Jul 1871	Stamp & Co
204	Archdruid ss	20 Mar 1871	29 Apr 1871	E Shotton & Co
205	Ravensworth Castle ss	25 Nov 1871	13 Mar 1872	Northumberland Steam Shipping Co
206	Anthony Strong ss	8 Apr 1871	15 Jun 1871	A Strong & Co
207	Warkworth Castle ss	17 Jun 1871	30 Sep 1871	Laws, Cleugh & Co
208	Monica [ss]	16 Aug 1871	20 Sep 1871	Stamp & Co
209	Pickwick [ss]	19 Aug 1871	20 Sep 1871	Bell & Co
210	Umzinto	3 Oct 1871	7 Oct 1871	Bullard, King & Co
211	Royal Standard [ss]	6 Jul 1871	13 Sep 1871	E Shotton & Co
212	Despatch ss	14 Sep 1871	15 Nov 1871	Banks & Mitchell
213	Crighton ss	28 Oct 1871	20 Jan 1872	P Dale & Co
214	Great Western	7 Mar 1872	23 May 1872	M Whitwill & Son
215	Coromandel ss	25 Apr 1872	23 Jul 1872	J & J Wait
216	Eliza Hunting	14 Dec 1871	3 Feb 1872	A Strong

Yard no	Name	Launched	Sailed	Owners
217	*Roma*	10 Jun 1872	3 Aug 1872	A Strong
218	*Argentino*	28 Mar 1872	25 May 1872	G Bell & Co
219	*Dorcas*	20 Jul 1872	14 Sep 1872	T C Stamp & partners
220	*Celerity*	17 Aug 1872	3 Oct 1872	Banks & Mitchell
221	*Royal Minstrel*	11 May 1872	29 Jun 1872	E Shotton & Co
222	*Eunice*	8 Aug 1872	17 Sep 1872	T C Stamp & partners
223	*Newbiggin*	22 Jun 1872	21 Aug 1872	G R Dawson & Co
224	*Cortes*	2 Nov 1872	17 Sep 1872	E Shotton & Co
225	*Marquis de Numez*	19 Sep 1872	3 Dec 1872	Oscar de Olivarria & Co
226	*Sam Weller*	12 Nov 1872	24 Jan 1873	G Bell & Co
227	*Pedro J. Pidal*	14 Dec 1872	2 May 1873	Oscar de Olivarria & Co
228	*Border Chieftan*	30 Jan 1873	25 Mar 1873	E Shotton & Co
229	*Lilibeo*	30 Nov 1872	2 May 1873	Trinacria Steam Shipping Co
230	[blank]	13 Mar 1873		J R Kelso
231	*Rosario*	17 Mar 1873	24 May 1873	G Bell & Co
232	*Barassa*	24 May 1873		T B Walker
233	*Echo*	10 Apr 1873	24 May 1873	D G Pinkney & Co

(Although not marked on original, some of the above are steamers according to *Lloyd's Register*.)

APPENDIX IV

SPECIFICATION OF IRON SAILING SHIP *ABEONA* SHIPYARD NO 95

Built in 1867 by Alexander Stephen & Sons for J & A Allan of the Anchor Line, Glasgow. Contract dated 21 Dec 1865 at a price of £16 5s per register ton which *Lloyd's Register* gives as 979. They give the dimensions as 210.3ft × 33.4ft × 21.0ft. As the completion date is 1867, construction work must have lasted more than twelve months, although the contract specifies nine.

This appears to be a standard printed contract for ships ranging in size from 700 to 799 tons, but these figures have been amended in ink to read '900 to 999' tons. This would have the effect of making the scantlings lighter although the clause at the end entitled 'Quality of Materials' states that the scantlings are 'meant as minimum sizes' and that if the Lloyd's Register surveyor should require an increase in them, then the cost would not be paid by the builder.

Two alterations in sizing can be noted: deck thickness increased from 3¾ins to 4ins; two bilge pumps increased from 6ins to 7ins.

A hand-written note pasted on to the inside of the cover reads: 'Verbally arranged with Mr Allan 2nd March 1866 – That the vessel is to be coated on bottom with Peacock's and not McInnes' paint as specified. [Words in specification already amended.] That the vessel is to have a Winch at after hatch instead of Capstan on quarterdeck, they paying the difference. That Greig's machine for bracing foreyard be found for the ship and charged extra, but no charge for fitting it.'

SPECIFICATION
OF AN
IRON SAILING SHIP,
Of about 990 Tons Register, to Class $\frac{A}{A}$ at Lloyds

PRINCIPAL DIMENSIONS

	Feet	Inches
Length of Keel and Forerake	200	0
Breadth, extreme,	33	2
Depth of Hold	21	0

Tonnage Register 990 to 999 Tons, but not to exceed latter.

General Description – The Vessel to be $\frac{A}{A}$ class at Lloyds, with a full East India outfit. To be built to the satisfaction of the Owners and their superintendent, and of the surveyors for Lloyds. The Vessel to be ship-rigged, and fitted with a half-poop, fitted in first-class style, according to an improved plan, say of the type of the new iron ship "City of Benares". No piece-work to be allowed in construction of the Vessel.

IRON-WORK

All the Iron Work to be in accordance with Lloyd's rules, and of the best quality; and the ship to be specially surveyed while building, and to be entered in Lloyd's book as an $\frac{A}{A}$ Ship. Butt straps of sheer strake and main stringer to be treble rivetted for 100 feet amidships. amidship.

Waterways – To have iron gutter waterways.

Stanchions in lower hold to be 3¼ inches diameter, and in 'tween decks 2¾ inches; the upper end to be fastened with the beam, and the hold beams to be fastened with four rivets through the keelson angle-irons, and double stanchions in way of hatchways, fitted as ladders. Stanchions to every hold beam from 10 feet abaft foremast to mainmast.

Rudder – To be made to ship and unship. Stock to be 6 inches diameter to where the back starts off; below this is to be 7 × 4, tapered to 3 inches as heel. Solid stop checks to be forged on the rudder post and rudder bands. Rudder frame to be 4 × 1¾ inch, plated with 5/16 inch plates, in one breadth, properly stiffened. Rudder head to be fitted with spare tiller and relieving tackles.

Bulwarks – Height to be about 4 3/12 feet from stringer to top of main rail, formed of plate 5/16 inch thick, stiffened, at distances of about 4 feet 6 inches, with stanchions of 1¾ inch iron, rivetted to a 6 × 3 × ½ inch angle-iron at top, and, to inner waterway, angle-iron at bottom. Bulwark plates to have double rivetted butts and single landings.

Hatch Combings – To be of ½ inch plates, with half round iron on upper edge. Upper deck combings to stand about 12 inches above the deck, 'tween deck do raised above deck plank.

Pall Bitt – Of greenheart or iron, about 19 × 15 inches, secured at deck and at foot by iron partners and knees, with ventilation to holds.

Hawse Pipes and Timberheads – To be supplied with two malleable cast-iron hawse pipes at bow, 2 cast cleats of similar iron at stern, and timberheads, mooring chocks, and pipes, as may be deemed necessary.

Mooring Bitts – Two pairs of short bitts to be fixed on main deck; one pair to be abreast of the quarter pipes, and the other pair abreast the bow pipes; one pair on poop; one pair on topgallant forecastle.

Smith Work – Iron bands to be fixed round the lower masts, 4 feet above the deck, fitted with belaying pins. 3 feet below each of these, another band to be fixed, having strong eyes for topsail sheets; the vessel to be fitted with iron cleats and belaying pins where required. Patent trusses to lower yards to have double topsail yards, and iron swivel parrels to topsail and topgallant yards; two sets of boat davits, two normans, two strong backs, awning stanchions (strong top ends), and all other smith-work for the rigging and decks; topgallant outriggers to be of wood or iron, with a bar across; all light ironwork about deck and hatch bars to be galvanized. Hoops for stay rollers; hoops or strong plates, with links, for yard slings; eyes and eye-bolts where required for rigging purposes.

WOOD-WORK AND GENERAL OUTFIT

Main Deck – To be of best Quebec yellow pine planks, to be 4 inches thick and 5 inches wide, fastened to deck beams by bolts and nuts (one bolt and nut in each plank in each beam). All the combings round the masts to be of iron; plank next water-ways to be teakwood, and to be not less than 8 inches broad; one plank of teak or hardwood for ring bolts, from fore-part of main hatch to forecastle on each side of boats.

Lower Deck – To be laid from a beam before the after hatch, aft, and from fore bulkhead forward, with 3-inch Quebec yellow pine planks, 6 inches wide, and caulked; planks to be fastened to the deck beams by wood screws. The middle part of lower deck to be formed into suitable hatches to Owners' satisfaction, with permanent combings of hardwood, to allow of cargo being stowed between the beams. The height from top of lower deck to upper side of main deck beams, along the centre line of ship, to be about 7 feet.

Half-Poop and Forecastle Deck – To be laid with best Quebec yellow pine planks, 3 inches thick and 5 inches wide, secured with nuts and screw bolts similar to upper deck.

Beams – To be lined with elm where not covered by deck.

Rails – Main rail to be of elm, faced with greenheart, 3¾ inches thick, with belaying pins. Topgallant bulwarks about 18 inches high, surmounted by a teak rail, and supported by teak stanchions, and all neatly pannelled.

Hold Ceiling – On flat of bottom, and in the bilges to the hold stringers to be ceiled, solid with 2½ inches elm, laid partly in hatches, as directed by Owners, to allow access to the skin for cleaning and painting. From turn of bilge upward to be ceiled, berth and space, with 2½-inch red pine planks. Pine shutters to be fixed under the upper deck waterway, so as to carry the condensed water or leakage between the ceiling and the skin.

Dunnage – Permanent dunnage to be put on in the usual way; sweating boards to be fitted in the usual way.

Windlass Bits – Of teak or greenheart, about 7 inches, secured to deck with strong wrought iron knees and angle-iron partners.

Windlass – Body to be of English oak or greenheart, with iron spindle in one piece; to be worked with Pow and Faucus's or other approved purchase, with double cross head and strong handles. Gryll's whelps and ends as required, Wardell's Patent Deck Stoppers.

Capstans – Three iron capstans with brass heads to be fitted complete with bars, &c; one on the forecastle, one on main deck, and one on poop deck.

Chain Lockers – Of iron of suitable size, with iron chain pipes, and strong clinching apparatus.

Masts and Spars – The fore and main lower masts and bowsprits to be of iron plates 7/16 and 3/8 inch thickness; to have double rivetted butt straps, and double rivetted lap joints. Cheek plates to be 9/16 inch in thickness, and masts adapted to ventilate 'tween decks and hold. The fore and main lower yards to be of cast rolled steel, from 5/16 to 4/16 inch in thickness, with 2 angle-irons the whole length, and two in centre about 12 feet long. To have steel rivets and treble rivetted butts; topmast, double topsail-yards, and jibboom, of pitch pine; or to be of cast rolled steel, if pitch pine cannot be had. Spars, other principal yards and booms, of red pine; small spars of spruce; boom irons to be fitted where required. Full set of studdingsail booms and yards to be supplied. Mizen mast and cross jack-yard to be of Oregon wood, or Vancouver's Island; mizen cap and fitting at mast head to be of brass.

Fife Rail – Of teak, with turned teakwood stanchions, to be fixed round the mainmast, and fitted with hardwood pins, &c, and sheaved complete.

Gipsy Winches – Two of each side fitted complete.

Boat Beams – Two strong gallows beams for boats over main deck, sufficiently supported by iron stanchions on rail; fitted complete with everything for securing the Boats.

Catheads – To be of English or African oak, and to be fitted with sheaves, stoppers, &c, complete.

Rigging – The Vessel to be rigged as a Sailing Ship, with all standing and running rigging and studdingsail gear. The standing rigging to be of Newall's first quality of charcoal wire galvanized, and served all over; the running gear to be of St Petersburg hemp, or best Manilla rope, at Owners' option; all chains and iron work for rigging to be of the very best quality, and chains Admiralty proved; treble topmast and double topgallant back stays, for the fore and main mast to be fitted.

Blocks &c – To be supplied with all blocks for rigging and all dead eyes; sheaves, where not of iron, to be of lignum-vitæ; blocks iron-bound where required; to have patent roller sheaves for all halyards and brace blocks. Blocks for studdingsail gear to be bushed and fitted complete for use. Davit blocks and falls fitted; cat and fish blocks, luff tackle and snatch blocks, and all gear required for the efficient working of the ship and her tackle. All sheaves to be fitted with brass bushes.

Steering Wheel – To be of mahogany, with lignum-vitæ nave and greenheart spokes, handsomely brass-bound, and to be fitted with a screw steering apparatus.

Winches – One double-handed winch to be fixed on main deck, at fore and main hatches; the former one fitted with gipsy ends.

Pumps – Two of 7 inches for main hold, and two of 7 inches for bilges, with fly-wheel gearing, as required. Sounding pipes, rods &c, complete. Two spare sets of upper and lower boxes. Head and stern pumps complete.

Figurehead – Trail boards, name boards, and stern carving, to be neatly carved and painted, and gilded in usual style. To have carved mahogany gangway boards on bulwarks, mounted with brass. The name boards to be made to unship at sea.

Half-Poop – Fitted to plan; the top to be approached at the forward end by two teak ladders or stairs, with brass-mounted steps and brass hand-rails, and the sides round the poop to be protected with galvanized-iron stanchions and double rails; the upper rail to be of teak. Forward of poop, a deck house to be fitted for officers, and another for galley, store, &c. The have side lights and stern lights as required. The combings of deck houses and poop to be of teak.

Accommodation (Seamen) – To be provided on the main deck under topgallant forecastle deck, and fitted with berths, lockers, water-closets, and seats, &c. The space under berths to be high enough to take in men's chests; side lights to be fixed where required.

Painting – The iron hull of the vessel, where not specified otherwise, together with all wood-work, to have three coats best oil paint.

Ventilators – Three 15-inch Ventilators to be provided for main hold; to be of galvanized sheet-iron, excepting the bell mouth top of that one which comes on the poop, which will be of brass; and all revolving with tightening screws.

Sundries – To be provided with iron chain gipsy on forward winch; side lights to be fixed in the peaks; to have a coal-hole in the fore peak, with scuttle and grating to communicate with main deck. All brass work that may be required to be of best quality and sufficient weight, – viz. sill plates for cabin; mountings &c, for gangway boards; hinges for skylights and forecastle, and cook-house; clasp and quadrants for skylights, &c. The ship's watermark to be cut with a chisel on each side of stem and stern. All locks and hinges throughout the ship to be of brass. The deck plan to be approved by Owners. The compasses to be adjusted at the expense of the builders. The Owners to take the vessel from this Harbour to the Gareloch for the purpose of adjusting.

INVENTORY OF OUTFIT AND STORES.
ALL OF BEST QUALITY TO OWNERS' APPROVAL.

Sails – To be made by A. Stephen & Sons, Glasgow, of the best Gourock canvas of extra quality, and to be the numbers given for each respective sail, and fitted with all rope, leather, and galvanized-iron thimbles and spectacle clew where required. To have –

1 Flying jib,	No. 5.	2 Mainsail,	" 2.
2 Standing jibs,	" 3.	2 Maintopsails, (say 4 in all,)	" 2.
2 Foretopmast staysails,	" 1.	2 Maintopgallant sails,	" 4.
1 Storm staysail,	" 1.	2 Main royal,	" 5.
2 Foresails,	" 1.	1 Main staysail,	" 2.
2 Foretopsails, (say 4 in all,)	" 2.	1 Main trysail,	" 2.
2 Foretopgallantsails,	" 4.	1 Main skysail,	" 6.
2 Royal	" 5.	1 Crossjack,	" 3.
1 Maintopmast staysail,	" 3.	2 Mizen topsail, (say 2 in all,)	" 3.
1 Maintopgallant staysail,	" 5.	3 Topmast studding sails,	" 4.
2 Mizen topgallantsail,	" 5.	4 Topgallant studding sails,	" 5.
2 Mizen royal,	" 6.	3 Royal studding sails,	" 6.
2 Spanker	" 2.	1 Lug sail, for long boat,	" 7.
1 Mizen topmast staysail,	" 5.		
1 Mizen topgallant staysail,	" 6.	All Fore and Aft Sails to be made of	
2 Lower studding sails,	" 4.	15-inch canvas.	
1 Main royal staysail,	" 6.		

Covers, &c – To be made of Gourock bleached canvas, and to be as follows, viz:-

3 Main hatch tarpaulins, tarred.	1 Bell cover.
3 Fore hatch tarpaulings, tarred.	1 Colour bag.
1 After hatch cover.	2 Covers for skylights.
3 Mast coats, (double each mast.)	2 Covers for chain pipes.
1 Steering wheel cover.	2 Windsails.
2 Binnacle covers.	Canvas cover for all the boats.

Awning – To extend from the after end of poop to the fore-part of top-gallant forecastle, to be in four pieces, and to be made of No. 3 Gourock bleached canvas; four side curtains, each about 26 feet long, of No. 3 canvas, to be furnished for side of vessel, aft.

Ship Chandlery – 13 bolts of Gourock bleached canvas, Nos. say $\frac{2}{2}$, $\frac{3}{8}$, $\frac{3}{4}$, $\frac{3}{5}$, $\frac{2}{6}$.

1 Patent deep-sea land, 32 lbs.	1 Coil 4-inch cordage.
2 Hand-lead lines, one 20 fathoms long, and one 25 fathoms long.	1 Coil 2$\frac{3}{4}$-inch cordage.
2 Hand leads, one 8 lbs and one 10 lbs.	1 Coil 3$\frac{1}{2}$-inch cordage.
26 Lbs Log lines.	2 Coils 3-inch cordage.
2 Log reels.	10 Coils assorted, from 20 thread down to 3 in addition.
2 28-sec, and 2 14-sec log glasses.	$\frac{1}{2}$ Coils 4$\frac{1}{2}$ and 5 inch lanyard rope. All the coils to be of Europe or Manilla, and to be each 100 fathoms long.
6 Sail hooks.	
4 Palms.	
6 Dozen sail needles.	4 Dozen fine 2-yarn, and 4 dozen 3-yarn.
6 Serving mallets.	2 Dozen Ambro' line, assorted.
6 Serving boards.	4 Dozen marline.
1 Shark hook.	4 Dozen houseline.
6 Hand stones.	5 Dozen seaming, and 2 dozen roping twine.
1 Hide service leather.	
$\frac{1}{2}$ Hide pump leather.	4 Fish lines, 16, 12, 8, and 6 oz.
1 Barrel Stockholm tar.	Signal halyards, one for each mast.
1 Barrel pitch.	Bolt rope, assorted, 2 cwt.
1 Barrel bright varnish.	1 Buoy rope.
20 Gallons black varnish.	1 11-inch hawser tarred Manilla, 90 fathoms long.
3 Cwt oakum.	
6 Sheets sheathing felt.	1 9-inch hawser tarred Manilla, 90 fathoms long.
50 Gallons boiled paint oil, in small iron tank, with tap.	
10 Gallons turpentine, in iron cans, with brass taps.	1 7$\frac{1}{2}$-inch hawser tarred Manilla, 90 fathoms long.
10 Gallons rape oil, in iron cans, with brass taps.	1 Ensign, 6 yards.
30 Gallons seal oil, in iron cans, with brass taps.	1 Union jack, 3 yards.
	1 Blue-peter, 3 yards.
	1 House flag, 8 yards.
4 Cwt black paint.	Marryat's code of signals with chest and book.
10 Cwt white paint.	
56 Lbs oxide of iron.	Commercial code with chest and book.
14 Lbs dryer.	1 Burgee.
1 Keg M'Innes's composition.	4 Cork fenders, stitched with hemp.
28 Lbs umber.	4 Life buoys.
3 Lbs chrome.	
1 Pot vermilion.	
2 Lbs black lead.	
2 Lbs glue.	
12 Lbs chalk.	
$\frac{1}{2}$ Cwt whiting.	

Spare Block, & c –

4 Single 10-inch blocks, bushed.	1 Dozen bushed sheaves, from 7 to 10 inches.
4 Single 9-inch blocks, bushed.	
6 Single 8-inch blocks, bushed.	1 Dozen steel pins.
6 Single 7-inch blocks, bushed.	12 Hickory handspikes.
18 Single bushed blocks, for deck leads.	

Ironmongery –

1 Grindstone, 20 inches diameter, and trough with iron hoops.	Pair Sugar tongs.
1 Cabin store with copper funnell.	1 Sugar nippers.
1000 4d clasp nails.	2 Funnels – viz., 1 tin and 1 copper.
500 6d clasp nails.	4 Water dippers – viz., 2 tin and 2 copper.
500 8d clasp nails.	
500 10d clasp nails.	2 Dust pans.
500 12d clasp nails.	1 Coffee-pot, block tin.
800 Boat nails, assorted.	1 Tea-pot, block tin.
200 3-inch batten nails.	1 Soup ladle, of metal.
100 2$\frac{1}{2}$-inch plate nails.	6 Dish covers.
500 clasp nails.	1 Set scales and weights.
500 clasp nails 2$\frac{1}{2}$-inch.	1 Salter's balance.
1000 Copper pump tacks.	1 Steelyard.
1000 Iron pump tacks.	1 Set of measures.
26 Lbs spikes.	2 Lime-juice measures.
1 Dozen clip hooks.	2 Vinegar measures.
2 Dozen fish hooks.	1 Coffee canister.
1 Dozen single hooks, assorted.	1 4-lb canister.
4 Dozen forelocks, assorted.	1 Large tea canister.
24 Marline spikes.	1 Small canister.
1 Cross-cut saw.	1 Sugar canister.
1 Hand-saw.	2 Pairs brass candlesticks.
Axe.	2 Pairs snuffers and tray.
Pair grains.	1 Duster.
Harpoon.	2 Leathers.
1 Screw wrench.	2 Pair carvers and one steel.
1 Pair rigging-screws, 18 inches long.	12 Ivory table knives.
1 Pitch pot, 4 gallons.	12 Ivory dessert knives.
1 Pitch ladle.	3 Canisters polishing powder.
18 Scrapers.	1 Box rouge.
12 Mast knives.	6 Bottles blacking.
12 Round-mouthed ballast spades, No. 3.	12 Bath bricks.
	6 Balls cotton.
1 Black jack.	6 Rolls flat wick.
1 Spunyarn winch.	$\frac{1}{2}$ Gross matches.
1 Knife board.	2 Pairs crate hooks, one large and one medium size, with chains.
Copper pump.	
Poop bell, engraved.	3 Pairs can hooks.
Hand bell.	2 Chain puncheon slings.
3 Galvanized tanks – viz., one for lamp oil (45 gallons), and two for paint oil (35 gallons), each to have brass taps and holes at top of each for cleaning them out, with screwed covers.	3 Crow bars.
	24 Connecting links.
	Grapnell, 30 lbs weight.
	Brass padlocks, for hatches.
6 Tanks for paint.	6 Deck lights.
4 Oil feeders.	1 Brand iron with ship's name.
2 Pairs lamp scissors.	1 Fog Horn.
2 Spirit taps.	28 lbs sheet lead.
1 Wine funnel.	6 Sash-tools.
1 Pewter jug.	2 Plate brushes.
1 Shaving can.	24 Ground paint brushes.
1 Rat Trap.	6 Pencil brushes.
1 Plate basket.	2 Tar brushes.
1 Filter.	1 Hearth brush.
2 Coffee mills.	1 Long brush.
3 Waiters.	1 Crumb brush.
2 Corkscrews.	1 Scouring brush.
Cheese tray.	1 Set shoe brushes.
Bread basket.	8 Pairs scrubbers.
Candle box.	3 Deck scrubbers.
	6 Dozen besoms.

Electro-Plate –

1 Tea pot.	12 Egg spoons.
1 Coffee pot.	6 salt spoons.
1 Cream jug.	4 Mustard spoons.
1 Sugar basin.	1 Soup ladle.
12 Table forks.	2 Sauce ladles.
12 Dessert forks.	1 Tureen.
12 Table spoons.	1 Set cruet stand.
12 Dessert spoons.	2 Butter knives.
12 Tea spoons.	1 Toast Rack.

Lamps –

Signal lamps, as per Board of Trade Regulations, including anchor lamp.
1 Deck lantern.
2 Hold lanterns.
1 Dark lantern.
1 Flash lamp.
2 Forecastle lamps.
1 Lamp for petty officers and boys.
1 Cook's lamp.
1 Cabin lamp.
1 Lamp for Captain's room.
1 Lamp for first mate.
1 Lamp for second mate.
1 Lamp for steward.

Galley –

1 Cooking range complete for 40 hands, with condenser approved by Owners, with utensils as follows, viz.:-
1 10-gallon boiler and tap.
8 Sauce pans.
2 Frying pans.
1 Cullender.
1 Tormentor.
1 Potato steamer.
1 Copper kettle.
1 Gridiron, fluted.
1 Bread grater.
1 Pepper mill.
1 Pepper box.
1 Spice box.
1 Flour box.
1 Vegetable grater.
1 Flour sieve.
1 Wire sieve.
2 Iron bake pans.
2 Tin bake pans.
1 Dozen patty pans.
4 Bread tins (assorted).
1 Melon mould.
2 Pudding moulds.
1 Dough basin.
1 Egg whisk.
18 Skewers.
1 Rolling pin.
1 Saw.
1 Cleaver.
1 Axe.
1 Cook's stone.
2 Mincing knives.
2 Cook's knives.
2 Ladles.

Anchors and Cables –

3 Bower anchors, Trotman's patent.
1 Stream anchor, heavy, Trotman's patent.
2 Kedge, or 3 if required by Lloyds.
300 Fathoms stud chain cable, Admiralty proved.
90 Fathoms stud stream cable, Admiralty proved.

The cables and anchors to be tested at public testing machines to Admiralty proof, and all to be of the description Owners may require, and to be in accordance with Lloyd's Rules for a vessel of this tonnage.

Guns, &c –

1 Six lb iron carronades, mounted complete.
4 Best percussion muskets and bayonets.
2 Revolver pistols.
Copper magazine.
12 Rounds shot balls.
1 Dozen sky rockets.
12 Woollen cartridges.
Box of patent blue-lights, with discharger.
12 Pairs police handcuffs.
50 Ball cartridges.
20 Pistol cartridges.
8 Lbs best powder.
2 Boxes caps.

Cooperage –

12 Deck buckets, for quarter-deck, brass bound.
12 Deck buckets for main deck, galvanized hoops.
12 Mess kids.
3 Harness casks.
3 Water kegs for crew, 15 gallons each.
4 Casks, 15 gallons each, with galvanized taps.
2 Casks, 60 gallons each.
1 Wash-deck tub.   4 Bread barges.
1 Nun buoy.
4 Tar buckets.
1 Wood funnel.
2 Pump cans.
2 Oval breakers.

Compasses, &c –

1 Dolphin binnacle with lamps.
1 Dipping compass for ditto.
1 Port needle for ditto.
1 Binnacle for fore part of poop.
1 Azimuth compass for ditto.
1 Cabin ditto.
1 Spare brass compass.
6 Spare glasses for binnacles.
1 Telescope.
1 Night Glass.
1 Barometer.
1 Thermometer.
1 Timepiece, (best quality).
1 Half-hour glass.
1 Brass speaking trumpet, with ship's name on it.
The placed compasses to be corrected by magnets.

Spare Spars –

1 Spare lower yard.
1 Spare topmast.
1 Spare topsail yard or jibboom.
1 Spare topgallant mast or yard.
6 Small spare spars.
Spare planks, assorted.

Stationery –

1 Wages book.
2 Cargo books.
2 Log books.
2 Log slates.
1 Plain slate.
1 Inkstand.
6 bottles black ink.
1 Gross quills.
1 Bottle red ink.
3 Quires writing paper.
2 Nautical almanacs.
50 Envelopes.
6 Slate pencils.
1 Disbursement book.
1 Account book.
6 Small memorandum books.
1 Box steel pens.
6 Sheets blotting paper.
12 Black lead pencils.
1 Piece India-rubber.
1 Case for papers.
1 Box wafers.
4 Sticks wax.

Glass and Crockery Ware –

2 Quart decanters, cut.
2 Pint decanters, cut.
1½ Dozen tumblers, cut.
2 Dozen wines, cut.
4 Round salts, pressed and cut.
2 Dozen dinner plates.
2 Dozen soup plates.
2 Dozen pudding plates.
2 Dozen cheese plates.
10 Flat meat dishes.
4 Vegetable dishes.
2 Spare covers.
6 Sauce tureens, complete.
2 Butter boats and stands.
1 Well dish.
1 Fish drainer.
1 Salad bowl.
4 Dessert dishes.
18 Dessert plates.
18 Egg cups.
18 Tea cups and saucers.
18 Coffee mugs and saucers.
2 Round sugar boxes.
2 Butter tubs.
2 Cream jugs.
6 Slop basins.
6 Pie dishes.
4 Stone jugs.
1 Brush tray.
6 Chambers.

Furniture and upholstery –

A mahogany or oak table with guards.
Oil cloth for oak table with guards.
A sideboard of oak or mahogany with mirror.
2 Arm chairs, swivel seated, and strong backs, upholstered.
2 Moveable seats, upholstered.
6 Camp stools, with Brussels carpet seats.
12 Table cloths.
4 Dozen towels, assorted.
2 Table covers.
Oil cloth or carpet matting for cabin floor.

Boats – 1 Long Boat or Launch, carvel-built, or two Life-boats, in Owners' option.
1 Life-boat, clinker-built, fitted with buoyant apparatus, 24 × 6.6 × 2.6.
1 Cutter, clinker-built, fitted with buoyant apparatus, 24 × 6 × 2.6.
1 Gig, clinker-built, fitted with buoyant apparatus, 22 × 5 × 2.2.
Copper fastened, and fitted with back boards, yoke and iron rowlocks, all to have iron stem and heel plates, and to be fitted with brass plugs.
All iron work on boats to be galvanized. 24 Ash oars. Masts for two of the boats.
The boats to be of the sizes required by Lloyd's and Board of Trade, and fitted with davits and tackle complete.

Pumps – 1 Double action air-pump of gun metal, with 166 feet of 2½ vulcanized India rubber hose, in three lengths, with brass couplings attached to head or stern pump.

Engineer's Stores –

24 ¾ Belts and nuts.	6 Steel sets and 2 punches.
1 Cwt assorted rivets.	2 Pairs smiths' tongs.
2½ Cwt Staffordshire plates.	7 Steel caulking tools.
1 Ratchet brace.	1 Portable bellows and hearth.
7 Cwt Staffordshire angle-iron.	1 Pair rivet tongs.
6 Steel drills.	1 Keg borings.
10 Hand chisels.	2 Stripping and 1 rivetting hammer.
3 Spanners.	1 Anvil.
6 Steel drifts.	Sal-ammoniac.

Sundries –

Ship's bell.	2 Devil's claws.
Carpenter's bench and vice.	3 Cargo gins and 2 chains.
2 Teak or galvanized ladders for topgallant forecastle.	1 Dozen spare eye bolts.
2 Teak gangway ladders.	Water tanks, to contain 4000 gallons, properly cemented and fitted with pipes, pumps, &c, complete.
1 Hold ladder.	6 Bread tanks, iron, galvanized.
1 'Tween deck ladder.	Pig stye.
1 Rope ladder for side of ship.	Hen coops, double fronted.
Also, light-wooded side ladder for passengers.	2 Hardwood gangway chafing boards, for main rail.
1 Copper hand pump, for tanks.	4 Rolling fenders.
2 Dozen wood belaying pins (spare)	2 Hardwood boards on each side, for side fender ropes.
1 Dozen iron belaying pins (spare)	Rail chafing plates, to fit on main and topgallant rails, of galvanized iron.
3 Spare washers and glasses for lower side lights.	Medicine chest, complete as per Act.
18 Chain hooks.	
2 Fish hooks, and chains for anchors.	
2 Stoppers and shank painters.	

The vessel to be coated with solid cement in the inside of the bottom, up to the bilges. To be also coated with Peacock's patent composition (or other composition of equal value) on the outside, up to the loadwater line.

Painting – The whole of the ship, deck-work, cabins, masts, yards, spars, boats, &c, &c, inside and outside, to have three coats of best oil paint; and the deck work and spars to have an additional finishing coat when all is rigged up. (See memo as to painting.)

Quality of Materials, &c – The hull to be built of Consett Crown or Glasgow boiler plate-iron, tested and free from blisters, cracks, or flaws. The timber and all other materials to be also of the best quality. All the upper and lower deck planks and ceiling to be cut and exposed to the air to season; and the vessel to be built, completed and efficiently equipped in all respects, as herein described, in a thoroughly substantial and first-class manner. *No extras* to be charged unless ordered in writing. *Sizes* — When sizes are given in this Specification, it is meant as minimum size. Should Lloyd's surveyor, in classing, require more, it is to be put in free of charge.

Completion and Delivery – The vessel to be built under special survey, and classed A at Lloyds. The cost of Lloyd's survey and certificate to be paid by the builders. The vessel to be delivered in nine months from date of contract. The owners to have the right of appointing a superintendent.

Insurance – The ship to be insured by the builders against fire while in course of construction, and until delivered over to the Owners.

A neatly finished model to be supplied.

Drawings, showing deck arrangements, dimensions and capacity of holds, sizes of hatches, and a displacement scale, to be furnished by builders.

It is understood that this Specification, although detailing pretty fully the hull and outfit of the vessel, does not describe minutely everything required to complete the ship; and that such requirements will be supplied by the builders, although not thus fully described.

APPENDIX V

STANDING RIGGING SIZES OF BARQUENTINE *UNION* (1867)

Taken from Plan in Science Museum, London, no C/7/28; plan drawn on tracing linen.

Fore and main shrouds	6in hemp; lanyards 3¼in
Mizzen shrouds	5¼in hemp; lanyards 2¾in
Fore topmast backstays	5¼in hemp
Fore topgallant backstays	3¼in hemp
Fore royal backstays	2¼in hemp
Main inner spreader stay	3in hemp
Main outer spreader stay	2½in hemp
Mizzen spreader stays	2½in hemp
Main topping lift	3½in hemp
Mizzen topping lift	3in hemp
Fore stay	3¼in wire double
Fore topmast stay	2½in wire double
Fore standing jib stay	2¼in wire
Fore topgallant stay	2in hemp
Fore royal stay	1½in hemp
Main stay	3½in wire
Main middle stay	2¾in wire
Main topmast stay	2¼in wire
Main topgallant stay	1½in wire
Mizzen stays	2½in wire
Mizzen triatic stay	1¾in wire
Jibboom shrouds	2¼in wire
Flying jibboom shrouds	1¾in wire

APPENDIX VI

IDENTIFICATION OF NAMES OF SHIPS LISTED IN TABLE 1 OF APPENDIXES TO *REPORT MADE TO THE COMMITTEE OF LLOYD'S REGISTER OF BRITISH AND FOREIGN SHIPPING BY THE SOCIETY'S CHIEF SURVEYOR AND HIS ASSISTANTS CONCERNING THE DISMASTING OF LARGE IRON SAILING SHIPS* (1886).

Table I is entitled: 'Sizes of Masts, Yards, Bowsprits and other Spars'.

As stated in the text towards the end of Chapter Five, spar dimensions were given in this table of 82 unnamed ships, but it has been possible to assign names to all except two by means of the particulars given. These consisted of the rig, date of build, under deck tonnage and register dimensions. Most of the identification work has been done by Roderick Glassford and the late John Lyman, and I hope I will be forgiven for now revealing their research. The shipbuilders' names were not given in the Table, but John Lyman added them. The ships are listed in ascending order of size according to tonnage.

No in Table	Ship's Name	Date of Build	Shipbuilder
1	*Lucy Compton*	1875	Cole Bros; Newcastle
2	(?*Dunholme*	1865	Crown; Sunderland)
3	*Southwick*	1870	Crown; Sunderland
4	*Hope*	1871	Crown; Sunderland
5	*Cumbria*	1874	Bartram, Haswell; Sunderland
6	*Clan MacLeod*	1874	Bartram, Haswell; Sunderland
7	*Loch Fleet*	1872	Dobie; Glasgow
8	*Isle of Anglesea*	1872	Dobie; Glasgow
9	*Lanarkshire*	1873	Dobie; Glasgow
10	*Clan Campbell*	1875	Bartram, Haswell; Sunderland

11	*Kingdom of Sweden*	1875	Mounsey; Sunderland	46	*Haddon Hall*	1868	Royden; Liverpool
12	*Fernglen*	1874	Blumer; Sunderland	47	*Buckinghamshire*	1868	Barclay, Curle; Glasgow
13	*Eden Holme*	1875	Bartram, Haswell; Sunderland	48	(?*Blair Drummond*	1874	Caird; Greenock)
14	*Falcon*	1859	Steele; Greenock	49	*Niobe*	1874	Steele; Greenock
15	*Oregon*	1875	Mounsey; Sunderland	50	*Peter Stuart*	1868	McMillan; Dumbarton
16	*Alastor*	1875	Mounsey; Sunderland	51	(?*Linguist*	1874	Mounsey; Sunderland)
17	?	1859		52	*Loch Maree*	1873	Barclay, Curle; Glasgow
18	*Ariel*	1865	Steele; Greenock	53	*Stockbridge*	1869	Oswald; Sunderland
19	*Andes*	1874	Osbourne; Sunderland	54	*Blairgowrie*	1875	J & G Thomson; Glasgow
20	*Myrtle Holme*	1875	Bartram, Haswell; Sunderland	55	*Carbet Castle*	1875	Mounsey; Sunderland
21	*Waikato*	1874	Blumar; Sunderland	56	*Cairnbulg*	1874	Duthie; Aberdeen
22	*Dumbartonshire*	1874	Dobie; Glasgow	57	*British King*	1869	Royden; Liverpool
23	(?*West Riding*	1874	Dobie; Glasgow)	58	*Roderick Dhu*	1873	Mounsey; Sunderland
24	*Woollahra*	1875	Osbourne; Sunderland	59	*Lammermoor*	1874	Reid; Port Glasgow
25	*Waitangi*	1874	Blumer; Sunderland	60	*Loch Ard*	1873	Connell; Glasgow
26	?	1874		61	*Wallacetown*	1874	Oswald; Sunderland
27	*City of Glasgow*	1867	Barclay, Curle; Glasgow	62	*Respigadera*	1874	Oswald; Sunderland
28	(?*Gareloch*	1873	Dobie; Glasgow)	63	*Baron Colonsay*	1875	J E Scott; Greenock
29	*Timaru*	1874	Scott & Co; Greenock	64	*Duchess of Edinburgh*	1874	Mounsey; Sunderland
30	*Silverhow/Candida*	1875	Whitehaven Shipbuilding Co; Whitehaven	65	*Cambridgeshire*	1873	Cole Bros; Newcastle
				66	*Castle Roy*	1874	Elder; Glasgow
31	*Patriarch*	1869	Hood; Aberdeen	67	*Dunalistair*	1874	Mounsey; Sunderland
32	*Cashmere*	1868	Oswald; Sunderland	68	*Senator*	1874	Mounsey; Sunderland
33	*Caitloch*	1874	Duncan; Port Glasgow	69	*Mermerus*	1872	Barclay, Curle; Glasgow
34	*British Army*	1869	Oswald; Sunderland	70	*Penthesilea*	1869	Oswald; Sunderland
35	*Corona*	1866	Stephen; Dundee	71	*British Admiral*	1873	Royden; Liverpool
36	*Lactura*	1875	Baird & Brown; Glasgow	72	*Thomasina MacLellan*	1873	McMillan; Dumbarton
37	*Superb*	1866	Green; Blackwall, London	73	*Rydal Hall*	1874	Evans; Liverpool
38	*Martin Scott*	1875	J E Scott; Greenock	74	*Star of Bengal*	1874	Harland & Wolff; Belfast
39	*Carpathian*	1874	Humphrys & Pearson; Hull	75	*John Kerr*	1873	Reid; Port Glasgow
40	(?*Aros Bay/ Morayshire*	1875	Dobie; Glasgow)	76	*Chrysomene*	1873	Potter; Liverpool
				77	*Thessalus*	1874	Barclay, Curle; Glasgow
41	*Idomene*	1874	Oswald; Sunderland	78	(?*St Enoch*	1874	Dobie; Glasgow)
42	*British Commerce*	1874	Dobie; Glasgow	79	*Cilurnum*	1874	Palmer; Jarrow
43	*Norval*	1873	Watson; Sunderland	80	*Star of Russia*	1874	Harland & Wolff; Belfast
44	*Turkestan*	1874	Richardson, Duck; Stockton	81	*Stuart Hahnemann*	1874	McMillan; Dumbarton
45	*Loch Vennachar*	1875	Thompson; Glasgow	82	*Sobraon*	1866	Hall; Aberdeen

REFERENCES

CHAPTER 1

[1] William H Webb, *Plans of Wooden Vessels*, (New York 1895). An appraisal of design is given with each vessel, as well as measurements and some passage times.

[2] Howard I Chapelle, *The National Watercraft Collection*, (Washington DC, 1960), United States National Museum Bulletin no 219.

[3] Henry Hall, *Report on the Ship-Building Industry of the United States*, (New York 1882, reprint New York 1970), chapter V.

[4] Report by a Committee of the House of Representatives, *Causes of the Reduction in American Tonnage and the Decline of Navigation Interests* (1870).

[5] Grahame E Farr, *Chepstow Ships*, (Chepstow 1954), p 184.

[6] John Lyman, 'Iron and Steel Sailing Vessels Built in Germany', *Log Chips*, vol 2, November 1951, p 105 and January 1952, pp 118-120; also W Laas, *Die Grossen Segelschiffe* (Berlin 1908), pp 82-97.

[7] John Lyman, 'Sailing Ships Built in the Netherlands since 1869', *Log Chips*, vol 1, May 1950, pp 143-46, and vol 2, July 1950, pp 11-12.

[8] Vice-Admiral Paris, *L'Art Naval a L'Exposition Universelle de Paris en 1867*, (Paris *c*1869), vol 1 (text), p 469. Vol II consists of plates only.

[9] George Moorsom, *A Brief Review and Analyses of the Laws for the Admeasurement of Tonnage*, (London 1852), chapter III, esp p 78; see also David R MacGregor, *Fast Sailing Ships 1775-1875*, (Lymington, Hants, 1973) p 143.

[10] Lawrence A Harper, *English Navigation Laws*, (New York 1939, reprint 1964), p 361.

[11] Partial list of Custom House clearances, prepared by R S Craig.

[12] *Sydney Morning Herald*, 16 May 1853, quoting Tonge, Curry & Co's circular for 1852; *ibid*, 24 May 1854, for 1853 circular.

[13] *Argus*, (Melbourne) 23 Mar 1855, quoting Curry & Co's circular for 1854.

[14] P P, 'Mortality on Emigrant Ships', 1852-3, XCVIII, pp 327-52.

[15] *Australia and New Zealand Gazette*, 29 Jan 1853.

[16] P P 'Mortality on Emigrant Ships', *op cit*.

[17] *Australia and New Zealand Gazette*, 10 Feb 1855, p 138.

[18] *Argus* (Melbourne), 23 Mar 1855.

[19] B R Mitchell, *Abstract of British Historical Statistics*, (Cambridge 1962), pp 217-18.

[20] W S Lindsay, *History of Merchant Shipping and Ancient Commerce*, (London 1876), vol III, pp 618-19.

[21] Mitchell, *Abstract of British Historical Statistics*, *op cit*, table on p 223.

[22] Harper, *English Navigation Laws*, *op cit*, pp 362-63.

[23] Roger Prouty, *The Transformation of the Board of Trade 1830-55*, (London 1957), p 92.

[24] Mitchell, *Abstract of British Historical Statistics*, *op cit*, p 222.

[25] Surveyors of Lloyd's Register, *Report . . . on the Dismasting of Large Iron Sailing Ships*, (London 1886), p 168

[26] David R MacGregor, *The China Bird*, (London 1961), chapter 6.

[27] Gerald S Graham, 'The Ascendancy of the Sailing Ship 1850-85', *Economic History Review*, vol IX, pp 74-88.

CHAPTER 2

1 Alexander Stephen & Sons, diary of Alexander Stephen snr, summary for 1850.

2 *The Times* 7 March 1855, p 10, quoting P P return. This average has been calculated from 7165 ships of 2,169,620 tons.

3 [Sir A Murray Stephen], *A Shipbuilding History 1750-1932*, (Glasgow *c*1932), pp 195 and 198.

4 *Ibid*, p 195.

5 *Ibid*, p 198; also study of the ship plans.

6 Alexander Stephen & Sons diary, 29 July 1858.

7 *Ibid*, 28 April 1859.

8 Alexander Stephen & Sons, Letter Book 'A', fo 139.

9 Alexander Stephen & Sons, diary, 6 May 1858.

10 Alexander Stephen & Sons, Letter Book 'A', fo 21 and 22, 10 May 1856.

11 Alexander Stephen & Sons, diary, 27 Aug 1858.

12 Alexander Stephen & Sons, diary, 7 April 1858.

13 *Ibid*, 8 April 1859.

14 *Ibid*, 9 November 1857.

15 *Ibid*, 26 February 1858.

16 Alexander Stephen & Sons, Letter Book 'A', fo 175, dated 3 Feb 1858.

17 *Ibid*, fo 178, dated 9 Feb 1858.

18 *Ibid*, fo 182, dated 15 Feb 1858.

19 *Ibid*, fo 200, dated 12 April 1858; also diary entry dated 26 Feb 1858.

20 Alexander Stephen & Sons, Letter Book 'A', fo 190, dated 1 Mar 1858.

21 Alexander Stephen & Sons, diary, dated 10 May 1858.

22 Alexander Stephen & Sons, Letter Book 'A', fo 312, dated 3 Dec 1858.

23 NMM, L R survey reports, Iron ships, no 1757.

24 Bideford Public Library, Groscombe Bequest 1945. W Groscombe was master of the ship, 1861-66.

25 The best work yet published on Clydeside shipbuilders is by John Shields, *Clyde Built*, (Glasgow 1949), but a more comprehensive work is badly needed. In the *Rise and Progress of the City Line* (Glasgow 1908) John Smith comments on the Clyde shipbuilders.

26 Basil Lubbock, *The Colonial Clippers*, (Glasgow, 3rd ed, 1924), p 210.

27 Plans of ships inspected at premises of Barclay, Curle & Co, Glasgow; now lodged at NMM.

28 *Glasgow Herald*, 13 June 1853.

29 Alexander Stephen & Sons, diary, 7 Feb 1856.

30 List of ships built by R Steele & Co transcribed from a yard list loaned to me by James Steele (died 1955).

31 J W Smith and T S Holden, *Where Ships are Born, Sunderland 1346-1946*, (Sunderland 1947), p 93; figures for years 1845 and 1850 amended from 'Sunderland Ships; or . . . rise and progress of shipbuilding on the Wear', *Nautical Magazine*, 1852, vol XXI, p 593.

32 *The Times*, 9 Jan 1854, p 5.

33 'Sunderland Ships', *Nautical Magazine, op cit*, p 592.

34 Smith and Holden, *Where Ships are Born, op cit*, pp 18-19; undated obituary notice on William Pile jnr from which Smith and Holden also obtained much material; I am also grateful to Peter Barton for his notes on John and William Pile.

35 MS list of ships built by William Pile jnr from no 52 in 1857; copied from original notebook kept by Thomas C Stamp, Pile's cashier, and loaned me by his great-grandson, J G M Stamp of Newcastle.

36 *Illustrated London News*, May 1851.

37 'Sunderland Ships', *Nautical Magazine, op cit*, pp 590-91.

38 *Illustrated London News*, 9 Oct 1852, and *The Times*, 2 Oct 1852, p 8.

39 NMM, L R survey reports, Iron Ships, box 2.

40 Science Museum, London, plan no C/3/6.

41 N C Kierkegaard, *Plancher till Praktisk Skeppsbyggnadskonst*, (Gothenburg 1864), plate IX. Plan reprinted in Tre Tryckear, *The Lore of Ships*, (London 1964), p 23.

42 John F Gibson, *Brocklebanks 1770-1950*, (Liverpool 1953), vol I, p 142.

43 Lloyd's Register of Shipping, Visitation Committee Reports, annual visit of 1855.

44 There is some doubt as to who designed the *Royal Charter*, as the name of the Bristol builder, William Paterson, appears as the shipbuilder on her official register. See Arthur C Wardle, 'When Chester Built Ships', article probably published in *Liverpool Echo*, *c*1940-45; and Grahame Farr, *The Steamship Great Britain*, (Bristol 1965), p 17.

45 Liverpool Museums, Shipping Collections, and MS lists of shipbuilders with additional notes by Arthur C Wardle.

46 NMM, Merchant Ship Plans, nos T 15001 and T 15001A.

47 P P Liverpool Compass Committee, Third Report to the Board of Trade, (London 1862), especially pp 8, 25 and 36.

48 Bristol University Library, Brunel Papers, letter from Bradford Leslie to I K Brunel dated Manchester 26 March 1857.

49 MS shipbuilding lists compiled 1948 by W Stewart Rees, and now in possession of W Salisbury.

50 Liverpool Museum, Transport Section. A C Wardle's Notebook I, pp 68 and 91, provided much data on Hodgson's career.

51 Lloyd's Register of Shipping, Visitation Committee Reports; printed correspondence between Edward Bates and Lloyd's Register, Feb and March 1858.

52 NMM, L R Survey Reports, boxes 37-41; also, Philip Banbury, *Shipbuilders of the Thames and Medway*, (Newton Abbot 1971).

53 Lloyd's Register of Shipping, Visitation Committee Reports, annual visit of 1852.

54 *Ibid*, years 1854 and 1857.

55 NMM, L R survey reports, Portsmouth [?] no 896.

56 *The Times*, 5 Dec 1854, p 8.

57 Grahame Farr, *Shipbuilding in North Devon*, National Maritime Museum Monograph No 22, (Greenwich 1976); also L R survey reports, Bideford (beginning report no 701).

58 From note in R H Gillis collection, citing *Royal Cornwall Gazette*, 7 Sept 1855. I have not verified this.

59 Henry Hall, *Report on the Ship-Building Industry of the United States*, (New York 1882, reprint New York 1975), p 93.

60 'Log Chips', *Boston Merchant Vessels 1851-1856 as written by Duncan McLean for 'The Atlas' of Boston*, (Chapel Hill, North Carolina, 1975, facsimile reprint), p 39.

61 *Ibid*, p 4.

62 *Ibid*, p 3.

63 *Ibid*, p 36.

64 *Ibid*, pp 33 and 47. John Lyman compiled this facsimile reprint.

65 Richard C McKay, *Some Famous Sailing Ships and their Builder Donald McKay*, (New York 1928), pp 371-72.

66 *Tasmanian Daily News*, 4 Sept 1855.

67 *Ibid*.

68 Octavius T Howe and Frederick C Matthews, *American Clipper Ships, 1833-1858*, (Salem, Mass, 1926), vol I, pp 135-36.

69 Stanley T Spicer, *Masters of Sail*, (Toronto 1968), pp 84 and 193.

70 Frederick William Wallace, *Wooden Ships and Iron Men*, (London 1924), p 57.

71 *Illustrated London News*, 4 Sept 1852.

72 Richard Rice, 'The Wrights of Saint John: A Study of Shipbuilding and shipowning in the Maritimes, 1839-1855', in David Macmillan, ed, *Canadian Business History*, (Toronto 1972), pp 317-36; see also Esther C Wright, *Saint John Ships and Their Builders*, (Woodville NS, 1976).

73 Rice, *The Wrights of Saint John, op cit*.

74 *Mercury* (Liverpool), 3 February 1852. Transcribed from an old hand-written copy received in November 1971 from Richard Rice, but I have not checked it against the original newspaper; however I have omitted some of the too-numerous commas.

75 Frederick William Wallace, *Record of Canadian Shipping*, (Toronto 1929), p 287.

76 A tracing of *Inkermann*'s plan was sent to me in 1954 by George MacBeath, who was then Curator of the Department of Canadian History.

77 Wallace, *Wooden Ships and Iron Men, op cit*, p 73.

CHAPTER 3

1 For particulars about *Kent*, see Lubbock, *The Blackwall Frigates, op cit*, pp 185-91; and *Mercantile Marine Magazine*, *c* 1858.

2 Letter from G Coleman, *Melbourne Argus*, 10 Feb 1854.

3 Letter from Charles MacDonnell, *Melbourne Argus*, 8 Feb 1854.

4 *The Australia & New Zealand Gazette* gave date of arrival in Melbourne as 24 July, but this may only be date of passing through Port Phillip Heads.

5 *Illustrated London News*, 24 Dec 1853.

6 *Sydney Morning Herald*, 16 March 1854, quoting *Sunderland Times*, 3 Dec 1853.

7 *Illustrated London News*, June 1851, an account of *Vimeira's* launch.

8 W H Coates, *The Good Old Days of Shipping*, (Bombay 1900), p 67. This useful work was recently reprinted; it pre-dated Basil Lubbock's first book by ten years.

9 Alexander Stephen & Sons, small jotting book, beginning March 1860; note dated July 1860.

10 *Illustrated London News*, 11 Aug 1855.

11 L R Visitation Committee Reports, year 1855.

12 *Ibid*.

13 J W Smith and T S Holden, *Where Ships are Born; Sunderland 1346-1946*, (Sunderland 1947), pp 11-13; and Sir James Laing & Sons, data book of ships built.

14 Alexander Stephen & Sons, half-model; lines taken off by the author.

15 Alexander Stephen & Sons, sail plan traced by the author.

16 Alexander Stephen & Sons, Letter Book 'A', 4 July 1858.

17 Alexander Stephen & Sons, Alexander Stephen jnr's notebook 'B' entry dated Dundee 4 April 1856.

18 Alexander Stephen jnr's diary for 1858 is used to cover the description of building *Eastern Monarch* and *Tyburnia*.

19 Alexander Stephen & Sons, Letter Book 'A', dated 10 Feb 1858.

20 L R, Visitation Committee Report 1858.

21 Alexander Stephen & Sons, diary, 23 and 26 February 1859.

22 *Ibid*, 7 to 28 July 1860.

23 *Ibid*, 2 and 10 August 1860.

24 W I Downie, *Reminiscences of a Blackwall Midshipman*, (London 1912), pp 142-43.

CHAPTER 4

1 *The Times*, 7 Mar 1855, p 10, quoting figures in a Parliamentary return, from which those given here have been calculated.

2 List supplied by R S Craig, compiled from Port Clearance books, London Custom House Library.

3 N C Kierkegaard, *Plancher till Praktisk Skeppsbyggnadskonst*, (Gothenburg 1864), the plans come in a large folio.

4 NMM, L R Survey Reports, Aberdeen, no 1583.

5 Science Museum, London, Sailing Ship Collection, Plan no C/7/21.

6 NMM, L R Survey Reports, Iron Ships, no 823.

7 Howard I Chapelle, *The National Watercraft Collection*, US National Museum Bulletin 219, (Washington 1960), p 70.

8 Stanley T Spicer, *Masters of Sail*, (Toronto 1968), p 33.

9 Science Museum, Sailing Ship Collection, plan no C/2/14.

10 NMM, L R Survey Reports, Newcastle, box 1851-55.

11 Michael Bouquet, *No Gallant Ship*, (London 1959), pp 108-11.

12 NMM, L R Survey Reports, Shoreham box.

13 List of names from [Sir A Murray Stephen], *A Shipbuilding History 1750-1932*, (Glasgow 1932), pp 198-201; dimensions and net register tonnages from *Lloyd's Register*.

14 Howard I Chapelle, *The National Watercraft Collection, op cit*, p 72.

15 NMM, L R Survey Reports, Iron Ships, no 2339.

16 Basil Lubbock, *Last of the Windjammers*, (Glasgow 1927), vol I, p 425.

17 Basil Greenhill, 'Note on the Lisslie Collection of Ships' Drafts', *MM*, 1961, vol 47, p 58. On page 59 it states that only one plan, that of the yacht *Ventura*, had been identified and does not mention that of the *Mary Lord* by name; but her name is written vertically in the bottom left-hand corner of the sail plan.

18 NMM, L R Survey Reports, Bideford box.

19 Grahame Farr, *Shipbuilding in North Devon*, National Maritime Museum Monograph no 22, (Greenwich 1976).

20 These terms occur in the Builder's Certificate which the cost account of each ship contains.

21 See plans in Science Museum sailing ship collection.

22 See Basil Greenhill, 'Note on "Barrow Flats"', *MM*, 1961, vol 47, pp 149-51.

23 Inkerman Rogers, *A Record of Wooden Sailing Ships and Warships built in the Port of Bideford: from the year 1568 to 1938*, (Bideford 1947), pl XI.

24 *The Times*, 7 September 1855, p 9.

25 NMM, L R Survey Reports, Newcastle.

26 John Lyman, 'The Largest Two-Masted Schooner', *Log Chips*, (Washington), 1948, vol I, p 28.

27 Published 1948.

28 Basil Lubbock, 'Ships of the Period and Development in Rig', C Northcote Parkinson, ed, *The Trade Winds*, (London 1948), p 95.

29 *Comet* (Guernsey), 11 Mar 1852. Transcription made by J D Attwood; it has not been verified.

30 Carl C Cutler, *Queens of the Western Ocean*, (Annapolis 1961) pp 551-62; also, Charles S Morgan, 'New England Coasting Schooners', *American Neptune*, vol XXIII, 1963, p 8.

31 John P Parker, *Sails of the Maritimes*, (Halifax 1960), pp 47 and 64-66.

32 See Howard I Chapelle, *The Search for Speed under Sail 1700-1855*, (New York 1967), plate XV, pp 385, 387-88.

33 Henry Cheal jnr, *The Ships and Mariners of Shoreham*, (London 1909), pp 65-66.

34 *Ibid*, p 66.

35 N C Kierkegaard, *Plancher till Praktisk Skeppsbyggnadskonst*, (Gothenburg 1864), plate III. He also gives a lines plan.

36 Hans Szymanski, *Deutsche Segelschiffe*, (Berlin 1934), p 27.

37 Tyrrel E Biddle, *A Treatise on the Construction, Rigging & Handling of Model Yachts, Ships & Steamers*, (2nd ed, London 1883), pp 58-59 and Plate IV.

38 Captain John Smith, *Rise and Progress of the City Line*, (Glasgow 1908), pp 63-64. Robert and George Smith were two of the partners but were probably not related to the author of the book.

39 Szymanski, *Deutsche Segelschiffe, op cit*, plate 44.

40 John Lyman, 'Early Barkentine Illustrations', *American Neptune*, 1947, vol VII, pp 315-16; Griffiths' sail plan is reproduced in this article.

41 Mystic Seaport Library, American ship *Cremorne*, log no 5, (1861-66).

42 Rogers, *Wooden Sailing Ships Built in Bideford, op cit*, pp 31, 38-39.

43 Science Museum, Sailing Ship Collection, Geddie plans, no C/7/4.

44 Painting reproduced in Andrew Shewan, *The Great Days of Sail*, (London 1927), frontispiece. Spar dimensions copied from cost account of Alexander Hall & Sons extracted by James Henderson.

45 Seen by John Lyman when reading this paper for 1863 period.

46 Magnus Catling, 'The Bluejacket', *The Norfolk Sailor*, 1965, no 10, pp 17, 18, 23 and plan as centrespread.

47 NMM, L R survey reports, London no 19078.

48 *Ibid*, no 19091.

49 See Frank G G Carr, *Sailing Barges*, (London 1951), chapter VII.

CHAPTER 5

1 Liverpool Museum, Shipping Collection: List of Ships built by Jones, Quiggin & Co.
2 W J Macquorn Rankine, (editor), *Shipbuilding, Theoretical and Practical*, (London 1866), plates F 1-5. This is a large unwieldy book, and sometimes the plates are bound in with the text and at other times separately.
3 Liverpool Museum, ships built by Jones, *op cit*.
4 N C Kierkegaard, *Plancher till Praktisk Skeppsbyggnaskonst*, (Gothenburg 1864), plates only.
5 Mariner's Museum, Newport News, Hillmann Collection.
6 W Rickmer Rickmers, *Rickmers a Century 1834-1934* (Munich 1934), pp 17-28 and Appendices 4(a) and 5[?](a).
7 W Laas, *Die Grossen Segelschiffe* (Berlin 1908), p 23 and Appendix II.
8 Olof Hasslöf and others (editors), *Ships and Shipyards, Sailors and Fishermen* (Copenhagen 1972) p 69.
9 Alexander Stephen & Sons, diary, 29 July 1858 and 28 April 1859.
10 The first book was actually written by Sir Alexander Murray Stephen (although not acknowledged to him), *A Shipbuilding History 1750-1932*, (privately printed 1932). There are 87 pages of advertising included. The second book was written by John L Carvel, *Stephen of Linthouse, 1750-1950* (privately printed 1950). This second book actually contains an index covering 7½ pages, but no advertising.
11 Alexander Stephen & Sons, diary, 15 Dec 1862.
12 Basil Lubbock, *The Last of the Windjammers*, (Glasgow 1935, vol II), pp 14-15.
13 Alexander Stephen & Sons, diary, prices taken from quotations recorded in daily entries.
14 Captain John Smith, *Rise and Progress of the City Line* (Glasgow 1908) p 92.
15 Basil Lubbock, *Last of the Windjammers*, (Glasgow 1927, vol I) p 192.
16 *Ibid*, p 193.
17 Plans of Barclay, Curle & Co's ships inspected 1961 on firm's premises; plans now lodged at NMM.
18 Charles Chapman, *All About Ships*, (London 1869), p 372.
19 Particulars obtained from data book seen at Barclay, Curle & Co in October 1961, and from Liverpool Underwriters [Red] Registers.
20 Smith, *Rise of City Line, op cit*, p 90.
21 From a list of sailing ships built by Charles Connell & Co which was compiled by Richard Wilford and sent to me by Karl Kortum in 1969.
22 Lubbock, *The Last of the Windjammers, op cit*, vol I, p 141.
23 *Ibid*, p 280.
24 *Ibid*, p 141.
25 Reissued in book form in 1886 as *Report made to the Committee of Lloyd's Register of British and Foreign Shipping by the Society's Chief Surveyor and his Assistants concerning the Dismasting of Large Iron Sailing Ships*. Amongst the tables at the rear of the book are detailed spar dimensions of 82 unnamed ships.
26 Lubbock, *Last of the Windjammers, op cit*, vol I, p 158.
27 Lloyd's *Report on Dismasting, op cit*, p 6, para 15.
28 *North British Daily Mail*, 5 Aug 1875.
29 Letter in possession of Dr and Mrs Donald.
30 Alexander Stephen & Sons, diary, 14 Nov 1863.
31 *Ibid*, 4 Nov 1863.
32 Oil painting by F B Spencer, seen at Coe's Auction Rooms, South Kensington, on 31 Jan 1967, but painting withdrawn from sale; also photograph in Aberdeen Museum.
33 Cost Account of A Hall & Sons, transcribed by James Henderson.
34 *Nautical Magazine*, vol XLVI, November 1877, pp 1031-1044.
35 List of ships built by William Pile beginning with no 52 launched in 1858 loaned to me my J G M Stamp, a great-grandson of Mr Stamp, in October 1956.
36 R Martin, *Historical Notes of West Hartlepool and its Founder*, (West Hartlepool 1924), esp pp 27, 41 and 78-80.
37 J F Clarke, 'The Changeover from Wood to Iron in the North-East Shipyards'; paper received *c*1960.
38 MS table of gross earnings of Nicholson ships; transcribed 1955 from original in possession of B E Nicholson.
39 *Annan Observer*, 1863, no 202. Actual date unknown, but approximately 8 July.
40 Lubbock, *Last of the Windjammers, op cit*, vol I, p 168.
41 This letter and others were found in an envelope rolled up inside the plans of *Shenir* in Alexander Stephen & Sons' plan store in 1961.
42 Data supplied by Daniel Hay, Borough Librarian, Whitehaven.
43 NMM, PLAN NO T 16001, box 300; there is no body plan, sheer elevation or lines but the sail plan, midsection and general arrangement are shown in detail.
44 Lubbock, *Last of the Windjammers, op cit*, Vol I, pp 467-69.
45 *Ibid*, p 127.
46 *Ibid*, pp 155-57
47 P Barry, *Dockyard Economy and Naval Power*, (London 1863), p 306.
48 See *Log Chips*, (editor John Lyman), February 1958, vol IV, p 72.
49 Robert G Albion and others, *New England and the Sea*, (Middletown, Conn, 1972), pp 161-62.
50 Frank W Thober, 'Square Riggers Built in the US since 1870', *Log Chips*, July 1952 vol II, p 12.
51 Henry Hall, *Report on the Ship-Building Industry of the United States*, (New York 1970, reprint of 1882 ed), p 103.
52 F W Wallace, *Wooden Ships and Iron Men* (Belleville, Ont 1976, reprint of 1937 ed), p 192. The 1976 edition has an index and the page numbers appear to be the same as in 1937.
53 The full title to the report on dismasting appeared in the note against reference number 25.
54 *Ibid*, pp 11-12.
55 *Ibid*, p 169.
56 F L Middendorf, *Bemastung und Takelung der Schiffe*, (Berlin 1902).
57 *North British Daily Mail*, 30 Dec 1875.
58 *Log Chips*, 1953, vol III, pp 70, 81 and 94.
59 Lubbock, *Last of the Windjammers, op cit*, vol I, p 188.

CHAPTER 6

1 Basil Greenhill, *The Merchant Schooners*, (London 1957), vol II, pp 66-72.
2 Howard I Chapelle, the *National Watercraft Collection*, United States National Museum Bulletin no 219, (Washington 1960), pp 72-73.
3 Plans in possession of John Bigelow. The assistance of Charles Armour who traced the old plans and made them available to me, is gratefully acknowledged.
4 Basil Greenhill, *Westcountrymen in Prince Edward's Isle*, (Newton Abbot 1967), p 200.
5 John Lyman, 'Sailing Ships Launched in the United Kingdom, 1876', *Log Chips*, (Washington), 1959, vol 4, pp 81-84 and 93-96; not completed for coast of East Scotland.
6 C Knijpenga, 'Sailing Ships Built in the Netherlands since 1860', *Log Chips, op cit*, 1950, vol I, p 146.
7 J Malling, 'Square-Riggers built in Denmark since 1869', *Log Chips, op cit*, 1954, vol 3, pp 11-12.
9 See Robert Craig, W.H. Nevill and the Llanelly Iron Shipping Company', *National Library of Wales Journal*, 1958, vol X (Aberystywyth), pp 265-80. I am grateful to Robert Craig for permission to make such full use of his valuable article.
10 *Ibid*, p 269.
11 Grahame Farr, *Ship Registers of the Port of Hayle*, National Maritime Museum Monograph no 20 (Greenwich 1975), Appendix J.
12 Lines taken off half-model by William Salisbury.
13 Sail plan in Whitehaven Library and Museum.
14 Basil Greenhill, *The Merchant Schooners*, (London 1951, vol I) pp 90-91.

[15] Science Museum, neg no 7507.

[16] Chapelle, *National Watercraft Collection, op cit,* pp 74-82.

[17] *Ibid,* pp 85-86.

[18] John Lyman, 'Three-Masted Schooners of 1875', *Log Chips, op cit,* 1954, vol 3, p 106.

[19] John Lyman, 'Three-Masted Schooners Built on the Pacific Coast', *Log Chips, op cit,* 1951, vol 2, p 87.

[20] Greenhill, *The Merchant Schooners, op cit,* vol I, p 128.

[21] Alexander Stephen & Sons, diary, prices and data from daily entries.

[22] G W Laird Clowes, *Sailing Ships, their History and Development,* Science Museum Handbook, (London, 1948, 3rd ed, revised by E W White), part II, p 100.

[23] Whitehaven Public Library and Museum, William Kennaugh's account book.

[24] Charles A Armour and Thomas Lackey, *Sailing Ships of the Maritimes* (Toronto 1975), pp 146-47.

[25] Ch Eitrem, *Sjømannsliv,* (Oslo 1948), p 64. Reference received from John Lyman; I have not checked it myself.

[26] Altonaer Museum in Hamburg, *Schiffsporträts,* (c1970), p 53, fig 97.

[27] Hans Szymanski, *Deutsche Segelschiffe,* (Hamburg 1972, reprint of 1934 ed), fig 192.

[28] P A Eaddy, *Sails Beneath the Southern Cross,* (Wellington, New Zealand 1954), facing p 15.

[29] Captain Balsen, *The Shipmodeler* (Journal of Ship Model Maker's Club of New York), 1930, vol II, no 17, p 184.

[30] E A D [E A Dingley], 'Jackass Barques', *Sea Breezes,* 1927, vol 9, pp 325 and 348.

[31] Basil Lubbock, *Last of the Windjammers,* (Glasgow 1927), vol I, p 426.

[32] John Lyman, '*Zebina Goudey* a Jackass Barque', *MM,* 1971, vol 57, p 223.

[33] Tyrrel E Biddle, *A Treatise on the Construction, Rigging & Handling of Model Yachts, Ships & Steamers,* (2nd ed, London 1883), pp 58-59 and plate IV. The first edition of 1879 also carries this plate.

[34] D L Dennis, 'Topsail with a Baleston', *MM,* 1966, vol 52, p 156; see also A Balsen, 'Double Topsail Yards', *MM,* 1921, vol 7, p 350, includes diagram; Book Reviews, 'Bulletin 13, Amis du Musée de Marine', (Paris), *MM,* 1936, vol 22 p 127.

[35] G La Roërie and Commandant J Vivielle, *Navires et Marins de la Rame a L'Helice,* (Paris 1930), vol II, p 192.

[36] Greenhill, *Merchant Schooners, op cit,* vol 2, (1957), pp 92-95.

[37] *Ibid,* vol 1 (1951), plate 21.

[38] Frank G G Carr, *Sailing Barges,* (revised edition, London 1951), pp 124-26.

[39] Basil Greenhill and David R MacGregor, 'The *Mary* of Truro; the Life Story of a Coasting Smack', *MM,* 1960, vol 46, pp 81-87.

[40] *Royal Cornwall Gazette* 27 Jan 1860. This reference was seen in the collection of the late R H Ċ Gillis of Newquay, but has not been verified.

[41] I am particularly grateful to Grahame Farr for furnishing me with details of named trows from the Custom House Registers.

SOURCES

Those listed here are additional to those quoted in *Merchant Sailing Ships 1815-1850.*

PLANS, MODELS AND RELATED ARCHIVES

Dr Charles A Armour: plans of Canadian ships.

Barclay, Curle & Co, Glasgow: plans and shipyard lists (inspected on firm's premises).

Francis Russell Hart Nautical Museum at Massachusetts Institute of Technology: plans of American ships.

Frode Holm-Petersen: plans of Danish ships.

W Laas: sail plans from his book *Die Grossen Segelschiffe.*

Benjamin E Nicholson: half-models and accounts of ships built at Annan.

W J M Rankine: plan of *Formby* from his book *Shipbuilding, Theoretical and Practical.*

W Salisbury: plans of Blackwall frigates.

Alexander Stephen & Sons, Glasgow: plans and shipyard lists (inspected on firm's premises).

William H Webb: plans from his book *Plans of Wooden Vessels.*

SELECTION OF PRINTED WORKS

Albion, Robert G, and others, *New England and the Sea* (Middletown, Conn 1972).

Barry, P, *Dockyard Economy and Naval Power* (London 1863)

Blake, George, *Gellatly's 1862-1962* (Glasgow 1962)

Bouquet, Michael R, *No Gallant Ship* (London 1959)

Brett, Sir Henry, *White Wings* (Auckland vol I 1924, vol II 1928)

Carr, Frank G G, *Sailing Barges* (London 1931, revised ed 1951)

Cutler, Carl C, *Greyhounds of the Sea* (New York 1930)

Farr, Grahame, *Ship Registers of the Port of Hayle* (Maritime Monographs and Reports, Greenwich 1975)

Farr, Grahame, *Shipbuilding in North Devon* (Maritime Monographs and Reports, Greenwich 1976)

Griffiths, John W, *Treatise on Marine and Naval Architecture in Theory and Practice* (New York 1853)

Hall, Henry, *Report on the Ship-Building Industry of the United States* (New York 1882)

Hasslöf, Olof, and others, *Ships and Shipyards, Sailors and Fishermen* (Copenhagen 1972)

Kemble, John H, *San Francisco Bay* (New York c1957)

Kipping, Robert, *The Elements of Sailmaking* (London 1851)

Laas, W, *Die Grossen Segelschiffe* (Berling 1908)

Lissignol, E, *Navires en Fer A Voiles* (Paris 1866)

Lloyd's Register, *Report . . . concerning the Dismasting of Large Iron Sailing Ships* (London 1886)

Lubbock, Basil, *Colonial Clippers* (Glasgow 1924)

Lubbock, Basil, *The Down Easters* (Glasgow 1930)

Lubbock, Basil, *Last of the Windjammers* (Glasgow Vol I 1927)

Lyman, John (editor), *Log Chips* (Washington 4 vols 1948-1959)

MacGregor David R, *The Tea Clippers 1833-1875* (London 1983)

Mackrow, Clement, *The Naval Architect's and Shipbuilder's Pocket-Book* (London 1889)

Marryat, Captain, *Universal Code of Signals for the Mercantile Marine* (London)

Matthews, F C, *American Merchant Ships* (Salem 2 vols 1930 and 1931)

Norman, L, *Pioneer Shipping of Tasmania* (Hobart 1938)

Pollock, David, *Modern Shipbuilding and the Men Engaged In It* (London 1884)

Rankine, W J M, *Shipbuilding, Theoretical and Practical* (London 1866)

Ritchie, L A, *Modern British Shipbuilding: A Guide to Historical Records* (Maritime Monographs and Reports, Greenwich 1980)

Stammers, Michael K, *The Passage Makers* (Brighton 1978)

Underhill, Harold A, *Deep-Water Sail* (Glasgow 1952)

Underwriters' Registry for Iron Vessels (Liverpool from 1862)

Wallace, F W, *Record of Canadian Shipping* (Toronto 1929)

INDEX